Knowledge Management

Knowledge Management

An Integrated Approach

Ashok Jashapara
Loughborough University

FT Prentice Hall
FINANCIAL TIMES

An imprint of **Pearson Education**
Harlow, England • London • New York • Boston • San Francisco • Toronto • Sydney • Singapore • Hong Kong
Tokyo • Seoul • Taipei • New Delhi • Cape Town • Madrid • Mexico City • Amsterdam • Munich • Paris • Milan

Pearson Education Limited
Edinburgh Gate
Harlow
Essex CM20 2JE
England

and Associated Companies throughout the world

Visit us on the World Wide Web at:
www.pearsoned.co.uk

First published 2004

ISBN: 978-0-273-68298-1

British Library Cataloguing-in-Publication Data
A catalogue record for this book is available from the British Library

Library of Congress Cataloging-in-Publication Data
A catalogue record for this book is available from the Library of Congress

10 9 8 7 6
10 09

Typeset in 9/14.5 Stone Serif by 30
Printed and bound by Ashford Colour Press, Gosport

The publisher's policy is to use paper manufactured from sustainable forests.

This book is dedicated to the inspiring life of

Spud Bakhle
(1929–2003)

for our numerous conversations over a glass of wine

Brief contents

Contents

Part 5
Leveraging knowledge

Epilogue
Knowledge management

Companion Website resources

Visit the Companion Website at www.booksites.net/jashapara

For lecturers
● PowerPoint slides that can be downloaded and used as OHTs

Preface

The stimulus for this book came from the fact that I wanted a single knowledge management text for my postgraduate and doctoral students. During my deliberations, I was surprised that I could not find a single book that covered the breadth and range of material in knowledge management. Some of the scholarly offerings came from a human resource perspective, some from practitioner orientations, while others came from strong information systems directions. A cursory look at these texts showed that there was little crossover between these three dominant dimensions. Scholars from one perspective were rarely cited in the other and vice versa. The situation was as if each perspective of knowledge management was engrossed in its little world without having the language or foresight to engage in the other perspective.

Such a situation is not totally surprising given that knowledge management as a discipline is little over seven years old. There is currently a tremendous drive and popularity in knowledge management as practitioners and academics have accepted that we are collectively moving into a knowledge economy. To survive as individuals or organisations in this knowledge economy, we need tools and shared understanding of potential challenges and ways of dealing with them in knowledge-based organisations.

This book is intended for students and practitioners of knowledge management and recognises the relevance of the book for students from a multitude of different industrial sectors. The problems of managing knowledge and the everyday needs of knowledge workers are common across many sectors. This book should appeal to students and practitioners looking for a comprehensive coverage of theoretical debates and best practice in knowledge management. The book is likely to be challenging as it demands some philosophical introspection on the nature of knowledge given the argument that we cannot begin to manage knowledge until we know what knowledge is. Certain management or information systems aspects may also appear daunting to the uninitiated, particularly if this is not your background.

I suggest that you work through the uncomfortable feelings as I believe that the strength of this emerging discipline lies in an integrated approach to knowledge management. There are rich rewards as we move into a new paradigm of work. The material in this book is intended to provide you with some pertinent and practical frameworks as well as offer a source of stimuli to think and find out more in depth where needed. Even though there are questions within the text related directly to material found in each chapter, the 'Questions for further thought' were designed to help you think 'outside the box' using material from your experience and wider reading.

Ashok Jashapara
April 2004

About the author

Dr Ashok Jashapara is an internationally recognised expert in the field of knowledge management and Chair of the Knowledge Management Research Group at Loughborough University. He has considerable consultancy experience in Europe and the United States and has recently completed a knowledge management assignment for the United Nations in the Far East. He is Senior Lecturer in Knowledge Management in the most prestigious information science department in the UK. He has published widely in leading books and journals and has won a number of awards for his writing.

Acknowledgements

My special thanks go to my partner Karin. I would like to thank her for her tolerance of my many absences from family life, as well as practical and moral encouragement throughout the writing period. She was terrific! My two daughters, Nicole and Anna-Tina, have been an inspiration to me and I have valued their hugs and mischief when I have become overly involved with writing this book. My parents, Ramnik and Nilu, have also provided much-needed warmth and reassurance over the past year.

A large number of people have helped me with the preparation of this book, not least Jacqueline Senior at Pearson Education, whose assistance and advice guided my perceptions of a good textbook. I would like to thank colleagues in the Department of Information Science at Loughborough University for their kind words and feedback on chapters and early drafts of the book, in particular Professor John Feather, Professor Charles Oppenheim, Professor Ron Summers, Dr Mark Hepworth and Dr Ann O'Brien. A special acknowledgement goes to members of the Knowledge Management Research Group at Loughborough University who read draft chapters and gave me their valuable comments that helped improve the final version. I would like to single out Ray Dawson and Dr Tom Jackson in this regard.

I owe a debt of gratitude to my friends at the 'Swan and Greyhound' for their great forbearance at my ramblings when I have needed to talk to someone outside the confines of knowledge management. John Mack and Tony Zajciw at the 'Swan' have provided perfect diversions into conversations around the arts. Similarly, Glen Thumwood, Graham Farenden, Robin Page, Dick Smith and Dell Boy Morrison have provided much-needed humour, wit and hilarity to balance the seriousness of writing a book. I am similarly grateful to my biking friends Al, Onk, Stu, Debs, Ron, Chris, Donna and Blossom at the 'Coffin Scratchers' for the long bike rides and music festival diversions during the writing of this book. I cannot forget Roger Faulks and Manu Frosch at Swithland Woods for their friendship and tacit encouragement in this process.

Finally, I would like to thank the reviewers of the original proposal and draft chapters. They steered the book into new and uncharted waters and, while I do not claim to have incorporated all of their comments, they certainly caused some heart-searching reflection.

During the course of writing this book, my close friend, Spud Bakhle, died. I would like to dedicate this book to a celebration of his life and acknowledge our numerous conversations and ideas that have found their way into this book. Spud Bakhle was a Hegelian and Kantian scholar among other things and ideas around a dialectic are directly attributable to him.

Publisher's acknowledgements

We are grateful to the Financial Times Limited for permission to reprint the following material:

Knowledge management in law firms, © *Financial Times*, 8 November 2000; AMD, © *Financial Times*, 8 July 2002; Casmir, © *Financial Times*, 13 September 2001; Technip-Coflexip, © *Financial Times*, 16 October 2002; New twists for old tricks, © *Financial Times*, 6 November 2002; E-business KM Systems, © *Financial Times*, 6 March 2002; Crucibles of innovation, © *Financial Times*, 18 January 2002; Knowledge management strategy at BG, © *Financial Times*, 12 May 2000; Tough-Guy, Macho Culture, © *Financial Times*, 13 February 2002; Knowledge Ecology at Xerox, © *Financial Times*, 6 September 2002; War for talent, © *Financial Times*, 6 June 2001.

We are grateful to the following for permission to use copyright material:

Organisational Learning in the Design Industry, from *The Financial Times Limited*, 10 October 2000, © Aziz Cami; Outsourcing – Leave it to the experts from *The Financial Times Limited*, 24 November 2003, © Sarah Murray; Figure 1.5 © copyright The British Museum; Figures 1.6 (Scribe at Desk, Lansdowne 1179, f.34v.det) and 1.7 (page from Gutenburg Bible, C.9.3, page 1) by permission of the British Library; Figures 2.3 and 2.4 from *Sociological Paradigms and Organizational Analysis*, Heinemann, London (Burrell, G. and Morgan, M. 1979); Figure 2.5 reprinted from *Omega- The International Journal of Management Science*, 28, Goles, T. and Hirschheim, R., 'The paradigm is dead, the paradigm is dead … long live the paradigm: the legacy of Burrell and Morgan', 249–268, (2000), with permission from Elsevier; Figure 3.1 from *Experiential Learning: Experience as the Source of Learning and Development*, 1st ed., Pearson Education Inc (Kolb, D.A. 1984); Figures 3.4, 3.5, 3.6 and 3.7 from 'Organizational learning: the contributing processes and the literatures' in *Organization Science*, 2, 88–115 (Huber, G.P. 1991); Figure 4.12 is of The Starlight developed by John Risch at the Pacific Northwest National Laboratory and can be found at www.cybergeography.org/atlas/info_spaces.html; Figure 6.1 adapted from 'Of Strategies, deliberate and emergent' in *Strategic Management Journal* Vol. 6 No.3 (Mintzberg, H. and Waters, J.A. 1985) © John Wiley & Sons Limited. Reproduced with permission; Figure 6.3 from 'The effective organization: forces and forms' in *Sloan Management Review*, Winter, 93–107 (Mintzberg, H. 1991); Figure 7.3 from *Understanding Organizations*, Penguin Books Ltd (Handy, C. 1985); Figure 7.4 from *Corporate Cultures: The Rites and Rituals of Corporate Life*, Penguin Books Ltd (Deal, D.E. and Kennedy, A.A. 1988); Figure 7.6 from Organizational Culture Inventory by R.A. Cooke and J.C. Lafferty, 1983, 1986, 1987, 1989, Plymouth, Michigan, USA: Human Synergistics. Copyright 1989 by Human Synergistics, Inc. Adapted by permission; Figure 8.3 from *The Theory and Practice of Change Management*, Palgrave, Basingstoke (Hayes, J. 2002); Figure 8.4 from *Management of Organizational Behaviour: Leading Human Resources*, 8th ed. Prentice Hall Inc (Hersey, P. and K.H. Blanchard 2000); Figure 8.8 from *Employee Development Practice*, FT/Prentice Hall (Stewart, J. 1999); Figure 8.9 from *Strategic Management of Human Resources: A Portfolio Approach*, Jossey-Bass, San Francisco (Odiorne, G. S. 1984); Figure 9.2 from *The Learning Organization*, Gower, Aldershot (Garratt, B. 1987); Figure 9.3 from *The Learning Company: A Strategy for Sustainable Development*, McGraw-Hill, London (Pedler, M., Burgoyne, J. and Boydell, T. 1991), reproduced with the kind permission of the McGraw-Hill Publishing Company; Figure 9.5 from 'Cognition, culture and competition: an empirical test of the learning organization' in *The Learning Organization*, Vol. 10, No. 1, 31–50 (Jashapara, A. 2003); Figure 10.1 from *Intellectual Capital: Navigating in the New Business Landscape*, Macmillan Business, Houndsmills (Roos, J., Roos, G., Edvinsson, L. and Dragonetti, N.C. 1997); Figure 10.3 from 'The balanced scorecard as a strategic management system' in *Harvard Business Review*, Vol. 70, No. 1, 71–79 (Kaplan, R.S. and Norton, D.P. 1992); Figure 10.4 is taken from the following sources: *European Management Journal*, Vol. 14, No. 4, Petrash, G., 'Dow's journey to a knowledge value management culture', 365–373 © 1996, with permission from Elsevier; *Strategic Management of Professional Service Firms*, Handelshojskolens Forlag, Copenhagen (Lowendahl, B. 1997), © Copenhagen Business School Press, 1997, www.cbspress.dk; Danish Confederation of Trade Unions (1999) 'Your Knowledge – can you book it?', *International Symposium Measuring and Reporting Intellectual Capital: Experiences, Issues and Prospects*, Amsterdam; *Profiting from intellectual capital: extracting value from innovation* (Sullivan, P.H., 1998), © John Wiley & Sons Limited. Reprinted with permission; Intellectual Capital, Thomson Business Press, London (Brooking, A. 1996).

Whilst every effort has been made to trace the owners of the copyright material, in a few cases this has proved impossible and we take this opportunity to offer our apologies to any copyright holders whose rights we may have unwittingly infringed.

Discovering knowledge

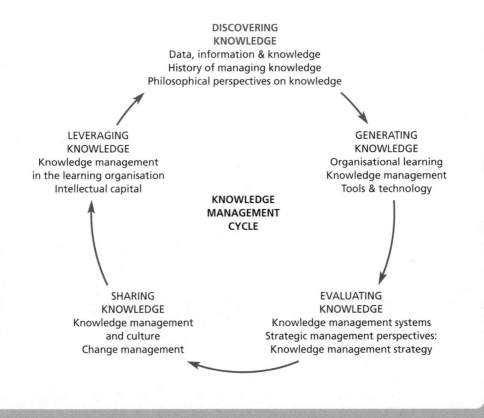

DISCOVERING
KNOWLEDGE
Data, information & knowledge
History of managing knowledge
Philosophical perspectives on knowledge

GENERATING
KNOWLEDGE
Organisational learning
Knowledge management
Tools & technology

LEVERAGING
KNOWLEDGE
Knowledge management
in the learning organisation
Intellectual capital

KNOWLEDGE
MANAGEMENT
CYCLE

EVALUATING
KNOWLEDGE
Knowledge management systems
Strategic management perspectives:
Knowledge management strategy

SHARING
KNOWLEDGE
Knowledge management
and culture
Change management

Chapter 1

Introduction to knowledge management

LEARNING OUTCOMES

After completing this chapter the reader should be able to:

- distinguish between different perspectives in the knowledge management (km) literature;
- explain the diversity of disciplines and content that make up the field of knowledge management;
- describe the differences between the terms data, information and knowledge;
- assess the differences in the management of knowledge from ancient to modern times.

MANAGEMENT ISSUES

An introduction to the discipline of knowledge management implies these questions for managers:

- What is knowledge management?
- How can knowledge improve actions in an organisation?
- What is the difference between information management and knowledge management?

Links to other chapters

Chapter 2   examines the history of philosophical thought on the notion of knowledge which links directly to the history of managing knowledge from the oral traditions to the storage of knowledge in libraries.

Knowledge management in law firms

As professions go, 'the oldest one is the biggest revenue generator on the internet', points out Paul Greenwood, director of knowledge and information at Clifford Chance, the law firm. Resist any temptation for cheap jokes about prostitution. Mr Greenwood's point is a serious one – and if he is right, the way legal services are delivered to clients could be transformed.

He argues that technology can be used to escape from labour-intensive models of delivering services face to face. 'The top musical performers of a few hundred years ago were strolling minstrels, earning a pittance because they had no leverage,' says Mr Greenwood. Now, because they can sell a single performance around the world, stars earn millions.

Clifford Chance aims to exploit its expertise in the same way, selling regulatory and legal advice online. It is putting money behind its hypothesis and claims to have spent a seven-figure sum developing NextLaw, its subscription legal advice service for e-business issues.

It is not the only enthusiast for online sales. Linklaters, another member of the 'magic circle' of UK law firms, has invested at least as much in its Blue Flag range of subscription services. It is also bullish about the future. 'We are seeing a lot of talk from our so-called major competitors but not a reshaping of the legal landscape, which is what Linklaters is committed to doing,' says partner Paul Nelson.

The company has invested 'very many noughts' in Blue Flag, with the ultimate aim of an initial public offering as a separate company. It is in the final stages of testing a capital markets product that combines documentation, online advice and transaction management. 'We have cracked it now and will roll it out to the rest of the firm, expanding into property, pensions and mergers and acquisitions,' says Mr Nelson. 'We are going to roll out into our Blue Flag effort everything that makes sense to "electronify".'

The two firms claim their approach is not only revolutionary but also streets ahead of their big US rivals. 'Remarkably, most US firms are not off the starting block,' says Christopher Millard of Clifford Chance. This is true to the extent that none of the leading New York firms sells advice online. Davis Polk & Wardwell offers 'custom publishing' – targeted information – but to selected clients only. Michael Mills, director of professional services and systems, admits: 'I don't know that we have a clear rationale for (this approach) except that it's what our clients seem to need. We're not nearly as big as Clifford Chance or Linklaters.'

Other US firms question their London rivals' claim to supremacy. 'Internal knowledge management is the area where the New York firms are investing and are probably ahead (of London),' says David Lopez, a partner at Cleary Gottlieb Steen & Hamilton. The firm says its focus on 'complicated, cutting-edge transactions' does not fit the online advice approach of breaking legal know-how into generic chunks that companies can use without consulting a lawyer face to face. 'If you are working in a field where the answers are more settled, the provision of interactive legal advice is easier because there is less ambiguity,' says Brent Miller, Cleary's director of knowledge management.

Allen & Overy (A&O), another UK magic circle firm, uses an analogous argument to explain why it has steered clear of selling online, despite investing an estimated £10 million ($14million) in e-business. 'What we've tried to do is focus our efforts very much on our core practice,' says partner Jonathan Brayne. 'What we've done will enhance about 75 per cent of our practice: the competition has opted to promote certain niche areas that lend themselves to selling over the internet, which represent, say, 10 or 15 per cent of revenues.'

A&O will shortly [early 2001] announce a client extranet – a system allowing global clients online billing and access to all their relevant documents. The service supplements A&O's Fountain product – designed to allow each lawyer electronic access to the firm's collective legal knowledge – and its NewChange document and transaction management system. NewChange also offers virtual deal rooms – secure websites to which teams of lawyers and bankers involved in a big transaction can gain access. To date it has opened 450 of these, involving 8,600 users.

A&O is not alone in offering such services. Linklaters in September [2000] launched what it claims is the 'most advanced extranet service yet offered to clients in the legal world'. But does this herald the start of a revolution in the legal services clients receive? Some lawyers are sceptical. 'It is a unique period for law firms – we are all jostling for position,' says Mr Brayne. 'But in a few years' time we'll be back to competing on whether we are good lawyers or not.'

Source: Article by Jean Eaglesham, *Financial Times*, 8 November 2000

Questions

1 Describe the advantages of a 'strolling minstrel' variety of lawyer over the computer savvy one.
2 Evaluate the shortcomings of law firms that consider e-business synonymously with knowledge management.

3 Discuss the most likely aspects of 'internal knowledge management' practices among New York law firms.

Knowledge management: an integrated approach

The aim of this book is to provide a comprehensive and integrated discourse on the various facets, emerging issues and perspectives on knowledge management. There are numerous accounts of knowledge management as a process and a continuous cycle and this representation has been used as a structure for this book, as shown in Figure 1.1. The generic activities in the knowledge management cycle are subdivided into the five parts of this book: discovering knowledge, generating knowledge, evaluating knowledge, sharing knowledge and leveraging knowledge.

▶ Part 1: Discovering knowledge

Part 1 explores all the different aspects related to the notion of knowledge and knowledge management. An historical perspective on how knowledge was managed across

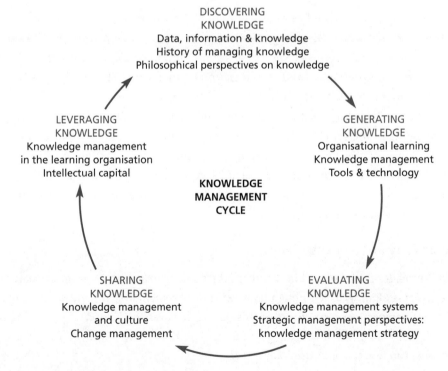

Figure 1.1 Knowledge management cycle

the centuries from the bardic oral tradition to the current digital revolution is provided. Philosophy is not often taught in our universities and its central role in understanding knowledge is examined. This will allow future students to move beyond the narrow logical behaviourist perspective of tacit and explicit knowledge that is currently in vogue in the literature.

- *Chapter 1: Introduction to knowledge management.* This chapter provides an exploration of the emerging discipline and forwards an integrated model. The differences between data, information and knowledge are examined. An historical perspective on knowledge management illustrates the central function of libraries in knowledge creation, sharing and transfer.
- *Chapter 2: Philosophical perspectives on knowledge.* This is a thought-provoking chapter exploring issues of ontology and epistemology. What is the nature of knowledge and reality? What are the aspects of knowledge that we can know? The contributions of major philosophers in the knowledge debate are examined and the current notions of knowledge in the knowledge management literature are assessed.

▶ Part 2: Generating knowledge

Part 2 is concerned with generating knowledge through people in the form of organisational learning and through the multitude of knowledge management tools and technology. This part aims to bridge the gap between two disparate literatures where there is often little overlap.

- *Chapter 3: Organisational learning.* This chapter outlines the nature of individual, team and organisational learning. An information processing perspective is adopted to examine the processes of knowledge acquisition, information distribution, information interpretation and organisational memory. The development of organisational routines and dynamic capabilities are discussed.
- *Chapter 4: Knowledge management tools and technology.* This chapter provides a grounding in the variety of knowledge management tools that can be used at different stages in the knowledge management cycle. These include ontology and taxonomy tools, information retrieval tools, personalisation tools, data mining tools, case-based reasoning tools, groupware tools, videoconferencing tools, e-learning tools and visualisation tools.

▶ Part 3: Evaluating knowledge

Part 3 provides the analytical backbone to the book by examining how to evaluate the effectiveness of knowledge through knowledge management systems and strategic management perspectives. The thrust of this part is to assess the impact of technological systems on management processes and to explore how these improved management processes can lead to competitive advantage.

- *Chapter 5: Knowledge management systems*. This chapter elaborates on a variety of knowledge management systems including document management systems, decision support systems, group support systems, executive information systems, workflow management systems and customer relationship management systems.
- *Chapter 6: Strategic management perspectives*. This chapter contrasts the difference between three dominant strategy schools of thought: industrial organisation, excellence and turnaround, and the institutionalist perspective.

▶ Part 4: Sharing knowledge

Part 4 presents the human resource aspects of sharing knowledge and implementing knowledge management initiatives. All too often such initiatives fail as the more subtle aspects of organisational culture, leadership and employee involvement interventions are overlooked. The ability to optimise knowledge sharing in organisations is a major challenge for knowledge management.

- *Chapter 7: Knowledge management and culture*. This chapters contrasts the literature on organisational climate and culture and explores the debates around knowledge-sharing cultures. Informal networks called 'communities of practice' are explained along with the role of storytelling and narratives within them.
- *Chapter 8: Change management*. This chapter provides the latest thinking on the effective implementation of knowledge management initiatives. It examines how high levels of commitment can be developed through leadership and a variety of human resource interventions. The role of politics in change management programmes is highlighted.

▶ Part 5: Leveraging knowledge

Part 5 explores the Utopian search for the fruits of knowledge management, namely, the quest for a learning organisation and the generation of high levels of intellectual capital. Knowledge is seen as the critical factor affecting economic growth and the different perspectives on how it can be cultivated and measured at an organisational level are examined.

- *Chapter 9: Knowledge management in the learning organisation*. This chapter contrasts the terms organisational learning and the learning organisation and articulates the diversity of US and UK models associated with the learning organisation. Empirical research in this field is assessed.
- *Chapter 10. Intellectual capital*. This chapter examines some of the limitations of traditional financial measures in performance measurement and the search for non-financial measures such as intellectual capital to supplement these conventional sources. Several models of intellectual capital are compared and generic notions of human capital, social capital, organisational capital and customer capital are presented.

Introduction

Knowledge management has similar parallels with the rise of English as an academic discipline in the early twentieth century. In the 1920s, it was unclear why anyone should study English and, by the 1930s, it was a question of whether students should study anything else at all. English was initially a poor man's Classics and was taught in working men's colleges and mechanic institutes. The subject was considered an upstart and rather amateurish affair compared with the traditional subjects such as Classics and philology. Similarly, knowledge management in the twenty-first century has risen from practitioner and consultancy knowledge and has only recently become a subject for academic study. Today English is often associated with creative or imaginative writing. However, in the eighteenth century, English covered all the valued writings in society including history, philosophy, essays, letters and poems (Eagleton 1999; Palmer 1965). Similarly, today knowledge management can be confused with information systems by some commentators and human resource management by others. In reality, it has roots in a wide variety of disciplines such as philosophy, business management, anthropology, information science, psychology and computer science.

In fashioning knowledge management into a serious discipline, this chapter will explore the nature of knowledge management and propose a definition of this field from an interdisciplinary perspective. To provide a balanced appraisal of the literature, a critical understanding of reservations in this field will be forwarded. The terms data, information and knowledge can often be used synonymously in the literature and the distinction between these terms is explored.

Knowledge, and the way it is managed, has been with humankind since the beginning of time. This chapter shall proceed to explore the history of knowledge management, taking a broad perspective and including the vital role of libraries in the ancient and modern worlds. The development of oral knowledge from the oral traditions to the first writing of cuneiform among Sumerians is discussed. A journey is conducted through the flourishing libraries in Ancient Greece and Rome such as the Alexandria library and the Ulpian library. The influence of Christianity in the rise of monastic and cathedral libraries is explained together with the emergence of early universities. The paradigm leap in knowledge creation and dissemination that has occurred through the development of print, computers and telecommunications is fully explored.

What is knowledge management?

In the post-industrial economy, sometimes termed the 'knowledge economy' (Bell 1973; Drucker 1992), knowledge management has become an emerging discipline that has gained enormous popularity among academics, consultants and practitioners. It has been argued that it is no longer the traditional industrial technologies or craft skills that drive competitive performance but instead knowledge that has become the key asset to drive organisational survival and success.

To the uninitiated reader, the multitude of offerings on knowledge management in books, journals and magazines can appear rather daunting and confusing at first. The fact is that it is a relatively young discipline trying to find its way and recognising that it has roots in a number of different disciplines. Some literature on knowledge management is heavily information systems oriented, giving the impression that it is little more than information management. Other literature looks more at the people's dimension of knowledge creation and sharing, making the subject more akin to human resource management. These are the two most common dimensions and there is often little crossover between them. Each world fails to comprehend the other as the language and assumptions of each discipline vary significantly. However, it is precisely these interdisciplinary linkages that provide the most rewarding advances in this field.

Given the interdisciplinary nature of this emerging field, conventional academic demarcations in traditional subject areas do not help. For example, it is relatively rare for computer or information science graduates to gain sufficient grounding in human resource management and vice versa with traditional business management students. This impasse is often based on fear on both sides about the nature and relative merits of their respective skills and expertise. Beyond these two dominant dimensions, there are some additional perspectives within the KM literature, ranging from strategy to cultural change management. It is not surprising that there is little coherency between these offerings as many authors orientate the subject area to their singular discipline perspective.

Pause for thought

What does knowledge mean to you? If you were asked to detail your specialist knowledge, how would you describe your knowledge? Have you ever thought of the market value of your knowledge and what this may be? Given that there is a competitive market for knowledge and skills, how do you ensure that your knowledge is state-of-the-art and kept up to date?

The strength and challenge of knowledge management as an emerging discipline comes from its interdisciplinary approach, as shown in Figure 1.2 (p. 10). For example, if knowledge management was purely information systems, current tools and business processes would suffice. However, the reality is that different information systems approaches such as data processing, management information systems and strategic information systems have been found wanting. There are numerous examples of major investments made in this area, particularly in the financial services sector, that have yielded little or no benefit to host organisations. Instead, the real synergies in knowledge management are more likely to occur from boundary-spanning individuals who can see beyond the narrow margins of their own disciplines and recognise the value of dialogue and debate with other disciplines.

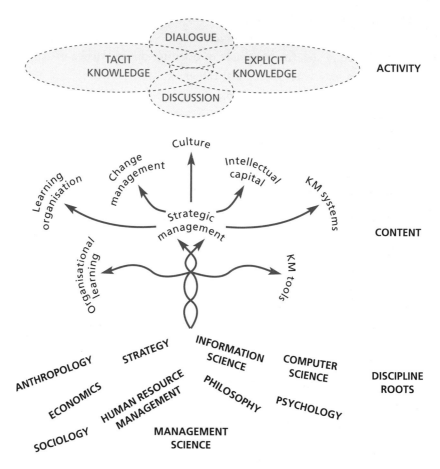

Figure 1.2 Tree of knowledge management – disciplines, content and activity

Given the multidisciplinary nature of knowledge management, it is not surprising that the variety of current definitions comes from a number of different perspectives, as shown in Table 1.1 (p. 11). Some come from an information systems perspective (Mertins *et al.* 2000) while others suggest a human resource perspective (Skyrme 1999; Swan *et al.* 1999a). A few definitions have begun to adopt a more strategic management perspective, recognising the importance of knowledge management practices for gaining competitive advantage (Newell *et al.* 2002; uit Beijerse 2000). However, none of these definitions expands on the alliances with particular strategic schools of thought, and the basic assumptions of the nature of competitive environments (such as highly turbulent) or strategic positioning (such as continuous innovation) need to be questioned (Newell *et al.* 2002). External environments may shift from turbulent to more stable environments over time and competitive environments may favour efficiency rather than innovation in a given period. The basic fact is that we live in uncertain times and any assumptions about competitive environments and approaches to organisational alignment and adaptability need to be considered carefully.

Table 1.1 Representative sample of knowledge management definitions

Author/s	Definition	Perspective
(Davenport and Prusak 1998)	'Knowledge management draws from existing resources that your organisation may already have in place – good information systems management, organisational change management, and human resources management practices.'	Integration (information systems and human resources)
(Swan *et al.* 1999b)	'... any process or practice of creating, acquiring, capturing, sharing and using knowledge, wherever it resides, to enhance learning and performance in organisations.'	Human resource process
(Skyrme 1999)	'The *explicit* and *systematic* management of *vital* knowledge and its associated *processes of* creating, gathering, organising, diffusion, use and exploitation, in pursuit of organisational objectives.'	Human resource process
(Mertins *et al.* 2000)	'... all methods, instruments and tools that in a holistic approach contribute to the promotion of core knowledge processes.'	Information systems
(uit Beijerse 2000)	'The achievement of the organisation's goals by making the factor knowledge productive.'	Strategy
(Newell *et al.* 2002)	'... improving the ways in which firms facing highly turbulent environments can mobilise their knowledge base (or leverage their knowledge "assets") in order to ensure continuous innovation.'	Strategy

From the definitions of knowledge management given in Table 1.1, it is clear that any advancements in this field need to adopt an integrated (Davenport and Prusak 1998), interdisciplinary and strategic perspective, as shown in Figure 1.3 (p. 12). The strategic purpose of knowledge management activities is to increase intellectual capital and enhance organisational performance (see Chapters 6 and 10). There is a human dimension of developing knowledge in individuals, teams and organisations and this fundamentally occurs through different learning processes (see Chapter 3). Once knowledge is created, the sharing of knowledge remains one of the fundamental challenges in this field. As human beings, we need support to help us explore and exploit knowledge (tacit – 'know how' – and explicit – 'know what', see Chapters 2 and 3) more fully. There is a wide variety of tools, technologies and systems that can fulfil these functions, such as the continuous cycle of knowledge creation, capture, organisation, evaluation, storage and sharing (see Chapters 4 and 5). However, KM tools and organisational processes are insufficient in themselves to achieve success. Many well planned initiatives have proved futile as they have failed to acknowledge the cultural and change management dimensions (see Chapters 7 and 8) of successful implementation.

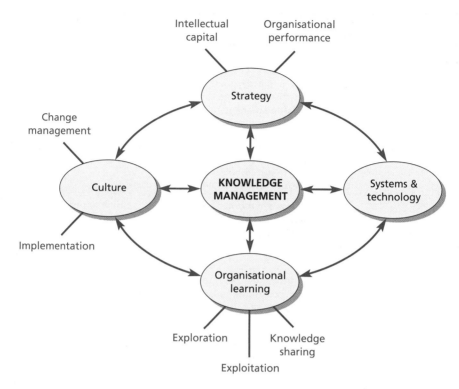

Figure 1.3 Dimensions of knowledge management

These different dimensions of knowledge management have been brought together into an integrated definition. From an interdisciplinary perspective, knowledge management can be defined as:

'the effective learning processes associated with exploration, exploitation and sharing of human knowledge (tacit and explicit) that use appropriate technology and cultural environments to enhance an organisation's intellectual capital and performance.'

Is knowledge management a fad?

As is common with any new field of discourse, knowledge management has its critics and antithesis. The most vociferous so far has come from information scientists who appear threatened by the prospect that it may marginalise their own discipline (Ponzi and Koenig 2002; Wilson 2002). This is clearly unjustified as information science is an essential component of knowledge management, although not the solitary one. A number of arguments have been put forward to show that knowledge management is no more than 'old wine in new bottles' where, like Alice through the looking glass, terms can mean what anyone chooses them to mean. Let us explore some of the arguments.

The first argument posed is that knowledge management is no more than a fad or a fashion. The difference between a fad and a fashion is the duration of time over which the phenomenon lasts. Fads develop a high level of interest in a short time, then die away. However, fashions have a much longer maturity of interest. Bibliometric techniques have been adopted to examine the volume of bibliographic records as an indicator of discourse popularity over time. The assumption is that knowledge management is similar to other management fads such as quality circles, total quality management and business process reengineering. However, the empirical evidence goes counter to these arguments. Bibliometric studies (1991–2001) show that knowledge management has had almost exponential growth in the past six years and shows no signs of abating (Ponzi and Koenig 2002).

The second argument posed by such critics is that knowledge management does not stand up to rigorous analysis as it has emerged from consultancy practice (Wilson 2002). This is clearly not the case as knowledge has roots within organisational learning and strategy literatures with a much older lineage of rigour. The organisation of knowledge was being considered by some scholars as early as the 1960s (Etzioni 1964). More recently, scholars have been debating the knowledge–based view of the firm (Grant 1996; Spender 1996) descending from a resource-based view of the firm (Barney 1991; Barney 2001) and institutional theory (Penrose 1959; Selznick 1957). At practitioner levels, there have been studies exploring knowledge management strategies and approaches in eminent journals such as the *Harvard Business Review* (Hansen *et al.* 1999; Nonaka 1991). The corpus of rigorous knowledge is emerging in this field, including critical analysis of the literature as well as alternative insights such as postmodernist orientations (Kalling and Styhre 2003; Styhre 2003).

The third argument against knowledge management is that many top business schools have failed to respond to these advances in knowledge management in their curricula (Wilson 2002). Some business schools may incorporate the material associated with knowledge management on a variety of modules such as strategic management, human resource management and information management strategy. It would be remarkable if any business school ignored the learning base associated with knowledge management. At some schools in the UK, such as the Open University Business School, there is a specialised module on knowledge management attracting a significant number of students. The knowledge management discipline is around seven years old and it is not surprising that some business schools have been pioneering in this new field whereas others have been assessing its likely impact.

The final argument is that knowledge management is no more than 'search and replace marketing' (Wilson 2002). This means that many software houses purely relabel their products with 'knowledge' or 'knowledge management' somewhere within their brand. There is certainly an element of this. Such organisations may be forgiven for cashing in on the popularity of knowledge management in the corporate marketplace. An example of this is Lotus Notes software relabelling itself as 'Knowledgeware' rather than groupware. However, knowledge management is more than software and systems, even though they are important aspects of it. Some confusion may arise when critics assume wrongly that knowledge management has developed an entirely new toolkit in the past five years rather than building and adapting existing information systems to serve its own ends. Future KM technologies are likely to explore ways of tapping into the vast reservoir of tacit knowledge in organisations.

A convincing counter argument against many critics is the clear empirical evidence demonstrating that knowledge management has become an accepted part of the corporate agenda, particularly among large firms. Specialist roles have emerged such as chief knowledge officers, knowledge managers and directors of intellectual capital (see Table 1.2 for a list of typical KM job titles). For instance, a survey conducted by KPMG Consulting in 1999 (KPMG Consulting 2000) of 423 organisations in the UK, mainland Europe and the US showed that 81 per cent were considering a KM programme, of which 38 per cent already had one in place. This survey was conducted predominantly among executives and chief executives of large organisations with a turnover exceeding £200 million a year. The survey confirmed that 64 per cent of these firms had a knowledge management strategy and the main drivers of KM strategy were senior management or board level engagement. The most common KM problems encountered were information overload, lack of time for sharing knowledge and the inability to use knowledge effectively. The main causes of failure in KM initiatives revolved predominantly around human resource issues. These included the lack of user uptake due to insufficient communication, inability to integrate KM practices with normal working practice, the lack of time to learn and the lack of adequate training. In addition to this survey, there are numerous well documented examples of firms engaged in KM strategies and practices, such as Buckman Laboratories and BP in the private sectors and World Bank and the United Nations in the public sectors.

Table 1.2 Some typical examples of knowledge management job titles

Typical knowledge management job titles advertised on the internet	
Chief knowledge officer	Director of knowledge management
Director of intellectual capital	Knowledge department manager
Knowledge manager	Knowledge economist
Knowledge consultant	Knowledge resources librarian
Knowledge management analyst	Knowledge administrator
Knowledge coordinator	Knowledge management project manager

What is the difference between data, information, knowledge and wisdom?

▶ Data

The dictionary definition of data is 'known facts or things used as a basis of inference or reckoning'. Let's try to unravel this multifaceted term and show that a definition of data depends on context. We acquire data from the external world through our senses and try to make sense of these signals through our experience. This external data becomes internal fact. The assumption about facts is that they are true. But our senses can play games with us. An example is the optical illusions of Escher's drawings that can be seen in two different ways. Escher made an art of creating impossible figures such as people ascending and descending stairs at the same time that were clearly contradictory. We can also exclude data in a number of ways that can affect our inference or reckoning of it. The first is by not focusing on the data, such as with the 'cocktail party' effect where we are bombarded with lots of data but are able to ignore most of it (background noise) and concentrate on the data of the person speaking to us. We also exclude data as our senses are not able to respond to signals such as ultraviolet light or ultrasound, and we may exclude data voluntarily by putting on a blindfold or inserting ear plugs (Meadows 2001) or involuntarily through data overload.

So far we have explored data from the perspective of the receiver of the signal. In this context, a signal is a set of data transmitted to our senses. What about the source of the signal and the channel or medium through which it is transmitted? Each one of these can have a distortion in them and affect the nature of data coming to us. The traditional game of 'Chinese whispers' at the dinner table shows how an initial message can become totally distorted by the time it has gone around the table.

There are differences between quantitative and qualitative data. For example, the numbers 72 and 83 per cent are pieces of data that can have multiple meanings and are highly context dependent. They may refer to mean examination scores or the performance of a new carburettor undergoing trials. Hence, the data is meaningless out of context and requires an association with something else. Qualitative data is much more troublesome as it depends on the perceptions of the transmitter and receiver of the data. Ten participants in a meeting are likely to provide ten totally different accounts of it depending on their perspective and their selective inclusion or exclusion of data. In this sense, data is also value laden. An example of this is two artists, one European and the other Chinese, who painted 'faithful representations' of the same landscape in the English Lake district (Gombrich 1960). To European eyes, the painting by the Chinese artist was typical of a Chinese painting. This example shows the 'conceptually saturated' character of observation and data where it is difficult to distinguish between what is observable (empirical) and what is unobservable (theoretical or conceptual). We may have 'sensations' in our eyes without concepts, but we have no perception of data without concepts (O'Connor and Carr 1982).

▶ Information

The dictionary definition of information is 'something told' or 'the act of informing or telling'. However, this doesn't help us distinguish between data and information. Information could be considered as 'systematically organised data' (Meadows 2001). The notion of systematic implies the ability to predict or make inferences from the data assuming it is based on some system. If we are given a sequence of odd numbers such as 7, 9, 11, 13, we can predict from the information that the next number in the sequence will be 15. To inform, the data needs to be organised. This may be done through some form of classification scheme to provide a framework for our thinking. For example, libraries classify their books using a bibliographic classification scheme. A common one is the Dewey Decimal Classification which is based on dividing all of knowledge into ten fields ranging from 0–999. Dewey has essentially followed a Darwinian model in which different aspects and parts of knowledge are related to each other either by direct descent or by collateral kinship. All knowledge is divided into *genera* and *species* using a similar approach to Darwin. The ten encompassing classes (000, 100 … 900) are subdivided, first into 401, 402 …, then 410, 411, and then by adding further numbers after the decimal point, which are related to numbers which can also appear before the point (an example is that the number after the decimal point is the same for the certain periods covered in related subject domains such as English history and English literature).

Another conception of information is data that is endowed with meaning, relevance and purpose. This meaning does not have to be a scientific meaning such as the Dewey classification system but may be a subjective meaning given by the receiver of the data or message. Information gives shape to the data and makes a difference to the outlook or insight of the receiver of the data. In this sense, it is the receiver of the data that determines whether a message is data or information. A consultancy report may be written to inform senior managers of critical issues but may be judged as ramblings and noise by the recipients (Davenport and Prusak 1998). Meaning in data often occurs through some form of association with experience or relationships with other data.

Pause for thought

From your experiences, can you describe situations where you have made decisions with wrong data or information? How do you guard against this? What strategies do you adopt to evaluate a situation with conflicting information or data? How do you manage 'noise' or irrelevant data or information related to a particular problem? How do you manage too much data or the problem of 'information overload'?

▶ Knowledge

In a practical sense, knowledge could be considered as 'actionable information', as shown in the hierarchy of data, information and knowledge in Figure 1.4 (p. 17). Actionable information allows us to make better decisions and provide an effective input to dialogue and creativity in organisations. This occurs by providing information at the right place, at the right time and in the appropriate format (Tiwana 2000). Knowledge allows us to act more effectively than information or data and equips us with a greater ability to predict future outcomes.

However, knowledge is much more complex than this simplistic notion. We have devoted the whole of the next chapter to exploring how western philosophers have grappled with the question of what is knowledge over the past two millennia. There is still no consensus on the nature of knowledge except that it is based on perception that can provide a rational justification for it. Such perceptions are based on our ontological and

Figure 1.4 **Data, information, knowledge and purposeful action**

epistemological assumptions of reality. Put simply, we all wear 'different coloured glasses' whether we are aware of it or not. These glasses have assumptions about reality, such as whether it is subjective or objective (ontology) and assumptions about what we can know (epistemology). Continuing this analogy, the knowledge of a certain phenomenon is likely to be different if one individual wears 'pink' glasses and another wears 'blue' ones. Hence, for example, it is no surprise that the knowledge of costs and benefits of organisational restructuring is often viewed very differently by the workforce and by senior management. The interpretation of the same data and information will vary significantly based on these perceptions and the original knowledge base of the individual.

The most common notion of knowledge in the current KM literature has its roots in the ideas of logical behaviourism based on the writings of Gilbert Ryle and Michael Polanyi. From this perspective, knowledge exists along a continuum between tacit knowledge (know how) and explicit knowledge (know what) (Polanyi 1967; Ryle 1949) (See Chapter 2 for more in-depth coverage of knowledge frameworks and typologies.) One of the major challenges in knowledge management is exploring creative ways to convert the tacit knowledge base in organisations into explicit knowledge (Nonaka 1994). Organisational routines, practices and norms can also act as part of this tacit knowledge base. Despite the logical behaviourist perspective of tacit and explicit knowledge being dominant at present, there are numerous alternative perspectives on the nature of knowledge. As the literature gains in maturity, it is likely that other perspectives such as postmodernism, critical theory and realism may provide new insights and advances in this field.

▶ Wisdom

Wisdom and truth have been shown to have higher qualities than knowledge in the hierarchy of Figure 1.4. These terms are even more elusive than knowledge. Wisdom is the ability to act critically or practically in a given situation. It is based on ethical judgement related to an individual's belief system. Wisdom is often captured in famous quotes, proverbs and sayings. Some examples of proverbs from around the world include the following:

- Children have more need of models than of critics (French).
- You can't see the whole sky through a bamboo tube (Japanese).
- There is plenty of sound in an empty barrel (Russian).
- Trust in Allah, but tie your camel (Muslim).
- Wonder is the beginning of wisdom (Greek).

Truth is even more problematic as there is a growing realisation that social phenomena are theory laden, as illustrated in the above example of the Chinese and European artists. Theory-neutral observations do not exist as our tacit theories or conceptions of the world affect our observations. The notions of 'truth' and 'objectivity' can appear meaningless if the social world can be understood only through particular ways of seeing. This implies that there are multiple truths rather than an absolute truth of social phenomena. A pessimistic outlook on information, knowledge and wisdom has been captured in the well cited lines from T.S. Elliot in the *Choruses* From *The Rock*:

> *Where is the life we have lost in living?*
> *Where is the wisdom we have lost in knowledge?*
> *Where is the knowledge we have lost in information?*

Early history of knowledge management: oral tradition to cuneiform

One of the oldest forms of managing knowledge is the oral tradition and the use of human memory to store knowledge. This oral transfer of knowledge occurs through a process of transmitting messages by word of mouth over time, as found in many bard traditions around the world. The process of transmission begins when messages are repeated over time and ends when they disappear for a variety of reasons. The message may represent news such as eyewitness accounts, hearsay or visions, dreams and hallucinations in some societies. The other group of messages are interpretations such as reminiscences of childhood, explanatory commentaries and historic tales, poetry, songs and sayings. Epic poems may be memorised to achieve a consistency over each recitation but the fact is that actual wordings are likely to change over time. Songs provide more faithful transmission of messages as their melodies act as mnemonic devices.

Pause for thought
Think about your work or social life. What are your difficulties in people giving you knowledge or information verbally? Despite these difficulties, what do you prefer about the spoken word over other forms of communication? Have you ever played Chinese whispers at dinner parties? What are the likely problems with passing down knowledge second, third or fourth hand? Are there similar problems with spoken knowledge being passed down over many years?

The unique characteristic of the oral tradition is that messages are intangible and accumulate interpretations as they are transmitted. Successive accumulation and selection of interpretations can mean that messages from the oral tradition become restrained by previous interpretations. Even though the reliability of messages from oral traditions may be questionable, they do provide inside knowledge of news or interpretations of a community of people.

The limitation of the oral tradition is the fallibility of our memories and the divergence or direct contradiction with written sources. This can occur when certain groups or individuals selectively discard certain knowledge and retain only that which they consider important at the time. People may also add new meanings to the old knowledge, giving a certain bias to the former knowledge. Oral traditions that are older than two or three generations can also suffer from the reliability of knowledge that is preserved (Vansina 1985).

Given the limitations of the oral tradition, the first signs of preserving knowledge through writing dates back to around 3000 B.C. The Sumerians settled in southern Mesopotamia and found that their rivers had a plentiful supply of good clay and reeds. They fashioned the clay into tablets, the reeds into three-cornered writing instruments or styluses and perfected a style of writing called cuneiform from simple lines and wedges (see Figure 1.5). The combination of these simple wedges (Latin *cunei*) and lines represented many hundred words and sounds. Scribes or '*dubsar*' underwent many years of training as apprentices to a headmaster or '*ummia*'. The scribes were highly venerated in this society, ranking just below high priests in social status. The knowledge recorded on these clay tablets ranged from administrative records, Hammurabi's laws and marriage contracts to legends and mythology.

Before long, collections of these clay tablets developed and the challenge became one of organising knowledge in tablets into some form of cataloguing system. In 1980, archaeologists discovered a room full of clay tablets at the ancient royal palace of Ebla in Syria dating back to around 2300 B.C. The Eblaites gave us our primitive form of catalogues in the shape of long lists of words, objects, place names and species. The palace

Figure 1.5 Example of cuneiform writing (this records delivery of 8 gin (about 64g) of gold by Lu-Ninshubur to the palace) © Copyright The British Museum

library provided a training ground for scribes and promoted the creation and preservation of knowledge similar in nature to our modern universities (Lerner 1998).

One of the greatest stores of knowledge in the ancient world covered over 10,000 works contained in 30,000 clay tablets found at Assurbanipal's palace library (around 650 B.C.) in Ninevah. These Assyrian collections were essentially archives created as a public memory for the state. Scribes and scholars were employed to compile, revise and edit different varieties of knowledge. The tablets were kept in earthenware jars, properly arranged on shelves in different rooms. Each tablet had an identification tag showing its precise location in a jar, shelf and room. There were also 'catalog' tablets in each room providing a brief description of the tablets and their location in the room (Harris 1995). Even though the library contained literary materials such as the *Epic of Gilgamesh*, omen texts tended to predominate, reflecting some of the preoccupations of that society. These included astrological omens, dream omens and practices to conduct exorcisms.

In Ancient Egypt, the chosen medium for transmission and storage of knowledge was papyrus. This was made from the stem of the common reed found growing abundantly on the Nile delta. Papyrus had the advantage over clay tablets of being much lighter, easily transportable and much less brittle. Papyrus was essentially used for less formal records. More formal records were inscribed on stone, as can still be seen on many Egyptian monuments today. The most famous library of Pharonic Egypt was the complex built by Rameses II called the 'sacred library' and inscribed with the phrase 'Healing place of the Soul' (Lerner 1998). The library contained texts on poetry, astronomy, history, engineering, agriculture and fiction that awaited the king in his afterlife.

Knowledge management in Ancient Greece and Rome

While literacy was the sole domain of scribes and scholars in Ancient Mesopotamia and Egypt, it was much more widespread in Ancient Greece. Books were written on papyrus even though parchment was also available. The central historic event of Ancient Greece was the Trojan Wars, captured and shaped by Homer in the epic poems of the *Iliad* and the *Odyssey*. These verses were recited and transmitted orally by generations of bards. One of the early concerns was to establish a complete text of Homer's epics. This was attempted in the sixth century B.C. by the tyrant Peisistratus who also founded the first public library in Athens (Lerner 1998).

The selling of knowledge through books was flourishing by the time of the famous philosopher Socrates in 400 B.C. A few decades later, book collecting became more common and it is most probable that Plato's Academy and Aristotle's Lyceum possessed their own private libraries. Alexander the Great, a Macedonian, recognised the contributions that books and libraries made in the classical Hellenic culture he had conquered. However, it wasn't until his death in 323 B.C. that Ptolemy I, one of his generals, became king of Egypt and commissioned the greatest library of antiquity in Alexandria. This library, known as a Museum, flourished for many hundreds of years, attracting many noted writers, poets, scientists and scholars and over 600,000 rolls of text. The Museum or 'the place of the Muses', included works of history, philosophy, music and the visual arts. In addition, it provided studies in language and literature and a multitude of commentaries, glossaries and grammar on notable texts such as the *Iliad* and the *Odyssey*. Rare and archaic words found in Homer were given meaning in a compilation by Philitas called *Miscellaneous Works*. This glossary of difficult or metaphorical words was a tremendous success among many avid readers of Homer. The great library of Alexandria came to an end in 48 B.C. when 400,000 rolls were accidentally destroyed in Caesar's brief Alexandrian war.

The main rival to the Alexandria library was the Pergamon, built in the time of Attalus I (247–197 B.C.). This possessed around 200,000 rolls and focused more on Homeric studies, geometry and art criticism. There was tremendous rivalry between Pergamon and Alexandria for scholarship and their collections. However, this came to an end in 41 B.C. when the Pergamon came under Mark Anthony's rule and he gave the entire collection of 200,000 rolls to Cleopatra, presumably in compensation for the losses by Julius Caesar in the library at Alexandria.

> **Pause for thought**
>
> Imagine that you were tasked to collect all the knowledge and received wisdom in your organisation. How would go about carrying out this assignment? Where would you start? For example, what do you think would be the most appropriate medium for storing your found knowledge? Do you think paper records could play a role? If so, how? How would you go about organising all the knowledge you had collected? What are the main difficulties with such an assignment?

Even though the Romans conquered Macedonia in 168 B.C., the invading forces were considerably influenced by the richness of Greek culture and their collections of books. Many of these books found themselves back in Rome as spoils of war. The learning captured in these books was revered by many generals such as Paulus Aemilius who developed one of the first notable Roman libraries (Harris 1995). Julius Caesar commissioned a public library in Rome to surpass the library in Alexandria, but the plan was never realised due to his untimely death.

The first public library in Rome was founded in 39 B.C. by a politician and general named Gaius Asinius Pollio. He had made a personal fortune from the conquest of Damatia and used part of this to amass a number of private collections and form a library in the Temple of Liberty (Atrium Libertatis) on the Aventine Hill, containing both Greek and Latin books. The tradition of founding public libraries continued throughout the Roman era, although private libraries were also common in this period and their size was often related to the wealth of the owner. One of the greatest of Roman libraries was probably the Ulpian library found in the Forum of Trajan and built by Emperor Trajan in 114 B.C. This was a public library on a grand scale, with two large chambers, one for the Greek collection and the other for the Latin one. Their sole purpose was to serve the readers of their collections in large sumptuous surroundings. The chambers were decorated with large sculptures, with lavish use of stone and marble throughout. Books were easily accessible to the reader and not stacked in vast rows, as was common in Greek libraries. The organisation of the library required the services of a specialist for cataloguing, reshelving and repairing damaged rolls. Some remains of the Forum of Trajan still exist in Rome near the Via dei Fori Imperiali (Casson 2001).

The knowledge contained in rolls among Roman libraries was susceptible to a number of hazards. These included frequent fires, insect attack on the rolls and dampness in the libraries. Various scholars and poets might also fall out of favour with an emperor and have their entire collection banished from library shelves. This occurred with Ovid under the rule of Augustus and the works of Livy and Virgil under the rule of Caligula (Wiegand and Davis 1994). Hence, the selectivity of knowledge from the oral tradition can apply equally to knowledge arising from written sources.

Management of knowledge in monastic and cathedral libraries

The rise of Christianity in the fourth century had a dramatic influence on the nature of knowledge that was collected and stored in libraries. Religion was elevated above other knowledge domains and libraries became associated more with churches and monasteries. The most common western library for the next millennia was found in a monastery where monks were involved with reading scripts, copying theological texts (scriptorium) and writing commentaries on key texts. This was the main form of learning in this period. The Bible was of course the core text and numerous volumes and print sizes would be kept. Other texts in these collections might include works by early church fathers, lives of martyrs and saints, church service books, Latin textbooks and classics, and local literature and history (Harris 1995). Many of these collections were kept in book chests or small closets and were closely guarded under lock and key. Monks were often allowed to gain access to only one book at a time.

Flavius Aurelius Cassiodorus, a politician and intellectual in Rome, abandoned public life around 550 A.D. to set up a model monastery called Vivarium. The name derived from a common daily activity conducted by monks of raising fish (*vivaria*). Cassiodorus's private collection became the core of the monastery's library which contained Christian writings and all the major 'pagan' Latin and Greek authors. His major contribution to monastic life was the publication of *Institutiones Divinarum et Saecularium Litterarum*. This provided the template for monastic practice and a curriculum of theological study which influenced many future monasteries and cathedral schools. Cassiodorus elevated the role of monks as scribes in the scriptorium (see Figure 1.6 (p. 23)) as one of the highest duties to God. Apart from reading and understanding the Bible, theological study included history, science and mathematics as part of understanding God's creation (Casson 2001; Lerner 1998). Similarly, a key figure in western monasticism was St Benedict. When he established Monte Casino and established his rule, a key element was the requirement on all monks to read and copy manuscripts. The scriptorium and the library became a central part of the Benedictine discipline. Like Cassiodorus, Benedict had been educated in the classical and Christian traditions and did not ban the reading or copying of pagan classical texts – a critical factor in their survival.

In the twelfth century, intellectual life was moving from the rural monasteries back to urban centres as there was a need to educate and train people in the growing and increasingly complex economies and governments of Europe. Cathedrals had traditionally acted as training grounds for monks in theology, music and canon law. They took on the new role and enlarged their book collections to include more secular interests such as arithmetic, rhetoric and astronomy. Some cathedral libraries such as Canterbury contained around 5,000 books by 1300. This led to the demise of many monastic libraries. The rule of Henry VIII in England led to a further fall in scholarly collections with the dissolution of the monasteries in the 1530s when numerous collections were scattered or destroyed (Harris 1995). Yet despite the loss of thousands of manuscripts, relatively little knowledge was lost compared with that lost in the fifth and sixth centuries when various Germanic tribes destroyed the western Roman empire.

At the same time as the emergence of cathedral schools, certain cities became renowned for groups of teachers with specialities in particular subjects such as law or theology. This started to attract many students and before long teachers and students were organising and regulatinge themselves. The resulting bodies were called universities or organised guilds. For example, the University of Paris evolved around 1200 and

Figure 1.6 Scribe comparing two texts in monastery

was renowned for theology. It gained recognition to certain rights and privileges through a charter from King Philip II. In 1167, some English students withdrew from the University of Paris and went back to England to form the start of Oxford University. The undergraduate student was more of a twelve-year-old schoolboy and the six-year curriculum contained the seven liberal arts (Lerner 1998). Surprisingly, classical literature from Greek and Rome was absent from this curriculum, being treated with great suspicion. The *trivium* helped to train the student in reasoning and argumentation:

- grammar;
- rhetoric;
- logic.

The *quadrivium* helped to train the student in the natural laws of the universe:

- arithmetic;
- geometry;
- music;
- astronomy.

The early university libraries resembled monastic libraries. They were normally formed through the bequests of ecclesiastical or lay patrons, such as the collection of Robert de Sorbonne which led to the founding of the Sorbonne in 1257. The predominant part of the collection was religious works, followed by classics and, lastly, the natural laws of the universe (mathematics, medicine, astronomy and law). There were strict rules and regulations on library membership and conduct in the library. For instance, students at Oxford could use the library only if they had studied philosophy for eight years, and there was a fine at the Sorbonne for leaving books lying open (Harris 1995). Books were expensive and knowledge was for the privileged few.

Paradigm shift from print to a digital age

The dramatic change in the storage and dissemination of knowledge came with the advent of print in 1455. Johann Gutenburg of Mainz is normally credited with the invention of printing in the west even though it is most likely to have been a Chinese invention in the eighth century. The first printed book in Europe was Gutenburg's 42-line Bible which resembled a fine manuscript. Manuscripts were expensive to produce, whereas printed texts cut the cost of books and allowed much wider dissemination. An example of Gutenburg's fine print is shown in Figure 1.7 (p. 25). Soon thousands of volumes were rolling off presses, with particular demand for Greek and Latin classics. These books found their way to private collections as well as to communal use in monasteries, cathedrals and the emerging universities.

The consequence of print was the striking rise in the size of libraries and their complexity. This gave way to modern librarianship so that basic functions of collection, organisation, preservation and access to this ubiquitous knowledge could be

Figure 1.7 Paradigm shift to print: an example of Gutenburg's print

conducted. In 1545, Conrad Gesner, father of modern bibliography, published his *Bibliotheca Universalis* to help keep track of the ever increasing volumes of books. An early attempt to index and find an appropriate classification scheme in libraries was made with the *Index Librorum Prohibitorum* in 1559.

The impact of this growth in libraries was to attract new readers and increase the levels of literacy among ordinary people. The introduction of printed texts also allowed lay people to have a private reading of the Bible which had been the select domain of monastic and cathedral libraries in the past. Around the seventeenth century, there was an explosion of learning and knowledge concerning science and it saw the formation of many learned societies which started to disseminate the latest thinking and specialist knowledge in their fields through journals (Eisenstein 1979; Wiegand and Davis 1994).

The next major quantum leap was the introduction of computers in the late twentieth century which resulted in an explosion of ways in which knowledge was captured, organised, stored, shared and evaluated. Digital computers operate by converting symbols, pictures and words into a binary digit called a bit (represented by 0 or 1). A string of eight bits is called a byte. The advancement of computer technology has meant that greater quantities of knowledge can be stored on computers at lower costs each year. A megabyte (million bytes) of computer storage capacity is fairly common for individual users and large organisations can have knowledge repositories measured in terabytes (1 trillion bytes). The increase in microprocessor power has meant that some powerful computers can process a single machine instruction in a nanosecond (a billionth of a second).

How important are computers in your everyday life? For example, do you feel you could live without them? As the power of computers and telecommunications has increased, what real differences have they made to your daily life? For example, how do computers assist you in making better quality decisions or storing your personal knowledge for later retrieval? Are there aspects of your personal knowledge that would be impossible to store in a computer?

The major impact of computers has come through telecommunications, allowing computers to link up and knowledge to be shared through networks across the world. This can be local area networks (LANs) in an organisation or more global networks such as the information superhighway (internet). Technology has also developed wireless communication where knowledge can be transferred over a mobile phone or through personal digital assistants (PDAs). The most common form of knowledge transfer is electronic mail. The physical separation of people over long distances has become less of a barrier. Groups of people can meet electronically over the phone through teleconferencing or can modify data files simultaneously through data conferencing or meet each other visually on video screens through videoconferencing. The World Wide Web is at the heart of this knowledge explosion, with a subsequent rise in publishing of knowledge over the internet. The increasing pace of technology development will provide new and exciting challenges for the future management of knowledge.

CASE STUDY

Destruction of ancient knowledge from war in Iraq

As the American juggernaut rumbles towards Baghdad, rival groups of academics, curators and collectors are scrambling to influence the cultural agenda of a post-war, post-sanctions Iraq. Leaders of US organisations representing archaeologists and other Near East scholars on one hand, and museum directors and collectors on the other are lobbying State Department and Pentagon officials. Their mission is to minimise destruction and looting of cultural property in the event of war, and with the White House sounding more bellicose by the hour these efforts have gained urgency.

Modern Iraq covers the region bounded by the Tigris and Euphrates rivers that gave rise to some of the earliest known civilisations. Its borders encompass some of the oldest evidence of agriculture and artefacts from the fourth millennium BC development of cuneiform writing. The country contains remnants of Sumerian, Akkadian, Assyrian and Babylonian empires, as well as biblical sites. A sustained air and ground war would almost certainly damage some of these treasures and open the way for

looting. For example, a bomb blast near the Arch of Ctesiphon in suburban Baghdad could crack or topple the third-century structure, which is the world's largest parabolic arch built of brick. The arch is perilously close to the Iraqi Atomic Energy Agency.

Representatives of museum directors, collectors, preservationists, Near East scholars and archaeologists late last month met in Washington with officials from the Defense Department and State Department to discuss their concerns. The talks were an opportunity to 'show our concern for antiquities sites and museums, as well as standing monuments', says McGuire Gibson, a professor of Mesopotamian archaeology at the University of Chicago and president of the American Association for Research in Baghdad. Professor Gibson has been leading efforts by the Archaeological Institute of America and the AARB, an academic group representing numerous disciplines. He has also presented to the Defense Department a detailed catalogue of about 4,000 Iraqi sites, only a fraction of the archaeologically significant locations in the country, which could number in the hundreds of thousands around the Tigris and Euphrates. 'In effect, the entire country is an archaeological site,' Gibson says.

Other interested groups include the American Council on Cultural Policy, which includes private collectors, museum directors and former government officials, and which works closely with the American Association of Art Museum Directors. Ultimately, the various organisations have different approaches to preserving antiquities. Scholars of the region, particularly archaeologists, have an interest in keeping artefacts in context, while collectors and museum directors are orientated towards acquisition.

None of the groups, however, has weighed in on the appropriateness of a war with Iraq. But recalling the belated and flawed communication between the US government and experts during the 1991 Gulf War, the experts 'want to point out what happened in the past and to try to suggest ways in which we can avoid that, if at all possible, or at least to mitigate the consequences,' says Jane Waldbaum, AIA president.

After the Gulf War, looting from museums and dig sites was widespread and Iraqi antiquities flooded the international market. Food shortages led people in the countryside to cultivate archaeological sites. With the prospect of renewed warfare, the AIA and AARB have urged the government to observe international treaties on cultural property, to work to minimise damage to archaeological sites and artefacts, to prevent looting, and to facilitate the preservation of Iraqi cultural heritage in the wake of any conflict.

International law enforcement agencies must be vigilant against illicit trade in Iraqi antiquities, says Patty Gerstenblith, a professor at DePaul University School of Law. The scholarly groups also urged compliance with the 1970 Unesco Convention on the Means of Prohibiting and Preventing the Illicit Import, Export and Transfer of Ownership of Cultural Property, a treaty signed by the US and UK, Iraq and more than 90 other countries.

Iraq's antiquities laws have their origins in the British administration of the League of Nations mandate following the first world war. 'We would want to ensure that the current Iraqi antiquities law is maintained and enforced,' says Jane Waldbaum. 'They have very strict requirements for the sale and removal of antiquities from the country. It's virtually prohibited.'

Unesco could have a role in determining future Iraqi cultural policy, if asked by a member state to intervene, according to Guido Carducci, chief of the organisation's International Standards Section in the Cultural Heritage Division. In working out the details, 'the antiquities department should be given the resources it needs to resume doing what it was

before. They were apparently a very well run antiquities service – one of the very best in the Middle East', according to Ashton Hawkins, president of the ACCP and former executive vice president and counsel to the Metropolitan Museum of Art in New York. He suggests that Iraq's prohibition on sales of antiquities is basically appropriate. At the same time, he argues that the proper role of an antiquities department is to identify and maintain seminal and emblematic artefacts and to consider the selective sale of the rest in order to fund preservation of the former. 'National patrimony doesn't consist of everything. It consists of the most important things,' he says.

Some US and international policies treat collecting as a contributing factor to looting. 'But on the whole, collectors stay away from that kind of material now. Reasonable intelligence (and) common sense should guide legitimate collecting. You should stay away from Iraqi material that might come on to the market in the next couple of years.'

It's not clear how the destruction of Iraq's cultural property would be treated under international law. Neither the US nor the UK is a party to the 1954 Hague Convention on the Protection of Cultural Property in the Event of Armed Conflict, although Iraq is one of the 103 state parties to the treaty. It bars the targeting of cultural sites unless militarily necessary and calls on parties to prevent looting and the export of cultural property from occupied countries. Carducci maintains that the Hague Convention's main strictures are established in customary international law, and that both the US and the UK accept this principle.

Unesco officials and western scholars say rebuilding the Iraqi antiquities agency and reviving the country's academic and professional infrastructure are keys to safeguarding its cultural heritage. But given the increasing odds of widespread devastation, Carducci does not sound optimistic. 'From a military point of view (protection of cultural property) is of course not the first priority. It's always been like that.'

Source: Article by Ted Bowen, *Financial Times*, 5 February 2003

Questions

1 How could vestiges of human knowledge such as the cuneiform writing from Ancient Iraq have been protected from the recent war?
2 Evaluate the difficulties of international law enforcement to protect Iraqi's cultural heritage.
3 Is the scattering of knowledge found among books and artefacts inevitable after a war as found in other episodes throughout history? How can this knowledge be preserved against future wars?

Summary

This chapter has elaborated on five key areas of knowledge management:

1 The different current definitions of knowledge management predominantly from information systems or human resource management perspectives. The diverse dimensions of knowledge management are brought together in an integrated definition from an interdisciplinary perspective.

2 The arguments providing an antithesis to the emerging field debating that it is no more than 'old wine in new bottles'.

3 The distinction between data, information and knowledge, particularly acknowledging the role of the sender, receiver and medium of the messages and signals.

4 The bardic oral traditions presented as the earliest form of managing knowledge in civilisation and their strengths and limitations. The movement of knowledge from word of mouth to writing cuneiform on clay tablets is explained.

5 The central role of libraries in knowledge creation and dissemination from Ancient Greece to the formation of university libraries. The quantum leap in knowledge transfer occurring from the invention of print and the development of computers and internet technologies are discussed.

QUESTIONS FOR FURTHER THOUGHT

1 Given the highly specialised nature of traditional academic research, how can interdisciplinary research in fields such as knowledge management succeed and provide fresh insights?

2 What is the difference between information and knowledge management?

3 What are the strengths and shortcomings of academic knowledge and practitioner knowledge?

4 What does knowledge management mean to a small organisation?

5 How do you overcome the 'theory laden' nature of observations among managers in organisations?

6 What are the difficulties in the notion of knowledge as 'actionable information'?

7 How can lessons from the old bardic traditions assist modern-day knowledge management?

8 What are the advantages and disadvantages of different writing media such as clay, papyrus and parchment for storing knowledge?

9 How fallible is modern-day storage of knowledge on computers when many software programs become obsolete in less than ten years? How easy will it be to decipher the bytes on CD-ROMs in 1,000 years?

10 What lessons can we draw from ancient libraries and librarianship for the creation, storage and preservation of knowledge?

Further Reading

1 Newell *et al.* 2002 is a good all-round book on knowledge management predominantly from a human resource perspective and contains some good case study material.

2 Davenport and Prusak 1998 helped popularise the field of knowledge management and comes from a consultancy and practitioner background.

3 Harris 1995 provides an excellent historic background on the development of libraries and the management of knowledge through the ages.

References

Barney, J. B. (1991) 'Firm resources and sustained competitive advantage', *Journal of Management*, 17(1), 99–120.

Barney, J. B. (2001) 'Resource-based theories of competitive advantage: a ten-year retrospective of the resource-based view', *Journal of Management*, 27, 643–650.

Bell, D. (1973) *The Coming Post-industrial Society*, Basic Books, New York.

Casson, L. (2001) *Libraries in the Ancient World*, Yale University Press, New Haven.

Davenport, T. H. and Prusak, L. (1998) *Working Knowledge: How Organizations Manage What They Know*, Harvard Business School Press, Boston, MA.

Drucker, P. (1992) 'The new society of organizations', *Harvard Business Review*, September/October, 95–105.

Eagleton, T. (1999) *Literary Theory: An Introduction*, Blackwell Publishers, Oxford.

Eisenstein, E. L. (1979) *The Printing Press as an Agent of Change*, Cambridge University Press, Cambridge.

Etzioni, A. (1964) *Modern Organizations*, Prentice-Hall, Englewood Cliffs, NJ.

Gombrich, E. G. (1960) *Art and Illusion*, Phaidon, London.

Grant, R. M. (1996) 'Toward a knowledge-based theory of the firm', *Strategic Management Journal*, 17, 109–22.

Hansen, M., Nohria, N., and Tierney, T. (1999) 'What's your strategy for managing knowledge?', *Harvard Business Review*, March–April, 106–16.

Harris, M. H. (1995) *History of Libraries in the Western World*, The Scarecrow Press, London.

Kalling, T. and Styhre, A. (2003) *Knowledge Sharing in Organizations*, Copenhagen Business School Press, Copenhagen.

KPMG Consulting (2000) 'Knowledge Management Research Report 1999', Atos KPMG Consulting, London.

Lerner, F. A. (1998) *The Story of Libraries: From the Invention of Writing to the Computer Age*, Continuum, New York.

Meadows, J. (2001) *Understanding Information*, K.G. Saur, München.

Mertins, K., Heisig, P. and Vorbeck, J. (2000) *Knowledge Management: Best Practices in Europe*, Springer-Verlag, New York.

Newell, S., Robertson, M., Scarbrough, H. and Swan, J. (2002) *Managing Knowledge Work*, Palgrave, Basingstoke, Hampshire.

Nonaka, I. (1991). 'The knowledge-creating company', *Harvard Business Review*, 69 (November–December), 96–104.

Nonaka, I. (1994) 'A dynamic theory of organizational knowledge creation', *Organization Science*, 5(1), 14–37.

O'Connor, D. J. and Carr, B. (1982) *Introduction to the Theory of Knowledge*, Harvester, Brighton.

Palmer, D. J. (1965) *The Rise of English Studies*, Oxford University Press, London.

Penrose, E. T. (1959) *The Theory of Growth of the Firm*, Blackwell, Oxford.

Polanyi, M. (1967) *The Tacit Dimension*, Doubleday, New York.

Ponzi, L. J. and Koenig, M. E. (2002) 'Knowledge management: another management fad?', *Information Research*, 8(1), 145.

Ryle, G. (1949) *The Concept of Mind*, Hutcheson, London.

Selznick, P. (1957) *Leadership in Administration: A Sociological Interpretation*, Row, Peterson and Co., Evanston, IL.

Skyrme, D. J. (1999) *Knowledge Networking: Creating the Collaborative Enterprise*, Butterworth-Heinemann, Oxford.

Spender, J. C. (1996) 'Making knowledge the basis of a dynamic theory of the firm', *Strategic Management Journal*, 17, 45–62.

Styhre, A. (2003) *Understanding Knowledge Management – Critical and Postmodern Perspectives*, Copenhagen Business School Press, Copenhagen.

Swan, J., Newell, S., Scarborough, H. and Hislop, D. (1999a) 'Knowledge management and innovation: networks and networking', *Journal of Knowledge Management*, 3(4), 262–275.

Swan, J., Scarborough, H. and Preston, J. (1999b) 'Knowledge management – the next fad to forget people?', *Proceedings of the 7th European Conference on Information Systems*, Copenhagen.

Tiwana, A. (2000) *The Knowledge Management Toolkit*, Prentice Hall, Upper Saddle River, NJ.

uit Beijerse, R. P. (2000) 'Knowledge management in small and medium sized companies: knowledge management for entrepreneurs', *Journal of Knowledge Management*, 4(2), 162–179.

Vansina, J. (1985) *Oral Tradition as History*, James Currey Ltd, London.

Wiegand, W. A. and Davis, D. G. (1994) *Encyclopedia of Library History*, Garland, New York.

Wilson, T. D. (2002) 'The nonsense of "knowledge management"', *Information Research*, 8(1), 144.

Chapter 2

Philosophical perspectives on knowledge

LEARNING OUTCOMES

After completing this chapter the reader should be able to:

- describe the underlying philosophical traditions and their quest for knowledge;
- evaluate the competing paradigms in knowledge management;
- identify and understand the current typologies of knowledge within the knowledge management literature.

MANAGEMENT ISSUES

The philosophical perspectives on knowledge imply these questions for managers:

- What are the problems of an action-oriented organisation?
- How can reflection be incorporated into organisational routines?
- How can tacit and explicit knowledge be managed effectively?
- How can 'past experience' be stored in a manner that is useful and meaningful to staff on a daily basis?
- Can a philosophical understanding promote double-loop learning in organisations?

Links to other chapters

Chapter 3   to understand some of the philosophical underpinnings of theory linked to individual, group and organisational learning.

Chapter 9   to recognise the different approaches to cultural management and their philosophical bases.

Plato and leadership

FT

The cult of the celebrity chief executive is closely connected with the current malaise in the business world. Pioneering, risk-taking CEOs were allowed to create their own myths in the 1990s and the leadership archetypes, fawned over by business schools, reflected the fashion. Crass as it now seems, swashbuckling figures from the past who rallied their troops, junked all rule books and refused to give in, despite hopeless odds – the Nelsons, Churchills, Shackletons – were seen as sensible paragons for other people who spend their lives travelling to meetings.

But it has taken Enron *et al.* to make a more contemplative leadership style seem suddenly compelling. Leaders who plug away diligently for decades, know their markets and organisations intimately, see a quick buck as beneath them, and who salute the importance of stability, balance and service in management are the new heroes and heroines – requiring entirely different exemplars.

Plato believed leaders required a grounding in disciplined thought: 'Until kings become philosophers and philosophers kings, things will never go well with the world,' he said. When he founded his Academy in 387BC – an institution which was to last 500 years – it was partly with a view to 'turning around' Athens, which, following the death of Pericles, had fallen into a kind of destructive circularity in which self-serving individual leaders could too easily overwhelm the needs of the community.

Moral confusion, Plato believed, was responsible for Athens' defeat in the Peloponnesian war. History does not record the Attic version of 'ethical deficit'. Unlike Heraclitus, the philosopher of flux and precursor of complexity theorists, Plato was concerned with the source of permanent moral values, which he believed could be accessed by reasoning. The point of philosophy was not happiness or pleasure, but knowledge, which he defined as the justification underpinning truth.

The one who knows is the one who can justify. Good judgement was emblematic of the character and values necessary among those entrusted with leadership – a concern that has rarely been more contemporary. Indeed, Carly Fiorina, chief executive of Hewlett-Packard, sounded most Platonic recently when she said: 'Good leadership means doing the right thing when no one's watching.'

Pre-empting modern educationists, Plato banned lecturing in the Academy, instead preferring joint analysis by students and teachers. This was the method of his mentor and protagonist of many of his dialogues, Socrates. History views Socrates warmly, although he often maddened his contemporaries, not just with his lax sanitation and drunkenness, but also by trapping them in conceptual mazes. If someone suggested that justice lay in giving people their due, Socrates would ask whether they thought it wise to return a sword to a lunatic.

However, when Socrates said that nothing should be taken for granted, the point was not empty cynicism but profound respect for truth. Wisdom could be approached only by rigorous teleological questioning, slicing through false argument and circling ever nearer to the goal of truth even if, finally, it proved unattainable. The exercise of doubt was critical: a useful principle in the selection of non-executive directors.

Business leaders, of course, need to come to decisions. But a Socratic approach to refined decision-making has had many supporters. In *The Effective Executive*, Peter Drucker wrote: 'Decisions are not made well by acclamation. They are made well only if based on the clash of conflicting views, the dialogue between different points of view, the choice between different judgments. One does not make a decision unless there is disagreement.'

Faced with a consensus on the board, Alfred Sloan, of General Motors, feared making a rash choice: 'I propose we give ourselves time to develop disagreement and perhaps gain some understanding of what the decision is all about.'

Among Plato's adversaries were the Sophists. The Sophists were popular among the new Athenian rich as teachers of oratory and rhetoric – forefathers, perhaps, of today's communication coaches. They advocated that the term 'good' was really synonymous with being influential and successful. Words such as 'loyalty', 'justice' and 'truth' were subjective inventions with their own private meaning for individuals. Thrasymachus, one of the more skilful Sophists, even argued that moral codes were a racket aimed at masking the fact that the strong dominate the weak. The wise man does as he likes, but avoids being caught.

Against such views, Plato assembled many arguments, some of which seem flaky today (arguing that human beings aren't designed to be immoral, for instance). But among his best was the highly modern idea that morality underpins life in a community and that trust is in the long-term interest of all. Leaders were repositories of collective behaviour, he argued, so they had to exercise self-discipline in leading 'for the broad good' and avoid the temptation to play to select audiences or mass fashions.

In the 20th century, Plato's 'benevolent guardians' were found to be no good at running countries. But there are strong grounds for hoping they may fare rather better at running companies, not least because they would understand the efficiency of trust. Plato would have applauded parts of Douglas McGregor's Theory X and Theory Y. 'Trust is a delicate property of human relationships. It is influenced far more by actions than by words. It takes a long time to build, but it can be destroyed very quickly.'

He would also have favoured the doctrines of Warren Bennis, the doyen of leadership gurus, who described the best leaders as 'ideas people, conceptu-alists'. Bennis said there are four factors in great leadership – managing attention, managing meaning, managing trust and managing self – and emphasised the importance of longevity, of leadership as a life's work. 'The worst problem in leadership is, basically, early success,' he said.

Source: Article by Stephen Overell, *Financial Times*, 24 February 2003

Questions

1 What are the merits of a 'thinking' style of leadership (Plato) over a 'doing' style of leadership (Aristotle)?
2 Why does Plato advocate that leaders (kings) need to become philosophers?
3 How can a Socratic approach be destructive to organisations.

Introduction

Much of the current literature in knowledge management is based on the writings of two philosophers, Gilbert Ryle and Michael Polanyi. These names and their ideas of logical behaviourism come out predictably within the literature and there seems to be relatively little questioning of their underpinnings. This chapter intends to explore the nature of knowledge more fully to enable the reader to gain a firm grounding of the different perspectives and to engage in some level of philosophical introspection. For example, the reader may find the competing postmodernist notion of production and consumption of knowledge much more attractive than the traditional viewpoint of logical behaviourism.

As a starting point, this chapter begins by looking at how western philosophers have grappled with the 'knowledge' question over the centuries. This forms the rich tapestry against which one can develop new perspectives and understandings of knowledge. As a way of aiding the uninitiated reader, western philosophers have been grouped into idealist and empiricist perspectives, as shown in Figure 2.1 (p. 34). This simplistic notion can act as a useful basis for the reader's future inquiry into the debates surrounding knowledge.

A closer examination is made of Gilbert Ryle's notion of 'knowing how' and 'knowing that' and Michael Polanyi's understanding that these concepts exist along a continuum rather than occurring as distinct separate entities. The myriad epistemological positions are developed using Burrell and Morgan's framework and four common philosophical positions are explored in greater detail: positivism, constructivism, postmodernism and critical realism. The aim is to enable the reader to have a greater understanding of the assumptions behind the writings of different scholars in the area of knowledge management.

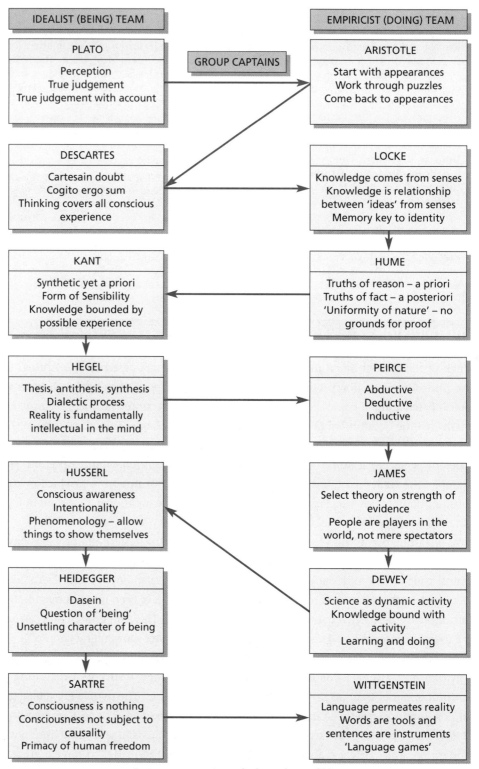

Arrows represent rough chronology of ideas

Figure 2.1 Idealist and empiricist perspectives on knowledge

The different typologies of knowledge within the current knowledge management literature are forwarded to avoid confusion between different terminology used to describe the same concepts of 'knowing how' and 'knowing that'. A realist theory outlining the structure of knowledge based on 'past experience' is presented that builds on Ryle's concepts and suggests that the occurrence of a reflection phase may determine the difference between single-loop and double-loop learning within the structure of knowledge.

What is knowledge? Philosophers from Plato to Wittgenstein

▶ Plato

Plato (427–347 BC), as a pupil of Socrates, wrestled with a wide variety of moral and philosophical questions in the form of dialogues. He expressed his 'idealist' doctrine mainly through the mouth of Socrates in the form of 'Socratic questioning'. Socrates would start with a concept and get his pupils to understand the problems with the concept until they formed an answer to the problem. In subsequent dialogue, Socrates would then show the inadequacy of their answers by revealing contradictions within them. The end result was not to provide a firm answer but to gain a better grasp of the problem. As such, Plato believed that 'conclusions' did not have any special status as our assumptions and beliefs are open to perpetual questioning.

In a later dialogue, *Thaetetus* (360 BC), Plato explores the nature of knowledge. Is knowledge purely subjective and why is it better than opinion? Plato provides three answers to the question of 'What is knowledge?':

● Knowledge is perception.
● Knowledge is true judgement.
● Knowledge is true judgement together with an account.

Each answer is knocked down in true Socratic style. There is no consensus to this day about knowledge except that it is derived from perception that can provide a rational justification for it.

▶ Aristotle

Aristotle (384–322 BC), Plato's star pupil, saw philosophy as an on-going attempt to explore the complexities of human experience. After a sharp reaction against Platonism, he achieved a synthesis of the natural and rational aspects of the world in *The Metaphysics* (350 BC). In every area, his approach was to start with 'appearances' (ordinary beliefs and language), work through puzzles (work through contradictions and find beliefs that were most basic and central) and come back to 'appearances' with increased structure and understanding.

Reflect on your way of looking at the world. Have you ever done any philosophical introspection to understand your own position in amongst the diverse ways of looking at the world? Are you more of a thinker or a doer? Do you think that this has any impact on how you see the world? Have you ever thought about the effect that diverse ways of thinking about a problem may have on the functioning of a team? What do you think could be the implications of this?

Descartes

René Descartes (1596–1650), a rationalist philosopher, struggled with the question 'Can we know anything for certain and, if so, how?' He saw 'certainty' as a state of mind and 'truth' as a property of statements about the external world. He developed scepticism to an art form and promoted doubt as a method which later became known as 'Cartesian doubt'. In *Meditations* (1641), Descartes provides three stages of doubt in order to know something:

1 Lay aside things on common-sense grounds that are doubtful.
2 Doubt that at any given moment you are awake or perceiving anything at, i.e. you may be dreaming.
3 Imagine that a malign spirit or a malicious demon has the sole intent to deceive you.

This led Descartes to his first certainty:

> *'Cogito ergo sum' or 'I think, therefore I am.'*

In *Meditations*, Descartes sees 'thinking' to mean all forms of conscious experience including pain, perceptions and feelings. The true value of Descartes comes from his questioning different aspects of knowledge:

- What do I know?
- What can I doubt?
- How can I know whether any of my beliefs are true?
- What is the difference between my beliefs and prejudices?
- Is there room for scepticism?

Locke

John Locke (1632–1704), an empiricist, believed that everything we conceive or construct has come from experience. His dictum was:

> *'Don't blindly follow convention or authority. Look at the facts and think for yourself.'*

In an *Essay Concerning Human Understanding* (1690), he develops the concept of 'idea' as something sensory that has the properties of a sensory image before the mind. An 'idea' can also cover thoughts, pains and emotions. He views reasoning as a mental operation of these 'ideas' which leads to knowledge or belief. In this sense, knowledge is a perception of relationships between ideas. He accepts that our senses provide us with knowledge of the existence of things but not knowledge of their nature or essence. Locke saw Newton's laws as a kind of crude fact. They were a good description of how things behave but not an explanation. He was keen to point out Newton's most quoted words: 'Hypotheses non fingo' ('I'm not offering explanations'). Locke saw memory as key to personal identity as each person's awareness of history makes them the individual they are.

▶ Hume

David Hume (1711–76) knocked the bottom out of science with his insights into causal links. He acknowledged that one could make 'inductive inferences' about 'matters of fact' such as A causes B from observation of A followed by B, such as day follows night and night follows day. But he argued that past experience could not justify a conclusion about future behaviour. Even though defenders of induction invoked the principle of 'uniformity of nature', there were clearly no grounds to prove that this principle was correct. This insight showed that scientific laws gained through observation were no longer universal statements as previously held (Hume 1739). Subsequently, the doctrines of 'logical positivism' have been derived from Hume. He divided propositions into 'truths of reason' (analytic or a priori – from theory) and 'truths of fact' (synthetic or a posteriori – from practice).

▶ Kant

In *Critique of Pure Reason* (1781), Immanuel Kant (1724–1804) suggested a third proposition to Hume's truths of reason and truths of fact. This proposition was synthetic yet a priori, namely the Form of Sensibility, and concerned space and time. He argued that space and time were inescapable modes of experience and could be specified in an a priori manner (space with geometry and time with arithmetic). He saw knowledge as bounded by 'possible experience'.

▶ Hegel

Georg Wilhelm Friedrich Hegel (1770–1831) viewed the primary goal of knowledge as the greater development of the mind towards freedom. In *The Philosophy of History* (1837), he considered all concepts historically as part of a 'dialectic process'. Using the example of Greek society, the dialectic process starts with a 'thesis' where there is harmony between reason and desire in society. However, he argues that this stable condition cannot persist indefinitely and gives rise to its 'antithesis' through 'Socratic questioning' and the subsequent breakdown of Greek society. In turn, the dialectic process moves forward to create 'synthesis' of these opposing views to give way to a new thesis. Hegel's view of reality is 'Geist' (mind or spirit) which is fundamentally mental or intellectual in nature.

▶ Pragmatists

The primary contribution of the American Pragmatists (Peirce, James and Dewey) towards knowledge was to create a link between belief, meaning, action and inquiry. Charles S. Peirce (1839–1914), often seen as the father of pragmatism, was principally focused on the question of how we are able to investigate the world rationally. In his *Theory of Inquiry* (1867), he suggests that we inquire by testing hypotheses and holding certain beliefs constant that may be revisable or fallible. In scientific inquiry, he proposes the following phases in the development of knowledge:

● 'abductive' inquiry – presenting theories for consideration;
● 'Deductive' inquiry – preparing theories for test;
● 'inductive' inquiry – assessing results of the test.

William James (1842–1910) presents a pragmatic theory of truth where our beliefs need to be in accord with the underlying evidence (1909). For instance, he suggests that our preferences for one theory over another need be based purely on the strength of the competing evidence. In circumstances where evidence is equal, James suggests that we can use other criteria such as bias. He views people as players in the world rather than mere spectators.

John Dewey (1859–1952) applied Peirce's theory of inquiry to social and political philosophy. In *The Quest for Certainty* (1929), he sees science as an activity and process of 'inquiry' that is essentially dynamic in nature. He is against a 'spectator' view of knowledge. Instead, he views human activity as a concern for survival in a dynamic environment where knowledge is the most important survival mechanism. For Dewey, knowledge was closely bound with activity, and notions of truth and meaning also needed to have some connection with it. Dewey made a significant contribution to the philosophy of education (Dewey 1899) by highlighting the interconnectedness of learning and doing and the need to encourage children to learn by doing, by activity and by adopting a problem-solving approach.

▶ Phenomenology and existentialism

Edmund Husserl (1859–1938) influenced a number of philosophers such as Heidegger, Sartre and Merleau-Ponty and established a movement known as phenomenology. In addition, he made a crucial impact on the development of continental and analytic philosophy.

Pause for thought

On many levels, the pragmatist perspective may be considered to be the most appropriate one for managers. What do you think are the strengths and limitations of this perspective? Can you think of any circumstances when a pragmatist perspective could be detrimental to an organisation? Why do you think problem solving could be enhanced by this perspective?

In his masterpiece *Logical Investigations* (1901) Husserl starts his general theory of knowledge on the basis of our conscious awareness being undeniably certain. He continues that our consciousness is always an awareness of something and, in practice, it is difficult to distinguish between states of consciousness and objects of consciousness. He calls the directedness of mental content 'intentionality' and the aspect of the mind that accounts for this directedness 'intentional content'. He argued, for example, in his account of intentionality that it didn't matter whether there was a chair out there or not. He could bracket it and perform a 'phenomenological reduction'. This meant that all that was needed was that he took there to be a chair in the world of objects. He further argued that no one could experience anything without this directed mental content (intentionality). This became his unquestionable foundation for all understanding. For Husserl, phenomenology was allowing things to show themselves as they are in themselves.

Martin Heidegger's (1889–1976) predominant philosophical preoccupation was to answer the 'question of being'. In *Being and Time* (1927), he views human beings as 'Dasein', meaning existence, and sees activity characterised by humans coping in certain situations. Heidegger suggests that we become 'Dasein' when we conform to public norms and become socialised in shared coping skills. Any Dasein is aware that the way of the world is ungrounded. He uses the word 'Unheimlich' (not being at home) to describe the anxiety in the form of guilt caused by the unsettling character of just being. This notion is taken up by existentialists in their liberation philosophy to accept no meaning in Dasein and the unsettling groundlessness of experience.

Jean-Paul Sartre (1905–80) was a student of Husserl and Heidegger and was also greatly influenced by Descartes' notion of human consciousness as free and distinct from the physical universe. In *Being and Nothingness* (1943), Sartre describes consciousness as 'nothing' ('not-a-thing') but an activity ('a wind blowing from nowhere towards the world'). As consciousness is nothingness, it is not subject to the rules of causality. This is fundamental to Sartre's thesis as it forwards the primacy of human freedom. He argues that consciousness is always self-determining and follows a playful paradox:

'It is always what it is not, and is not what it is.'

▶ Wittgenstein

Ludwig Wittgenstein (1889–1951) was primarily concerned with the role of language in human thought and life. In *Tractatus Logico-philosophicus* (1922), Wittgenstein argues that if language represents reality and sentences represent states of affairs, there must be something in common between sentences and states of affairs. As part of his 'picture theory of meaning', he regards sentences as a picture of possible fact and the fundamental unit of meaning. Furthermore, he views the arrangement of words ('names') in sentences corresponding to possible arrangements of objects in the world. This leads to his premise that the structure of the real world determines the structure of language.

In his later work, *Philosophical Investigations* (1953), Wittgenstein employs a 'tool' conception of meaning whereby words are tools and sentences are instruments. The meaning of a word is its use in language and the structure of language determines how we perceive the real world. Language is not strictly held together by a logical structure, as argued earlier in the *Tractatus*, but consists of a multiplicity of simpler substructures or 'language games'. In this analysis, as language permeates all thinking and human experience, the notion of thinking can exist only with expressions. This resulted in some controversy over the 'private language' argument where critics argued that individuals could use words to name private sensations that no one else understood.

Contemporary philosophers: Ryle, Polanyi and Macmurray

The most dominant concepts within the current knowledge management literature are the notions of 'tacit' and 'explicit' knowledge (Nonaka 1994). The underlying philosophy of these constructs can be traced back to Gilbert Ryle (1900–1976) and Michael Polanyi (1891–1976). In the same period that Wittgenstein held the Chair of Philosophy at Cambridge, Ryle held a similar Chair of Philosophy at Oxford. In *The Concept of Mind* (1949), Ryle's major work, his philosophy of mind is focused on a destruction of Cartesianism. He argues that the world of experience is composed of two entities: physical things and mental things.

Ryle's most important contribution is demonstrating the difference between 'knowing how' and 'knowing that'. He makes a distinction between intelligence ('knowing how') and possessing knowledge ('knowing that'). For him, intelligence can have meaning only in activity and is associated with the ability of a person to perform tasks. It is the action that exhibits intelligence. In contrast, 'knowing that' is holding certain bits of knowledge in one's mind such as the names of Snow White's seven dwarfs. He defends his type of logical behaviourism by arguing against the Cartesian idealism that sees knowledge and intelligence as part of the same mental process. He contends that when a person does something intelligently, they are doing only one thing, not two. Knowing how cannot be defined in terms of knowing that. For instance, a chef doesn't recite his recipes to himself (knowing that) before he can cook according to them (knowing how).

Michael Polanyi comes from a similar behaviourist background as Ryle in his book *The Tacit Dimension* (1967) and develops the notion of tacit knowledge from a number of experiments involving hypothetical shock treatments reminiscent of the stimulus-response model of behaviour (Skinner 1938). His starting point of human knowledge is 'the fact that we can know more than we can tell'. He uses Ryle's distinction between 'knowing that' and 'knowing how' and suggests that each aspect of knowing is ever present with the other. They are not distinct entities and his assumption is that they exist together along a continuum, as shown in Figure 2.2 (p. 41). He uses the example of riding a bicycle and the need to have tacit knowledge to stay upright. Staying upright and engaged in the activity of riding is part of 'knowing how' to ride a bicycle. However, many people may find it difficult to articulate clearly (knowing that) what keeps them upright.

Figure 2.2 Philosophy of Gilbert Ryle and Michael Polanyi

How appropriate do you believe it is to define and classify roles in organisations under 'know that' and 'know how'? When employers ask for skills and experience in person specifications, are they purely looking for 'know how'? Passing a football around an organisation provides a useful metaphor for knowledge sharing in organisations. What is wrong with this metaphor? Can you think of a better metaphor for describing knowledge in organisations?

A recent revival in the writings of John Macmurray, a realist philosopher who held the Grote Chair of Philosophy of Mind and Logic at London University from 1928 – 44, saw realism as the unity of theory and practice. The realist position represented a radical departure from the dominant European idealist tradition which divorced theory from action. Macmurray (1933) believed the primary function of thought was to enable action to become 'effective' and 'right'. He insisted that action was more primary than thought with the assertion that:

> *'Thought begins only where action fails.'*

Macmurray (1961) claimed that western philosophy had become ensnared by adopting a position that was theoretical and egocentric. The self was treated as pure, withdrawn and a detached subject. He recognised that to isolate mental activity as the distinctive feature of the self was to exclude the possibility that action, the material world and other persons were of definitive importance in understanding what it is to be human. He suggested (1957) that we substitute the Cartesian dictum:

> *'Cogito ergo sum' (I think, therefore I am)*
>
> with
>
> *'Ago ergo sum' (I do, therefore I am).*

Burrell and Morgan's framework on philosophical paradigms

Burrell and Morgan (1979) have left a lasting legacy in the field of organisational studies by developing our understanding of the production of knowledge. As shown in

Figure 2.3 **Assumptions about social science research (adapted from Burrell and Morgan 1979)**

Figure 2.3, they begin their analysis by examining the ontological assumptions which may underly any epistemological positions and assumptions. Ontology relates to our assumptions of reality and epistemology relates to our grounds of knowledge and what we can know. In turn, Burrell and Morgan argue that it is the epistemological assumptions together with assumptions about human nature that determine the nature of methodology chosen by a particular perspective. The assumptions of human nature are principally focused across the polarities of free will and determinism.

From these assumptions, they produce a map of four 'sociological paradigms' by mapping the major belief systems of academics along a subjective–objective dimension and a free will (sociology of radical change) – determinism (sociology of regulation) dimension (see Figure 2.4 (p. 43)). Paradigm is used to mean a 'commonality of perspective which binds together the work of a group of theorists'. The functionalist paradigm is concerned with a positivist, realist and social engineering perspective where organisational life is about creation and control and not letting matters fall apart. The interpretivist paradigm seeks to understand reality through the realm of individual consciousness and subjectivity. The radical structuralist paradigm emphasises the need to overthrow or transcend limitations placed on social and organisational arrangements by analysing economic power relationships. The radical humanist paradigm seeks radical change and emancipation by overcoming distorted ideologies, power and psychological compulsions and social constraints.

The dominance of the functionalist paradigm and the paucity of radical structuralist or humanist perspectives in knowledge management research makes the current reality of research resemble much closer the representation forwarded by Goles and

Figure 2.4 Burrell and Morgan's four paradigms and different epistemologies (adapted from Burrell and Morgan 1979)

Hirschheim (2000), as shown in Figure 2.5 (p. 44). This position has arisen from similar searches for respectability of young and emerging fields to align themselves to the more respectable 'hard' sciences and the failure of young researchers exploring different paradigms to get published or obtain tenure due to the well-meaning constraints of academic departments and journal editors. In addition, radical humanist and structuralist perspectives can be seen as a threat to traditional organisations as they advocate some form of rebellion against the current orthodoxy. In some quarters, this may be seen as an unwelcome insurgence, in others as transformation of the organisation. Fortunately, there has been a positive development of Burrell and Morgan's contention that the four paradigms are mutually exclusive and a greater move towards multiparadigm research. Gioia and Pitre (1990) argue that the four paradigms can be bridged by transition zones and provide examples of structuration theory, critical theory, Marxism, Weberian theory and solipsism that can exist in more than one paradigm.

Pause for thought

Look closely at Burrell and Morgan's (1979) four paradigms. Why do you think that there has been almost negligible management research from a 'radical humanist' or 'radical structuralist' perspective? What are the problems of 'free will' assumptions in management research? Do you believe that the objective scientific approach is the best perspective for management research and organisational problem solving? What may be some of the limitations of this approach?

Figure 2.5 Proportional representation of Burrell and Morgan's four paradigms in knowledge management research (adapted from Goles and Hirschheim 2000)

Competing philosophical positions in knowledge management: positivism, constructivism, postmodernism and critical realism

Given the large array of philosophical positions, it is not astounding that there are often 'paradigm wars' between adherents of different epistemologies. It is also not uncommon to find open warfare within the same camp where further distinctions of epistemology are made by adding prefixes such as radical, post, critical and neo to the philosophical positions. As positivist science tends to dominate research, there is an uneasy tension between positivists and anti-positivists. The positivists view social phenomena as essentially not different from the natural sciences with a distinct and independent subject–object relationship as shown in Figure 2.6 (p. 45). In the 'naturalism debate', the argument against this position is that the social world is radically different from the natural world. The independent subject–object framework excludes social relations where subjects (let's say academics) may have their own language community as well as being engaged as objects of the social phenomena (see Figure 2.6).

Another argument against the positivist stance is that social realities are often not directly observable. This implies that knowledge of social phenomena is not as certain as in the natural sciences as there are no ways of justifying or falsifying general statements. Similarly, such knowledge does not tend to produce universal laws and logically coherent theories.

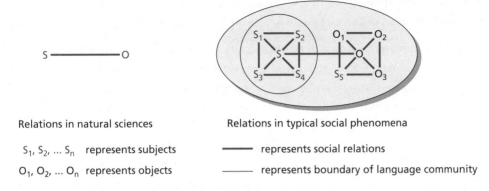

Relations in natural sciences   Relations in typical social phenomena

$S_1, S_2, ... S_n$ represents subjects   ——— represents social relations

$O_1, O_2, ... O_n$ represents objects   ——— represents boundary of language community

Figure 2.6 **The naturalism debate (adapted from Sayer 1992)**

Criticism of the positivist stance is also levelled at its underlying premise that the social world is characterised by a closed system. The absence of constant conjunctions in the social world is echoed in the physical world. A closed system is one where such conjunctions are invariant while open systems are those in which events do not follow a regular, fixed and repeated pattern. In reality, it is almost impossible to create a closed system in the social world similar to those obtained from laboratory practices. Some commentators have argued that the variability of events in the social world may not be due to the inherent uncertainty and chaos as suggested by the 'turbulent environment' thesis but rather the conjunction of real causal mechanisms at work in open systems.

In their classic *The Social Construction of Reality* (1966), Peter Berger and Thomas Luckmann examine common-sense knowledge of what individuals take for granted as real. They recognise that the 'obvious' facts of social reality may differ among people of differing cultures and even within the same culture. The objective becomes the analysis of the processes by which people come to perceive what is 'real' to them. The constructivist perspective argues that our social and organisational surroundings possess no ultimate truth or reality but are determined by the way in which we experience and understand the world we construct in our interaction with others. Critics of this position have argued that social constructivists selectively view certain features of social reality as objective and others as socially constructed. In addition, this perspective fails to accept that there may be broader social forces such as capitalism or materialism that act as powerful influences on observable social outcomes.

One of the main exponents of a 'postmodern' perspective is Jean-François Lyotard in his book *The Postmodern Condition* (1984). He argues that the notion of history shaping phenomena and leading to progress has collapsed. He contests that there are no longer any 'grand narratives' or metanarratives of history or society that make sense. As individuals are engaged in countless videos, films, TV programmes and websites, they come into contact with a multitude of ideas and values that no longer have a basis in their personal or external history. He rejects two influential metanarratives on the goals of knowledge and asserts that there is no ultimate proof for settling disputes over these goals that:

- knowledge is produced for its own sake;
- knowledge is produced for people in a quest for emancipation.

Another important theorist of postmodernity is Jean Baudrillard (1988). He contends that electronic media have destroyed our relationship to the past and reversed the Marxist theory that history and economic forces shape society. Instead, he argues it is signs and images from electronic communication and mass media that influence people's lives.

Michel Foucault is another key contributor to postmodern thought even though he refuses to call himself a postmodernist. He forwards important ideas about the relationships between power, ideology and discourse. The role of discourse is central to understanding power and control in society. Power works through discourse to shape popular attitudes towards social phenomena. For example, expert discourses can become powerful tools to restrict alternative ways of thinking. In this way, Foucault (1980) argues that knowledge becomes a force for control and is linked to technologies of surveillance, enforcement and discipline.

Critics of the postmodernism viewpoint argue that attempts to understand social phenomena or change the world for the better are doomed by this perspective. Also, it impedes any development of general theories of the social world that can help us to intervene and shape matters in a positive manner. One of the central planks of postmodern theory was the discovery of the complexity of the social world, language and meaning. For some critics, there was no possibility to encapsulate the complexity such that postmodern theory became the complexity itself. This is reflected in the wildly conflicting theories, practices and knowledge gained under the umbrella of postmodernism. Some critics of postmodernism have argued that its influence is going out of fashion at the start of the twenty-first century and that its most radical propositions are no longer outrageous and have a clichéd ring about them. In opposition to the ambiguity and complexity of this perspective, it is suggested that the clarity and simplicity of a critical realist perspective may provide the explanatory power and utility to follow the potential demise of this school of thought.

From a realist perspective, there are four misconceptions about knowledge (Sayer 1992), as shown in Table 2.1 (p. 47). First, knowledge can come from participation and interaction with others as well as observation. Secondly, spoken and written forms of language are not the only ways to communicate, appreciate and apply knowledge. Everyday skills such as feelings of sight, sound and smell can give knowledge about, say, being in a large crowd or a threatening environment. Thirdly, knowledge is not a finished product but rather an 'ever present' and 'continually reproduced' outcome of individuals. Lastly, science cannot be assumed to be the highest level of knowledge derived from the first three misconceptions.

Table 2.1 Four misconceptions of knowledge (Sayer 1992)

1 That knowledge is gained purely through contemplation or observation of the world.

2 That what we know can be reduced to what we say.

3 That knowledge can be safely regarded as a thing or product that can be evaluated independently of any consideration of its production and use in social activity.

4 That science can simply be assumed to be the highest form of knowledge and that other types as dispensable and displaceable by science.

To ask for the cause of something is to ask what 'makes it happen', what 'produces', 'generates', 'creates' or 'determines' it. These are all metaphors by which change can occur (Bhaskar 1975). Realism does not view causality as a relationship between discrete events. Instead, realism is concerned with the 'causal powers' or processes and structures that operate in the social world, as shown in Figure 2.7. The causal powers can exist whether or not they are exercised. For instance, unemployed workers have the power to work even though they are not doing so now. Knowing an event 'A' has been followed by an event 'B' is not enough – we need to understand the continuous process by which 'A' produced 'B'. The process of change usually involves several causal mechanisms. Depending on the conditions, operation of the same process can produce different results or, conversely, operation of different processes may produce the same results. The underlying structures can be identified through abstraction and looking for what might produce the effects at issue. Examples of structures are bureaucracies, religious structures and structure of industries.

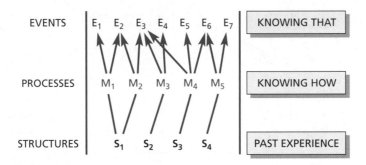

Figure 2.7 Realist theory of explanation

Pause for thought

How would you describe your own knowledge? Do you use words such as 'know how' and 'know that'? Spend some time thinking about your own knowledge and make a list of words that describe your knowledge base. Can you recognise any similarities or differences in the words that you have used? Do your descriptions compare with any words found in this chapter? If you have some atypical words and descriptions, could they be used to formulate a new theory of knowledge?

Current 'knowledge' frameworks within the knowledge management literature

Knowledge can have a nebulous connotation and can become confused with data and information, especially when the terms are used interchangeably in organisations. Davenport and Prusak (1998) view data as discrete objective facts about events that may take the form of structured records of transactions in organisations. In contrast, information is seen as a 'message' or flow of messages that informs the data and makes some difference in outlook or insight to the receiver. Knowledge arising from this data and information has taken the form of a logical behaviourist perspective within the current literature and can be distinguished along the continuum of 'knowing how' and 'knowing that' (Polanyi 1967), as shown in Table 2.2.

Table 2.2 Typologies of knowledge

	KNOWING HOW		CONTINUUM		KNOWING THAT
Kogut & Zander (1992)	Know-how				Information
Nonaka (1994)	Tacit				Explicit
Blackler (1995)	Embrained	Embodied	Encultured	Embedded	Encoded
Spender (1996, 1998)	Individual/Implicit Social/Implicit		Social knowledge		Individual/Explicit Social/Explicit
Brown & Duguid (1998)	Know-how				Know-that
Davenport & Prusak (1998)	Experience	Insight	Values	Data	Information
Cook & Brown (1999)	Knowing (tacit)		Discourse		Knowledge (explicit)
Pfeffer (1999)	Knowing-Doing				Knowledge
Hassard & Kelemen (2002)	Processual – knowing the world		Cultural practices		Being in the world
Newell et al. (2002)	Processual perspective				Structural perspective
Orlikowski (2002)	Knowing				Knowledge

Kogut and Zander (1992) categorise knowledge as a difference between know-how and information based on a similar distinction between declarative and procedural knowledge as used in artificial intelligence. Nonaka (1994) makes a distinction between tacit and explicit knowledge based on Polanyi's (1967) original categories. He develops a hypothesis for the four modes of knowledge conversion as:

- from tacit knowledge to tacit knowledge: process of 'socialisation' through shared experience and interaction;
- from explicit knowledge to explicit knowledge: process of 'combination' through reconfiguring existing knowledge such as sorting, adding, recategorising and recontextualising explicit knowledge can lead to new knowledge;
- from tacit knowledge to explicit knowledge: process of 'externalisation' using metaphors and figurative language;
- from explicit knowledge to tacit knowledge: process of 'internalisation' through the learning process.

Blackler (1995) provides a more detailed framework of the five types of knowledge found in organisations. As shown in Table 2.2, embrained and encoded knowledge corresponds with 'knowing how' and 'knowing that' respectively and the three further forms of knowledge are forwarded to exist along the continuum of knowledge. It is important to clarify here that different terms are used for the same concept within the literature, as illustrated in Table 2.2. For example, the action-oriented concept of 'knowing how' (Polanyi 1967) is treated as implicit knowledge (Spender 1996, 1998), experience (Davenport and Prusak 1998), knowing (Cook and Brown 1999; Hassard and Kelemen 2002; Orlikowski 2002), knowing-doing (Pfeffer and Sutton 1999), and a processual perspective (Newell *et al.* 2002). Similarly, 'knowing that' has been considered as information (Davenport and Prusak 1998; Kogut and Zander 1992), explicit knowledge (Cook and Brown 1999; Spender 1996, 1998), knowledge (Orlikowski 2002; Pfeffer and Sutton 1999) and the structural perspective (Newell *et al.* 2002). Are these reworkings purely another form of old wine in new bottles?

Hassard and Kelemen (2002) provide a refreshingly different perspective of knowledge from the postmodern tradition. They draw heavily on Lyotard (1984) and Foucault (1980) and view knowledge as 'a set of cultural practices situated in and inextricably linked to the material and social circumstances in which it is produced and consumed'. Production of knowledge relies on resources cut away from its original creation and consumption of knowledge occurs through 'being in the world' and social participation in a community of practice.

A realist theory of the structure of organisational knowledge

If one adopts a realist theory of knowledge, one can conceptualise 'knowing that' as the events in social phenomena characterised by the production of knowledge. Similarly, 'knowing how' can be visualised as the processes and mechanisms that produce the 'knowing that'. However, there is nothing within the current literature to illustrate the structure of knowledge that informs 'knowing how' and 'knowing that'. It is argued here that the primary structure of knowledge is past experience, as shown in Figure 2.8 (p. 44). The past experience of human actors shapes the broad social, economic and political networks within organisations.

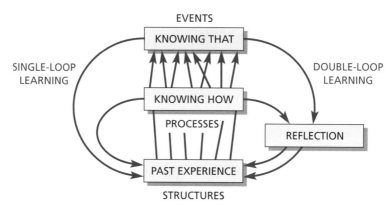

Figure 2.8 Structure of knowledge: routines and revolution

If a person is confronted with a totally new situation, it is likely that the person will predominantly have recourse to their past experience and intuition to determine how to manage in a given environment. This is closely linked with the process of sense making (Weick 1995) whereby people turn knowledge into action. Intuition is assumed to be an innate behaviour embedded within the fabric of experience. Past experience is developed and nurtured in the form of a learning cycle informed and reinforced by 'knowing how' and 'knowing that', as shown in Figure 2.8. It is argued that these behavioural cycles will produce organisational routines (Nelson and Winter 1982) and single-loop learning (Argyris and Schon 1978) within organisations whereby these processes maintain the central features of the organisation's 'theory in use' by detecting and correcting errors within a given system of rules. Individuals may take risks but this will still be based on past experience, even though it is partial and difficult to justify.

In contrast, it is proposed that if a 'reflection' phase is incorporated regularly into the cycle of 'knowing how' and 'knowing that' such that the underlying assumptions and values of an organisation are questioned, this is likely to result in the higher cognitive level within organisations referred to as double-loop learning (Argyris and Schon 1978). This is more likely to lead to 'revolutions' in organisational thinking which may not always lead to the positive organisational outcomes envisaged. Double-loop learning can potentially result in a destabilising force within any organisation.

CASE STUDY

AMD

Jerry Saunders, chief executive and co-founder of AMD, has just rung you (Hans-Raimund Deppe) as the new general manager of the Dresden plant in former communist eastern Germany. He has congratulated you on your successful appointment and transition from the semiconductor subsidiary of Siemens. He reiterates that he has high hopes in your abilities to take over from the successful start-up established by your predecessor Jim Doran.

However, he has some serious concerns about the plant and wants to talk to you in person in three days' time. He will be flying in directly from the headquarters office in California for this meeting.

You are aware that Jerry Saunders will soon be retiring from the company and his overarching vision is to be a sizeable competitor to the virtual monopoly established by Intel in the semiconductor market. His main concern is how you intend to deliver on the projections of growth with a comparatively untrained workforce. Dresden has always been a risky venture for him and he is keen to see it succeed in an environment of highly changing technologies. You are now presiding over a $600 million expansion to push up production at Dresden.

The production of microprocessors was started at this plant three years ago and employs 1,900 people. Your annual production target is set to reach 40m–50m chips next year. This will enable AMD to fulfil its dream of growth, assuming that there isn't a downturn in the global market for microprocessors. Jerry Saunders is keen to understand the detail of how you will make this happen.

During the start-up phase, twenty staff were brought in from offices in California to lend their expertise to the venture. In a dramatic move, 150 of the more highly qualified workers were sent to the US for up to a year immediately before the plant began production. They learnt about the more esoteric aspects of making silicon circuits using a new process to be employed at the Dresden plant. This used copper rather than aluminium within each chip to make the interconnections between different groups of transistors. In addition, the plant workers had to learn how to use a new generation of wafer steppers. These are machines that define the size of electronic patterns on individual chips so that the spacing between individual circuits can be reduced to enable more circuits to be packed inside each chip.

By the end of the year, the Dresden plant is due to make all the company's chips including the new high-performance Hammer microprocessor with a feature size of 0.18 micrometres. On the downside,

you are aware that the factory is not equipped to make chips using the new technology based around 300mm diameter wafers instead of the current 200mm wafers used at Dresden that contain fewer chips. It is also almost certainly too expensive to switch the plant to the new technology. This raises concerns in your mind about whether the plant could survive more than five to seven years in its current state. Intel has already invested in 300mm wafer technology and by the end of the year will have five microprocessor factories capable of making chips with 0.13 micrometre line widths. The key issue is how to compete with Intel on these terms and to reduce their supremacy of the market. Last year, AMD accounted for an estimated 20 per cent of all microprocessor shipments while Intel was almost totally responsible for the rest.

Source: Article by Peter Marsh, *Financial Times*, 8 July 2002

Questions

1 Discuss how you will manage your meeting with Jerry Saunders and your action plan for the coming year.

2 Development and production of microprocessors involves some of the most advanced skills in any industry. How do you intend to develop the 'know how' and 'know that' at the Dresden plant given the rapidly changing technological environment?

3 How do you intend to set up 'communities of practice' between AMD's Californian workers and your Dresden staff to encourage knowledge sharing and innovation? Can you see any problems that could arise from your interventions?

Summary

This chapter has elaborated four main themes:

1 The development of western philosophy with its perpetual quest for an understanding of knowledge underlies many contemporary justifications of the term. Broadly, western philosophy has created a distinction between the idealist philosophers who view knowledge as an entity within our minds and empirical philosophers who view knowledge as arising from our senses.

2 The notions of 'knowing that' and 'knowing how' arising from Gilbert Ryle and Michael Polanyi are considered to exist along a continuum rather than as separate entities. The current typologies of knowledge within the literature are expressed as a reworking of this form of logical behaviourism.

3 The competing philosophical positions are explored using Burrell and Morgan's framework, especially the more common perspectives of positivism, constructivism, postmodernism and realism in knowledge management research.

4 A realist theory of the structure of knowledge is presented based on 'past experience' to underpin the processes of 'knowing how' and the outcomes of 'knowing that'. It is argued that a reflection phase is primary in transforming organisational routines to double-loop learning in the underlying structure of knowledge.

QUESTIONS FOR FURTHER THOUGHT

1 Do you agree with the idealist notion that knowledge can only exist in our heads? If not, what alternative can you provide to our current conception of knowledge?

2 What are the strongest arguments against an empiricist perspective of knowledge?

3 Using Hegel's notion of the dialectic process, which one of the competing perspectives is likely to provide a credible antithesis to the dominant positivist paradigm in management research?

4 From Husserl's perspective, knowledge is linked to a directed mental content called 'intentionality' in our consciousness. What are the merits and drawbacks of this perspective in knowledge management?

5 What are the likely consequences of an almost total lack of regard of issues concerning language in knowledge management research?

6 How could a philosophical understanding of knowledge improve worker performance?

7 Philosophical debates are often excluded and denigrated as being esoteric and inappropriate for management. Can this position be defended in the further quest for knowledge?

8 If knowledge is not purely about what we can say, how can we incorporate other forms of communication such as non-verbal cues into our theory of knowledge?

9 What is the difference between data, information and knowledge in an organisation? How can a manager effectively transform data and information into effective knowledge? How can organisations manage competing and often conflicting interpretations of the same data and information? What are the drawbacks of relying on position power in these circumstances?

10 If the underlying structure of knowledge is past experience, what are the drawbacks of considering intuitions, hunches and insights as part of one's past experience?

Further reading

1 Magee, B. 2000 is an excellent introduction to the thinking of western philosophers in the form of a dialogue between Magee and academics who have spent a lifetime studying particular philosophers.

2 Ryle, G. (1949) acts as the basis for much of the philosophical assumptions around the notion of 'knowledge' in the current literature.

References

Argyris, C. and Schon, D.A. (1978) *Organizational Learning: A Theory of Action Perspective*, Addison-Wesley, Reading, MA.

Aristotle (1998) *The Metaphysics*, H. Lawson-Tancred, translator, Penguin Books, London.

Baudrillard, J. (1988) *Selected Writings*, Polity Press, Cambridge.

Berger, P.L. and Luckmann, T. (1966) *The Social Construction of Reality: A Treatise in the Sociology of Knowledge*, Penguin, New York.

Bhaskar, R. (1975) *A Realist Theory of Science*, Leeds Books, Leeds.

Blackler, F. (1995) 'Knowledge, knowledge work and organizations: an overview and interpretation', *Organization Studies*, 16, 1021–46.

Brown, J.S. and Duguid, P. (1998) 'Organizing knowledge', *California Management Review*, Vol. 40, No. 3, 90–111.

Burrell, G. and Morgan, M. (1979) *Sociological Paradigms and Organizational Analysis*, Heinemann, London.

Cook, S. D. N. and Brown, J. S. (1999) 'Bridging epistemologies: The generative dance between organizational knowledge and organizational knowing', *Organization Science*, 10(4), 381–400.

Davenport, T. H. and Prusak, L. (1998) *Working Knowledge: How Organizations Manage What They Know*, Harvard Business School Press, Boston, MA.

Descartes, R. (1996) *Meditations on First Philosophy*, J. Cottingham, ed., Cambridge University Press, Cambridge.

Dewey, J. (1990) *The School and Society and the Child and the Curriculum*, P. W. Jackson, ed., University of Chicago Press, Chicago.

Dewey, J. (1991) *The Later Works, 1925–1953*, J. A. Boydston, ed., Southern Illinois University Press, Carbondale, Il.

Drucker, P.F. (2002) *The Effective Excutive*, HarperCollins Publishers, New York.

Foucault, M. (1980) *Power/Knowledge*, Pantheon, New York.

Gioia, D. and Pitre, E. (1990) 'Multi-paradigm perspectives on theory building', *Academy of Management Review*, 15(4), 584–602.

Goles, T. and Hirschheim, R. (2000) 'The paradigm is dead, the paradigm is dead ... long live the paradigm: the legacy of Burrell and Morgan', *Omega – The International Journal of Management Science*, 28, 249–268, reprinted with permission from Elsevier.

Hassard, J. and Kelemen, M. (2002) 'Production and consumption in organizational knowledge: the case of the 'paradigms debate', *Organization*, 9(2), 331–355.

Hegel, G. W. F. (1997) *On Art, Religion, and the History of Philosophy*, J. G. Gray, ed., Hackett Publishing Co., Cambridge, MA.

Heidegger, M. (1978) *Being and Time*, Blackwell Publishers, Oxford.

Hume, D. (2000) *A Treatise of Human Nature*, D. F. Norton and M. J. Norton, eds, Oxford University Press, Oxford.

Husserl, E. (2001) *The Shorter 'Logical Investigations'*, D. Moran and M. Dummett, eds, Routledge, London.

James, W. (1990) *Pragmatism and the Meaning of Truth*, Harvard University Press, Cambridge, MA.

Kant, I. (1999) *Critique of Pure Reason*, P. Guyer and A. W. Wood, eds, Cambridge University Press, Cambridge.

Kogut, B. and Zander, U. (1992) 'Knowledge of the firm, combinative capabilities and the replication of technology', *Organization Science*, 5, 383–397.

Locke, J. (1998) *An Essay Concerning Human Understanding*, Wordsworth Editions Ltd, Ware, Herts.

Lyotard, J. F. (1984) *The Postmodern Condition: A Report on Knowledge*, G. Bennington and B. Massumi, translators, University of Minnesota Press, Minneapolis.

Macmurray, J. (1933) *The Philosophy of Communism*, Faber, London.

Macmurray, J. (1957) *The Form of the Personal: The Self as Agent (Vol. 1)*, Faber, London.

Macmurray, J. (1961) *The Form of the Personal: Persons in Relation (Vol. 2)*, Faber, London.

Magee, B. (2000) *The Great Philosophers*, Oxford University Press, Oxford.

Nelson, R. and Winter, S. (1982) *An Evolutionary Theory of Economic Change*, Harvard University Press, Cambridge, MA.

Newell, S., Robertson, M., Scarbrough, H. and Swan, J. (2002) *Managing Knowledge Work*, Palgrave, Basingstoke, Hampshire.

Nonaka, I. (1994) 'A dynamic theory of organizational knowledge creation', *Organization Science*, 5(1), 14–37.

Orlikowski, W. J. (2002) 'Knowing in practice: enacting a collective capability in distributed organizing', *Organization Science*, 13(3), 249–273.

Peirce, C. S. (1998) *The Essential Peirce: Selected Philosophical Writings, 1893–1913* (Vol. 2), N. Houser, ed., Indiana University Press, Bloomington, IN.

Pfeffer, J. and Sutton, R. I. (1999) 'Knowing "what" to do is not enough: turning knowledge into action'. *California Management Review*, 42, 92–3.

Plato (1992) *Thaetetus*, B. Williams and M. F. Burnyeat, eds, Hackett Publishing Co, Cambridge, MA.

Polanyi, M. (1967) *The Tacit Dimension*, Doubleday, New York.

Ryle, G. (1949) *The Concept of Mind*, Hutcheson, London.

Sartre, J. (1968) *Being and Nothingness*, Routledge, London.

Sayer, A. (1992) *Method in Social Science: A Realist Approach*, Routledge, London.

Skinner, B. F. (1938) *The Behaviour of Organisms: An Experimental Analysis*, Appleton-Century-Crofts, New York.

Spender, J. C. (1996) 'Organizational knowledge, learning and memory: Three concepts in search of a theory', *Journal of Organizational Change*, 9, 63–78.

Spender, J. C. (1998) 'Pluralist epistemology and the knowledge-based theory of the firm', *Organization*, 5(2), 233–56.

Weick, K. E. (1995) *Sensemaking in Organizations*, Sage Publications, Thousand Oaks, CA.

Wittgenstein, L. (1953) *Philosophical Investigations*, G. E. M. Anscombe, translator, Basil Blackwell, Oxford.

Wittgenstein, L. (2001) *Tractatus Logico-philosophicus*, Routledge, London.

PART 2

Generating knowledge

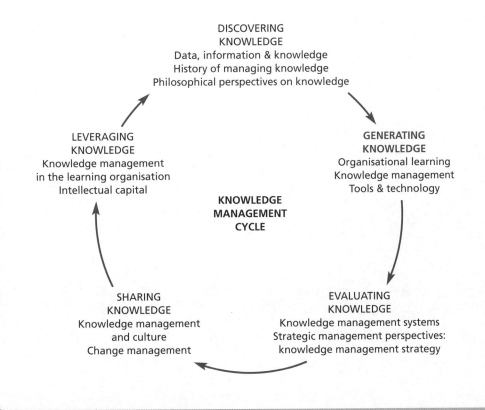

DISCOVERING
KNOWLEDGE
Data, information & knowledge
History of managing knowledge
Philosophical perspectives on knowledge

LEVERAGING
KNOWLEDGE
Knowledge management
in the learning organisation
Intellectual capital

GENERATING
KNOWLEDGE
Organisational learning
Knowledge management
Tools & technology

**KNOWLEDGE
MANAGEMENT
CYCLE**

SHARING
KNOWLEDGE
Knowledge management
and culture
Change management

EVALUATING
KNOWLEDGE
Knowledge management systems
Strategic management perspectives:
knowledge management strategy

Chapter 3

Organisational learning

LEARNING OUTCOMES

After completing this chapter the reader should be able to:

- understand cognitive and behavioural approaches to learning;
- contrast single-loop and double-loop learning;
- present the nature of organisational learning from an information-processing perspective;
- explain how organisational routines are changed and transformed to dynamic capabilities;
- describe the role of politics in organisational learning.

MANAGEMENT ISSUES

An understanding of individual learning, team learning and organisational learning implies these questions for managers:

- What learning environments can be developed to promote effective learning?
- How can complacency from successful ventures and defensive routines from failures be managed effectively?
- When is it appropriate to maintain stability or challenge status quo to promote organisational learning?
- Is an autocratic or participative leadership style more suitable for organisational learning?

Links to other chapters

Chapter 6   concerning how organisational learning can lead to competitive advantage.

Chapter 7   on the role organisational culture may have on the internal political climate and organisational learning.

Chapter 8   on the human resource interventions that can be adopted to foster knowledge sharing and organisational learning.

Organisational learning in the design industry

Attitudes to the design industry are changing. Increasingly, through government support and ongoing promotion by the Design Council, the value of design to business in its many forms has started to be more widely recognised. But there is more to do before the business community accepts design as an indisputable asset that adds value to the bottom line. As an industry, the onus is on us to change the business community's opinion, put design on the same level as other professional practices and convince business that our creativity adds real financial value.

This will become easier as businesses and designers understand more about how creative ideas are born. For too long, creativity has been viewed from a purely aesthetic perspective. Aesthetics are the packaging of an idea. The real equity lies in the idea itself and big creative ideas come from only one source – identifying the specific commercial issues a business is trying to solve. To do that we, as creatives, have to be able to understand business and how it works.

There are several elements of management and business practice we can draw on to help achieve this, not least the very language of business. As an industry we need to learn to talk in the same language as our clients, and marry effectively creativity and strategic thinking. Design businesses need strategists as well as creative thinkers to be involved in all parts of the process, so that the results will always be based on solid business reasoning that our clients can understand.

The industry also needs to learn to be more entrepreneurial in the way we gain our business understanding. In the past, our (design) agency has loaned people out to work in-house alongside our clients. This has helped us get better at identifying how design will add value to their business, and made us better able to express this using their language. The ability to embrace growth is another business quality we would do well to adopt, bearing in mind that 73 per cent of design businesses earn less than £1 million a year in fees. Too many agencies still fear the prospect of expansion, associating it only with a loss of creativity. But to keep up with the pace of our clients, and to support their changing needs, we must learn to view growth as an opportunity.

Growth is not just about more money, but about developing people. There is a war for talent out there, and we need to offer our people opportunities to develop their skills, or someone else will. We also need to implement the processes that go hand in hand with growth, such as better financial controls and people development skills.

Successful businesses embrace change and make it part of their culture. The design industry must do the same. Ironically, creative people are often the most intrinsically conservative, but to stand still in business is the biggest danger of all. If we are not as flexible as our clients in rapidly adapting to change, then how can we expect them to value us genuinely as business partners?

The design industry is reminiscent of a teenager on the brink of adulthood, looking to management and business for guidance in its evolution. In Britain, just 25 per cent of the industry accounts for 80 per cent of the fee income. If our industry is to develop and this ratio become more balanced, we need to address these aspects of the business world and start to operate more like consultants, selling design as a serious, professional, results-orientated activity.

But by the same token, clients need to learn from creatives to allow their own people to take more creative risks, which is, for us, a daily affair. And a lot of fun.

Source: Article by Aziz Cami, *Financial Times*, 10 October 2000

Questions

1 How can design organisations learn to be more entrepreneurial? What skills are required to enable them to act differently?
2 What conditions are necessary for design firms to innovate rather than following their traditional patterns?
3 How can the intrinsic creativity of design firms be channelled into effective business solutions?

Introduction

There is considerable fragmentation in the field of organisational learning and no single framework has successfully encapsulated the diversity of its offerings. The discipline of organisational learning has its roots in a number of wider disciplines of psychology, management science, sociology, strategy and cultural anthropology (Easterby-Smith 1997). The literature of organisational learning is much more mature than the relatively recent literatures of the 'learning organisation' and 'knowledge management' and provides an essential cornerstone for the emerging knowledge management literature.

This chapter begins by looking at how we learn as individuals and how we learn in groups. It examines the role of success and failure in organisational learning and forwards the proposition that moderate levels of failure may act as important drivers in the learning process. The notion of organisational learning is explored in terms of single and double-loop learning and two commonly cited frameworks are investigated – one from an ethnomethodology background and the other from an information-processing one. The information-processing perspective (Huber 1991) of organisational learning is further developed by considering the processes of knowledge acquisition, information distribution, information interpretation and organisational memory.

The role of 'unlearning' is examined together with its importance in preventing stagnation and inertia in organisations. A common response to familiar problems in organisations is to develop routines based on existing knowledge. Learning in the form of organisational routines is explored and how these routines change in response to performance gaps or new possibilities. It is assumed that many of these routines contain tacit knowledge and are stored as procedural memory in organisations. A recent conceptual development of organisational routines is the concept of 'dynamic capabilities'. The theoretical nature of these dynamic capabilities is explored and their role in highly volatile environments. A much neglected area of organisational learning is the impact of politics on learning. A model is forwarded showing a dialectic of cooperative and competitive environments linked to potential asymmetry of power relations, emotions and self-identities.

Individual learning

In an organisation's infancy or in micro-firms comprising a few members, organisational learning could be considered synonymous with individual learning. However, as organisations grow, a clear distinction develops between individual and organisational learning. But are they one and the same? Argyris and Schon (1978, p. 9) articulate this dilemma as follows:

'There is something paradoxical here. Organisations are not merely collections of individuals, yet there are no organisations without such collections. Similarly, organisational learning is not merely individual learning, yet organisations learn through the experience and actions of individuals. What, then, are we to make of organisational learning? What is an organisation that it may learn?'

The current theories of individual learning come from various branches of behaviourism and cognitive psychology. Some of the early behaviourist theories of individual learning were based on a stimulus-response model of behaviour (Gutherie 1935; Skinner 1938). These simplistic notions were extended by examining changes in response probabilities from various stimuli in the learning process. Further behavioural research in the 1950s was conducted on mechanisms of learning where learning became connected with an acquisition of associations, conditioned reflexes and stimulus-response bonds. Subsequent behavioural research explored the role of memory to understand the process of strengthening and weakening associations through rote verbal learning (Underwood 1964).

Another branch in learning theory came from cognitive psychology which saw learning as a change in states of knowledge rather than a change in the probability of response (Bruner *et al.* 1956). This information-processing perspective laid an emphasis on problem solving. Further research in this area moved to investigate memory structures, processing of information, organisation of knowledge and the process of problem solving (Klahr and Wallace 1976). The advent of the information-processing perspective has led to wide acceptance of computer simulation and modelling of the learning process.

Pause for thought   Spend five minutes thinking about the different learning practices in your organisation and make a list of them. Which ones have you found to be the most effective and why? What do you consider are the main strengths and limitations of external courses such as MBA programmes? How do you keep your knowledge up to date, particularly for internal promotion opportunities and in a highly changeable and competitive external job market?

A model of the learning process that is widely used in teaching, training and management is the Lewinian experiential learning model (Kolb 1984), as shown in Figure 3.1 (p. 61). Individual learning can be defined as (Kim 1993):

'increasing one's capacity to take effective action.'

The basic learning cycle from the experiential school of thought has appeared in a variety of different management guises: Deming's (1986) plan–do–check–act cycle, Schein's (1987) observation–emotional reaction–judgement–intervention cycle and Argyris and Schon's (1978) discovery–invention–production–generalisation cycle. Each of the four aspects of the learning process have been developed into learning styles to help individuals understand their strengths and weaknesses in the learning process. An

Figure 3.1 The Lewinian experiential learning model

instrument commonly used by trainers is the Learning Styles Questionnaire devised by Honey and Mumford (1986). This instrument provides individual profiles against the four learning styles, activist, pragmatist, reflector and theorist, which are directly related to the Lewinian learning model.

One of the main criticisms against this learning model is that it ignores the learner's motivation to learn. Without this motivation, or 'fire under the belly', it is unlikely that the individual will have any incentive to learn. How do we ignite this fire in individuals to foster learning in organisations? Also, learning models assume that feedback and reflection are central to the learning process. However, in many organisations, there can be a tendency towards an action-fixated non-learning cycle (Garratt 1987) where the reflection stage is ignored. People don't necessarily have time to think and reflect, being bombarded by urgent problems and pressing deadlines. Are there serious consequences for individual learning in the 'busy-busy' cultures and environments we inhabit? How is the space and time for reflection managed in organisations?

The traditional goals of the learning process are acquisition of knowledge (know what), development of skills (know how) and a change in attitudes of the individual learner. However, through introspection, a learner can also learn about their strengths and weaknesses as a learner. Bateson (1987) coined the phrase 'deutero-learning' for individuals who became effective at 'learning to learn' and more skilled at problem solving. Defensive routines can create blockages in deutero-learning and inhibit further learning. This is particularly evident among smart and professional people where there may be a disparity between what they say (their 'espoused theories') and what they believe (their 'theories in use') (Argyris 1991). The defensive reasoning often arises from smart people's high aspirations for success and their equally high fear of failure which may lead to embarrassment and feelings of vulnerability and incompetence.

Reg Revans (1977) developed the notion of 'action learning' from observing managers and recognising that their learning entails taking effective action rather than purely recommending or making an analysis of a given situation. He stressed the need to integrate cognition and action and theory and behaviour. Revans based his notion of learning on the simple mathematical equation:

L (Learning) = P (Programmed Learning) + Q (Questioning Insight)

Team learning

Team learning can be viewed as the capacity of a group to engage appropriately in dialogue and discussion (Senge 1990). There are three characteristics of effective team learning:

- ability to think insightfully about complex issues and bring together the collective intelligence of the team rather than the insight of the dominant individual;
- ability to provide innovative and coordinated action. This implies alignment of minds between team members and a conscious awareness of other team members and their actions. The example of great jazz ensembles provides a useful metaphor for spontaneous and coordinated action;
- ability to share practices and skills between teams in organisations.

Dialogue is the free and creative exploration of complex issues involving active listening and suspending one's own view. The purpose of dialogue is to go beyond one's own understanding and become an observer of one's own thinking. This means suspending one's own assumptions and playing with different ideas. Dialogue means letting go of power differentials between team players and treating each member equally. It means exploring our assumptions behind our closely held views. Dialogues are particularly useful for divergent thinking where we want a richer grasp of a complex issue rather than fostering agreement. All the early western philosophers such as Socrates, Plato and Aristotle used dialogue in their development of knowledge. Isaacs (1993) provides a useful analogy of the dialogue process when it works well:

> 'A flock of birds suddenly taking flight from a tree reveals the potential coordination of dialogue: this movement all at once, a wholeness and listening together that permits individual differentiation but is still highly interconnected.'

Discussion is complementary to dialogue and is best employed in situations of convergent thinking and decision making, as shown in Figure 3.2 (p. 63). In discussion, different views are presented and defended and there is the search for the best view and arguments to support the decision that needs to be made (Senge 1990). Discussions converge to a conclusion and a course of action. The assumption is that the best argument tends to win in discussions. However, it can be the best arguer using rhetoric or emotive language rather than logic that wins as objective criteria against which the quality of and validity of an argument are rarely tested.

However, there can be defensive routines that can block effective team learning, especially if an individual digs in their heels with their own perspective. This can lead to team conflict, entrenched views and a block of energy flow in a team. Often the defensive routines can arise from individuals not wishing to confront their own thinking to save themselves from threat or embarrassment. This enables them to maintain an air of confidence in a situation based on past judgements and obscures their ignorance.

The distinction between discussion and dialogue can be seen as the difference between decision making and sense making. Weick (2002) describes how a leading fire-fighter makes this distinction clear:

> *'If I make a decision it is a possession, I take pride in it, I tend to defend it and not listen to those who question it. If I make sense, then this is more dynamic and I listen and I can change it. A decision is something you polish. Sense making is a direction for the next period.'*

Drivers of organisational learning: success or failure?

Is failure a prerequisite to organisational learning? If it is, many organisations do little to cultivate it and learn the important lessons from it. Instead, we live in a dominant culture where failure and mistakes are often not tolerated, leading to behaviours where people don't talk about them, dissociate themselves from them and never freely admit to such experiences. Yet failures and mistakes occur on a daily basis in organisations and they can be costly if there isn't a culture of 'error harvesting' where people share their mistakes and hard-won lessons with fellow colleagues. In large organisations, this could prevent costly mistakes from recurring due to blame cultures that may be dominant. Successful forms of 'error harvesting' cultivated in organisations have included groups or work teams coming together on a regular basis and discussing problems, issues and collective appraisals on remedial measures and future actions. Such reflective group-ings have been called 'quality circles' or 'action learning groups' in the past.

What is the problem with success? Surely it provides a secure and reliable basis for future action? If certain practices, procedures and routines have worked in the past, why discard them for something new? Success tends to maintain the status quo

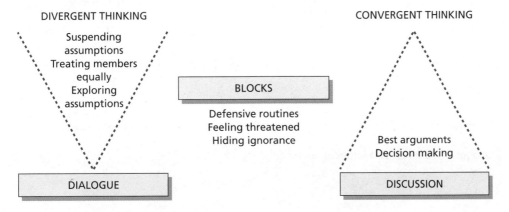

Figure 3.2 Team learning (Senge 1990)

and short-term stability as people are rewarded for their successes and follow their tried and tested ways. The danger is that success can lead to complacency, restricted search and attention, risk aversion and homogeneity (Sitkin 1992).

Success can lead to little motivation to change our ways as existing behaviours are reinforced. The tendency is towards risk-averse and conservative behaviours connected with innovation or decision making. Managers want to guard themselves against the embarrassment and dangers of undertaking risky options that may backfire. Firms prefer to pursue the traditional ways that have worked in the past and have led to their success. Given the nature of dynamic external environments, such 'play it safe' behaviours can provide reliable performance only in the short term. Some of the characteristics of success and failure in organisations are shown in Figure 3.3.

Pause for thought

Reflect on some successful projects or jobs based on your past experience. What specific lessons did you learn from them and did you use your experience on later projects? Similarly, now think of projects that were more like failures in your mind. How different were the lessons from these projects? What types of projects or jobs have you found valuable and have made a marked impression on you? Are there any connections with successful or unsuccessful projects?

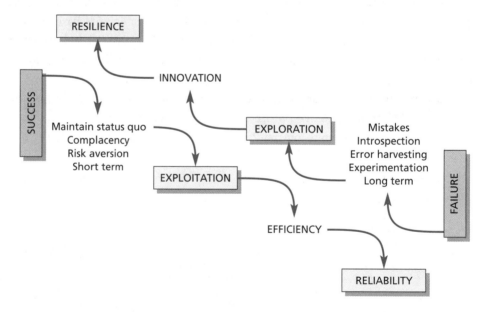

Figure 3.3 **Success and failure in organisations**

Failure allows organisations to learn through experimentation and making adjustments from their mistakes. Major failures are to be avoided as they can lead to the ultimate demise of any firm. However, modest failures could be tolerated to enhance the levels of risk taking and foster experimentation. Failure challenges traditional norms and promotes greater introspection and analysis of what went wrong. People tend to focus on the inconsistencies of the outcome and draw attention to problems that may have been overlooked. This stimulates much greater experimentation with new strategies, procedures and processes. Such varied outcomes and resulting capabilities can lead organisations to be more adaptable to unexpected environments. Hence, moderate levels of failure can lead to increased innovation and improve an organisation's resilience to adapt to differing environments. As Shakespeare reminds us in *Measure for Measure*:

> *'They say best men are moulded out of faults and, for the most, become much more the better for being a little bad.'*

It is clear that organisations can be weighed down by their history, their past experiences and traditions laid down by their founding fathers. But how far is history a driver for organisational learning? Organisational learning from history may be restricted to small samples of experience in any given situation (March *et al.* 1991). If an organisation's experience was successful in the past, the learning and behaviours may become embedded in its actions. If there are different perspectives and cultures in an organisation, this may lead to several different lessons being learnt from the same experience and increasing an organisation's repertoire of interpretations.

Single-loop and double-loop learning

The nature of organisational learning will depend to a large extent on one's definition of an organisation. If one views the organisation as a political entity, the level of organisational learning will depend on political theory and theory of socio-political movements. In a similar way, if one views the organisation as a culture, the level of organisational learning will depend on studies connected with anthropology, ethnomethodology and phenomenology. If one takes a cognitive school approach, organisational learning may be viewed as a distinction between cognition development and behavioural development (Fiol and Lyles 1985). These conceptions of organisational learning as a mental process have become embedded within the literature through the notions of single-loop learning (behavioural) and double-loop learning (cognitive) (Argyris and Schon 1978).

Single-loop learning refers to the process that maintains the central features of the organisation's 'theory-in-use' by detecting and correcting errors within a given system of rules. This means that, given any set of problems, an organisation is likely to act in the same traditional ways and patterns. In contrast, the higher cognitive level of double-loop learning is where current organisational norms and assumptions are questioned to establish a new set of norms. Firms do not continue with their age-old patterns but question their assumptions and values. This often leads to new ways of working and acting.

For example, a firm may be faced with the problem of drastically diminishing sales. The firm may place the blame for the problem on the poor sales force and introduce measures to make them work harder or face redundancy. This would be an example of single-loop learning where the firm responds in a tried and tested manner but assumes it can accomplish its goals by pushing harder. An example of double-loop learning would be if the firm tried to assess the problem more closely and look at the underlying assumptions. It might discover that the customers find its products or services dated, unappealing and poor value for money compared with competitive offerings. In this situation, the firm might decide to innovate its product or service by engaging the collective talents of its marketing, design and operations teams. The new product or service might compete more effectively in the changing competitive markets. Such measures would be an example of double-loop learning.

This example illustrates the difference between exploration and exploitation in organisational learning (March 1991). Exploration behaviours (double-loop learning) are where organisations engage in risk taking, play with ideas, experiment, discover and innovate. In contrast, exploitation behaviours (single-loop learning) are concerned with the refinement of existing processes and emphasise efficiency goals. Both behaviours are important for an organisation depending on the context. If efficiency is the driving force in the competitive environment, single-loop or exploitation behaviours become important. However, there can be a continual flux between exploitation and exploration as they compete for a firm's scarce resources.

As exploration behaviours require risk taking and experimentation, their outcomes can be less certain and have much longer time horizons. The exploration of new ideas, markets and relationships and their likely outcomes are much more ambiguous than exploiting and imitating current methods and relationships. It has been argued that as firms adapt to the changing environments by refining exploitation behaviours more rapidly than exploration ones, they are likely to be effective in the short term but self-destructive in the long term.

Organisational learning frameworks

In the organisational learning literatures, there is an underlying assumption that learning will improve a firm's performance. In contrast, a key premise in the strategy literatures is that this will be achieved by close alignment of the firm to its environment. A definition of organisational learning based on action that encompasses such assumptions is proposed by Fiol and Lyles (1985):

'Organisational learning means the process of improving actions through better knowledge and understanding'

A number of studies have investigated the disparate literatures of organisational learning and tried to chart its varied terrain (Crossan *et al.* 1999; Easterby-Smith 1997; Fiol and Lyles 1985; Huber 1991; Levitt and March 1988; Shrivastava 1983). Each examination has provided a somewhat different map of the landscape depending on the epistemological perspectives and backgrounds of the researchers. A recent ethnomethodology framework of organisational learning (Bontis *et al.* 2002; Crossan *et al.* 1999) builds on the tension between exploration and exploitation in organisations and places these notions at the heart of strategic renewal. Renewal is based on organisations exploring and learning new ways while at the same time exploiting what they have already learnt. This framework considers organisational learning at three levels: individual, group and organisational, as shown in Table 3.1. There are four learning processes that flow naturally from one to another without any clear distinction of where they begin or end. Also, there may be feedback loops from the learning processes between the three levels.

Table 3.1 Organisational learning framework (Crossan *et al.* 1999)

Level	Process	Inputs/Outcomes
Individual	Intuiting	Experiences Images Metaphors
	Intepreting	Language Cognitive map Conversation/dialogue
Group	Integrating	Shared understandings Mutual adjustments Interactive systems
Organisation	Institutionalizing	Routines Diagnostic systems Rules and procedures

The four learning processes entail:

- *Intuiting.* This is largely a subconscious process that often requires some form of pattern recognition. For instance, an expert may be able to foresee a pattern in a problem that a novice may not. This pattern recognition will support exploitation. However, intuition is also important for exploration to help generate new insights and novel applications. Metaphors and the use of imagery can help provide the language to communicate one's insight to someone else.
- *Interpreting.* This is the process of explaining through words and/or actions an insight or an idea to one's self or to another person. We develop our own cognitive map of a domain and can interpret the same stimulus differently due to our established cognitive maps. In a group situation, this can result in multiple and potentially conflicting interpretations of the best course of action.

● *Integrating*. This learning process is about developing shared understanding and taking coordinated action through mutual adjustment. Group dialogue and story-telling are seen as major tools for developing new and deeper shared understandings.

● *Institutionalising*. This learning process is to ensure that routinised actions occur. Successful actions over time often become embedded in organisational routines. Such routines have an effect on the systems, structures and strategies of an organisation. One characteristic of institutionalisation is the endurance of the behaviour over a period of time.

This model proceeds to suggest a dynamic between the four learning processes through 'feedforward' and feedback loops. It does not elaborate on how these processes assist organisations to find the balance between exploration and exploitation behaviours which are seen as critical for strategic renewal. Most of the innovation in this 4I framework rests on the entrepreneurial intuiting in the first individual phase. Without the 'feedforward' loops, it is unlikely that the institutionalised organisational routines would be challenged, with a consequence of exploitation behaviours predominating within any organisation. How could managers balance the wisdom of their experts with the uneasy flair of the entrepreneurs? What effect would culture have on strategic renewal? Dialogue may be valuable for developing divergent thinking but what are the implications for actions requiring convergent thinking and decision making?

One criticism of this 4Is model is the tendency in management literature towards prescriptions related to certain characters of the alphabet:, 4Ps in marketing and 4Is in action learning (Mumford 1991). What distinguishes the effectiveness of Mumford's model based on 4Is of interaction, integration, implementation and iteration over the Crossan *et al.* one? There appear to be similarities between interaction in one model and interpreting in another, integration occurs in both models, and iteration could be seen as a form of the feedback loops leading to institutionalisation.

Most empirical research in organisational learning tends to be qualitative in nature and it is relatively uncommon to find many quantitative studies. This is mainly related to the difficulties of developing valid instruments that measure organisational learning. One can always develop a multitude of items from pilot interviews and theoretical frameworks related to organisational learning. From statistical analysis, one can demonstrate the strength of reliability of these constructs relatively easily. However, we still don't know whether what we are measuring is really organisational learning. Evidence for validity of these instruments is often found wanting. The main reason is that there isn't a singular valid instrument in the public domain that has the consensus of this academic community. If this was the case, one could develop new instruments confidently, knowing that an element of a valid instrument was contained within the questionnaire for empirical testing.

The second major issue is around sampling. Who do you send your questionnaires to? How many people need to be sampled within a firm to get a reliable sample?

Assuming that the research has limited resources, do you sample many people in a few firms or a few people in lots of firms to get greater generalisations from the results? Some researchers have surveyed a single senior executive from each firm, assuming that their position is likely to give them a 'helicopter view' of the organisation. Given the complexity of these methodological issues, can the results from quantitative studies of organisational learning be meaningful?

One of the seminal papers in this discipline comes from Huber (1991) who attempts to understand and evaluate the diverse literatures of organisational learning under four constructs, as shown in Figure 3.4. He adopts an information-processing perspective defining organisational learning as follows:

> 'An entity learns if, through its processing of information, the range of its potential behaviours is changed.'

This framework adopts a behavioural rather than a cognitive perspective of learning and assumes that the four constructs are inter-related. No attempt is made to show how the processes in each construct integrate with one another. Knowledge acquisition is seen as the process by which knowledge is obtained. Information distribution is the process by which information is shared, which can often lead to new information or understanding. Information interpretation is the process by which information is given one or more interpretations. Organisational memory is the means by which knowledge is stored for future use (Huber 1991).

The main criticisms of this perspective are around the problems of implementing organisational learning (Easterby-Smith 1997):

- Political behaviours in organisations are not considered in the framework and can lead to distortion and suppression of information. The political climate can also lead managers to make decisions based on irrational grounds. The framework could be considered as politically naïve.
- As the framework adopts a behavioural rather than a cognitive perspective, there is a danger that it may lead to a tendency towards exploitation rather than exploration in organisations.
- Behavioural perspective may create a tendency to hold on to old views and practices rather than questioning them.

Figure 3.4 Organisational learning framework (Huber 1991)

Knowledge acquisition

Organisations acquire new knowledge through the processes of congenital learning, experiential learning, vicarious learning, grafting, and searching and noticing (Huber 1991), as shown in Figure 3.5. Congenital learning is the learning influenced by the founding fathers of the organisation. This inherited knowledge can affect the way a firm acts and interprets new knowledge. Experiential learning is acquired from direct experience and can be found in a number of guises:

- Organisational experiments may take the form of pilot studies with feedback of findings and recommendations to the organisation.
- Move from behavioural learning to cognitive learning through questioning key assumptions and values.
- Enhancing adaptability as an experimenting organisation with a greater emphasis on exploration rather than exploitation.
- Unintentional learning through the haphazard and multi-faceted lives of workers.
- Learning curves or 'learning by doing' show that as an organisation produces more of a product, the unit cost of production decreases at a decreasing rate. The beauty of this experiential learning is that performance over time can often be predicted using a mathematical model. Such learning can be explained through individuals learning over time as well as the organisation, such as the effective use of technology (Yelle 1979). Effective decisions can be made by managers on how best to balance technology against working practices (Epple *et al.* 1996).

Often organisations don't have the time to gain certain knowledge to meet competitive pressures. They may seek to borrow competitors' strategies, practices and technologies. Such learning is termed vicarious learning and it adopts imitation or mimicry of other firms. Gaining the 'know how' of other firms is termed 'corporate intelligence' and can be gained from consultants, professional meetings and publications.

Knowledge can also be acquired by 'grafting' or employing new members with the knowledge and skills lacking within the organisation. This may be seen as preferable to developing the knowledge and skills in-house through various human resource interventions. On a bigger scale, firms engage in acquisitions of other companies where the acquisition may have core competences lacking within the parent firm.

Figure 3.5 **Knowledge acquisition constructs (Huber 1991)**

Pause for thought

Benchmarking is all the rage in some organisations. What do you think are the problems of this form of vicarious learning? Similarly, what are the advantages and limitations of using off-the-shelf solutions compared with building them in-house? From your experience in organisations, what do you feel hinders them from learning? Many organisations seem to make the same mistakes over and over again. What do you believe could help organisations break such detrimental cycles?

Firms also acquire knowledge through intentional search and unintentional noticing behaviours. Organisational search can take a number of forms (Huber 1991):

- scanning – a monitoring behaviour of organisations often conducted by senior managers searching for non-routine but relevant information;
- focused search linked to a particular organisational problem;
- performance monitoring of internal targets and measures as well as satisfying the needs of external stakeholders.

Information distribution

In small organisations, information distribution may remain at a very informal level. However, the quality of information distribution may lead to new or more broadly based organisational learning. Such information sharing can enable the development of new information as well as new understanding (Krone *et al.* 1987). Information distribution highlights the role of organisational communication and the nature of the internal political environments (Jashapara 1993) which may aid or hinder such communication. There are technological aspects (see Chapter 5) of knowledge storage and retrieval as well as social capital aspects such as the relationships between employees (see Chapter 10) that will have an impact on the nature of information distribution within an organisation.

Information interpretation

Information interpretation can be seen as the process by which information is given meaning and the development of shared understanding (Daft and Weick 1984; Huber 1991). Is the goal to develop similar understandings or diverse understandings within organisations? Would similar understandings result in greater cooperation and coherence whereas more diverse understandings would lead to greater strife and conflict? The shared understandings and interpretations of new information are affected by cognitive maps and framing, media richness, information overload and unlearning, as shown in Figure 3.6 (p. 72).

Figure 3.6 Information interpretation constructs (Huber 1991)

A person's existing cognitive map determines how a piece of information is interpreted. They may be influenced by their position within an organisational hierarchy, previous experience and their current working team and environment. To establish uniformity of shared interpretation, there needs to be uniformity in cognitive maps among the team. This is easier when new information is framed in a consistent and familiar manner. If new information is framed in a different manner around different divisional units, it is likely that there will be a diversity of shared understandings of the information.

Media richness is the communication medium's capacity to change mental representations within a specific time interval (Huber 1991). Managers often explore the most effective media to communicate their message to develop shared meaning. For example, the use of e-mail as opposed to face-to-face meetings to transmit a message may convey very differing messages. Face-to-face communication has much greater richness as it displays the person's tone of voice and body language as well as the words, unlike the monotone nature of e-mails.

Information overload has a direct effect on an individual's capacity to interpret information. In group situations, information overload may result in disparities of shared understandings due to different levels of overload within the same group. Even if there are consistencies in the levels of overload within a group, there are likely to be diverse interpretations of the same message as individuals respond more to their own internal state and perceptions than to the external stimulus.

Pause for thought

We live in a world where we are bombarded with information and countless e-mails every day. From your experience, describe your perceptions of information overload on your job. How do you manage large quantities of information? If you discard much of this information, how do you know what to discard? How does information overload affect your emotions and reasoning? What practical strategies have you developed to cope with information overload?

Unlearning is the process by which individuals discard obsolete or misleading knowledge (Hedberg 1981). At an organisational level, unlearning can have the effect of blocking the firm in areas where it used the misleading knowledge or behaviours. It can also activate a firm to search for knowledge or behaviours to replace the obsolete ones and encourage it to become more open to new forms of learning and knowledge. Further elaboration of unlearning is provided on page 73.

Organisational memory

The old oral traditions utilised the human memory and highlighted its limitations. Long periods of time were spent memorising information, leaving little room for critical evaluation. In an organisational context, organisational memory may reside in people's minds as repositories of organisational knowledge. However, as people leave a firm, this precious organisational memory may be lost for ever. This 'soft' form of organisational memory can be invaluable in a variety of circumstances:

- diagnosing an error in a complex piece of technology;
- knowledge of organisational skills, experts and resources;
- locating non-traditional information sources.

In the psychology literature, a distinction is made between semantic (general) and episodic (context-specific) memory (Stein and Zwass 1995). Semantic memory comes from shared interpretations of significant events that are not personally experienced and may take the form of handbooks and procedural manuals. Episodic memory is shared interpretations and collective understandings of personally experienced events.

The 'hard' forms of organisational memory relate to storage and retrieval processes and computer-based organisational memory, as shown in Figure 3.7. The latest KM component technologies related to effective storage and retrieval and data warehouses are discussed in Chapters 4 and 5. Such notions of organisational memory treat the construct as a set of repositories of stored information from an organisation's history. The repositories may contain knowledge about individuals, culture, transformations, structure and ecology (Walsh and Ungson 1991).

Unlearning

Do organisations exist in closed or open systems? Often the tendency among decision makers is to treat their subsystems and environments as closed systems, leading to a perception of stability in organisational learning. This is fine if environmental changes are low, stable and predictable. Typically after some delay, organisations will respond to environmental changes by adjusting their goals and expectations and modifing their decision-making behaviours. In benevolent environments, there is little incentive for organisations to change their ways, which ultimately can lead to inertia and stagnation.

Organisational memory → Storing and retrieving information
→ Computer-based organizational memory

Figure 3.7 Organisational memory constructs

However, if the environmental changes are more substantial and discontinuous, the traditional responses may need to be reconsidered, deleted and replaced to ensure organisational survival. This is known as unlearning.

> *'Unlearning is a process through which learners discard knowledge. Unlearning makes way for new responses and mental maps.'* (Hedberg 1981)

Successful behaviours in the past may no longer provide a valid response to future levels of environmental uncertainty. This requires organisations to pull down obsolete mental maps showing the correct ways of doing things and starting afresh. If they don't do this, the environmental discontinuities may threaten an organisation's survival. The effective response in these circumstances is to unlearn old behaviours and learn new ones.

Unlearning is a difficult and cumbersome process as it threatens the organisation's way of doing things. To external observers, organisations undergoing unlearning can appear incompetent and ineffectual. On the inside of organisations, unlearning can lead to disorientation and upheaval where traditional benchmarks are lost. Unlearning has three modes of operation (Hedberg 1981):

● challenge and negate (disconfirmation) processes for selecting and identifying stimuli. People and organisations unlearn their world views;
● challenge and negate (disconfirmation) any connections between stimuli and responses so that people don't know what responses to make to particular stimuli;
● challenge and negate (disconfirmation) any connections between responses so that people no longer know how to assemble responses to new situations.

Unlearning can be unnerving at an individual level as the traditional points of reference are lost. So what can act as useful triggers for unlearning in organisations? Effective triggers include problems, which can arise from cashflow shortages, declining revenues and profits, financial losses and criticisms from stakeholders. Problems typically arise from the gap between performance and expectations. Organisations do not respond in new ways to all problems. The deviation between performance and expectations needs to be large before any adjustments or reorganisations are likely to occur, as shown in Figure 3.8.

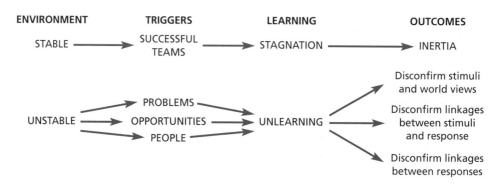

Figure 3.8 Environments and unlearning

Problems are not the only triggers, otherwise problem-ridden organisations would be the best innovators (Hedberg 1981) and this is clearly not the case. The dilemma for many organisations undergoing major problems and crises is that they cannot afford to take the necessary risks implied in the unlearning process. Opportunities in the external environment such as development of niche markets can also provide triggers for unlearning.

The third trigger for unlearning is people, particularly when key individuals leave the organisation, taking with them the experiences of procedures and processes from the organisational memory.

Organisational routines

Organisational routines are an important aspect of organisational learning as they help us to understand the interplay between an organisation's structure, its processes and its actions. Originally, routines were associated with an organisation's operating procedures and resembled the mechanical notions of computer programs with their routines and subroutines (Cyert and March 1963; March and Simon 1958). This included an organisation's norms, conventions, rules and procedures and the way it operates on a daily basis. They helped contribute to an organisation's stability. These routines were embedded in the organisation's culture, beliefs and frameworks and could often contradict rules found in operating manuals. In general, the routines were seen as independent of individual actors and capable of surviving significant turnover in personnel (Levitt and March 1988). Routines also explained the inertia within organisations through repeated patterns of behaviour bound by rules and customs (Nelson and Winter 1982). Such routines were seen as regular and predictable patterns of behaviour. In new circumstances, an organisation might draw from a pool of alternative routines (Levitt and March 1988).

Routines can be communicated through a variety of channels such as imitation, socialisation, education and personalisation processes, and become part of the collective memory. It was initially assumed that organisational routines did not change, but increasing empirical research shows that routines *are* subject to change (Feldman 2000; Pentland and Rueter 1994). A number of definitions of this phenomenon are forwarded in the literature:

> 'An executable capability for repeated performance in some context that has been learned by an organization in response to selective pressures.' (Cohen *et al.* 1996)

> 'An organizational routine is not a single pattern but, rather, a set of possible patterns – enabled and constrained by a variety of organizational, social, physical and cognitive structures – from which organizational members enact particular performances.' (Pentland and Rueter 1994)

> 'Recurring patterns of behaviour of multiple organizational members involved in performing organizational tasks.' (Feldman and Rafaeli 2002)

Cohen and Bacdayan (1994) have argued that organisational routines are stored as procedural memory. They make a distinction between 'procedural' memory and 'declarative' memory arising in the psychology literature. Procedural memory stores the cognitive and motor skills associated with an individual's skilled actions and could be considered as the individual 'know how'. By nature, it is tacit, relatively automatic and difficult to articulate. In contrast, declarative memory is the repository of facts, propositions and events and similar to an individual's 'know what' or explicit knowledge. The difference is similar to the more static notion of 'organisation' compared with the more dynamic process of 'organising' (Weick 1979).

Routines are an important part of an organisation's competence and without them organisations would lack efficient methods of collective action. However, routines can have detrimental consequences if they are automatically transferred to inappropriate new situations. Working routines are seen as much more than standard operating procedures as official documents may or may not be followed. What happens in reality is similar in distinction between espoused theories and theories-in-use in organisations (Argyris and Schon 1978). They are produced gradually over time through multi-actor learning engaged in a particular routine. The tacit and multi-actor nature of organisational routines makes them difficult to research effectively as the problem entails surfacing, verbalising and externalising an organisation's 'unconscious' memory (Cohen and Bacdayan 1994). Changes in habitual routines in groups can be triggered in a number of ways (Gersick and Hackman 1990):

● encountering a novel state of affairs;
● experiencing a failure;
● reaching a milestone in the life or work of the group;
● receiving an intervention that calls members' attention to their group norms;
● having to cope with change in the structure of the group itself.

Pause for thought

As human beings, we have been considered as creatures of habit. Such habits in organisational terms may be considered as routines. How do you believe that such stable patterns of behaviour or organisational routines can aid or hinder organisations? From your experience, do you feel that all processes, no matter how new or innovative, inevitably lead to organisational routines? Is it worth actively discouraging such routines in organisations? If so, how?

An alternative conception of organisational routines is one that resembles a set of possible patterns that are neither fixed nor automatic. A novel representation of routines is to use a grammatical model (Pentland and Rueter 1994). The 'grammar' analogy to routines allows actors to use a set of possibilities to accomplish a task without specifying a fixed outcome. This model acknowledges the importance of both the structure and agency (actor) within routines rather than the earlier fixation on operating procedures and the traditional elements of stimulus and automatic response. This approach concurs with social theory that regards routines in social activity as achieved through considerable effort (Giddens 1984).

A similar metaphor which demonstrates the stability and adaptability of routines is the ballroom dance (Feldman and Rafaeli 2002). Individual actions in dances are scripted beforehand but dances can allow flexibility depending on the context. Dancers will adapt their styles to this context depending on the number of other dancers on the floor, any obstructions in the floor, the competence of their partner and whether or not they have danced the particular number before. Communication between the dancers (similar to organisational routines) will allow flexibility in the dance to occur. Empirical research suggests that changes in organisational routines can occur due to a number of reasons (Feldman 2000):

- *Repairing* routines so that participants can produce intended and desired outcomes. This occurs when actions do not produce the intended outcome or produce an undesirable outcome.
- *Expanding* routines so that participants can produce new possibilities from outcomes. The changed routine takes advantage of new possibilities.
- *Striving* routines so that participants can respond to outcomes that fall short of ideals. This attempts to attain something that is difficult by nature.

Success and failure in outcomes can have a major impact on routines. Favourable performance with an inferior routine can lead to its perpetuation and the denial of a superior routine can lead to a competency trap (Levitt and March 1988). Sub-optimal performance may persist with the use of familiar procedures, practices and technologies. Success reinforces successful routines whilst inhibiting other routines. As outlined earlier in this chapter, failure or significant performance gaps may be the necessary determinant to change organisational routines as organisations search for ones that can match their desired outcomes.

Recent research has tried to unravel the processes that contribute to the stability and change of organisational routines (Feldman and Rafaeli 2002). The starting point in this theory is that organisational routines are a form of coordination used in organisations. The routines make 'connections' where connections are defined as the interactions between people that enable them to transfer information. The outcomes of the connection process are social support and information transfer (note the similarity to social capital and knowledge transfer). The encounters in connections create variations in strong and weak ties between organisational members.

The connections enable shared understandings to occur. These arise through verbal as well as non-verbal communication. The coming together of people in a routine allows different interpretations to be explored and the development of a common understanding. These understandings include aspects of the organisational context, performance expectations, power relations and organisational identity. The organisational context concerns what an organisation does and why, as well as who are the critical stakeholders. The power relations allow participants to understand the hierarchy and their status within the organisation. This theory assumes a time delay between routines and their development of connections and shared understandings and rather like the same notion in social theory needs to be worked on over time. A model providing a synthesis of the organisational routine literature is shown in Figure 3.9 (Cohen and Bacdayan 1994; Feldman and Rafaeli 2002). A useful anology to describe organisational routines was expressed vividly by an anonymous reviewer as follows:

> 'Routines are like ruts in a well-travelled road. They do not exactly determine where the next wagon will go, but neither do they merely describe where past wagons have gone.' (Pentland and Rueter 1994)

Dynamic capabilities

Dynamic capabilities as a concept is a relatively new phenomenon and has evolved from research on organisational routines. In fact, there is confusion within the literature about where organisational routines end and dynamic capabilities begin. It is fair to say that the literature on dynamic capabilities is based predominantly on theoretical developments rather than on empirical research. On a simplistic level, dynamic capabilities have been considered as 'routines to learn routines', similar to the notion of deutero-learning (learning to learn). The following definitions of dynamic capabilities illustrate some of the variations in the field:

> 'Firm's ability to integrate, build, and reconfigure internal and external competences to address rapidly changing environments.' (Teece *et al.* 1997)

Figure 3.9 **Organisational routines (adapted from Cohen and Bacdayan 1994; Feldman and Rafaeli 2002)**

*'The firm's processes that use resources – specifically the processes to integrate, reconfig-
ure, gain and release resources – to match and even create market change. Dynamic
capabilities thus are organizational and strategic routines by which firms achieve new
resource configurations as markets emerge, collide, split, evolve, and die.'* (Eisenhardt
and Martin 2000)

*'A dynamic capability is a learned and stable pattern of collective activity through which
the organization systematically generates and modifies its operating routines in pursuit
of improved effectiveness.'* (Zollo and Winter 2002)

So are organisational routines and dynamic capabilities synonymous concepts? The key
distinction appears to be the level of change encountered as a factor of market
dynamism. In stable or static environments and market conditions, organisational routines predominate, characterised by stable patterns of behaviour. The routines can be
complex but are predictable and build on existing knowledge. They evolve slowly over
time and exhibit qualities of single-loop learning. However, in moderately dynamic or
highly volatile markets, the use of organisational routines can prove hazardous in their
automatic response to changed stimuli. Organisations can learn to adapt their routines to
the changed circumstances, which leads to the development of dynamic capabilities. If
this does not occur, core competencies can become core rigidities (Leonard-Barton 1992).

The fine line between organisational routines and dynamic capabilities arises due to
models that highlight similar stable and predictable modes of activity for each phenomenon (Zollo and Winter 2002). In this conception, dynamic capabilities can be
viewed as modified operating routines following predictable mathematical arrangements, as shown in Table 3.2. The primary distinction is systematic learning, which
implies a stable pattern of learning not dissimilar to single-loop learning. What happens in highly volatile market conditions when organisations cannot rely on
systematic learning and existing knowledge? Do organisations fall back on their old
tried and trusted learning mechanisms in the vain hope of achieving desired outcomes?

Table 3.2 Dynamic capabilities (adapted from Zollo and Winter 2002)

Dynamic capabilities =	Systematic learning + Organisational routines
Systematic learning =	Experience accumulation + Knowledge articulation + Knowledge codification

Experience accumulation is perceived as occurring from learning investments aimed at
developing a collective understanding of action-performance linkages. A principal aspect
of the learning process is 'knowledge articulation' when groups of people come together
in a variety of circumstances such as meetings and debriefing sessions and make their
understandings and interpretations of a situation explicit. This does not imply that there
needs to be agreement within the group, but through a process of dialogue and discussion, a shared understanding is developed. Given that much of the knowledge is likely to
be tacit, this process of externalisation is important to make the knowledge explicit.

Knowledge codification as part of the systematic learning allows further reflection on existing routines to help understand which routines work, which don't work, and why (Zollo and Winter 2002). Knowledge codification may take the form of developing manuals, decision-support systems and blueprint guides of best practice.

Eisenhardt and Martin (2000) provide a clearer distinction between organisational routines and dynamic capabilities. They suggest that in stable and moderately dynamic market conditions, collective organisational activity resembles traditional predictable routines where managers rely heavily on their existing tacit knowledge. However, in high-velocity and volatile markets, organisational activity tends towards dynamic capabilities where managers rely much less on existing knowledge due to the ambiguity of the situation and more on situation-specific new knowledge. In these uncertain environments, the dynamic capabilities are composed of simple routines consisting of very few rules and a greater tendency towards improvisation. Flexibility of response becomes an important determinant. Dynamic capabilities possess a number of key attributes (Eisenhardt and Martin 2000):

- equifinality – firms develop similar dynamic capabilities even though they may have different starting points and take unique paths;
- commonality of dynamic capabilities – such routines are transferable between contexts and industries;
- idiosyncrasy – firms may have commonalities in their dynamic capabilities but differ in their levels of detail (firm specific) which leads to competitive advantage;
- prototyping – often used to test and gain new knowledge quickly through small losses and feedback;
- real-time information – to allow adjustment and adaptation to occur due to changing circumstances;
- multiple options – parallel consideration of alternatives to allow managers to act confidently and quickly;
- path dependent – a firm's investments in certain routines historically tend to constrain its future behaviour.

Dynamic capabilities can lead to competitive advantage if they are valuable, rare, inimitable and non-substitutable (VRIN attributes). However, it has been argued that they are necessary, but not sufficient, conditions for sustainable competitive advantage (Eisenhardt and Martin 2000). Their idiosyncratic nature may give them short-term competitive advantage, but this cannot be sustained as they are substitutable due to their equifinality and commonality characteristics.

Politics and organisational learning

The impact of politics and power relations has received little attention within the literature until recently (Coopey and Burgoyne 2000; Knights and McCabe 1998; Nissley and Casey 2002; Vince 2001). Organisations exist in dynamic contexts where power relations may vary considerably, resulting in internal environments fluctuating between polarities of cooperative, consensual coalitions at one end and conflictive in-fighting from deep political manoeuvrings at the other (Jashapara 2003).

In a broad societal context, politics can be seen as a way of ruling divided societies based on conciliation rather than on coercion or undue violence (Crick 1982). Linked with societal political structures is the notion of rights in most democracies: political rights, social rights and civil rights (Coopey and Burgoyne 2000). As organisations do not exist in a vacuum, the values and beliefs associated with these rights have a bearing on organisational political processes. Organisations also have a variety of leadership styles encompassing highly autocratic and highly participative ones. There is an inter-play between top-down power relations and bottom-up ones. The leadership and management styles as well as day-to-day relationships will have a bearing on assymetri-cal power relations within an organisation. An individual may not have position power but may have power gained through self -confidence and authority in their relation-ships. A model showing the interplay between power, emotions, identity and the dialectic of learning is provided in Figure 3.10.

The asymmetry of power relations gives rise to a variety of emotions such as joy or fear. Often our learning in organisations is driven purely by anxiety and the way we relate to people around us (Vince 2001). Such emotions and power relations will have an important bearing on the nature of learning spaces created in organisations. At an indi-vidual level, positive emotions are more likely to lead to greater self-expression in discussions and dialogue with other group members, leading to a more self-assured iden-tity. Even though there may be disagreements between organisational members, these organisational spaces are more likely to foster cooperative and partnership forms of working. In contrast, anxiety-driven emotions are more likely to result in the denial of

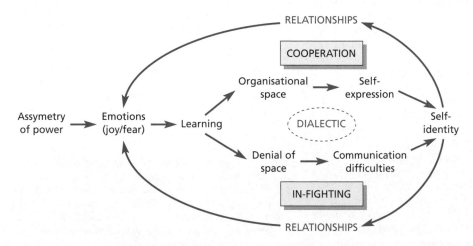

Figure 3.10 Politics and organisational learning (adapted from Coopey and Burgoyne 2000; Jashapara 2003; Vince 2001)

organisational learning space where individual views and opinions become marginalised. This can lead to communication difficulties where individuals knowingly collude, censor and subvert organisational processes to meet their own goals (Coopey and Burgoyne 2000). This behaviour has a direct impact on a person's self-identity and is likely to breed political infighting. The cycle of fear can perpetuate indefinitely as relationships reinforce an individual's emotional make-up. For organisational learning, this can invoke the politics of remembering or forgetting (Nissley and Casey 2002). The politics of remembering are often associated with positive experiences whereas the politics of forgetting involve discarding painful and negative experiences from a firm's history.

Recent empirical research shows that effective organisations tend to fluctuate between cooperative and competitive phases rather than becoming fixated on an idealised form (Jashapara 2003). This provides a creative dialectic between opposites. There may be limits to the levels of cooperation as ideology discourages change and if individuals perceive a need for change they may be forced to challenge the ideology which breeds politics. Cooperation is more likely to foster single-loop learning where existing routines are maintained and go unchallenged. In contrast, political environments are more likely to foster double-loop learning as underlying assumptions and values are questioned more frequently. Empirical research shows the need for a dialectic in the central ground between cooperation and competition to promote short-term stability and a healthy upheaval in underlying norms and patterns of behaviour.

CASE STUDY

Outsourcing – leave it to the experts

Faced with a tight schedule of product launches, Avaya – a spin-off of Lucent Technologies – needed a new approach to learning and development. Its geographically fragmented internal learning organisation was ill-equipped to provide the training necessary to accelerate the introduction of new products. Roughly 75 per cent of all learning events were instructor-led, which represented a hefty investment in both time and money.

Avaya decided to outsource its training to Accenture Learning. Accenture assumed the management of Avaya University and is now responsible for more than 1,800 product, technical and business courses. Using online programmes, classroom sessions and laboratory-based training, the company found it could deliver training quickly across a wide geographical range. An ability to roll out training to a large number of people at speed is often cited by training suppliers as one of the benefits of outsourcing. But many companies worry that, in the process, they will lose control of crucial elements of the business, such as values and company culture. The risk of valuable data falling into the wrong hands is another concern.

As the outsourcing industry matures, however, many of these fears can be allayed. In its early days, many simply handed over their non-core business processes to contractors and let them get on with it. Today, relationships with suppliers tend to be extremely close and bound by tight agreements.

'Actually, you gain control,' says Hap Brakeley, president of Accenture Learning. '[The supplier] is now managing that part of the business to specific objectives and service levels so companies feel they have more control. It's the same thing with content. You provide for the appropriate security and maintain the rights to the content.'

Jo Rawbone, training consultant at MaST International, a development and training consultancy, agrees. 'You're delivering to a standard that's been mutually agreed, that's probably tighter than would be set with an internal organisation. Because it's part of the contract, if the supplier fails, you can terminate the contract, whereas internally that takes much longer.'

These days, outsourcing suppliers recognise the need to spend time learning about the company and its culture, even going as far as getting up to speed on terminology used by employees.

Many companies prefer to develop a relationship with a supplier by simply buying its training materials before embarking on a full-blown outsourcing arrangement. 'They might start at the narrow end and, if the relationship is right, work up to the fat end of the wedge,' says Ms Rawbone. 'It's more challenging to secure a large outsourced contract with a client we've never worked with before as it requires a big element of trust.'

Building up trust means the supplier must invest time and energy in meeting the client's executives and managers both before the contract is signed and during the delivery of the training. 'It's about spending time with the organisation, understanding what makes it tick,' says Ms Rawbone. 'The aim is to become a seamless part of the organisation so that people don't realise it's being outsourced.'

But while training suppliers have matured, so have their clients and corporate learning departments are turning into savvy customers with strong views on how they want their training delivered.

With a growing range of training suppliers lining up to sell their services, there are certainly more options to choose from. For example, most business schools and universities have executive education departments, some of which are being spun off as profit centres catering to the corporate sector.

KPMG's UK learning and development unit is a case in point. The company, which provides audit, tax and advisory services, takes a mix and match approach to buying training, and outsourced resources include professional exam training and some elements of e-learning to reinforce the classroom-based training.

It also turns to external specialists for its leadership development. 'We're investing quite heavily around a broader set of leadership capabilities and there we look to partners with specialists in particular areas in different business schools,' says Julie Morgan, UK head of learning and development at KPMG, which enlists the expertise of specialists at institutions such as the London Business School, Cambridge's Judge Institute and Edinburgh business school.

However, Ms Morgan does not favour outsourcing the entire learning and development function. 'It's fine to outsource certain things like qualification training. There's no point in us reinventing the wheel and putting valuable resources into it when there are experts in the marketplace. And there's no competitive advantage to us having different training from the other firms,' she says. 'But when you're looking at what we are about, our values and business strategy, you don't get that if you have outsiders coming in.'

Source: Article by Sarah Murray, *Financial Times*, 24 November 2003

Questions

1 What are the benefits and limitations of outsourcing training and development to firms such as Accenture Learning?

2 Despite the rhetoric of seamless integration, how useful are outsourcing arrangements for atypical forms of learning and development?

3 What factors would govern your decision to adopt 'vicarious learning' such as outsourcing arrangements over 'grafting' an individual or a team with the prerequisite expertise into your organisation?

4 How could outsourcing arrangements help a firm gain competitive advantage?

Summary

This chapter has elaborated and argued five major themes associated with organisational learning:

1 Individual learning – the differences between a behavioural and a cognitive science perspective on learning. The central role of motivation in individual learning that is often overlooked in the traditional learning cycle. The importance of 'deutero-learning' or 'learning to learn'.

2 Team learning as a distinction between discussion and dialogue and its function in convergent or divergent thinking.

3 Organisational learning conceived as single-loop and double-loop learning and driven by moderate levels of failure and unlearning.

4 Adoption of an information-processing perspective linking organisational learning to knowledge acquisition, information distribution, information interpretation and organisational memory.

5 The development of organisational routines in stable environments and dynamic capabilities in more volatile market conditions.

QUESTIONS FOR FURTHER THOUGHT

1 Most individual learning theory tends to focus on how we can change the external environment to promote greater learning. How could we synthesise cognitive and behavioural approaches to better understand our internal learning mechanisms?

2 By nature, some team members may be more argumentative whereas others may be more reflective and deeper thinkers. How does one manage these two groups without developing defensive routines in specific circumstances where discussion or dialogue may be required?

3 What measures can be taken to promote 'error harvesting' and sharing mistakes in organisational environments where mistakes are concealed and never discussed?

4 What are the advantages of a 'dialectic' between single-loop and double-loop learning rather than a preoccupation with double-loop learning for organisational success?

5 In what circumstances is it most appropriate to use vicarious learning or grafting in organisations?

6 How can a diversity of interpretations be managed effectively in an organisation?

7 What issues need to be considered when transferring organisational routines within the same organisation or between organisations? How would global factors affect the transfer of these routines?

8 What managerial competences are required to manage dynamic capabilities?

9 It has been argued that competitive advantage occurs from the unique resource configurations and linkages between organisational routines. Given that routines are predominantly tacit in nature, how can managers develop them to ensure they possess VRIN attributes (valuable, rare, inimitable and non-substitutable)?

10 Knowledge sharing assumes a certain level of openness and cooperation between organisational members. What are the dangers of highly cooperative environments for organisational learning?

Further reading

1 Cohen and Sproull 1996 provides a good overview of the debates and thinking in the field of organisational learning.

2 Dierkes et al. 2001 offers a more theoretical perspective on some of the current debates in organisational learning and knowledge.

References

Argyris, C. (1991). 'Teaching smart people how to learn'. *Harvard Business Review*, 69(3), 99–109.

Argyris, C. and Schon, D. A. (1978) *Organizational Learning: A Theory of Action Perspective*, Addison-Wesley, Reading, MA.

Bateson, G. (1987) *Steps to an Ecology of Mind*, Jason Aronson, San Francisco, CA.

Bontis, N., Crossan, M. M. and Hulland, J. (2002) 'Managing an organizational learning system by aligning stocks and flows'. *Journal of Management Studies*, 39(4), 437–469.

Bruner, J. S., Goodnow, J. J. and Austin, G. A. (1956) *A Study of Thinking*, Wiley, New York.

Cohen, D. and Bacdayan, P. (1994). 'Organizational routines as stored procedural memory: evidence from a laboratory study'. *Organization Science*, 5(4), 554–568.

Cohen, M. D., Burkhart, R., Dosi, G., Egidi, M., Marengo, L., Warglien, M. and Winter, S. (1996) 'Routines and other recurring action patterns of organizations: contemporary research issues', *Industrial and Corporate Change*, 5(3), 653–698.

Cohen, M. D. and Sproull, L. S. (1996) *Organisational Learning*, Sage, London.

Coopey, J. and Burgoyne, J. (2000) 'Politics and organizational learning', *Journal of Management Studies*, 37(6), 869–885.

Crick, B. (1982) *In Defence of Politics*, Penguin, Harmondsworth.

Crossan, M. M., Lane, H. and White, R. (1999) 'An organizational learning framework: from intuition to institution', *Academy of Management Review*, 24(3), 522–37.

Cyert, R.M. and March, J. G. (1963) *A Behavioural Theory of the Firm*, Prentice-Hall, Englewood Cliffs, NJ.

Daft, R. L. and Weick, K. E. (1984) 'Toward a model of organizations as interpretation systems', *Academy of Management Review*, 9, 284–95.

Deming, W. E. (1986) *Out of the Crisis*, MIT Press, Boston, MA.

Dierkes, M., Antal, A. B., Child, J. and Nanaka, I. (2001) *Handbook of Organizational Learning and Knowledge*, Oxford University Press, Oxford.

Easterby-Smith, M. (1997) 'Disciplines of organizational learning: contributions and critiques', *Human Relations*, 50(9), 1085–1116.

Eisenhardt, K. and Martin, J. (2000) 'Dynamic capabilities: what are they?', *Strategic Management Journal*, 21, 1105–1121.

Epple, D., Argote, L. and Devadas, R. (1996) 'Organizational learning curves: a method for investigating intra-plant transfer of knowledge acquired through learning by doing', *Organizational Learning*, M. D. Cohen and L. S. Sproull, eds, Sage Publications Inc., Thousand Oaks, CA, 83–100.

Feldman, M. (2000) 'Organizational routines as a source of continuous change', *Organization Science*, 11(6), 611–629.

Feldman, M. and Rafaeli, A. (2002) 'Organizational routines as sources of connections and understandings', *Journal of Management Studies*, 39(3), 309–331.

Fiol, C. and Lyles, M. (1985) 'Organizational learning', *Academy of Management Review*, 10(4), 803–13.

Garratt, B. (1987) *The Learning Organization*, Gower, Aldershot.

Gersick, C. J. and Hackman, R. (1990) 'Habitual routines in task-performing groups', *Organizational Behaviour and Human Decision Process*, 47, 65–97.

Giddens, A. (1984) *The Constitution of Society: Outline of the Theory of Structure*, University of California Press, Berkeley, CA.

Gutherie, E. R. (1935) *The Psychology of Learning*, Harper & Row, New York.

Hedberg, B. L. T. (1981) 'How organizations learn and unlearn', *Handbook of Organizational Design*, P. C. Nystrom and W. H. Starbuck, eds, Oxford University Press, Oxford.

Honey, P. and Mumford, A. (1986) *The Manual of Learning Styles*, Peter Honey, Maidenhead.

Huber, G. P. (1991) 'Organizational learning: the contributing processes and the literatures', *Organization Science*, 2, 88–115.

Isaacs, W. H. (1993) 'Dialogue, collective thinking, and organizational learning', *Organization Dynamics*, 22(2), 24–39.

Jashapara, A. (1993) 'The competitive learning organization: a quest for the Holy Grail', *Management Decision*, 31(8), 52–62.

Jashapara, A. (2003) 'Cognition, culture and competition: an empirical test of the learning organization', *The Learning Organization*, 10(1), 31–50.

Kim, D. H. (1993) 'The link between individual and organizational learning', *Sloan Management Review*, Fall, 37–50.

Klahr, D. and Wallace, J. G. (1976) *Cognitive Development: An Information Processing View*, Halsted Press, New York.

Knights, D. and McCabe, D. (1998) 'When "life is but a dream": obliterating politics through business process reengineering?', *Human Relations*, 51(6), 761–798.

Kolb, D. A. (1984) *Experiential Learning: Experience as the Source of Learning and Development*, Prentice Hall, Englewood Cliffs, NJ.

Krone, K. J., Jablin, F. M. and Putnam, L. L. (1987) 'Communication theory and organizational communication: multiple perspectives', *Handbook of Organizational Communication*, F. M. Jablin, L. L. Putnam, K. H. Roberts and L. W. Porter, eds, Sage, Newbury Park, CA.

Leonard-Barton, D. (1992) 'Core capacities and core rigidities: paradox in managing new product development', *Strategic Management Journal*, 13, 111–125.

Levitt, B. and March, J. G. (1988) 'Organizational learning', *Annual Review of Sociology*, 14.

March, J. G. (1991) 'Exploration and exploitation in organizational learning', *Organization Science*, 2(1), 71–87.

March, J. G. and Simon, H. A. (1958) *Organizations*, Wiley, New York.

March, J. G., Sproull, L. S. and Tamuz, M. (1991) 'Learning from samples of one or fewer', *Organization Science*, 2(1), 1–13.

Mumford, A. (1991) 'Learning in action', *Personnel Management*, July, 34–37.

Nelson, R. and Winter, S. (1982) *An Evolutionary Theory of Economic Change*, Harvard University Press, Cambridge, MA.

Nissley, N. and Casey, A. (2002) 'The politics of the exhibition: viewing corporate museums through the paradigmatic lens of organizational memory', *British Journal of Management*, 13, S35–S45.

Pentland, B. T. and Rueter, H. H. (1994) 'Organizational routines as grammars of action', *Administrative Science Quarterly*, 39, 484–510.

Revans, R. W. (1977) *The ABC of Action Learning*, Action Learning Trust, Luton.

Schein, E. H. (1987) *Process Consultation: Lessons for Managers and Consultants*, Addison-Wesley, Reading, MA.

Senge, P. M. (1990) *The Fifth Discipline: The Art and Practice of the Learning Organisation*, Doubleday Currency, New York.

Shrivastava, P. (1983) 'A typology of organizational learning systems', *Journal of Management Studies*, 20(1), 7–28.

Sitkin, S. B. (1992) '*Learning through failure: the strategy of small losses*', *Research in Organizational Behaviour*, B. M. Staw and L. L. Cummings, eds, JAI Press, Greenwich, CT.

Skinner, B. F. (1938) *The Behaviour of Organisms: An Experimental Analysis*, Appleton-Century-Crofts, New York.

Stein, E. W. and Zwass, V. (1995) 'Actualizing organizational memory with information systems', *Information Systems Research*, 6, 2(85–117).

Teece, D. J., Pisano, G. and Shuen, A. (1997) 'Dynamic capabilities and strategic management', *Strategic Management Journal*, 18, 509–533.

Underwood, B. J. (1964) 'The representativeness of rote verbal learning', *Categories of Human Learning*, A. W. Melton, ed., Academic Press, New York.

Vince, R. (2001) 'Power and emotion in organizational learning', *Human Relations*, 54(10), 1325–1351.

Walsh, J. P. and Ungson, G.R. (1991) 'Organizational memory', *Academy of Management Review*, 16, 57–91.

Weick, K. E. (1979) *The Social Psychology of Organizing*, Addison-Wesley, Reading, MA.

Weick, K. E. (2002) 'Puzzles in organizational learning: an exercise in disciplined imagination', *British Journal of Management*, 13, S7–S15.

Yelle, L. E. (1979) 'The learning curve: historical review and comprehensive survey', Decision Sciences, 10, 302–328.

Zollo, M. and Winter, S. G. (2002) 'Deliberate learning and the evolution of dynamic capabilities', *Organization Science*, 13(3), 339–351.

Chapter 4

Knowledge management tools: component technologies

LEARNING OUTCOMES

After completing this chapter the reader should be able to:

- describe different component technologies found in knowledge management;
- explain the different technologies for capturing, organising, storing and sharing new knowledge;
- contrast the functions of different component technologies;
- feel confident about selecting appropriate knowledge management technologies for particular needs.

MANAGEMENT ISSUES

The use and application of knowledge management tools and technology implies these questions for managers:

- What KM tools are most appropriate for a given business problem?
- What is the nature of different KM tools and technologies?
- How do these technologies help capture and share the valuable tacit knowledge or 'know how' in an organisation?

Links to other chapters

Chapter 5   explains how the various KM component technologies are configured into a variety of knowledge management systems.

Chapter 6   looks at strategic perspectives for integrating technology and human aspects of knowledge management.

Chapter 8   examines the difficult aspects of implementing technological solutions within organisations.

Casmir

When Jim Hughes, co-founder of knowledge management company Casmir, recruited a new chief executive in March 2001 it was an intense experience. 'It was like giving my children to foster parents while still living in the same house,' says Mr Hughes. 'While I knew intellectually that it was the right thing for the business, emotionally it was difficult. And at the time I wasn't sure what it would mean for my role in the company.'

Mr Hughes, together with fellow academic Elaine Ferneley and PhD student Brendan Berney, set up Casmir in March 2000 to commercialise a collaborative search-engine technology that emerged from Mr Berney's PhD thesis at Salford University. None of the team had run a business but it was the height of the dotcom boom and they were seeing companies raising money for software projects that they felt were inferior to their own. So they decided to take the plunge.

With the help of a specialist university team, Casmir was spun out of the university, which retained a small shareholding in the business. Mr Hughes became managing director, Mr Berney was chief technology officer and Ms Ferneley took charge of operations. But 'there really wasn't very much specialisation; we would mostly sit and discuss things together, (as) we did in the university,' says Ms Ferneley.

A £30,000 start-up facility from the University of Salford Enterprise Board and some revenue from consultancy services kept Casmir afloat as its founders worked on the development of the Socialiser, an information-retrieval product for which the company had won a British Computer Society information technology award.

Last September, Casmir secured an investment deal through corporate financiers Altium Capital. Aim-listed development capital group Axiomlab invested £200,000 in the business and Internet Business Group a further £50,000, contingent on there being a new chief executive to strengthen the management team and add commercial focus.

It took about six months to find the right person. Sean Keenan, formerly director of the e-business division of Logical, an international e-business integration and services company, had vital commercial experience and understood the knowledge management business. Most important, he was someone they all felt they could work with.

In the month following Mr Keenan's arrival, there was a probationary atmosphere. He did not say or do much, they recall, but just watched and listened. And the founders were watching and waiting. Although

they had got to know Mr Keenan, they were nervous about the changes that he might make.

His first proposals came where they least expected – and provoked considerable resistance. With several programming projects running in parallel, Mr Keenan was afraid another year would go by before the company had a completed product to bring to the market. He said they must focus the development effort on one tightly specified version of the software – even though this involved adopting a radically different approach. 'I made clear that there wouldn't be enough money to finish the software if we pursued all our development plans and that we needed a basic version of the product before adding all the bells and whistles,' says Mr Keenan. 'Unfortunately we didn't have time to sit around and discuss things. It was a fiery meeting and harsh words were spoken. But in the end we managed to come to an understanding.'

For the founders, the initial months were difficult. 'At the beginning, we wanted to discuss all the decisions, as we had done previously,' says Ms Ferneley. 'But as we began to see Sean's impact on the business, we learnt to trust his judgement. It was still a bit of a surprise to discover that we had been doing so many things wrong.'

Mr Keenan's approach to the sales side of the business came as a shock to Mr Hughes. 'Where we had been happy with people showing interest in the software, (he) wanted to know their exact commitment: did they control a budget, or influence someone who did? Our prospects list was quickly whittled down by almost two-thirds,' says Mr Hughes.

Mr Keenan also tried to use his contacts to sell the Casmir software. Working closely with Mr Hughes and sales executives Mr Keenan had brought in from Logical, they developed low-cost pilot schemes to enable clients to get to know the company and the Socialiser product.

There are now several sites running the Socialiser software, including a Fortune 500 company. Such progress helped to persuade Axiomlab to put a further £500,000 into the business in May 2001 as part of a £1 million capital-raising exercise.

For the three founders, the new management structure is working well. Mr Hughes wishes it had happened earlier. 'For a start-up business, particularly coming from academia, exposure to the chill winds of commerce is vital. And the sooner the better. The cultures of academia and business are so different. Academics like to get a pat on the back, while in business it's all about cheques in the bank.'

Source: Article by Fergal Byrne, *Financial Times*, 13 September 2002

Introduction

For any aspiring purchaser of KM systems or technologies, the internet provides a multitude of vendors promising to transform your business. But where do you start? How do you understand the complexity of the offering and its effectiveness with your business problem? In the highly volatile market of software engineering, it is likely that many of these so-called 'market leaders' will cease trading in a few years' time. As an experiment in this book, it was found that fourteen 'market leaders' in KM tools (Mertins *et al.* 2000) had ceased trading in a two-year time frame.

So how can we decipher the offerings of the multitude of technologies in the market-place? The approach adopted in this chapter is to examine the component technologies that make up a knowledge management system or suite. The analogy of a hi-fi purchase is used where each item has a certain function and purpose. I have grouped various technologies in their ability to perform a knowledge function such as organising, capturing, analysing, storing and sharing knowledge, as shown in Figure 4.1. The

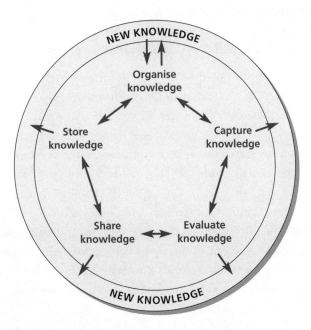

Figure 4.1 A typology of knowledge tools and component technologies

multitude of KM systems on offer in the marketplace is seen as a composite variation of a number of these component technologies. Firms may decide to buy different components off-the-shelf or develop their own tools to meet their needs.

As with purchasing hi-fi systems, one can purchase cheap or expensive KM technologies. Rather than becoming mesmerised by the power of these technologies, it is important to remain focused on the organisational needs that are driving the procurement of these technologies and whether an alternative may suffice; dare I say a telephone and e-mail! As a rule of thumb, experience shows that no more than one third of a knowledge management budget should be committed to technology (O'Dell *et al.* 2000). Often, the focus of technology is on hardware and software and managers can underestimate the value of knowledge content such as news feeds from Reuters. In a 1997 Ernst & Young survey, business managers indicated that the most important types of knowledge that would help them act effectively were (Smith and Farquhar 2000):

- knowledge about customers (97 per cent);
- knowledge about best practice and effective processes (87 per cent);
- knowledge about competencies and capabilities of their company (86 per cent).

In the same survey, it is noteworthy that 46 per cent of the 431 US and European executives felt that their organisations were good at generating new knowledge but only 13 per cent of the respondents agreed that their organisations were good at transferring existing knowledge (Ruggles 1998). The most common technologies employed by organisations were:

- creating an intranet (47 per cent);
- creating data warehouses (33 per cent);
- implementing decision-support tools (33 per cent);
- implementing groupware to support collaboration (33 per cent).

The predominant KM tools used today tend to focus on explicit knowledge and its reworkings even though the received wisdom acknowledges that it is the tacit knowledge or 'know how' that leads to greater effectiveness in organisations. The future challenge in this area is to develop tools to enable tacit knowledge to be made explicit in an easy and effortless manner. One approach may be the development of multimedia technologies such as digital video that capture and store an individual's 'know how' for storage, indexing and future retrieval via a search engine. This would enable a much richer form of communication between individuals and allow the addition of a diversity of audio-visual signals from the spoken word to tone of voice and body language.

Artificial intelligence (AI) is one of the oldest fields in computer science and provides the foundation for many KM technologies illustrated in this chapter. Artificial intelligence began by attempting to model the human mind and develop computer systems that would be as intelligent as humans. It has not reached this ambitious goal as yet but, it is fair to say, it has provided a lasting influence on the development of knowledge management tools. Artificial intelligence techniques have supported the development of tools in knowledge representation, knowledge search and acquisition as well as elements of intelligent agent technology. Major advances in many knowledge discovery tools could not have occurred without the support of artificial intelligence techniques.

Organising knowledge tools

▶ Ontology and taxonomy

Knowledge can come in a variety of forms: structured, semi-structured or unstructured, as shown in Figure 4.2. In order to organise this knowledge, one starts by gathering knowledge and working out a way to group, index or categorise it in some way. One could present a schema conceptualising a vocabulary of terms and relationships to represent the knowledge. This is called a 'knowledge map' or an 'ontology'. If each one of us tried to organise the same knowledge, we might come up with wide variations depending on our understanding and perspective on the subject. In an attempt to prevent this situation from occurring, we have developed 'ontologies' to improve our level of information organisation, management and understanding. Gruber (1993) defines ontology as:

'a formal, explicit specification of shared conceptualisation.'

This implies that a domain ontology provides us with a formalised vocabulary for describing a given domain. This is not the same as a philosophical understanding of 'ontology' which refers to our perceptions of 'the nature of being' and our assumptions of the nature of reality. In the context of KM tools, the term ontology is often used interchangeably with taxonomy as this may be the operational conceptualisation of a domain chosen by a user. To clarify the distinction, it is important to recognise that an ontology is an overall conceptualisation whereas a taxonomy is a 'scientifically based scheme of classification', as shown in Figure 4.3 (p. 94). An ontology may have non-taxonomic conceptual relationships such as 'has part' relations between concepts. In contrast, knowledge taxonomies generate hierarchical classification of terms that are structured to show relationships between terms. These ontologies and taxonomies have a significant impact on our ability to deal with vast amounts of information such as that found on the internet or corporate intranets.

Structured	Semi-structured	Unstructured
Financial data	Cases	Documents
Sales data	Policies	E-mails
Customer data	Procedures	Presentations
Demographic data	Action plans	Video

Figure 4.2 **Different forms of knowledge**

ONTOLOGY   TAXONOMY

⭕ ⭕ ● represent different ideas and concepts

Figure 4.3 Ontologies and taxonomies

The current norms are to generate ontologies manually. The English language comprises over half a million words and there is an almost infinite array of terms to convey the same concepts. This can present semantic complications and ambiguities in classifying, locating and retrieving knowledge. The scope of most ontologies is to provide a clear, consistent and coherent conceptualisation that is extensible and easily reusable. One doesn't want to reinvent the wheel each time new knowledge is added to a particular domain. Uschold and Gruninger (1996) have provided a useful approach to build ontologies manually to achieve these aims:

1 Identify purpose and scope.
2 Build the ontology via a three-step process.
   a) ontology capture – identify key concepts and relationships;
   b) ontology coding – commit basic terms such as class, entity and relations and choose a representation language or write the code;
   c) integrate existing ontologies.
3 Evaluate ontologies.
4 Document ontologies.
5 Provide guidelines for previous phases.

However, apart from being time consuming, manually generated ontologies have the added problem of being prone to errors and can pose difficulties in maintaining and updating them (Ding and Foo 2002). If there are significant delays in updating ontologies, this can cause problems in their usefulness and hinder their development. Some of these factors have driven the current impetus towards semi-automated and fully automated ontology generation systems.

Pause for thought

Reflect on all the different aspects of your knowledge that you use in everyday life. Spend five minutes drawing a map showing the diversity of your knowledge and the relationships between the various stands. You may find the analogy of a knowledge tree useful, with major branches and smaller branches of your knowledge. How could you replicate such an approach to develop an ontology for an organisation? What may be some of the limitations of this ontology? How could you get staff to cooperate in the development of your organisational ontology?

The current state-of-the-art ontology generation technologies still use some seed words provided by domain experts as the basis of ontology generation and have not yet reached their ultimate goal of using learning ontologies. Concepts are extracted from raw data using a variety of relatively mature techniques such as:

- 'part-of-speech (POS)' tagging to extract high-frequency words or phrases that could be used to define concepts and may perform a syntactic analysis;
- 'word sense disambiguation' to extract relations such as 'is-a' and 'associated with' where the distinction lies in the linguistic property of the nouns;
- 'tokenisers' to break strings into a series of tokens between two delimiting characters (such as the spacing between words) and determine the length of each string;
- 'pattern matching' – for example, a system may learn a semantic lexicon of paired words with their meanings and have the ability to extract phrase-meaning pairs from a document.

In recent years, automatic ontology generation or classification tools have advanced to such a point that they are comparable to manual classifiers of ontology in a well-organised operation. For example, the degree of accuracy of the best performing algorithms in automatic classifiers can exceed 85 per cent on good quality data (Marwick 2001). This degree of accuracy may be acceptable for many applications. A fundamental aspect of the current generation of automatic classifiers is their use of 'machine learning' to train themselves from example data which can give rise to refined distinctions given a wide variety of training data. Also, the new generation of classifiers have a high level of reuseability, enabling easy application to new domains and reducing overall costs of ontology generation.

Ontologies have been represented in a variety of ways depending on the technology. In their most simplistic form, they can be represented as a conceptual hierarchy similar to their related taxonomy. However, some classification tools use an algebraic extraction technique to generate a graph structure with thesaurus entries for all words. Others store the results of text processing into annotations using XML-tagged text (Ding and Foo 2002).

Current ontology generation tools are not free from problems. In part, this helps drive the next generation of tools. For example, there can be problems with the sense of a word in different contexts or the recognition of different phrases referring to the same concept. Machine learning techniques that enable the classifier tool to learn patterns can be helpful, but many of these learning relationships are highly complex. A general problem can be the 'shallow' semantics generated which can hide the richness and depth of any domain. Also, there may be differences between the automatic generation of ontologies and the schematic conceptions of a community or a group of experts. An almost classical conflict may arise from a group of artists who may have a loose and highly visual conception of their domain and the ontology engineer who may represent their ontology in a highly mathematical or hierarchical framework.

Ontologies are dynamic. Concepts and schemas do change their meaning and sense relations over time. How can we reuse existing ontologies and incorporate new meanings, relations, domains and knowledge over time? Given the overwhelming production of knowledge in organisations each year, there is likely to be a need to integrate existing ontologies with new domains. However, this can create numerous problems, such as semantic inconsistencies and differences in knowledge formats. Ontology mapping has developed as an area of research to address these problems. The current approaches for integrating a number of ontologies (see Figure 4.4 p. 97) include (Sofia Pinto *et al.* 1999):

- reusing available ontologies linking different domains;
- aligning ontologies by establishing links between them through some form of translation function using agent technology;
- merging ontologies to create a single ontology;
- integrating ontologies through clustering on the basis of similarities.

These approaches recognise that successful integration of ontologies requires a good understanding of semantics to reconcile semantic similarities, discrepancies, compatibilities, relevance and relativity. Semantics are concerned with the meanings individuals or groups give to a particular term or concept. It is understandable that confusion may easily arise from different communities associating different meanings or nuances of meaning to the same term. For example, the term 'elegance' may have connotations of aesthetics and beauty to an architect whereas the same term may imply optimal use of materials to an engineer.

Given the continual information overload problem in many organisations, there is a need to maintain and improve an existing ontology as it changes over time. Manual maintenance of ontologies can be tedious and time consuming. Hence, a variety of tools have been developed to assist the 'ontology editor' to semi-automate the tasks. Certain tools exist to acquire new concepts and place these within the domain ontology and some of these are based on machine learning techniques. It is notable that Tim Berners-Lee, inventor of the world wide web, believes that the information overload problems on the existing web will lead to a second generation which he calls a 'semantic web'. This will make explicit the semantics underlying all resources on the web and

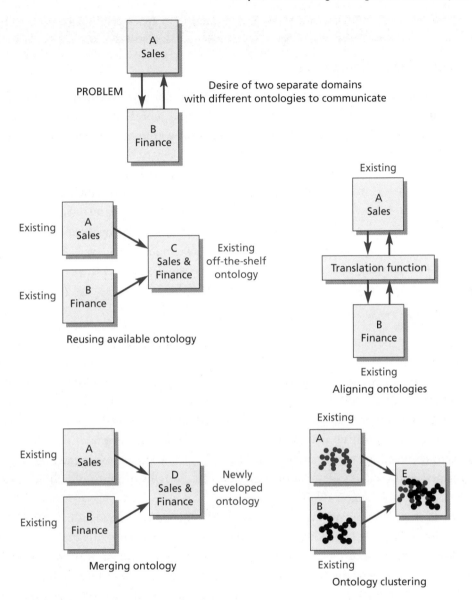

Figure 4.4 Ontology integration techniques

create a form of 'global' ontology. It is unclear whether this future 'global' ontology will be reused to create local ontologies by standardising concepts and the relations between them. An alternative route may be to use a universal classification system such as Dewey to represent a 'global' ontology in order to comprehend the whole of human knowledge, including that which is not yet known.

Capturing knowledge tools

▶ Cognitive mapping tools

In any given area of knowledge, each one of us has our own ontology or 'cognitive map' of that particular domain. The map is a visual representation of the domain which makes explicit mentally the concepts that exist within that domain and the relationships between them. In many cases, this map is likely to be tacit and unarticulated within an individual or an organisation. This tacit knowledge is a key source of competitive advantage as it is difficult to articulate, imitate, is context specific and has direct practical relevance (Ambrosini and Bowman 2002; Barney 1991; Grant 1996). Cognitive mapping provides a valuable tool to represent an individual's knowledge and experience and their view of reality (Eden and Ackermann 1998; Weick and Bougon 1986). The mapping process is based on Kelly's personal construct theory (1955). The structuring technique of idea generation is based on the premise:

'How do I know what I think until I hear what I say?'

Currently, the main application for cognitive mapping tools is in the area of mapping strategic knowledge (Huff and Jenkins 2002) through the use of causal maps. Causal maps are cognitive maps that can establish multiple relationships between entities through causal links. For example, entity A may 'cause' entity B and D and the complexity of other relationships can be depicted graphically, as shown in Figure 4.5. The advantage of causal mapping tools is that they provide a way of ordering and analysing something that is 'fuzzy' and vague and allow us to impose a structure on the fuzziness and visualise the relationships between concepts (Ambrosini and Bowman 2002; Weick and Bougon 1986).

In terms of strategic management, it is not the individual tacit maps but rather the organisational tacit knowledge that is likely to result in competitive advantage or greater effectiveness. If one views an organisation as a social system with interdependent parts (Gharajedaghi and Ackoff 1994), tacit organisational knowledge can be conceived as residing in a set of organisational routines (Grant 1996; Nelson and Winter 1982; Spender 1996). Nelson and Winter (1982) argue that these formal and informal routines are embedded in organisational activities and organisations remember them through action. These tacit routines are not codified and do not follow

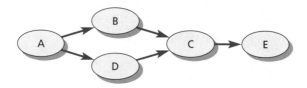

Figure 4.5 **Example of a cognitive map showing concepts and links**

standard rules and operating procedures. They are related to their specific context and, by implication, there are limits to the extent to which they can be articulated (Grant 1991). However, cognitive mapping tools allow us to reveal 'collective maps' of tacit routines from a process of group dialogue and discussion.

The most developed application of cognitive mapping tools has been in the field of strategy making to help surface and explore tacit knowledge, assumptions, assertions, values, beliefs, aspirations and concerns within a management team or board of directors (Eden and Ackermann 1998). This technique allows the important processes of 'sharing meaning' and 'making sense' to be facilitated and misunderstandings from implicit assumptions to be minimised. In a group situation, the technique supports important group processes such as negotiation and anonymity (Eden and Ackermann 2002). The resulting cognitive map comprises the collective thinking of a group of individuals which may contain conflicting views from a variety of perspectives.

The most common method of creating a cognitive map is through the 'oval mapping technique' and software that aids the mapping process (Decision Explorer™ [www.Banxia.com]) with effective representation, retrieval and analytical support, as shown in Figure 4.6. These visual thinking tools allow ideas and their relationships with other ideas to be made explicit. The process of oval mapping is as follows:

- Facilitator to ask group to focus on a question or issue.
- Ask participants to cover the working space such as a wall with flip chart paper.

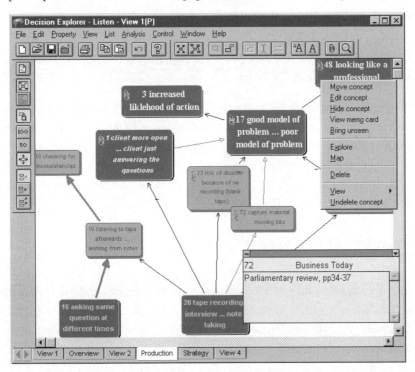

Figure 4.6 Cognitive mapping software: Decision Explorer ™

- Give participants a set of 'oval' cards and encourage them to focus on their expertise and record their views for public display.
- Ask participants to write one idea per oval preferably.
- Inform participants that no ovals will be removed (except in cases of total agreement by group) and they need to make disagreements explicit.
- Facilitator to organise ideas into clusters and subclusters. A 'dump' cluster can be used to give facilitator time, particularly where themes or patterns may not be self evident.
- Facilitator to elicit linkages between different ideas and clusters of ideas by looking at 'means and ends' or 'options and desired outcomes'. In essence, whether one idea causes or leads to another idea or cluster.

This public procedure, where each idea is considered equally valid, allows participants to look at the issues from alternative viewpoints and possibly change their position without the need to defend their own viewpoint. The process encourages social negotiation and greater commitment to the outcomes.

In strategy development, the causal maps are reorganised into clusters following a 'tear drop' model where aspirations and goals are at the top of the model (Eden and Ackermann 1998), as shown in Figure 4.7 (p. 101). These are the concepts with 'heads' but no 'out-arrows' in terms of consequences. The next layer of clusters are the issues or possible strategies supporting the aspirations and underlying them are the more detailed strategic options that impact on the potential strategies. Further analyses can be conducted on the cognitive map using the computer software such as:

- identifying the busiest concepts;
- calculating the centrality of a concept in the overall structure;
- exploring feedback loops.

In this example, cognitive mapping tools allow us to see how a business model or a livelihood scheme (for not-for-profit organisations) can be realised with the necessary intellectual and emotional commitment from key players. The logic and coherence of different parts of the map can be shared across the organisation to facilitate the change process by reducing the ambiguity of action programmes and demonstrating the impact of singular tasks on multiple objectives.

▶ Information-retrieval tools

The key goal in information retrieval is to retrieve knowledge that may be useful or relevant to a user. Traditionally, there have been two processes involved in information retrieval. First is the creation of an index that enables the location of a text and document structure. Textual data can be loaded into the system and en route it undergoes transformation such as the removal of common words. This is often referred to as a logical view of a document. An index has the advantage of speeding up the retrieval process and reducing the computational costs. Otherwise each record would have to be

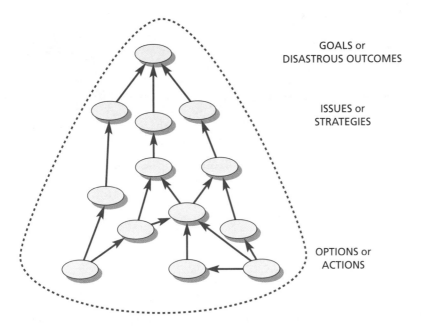

GOALS or
DISASTROUS OUTCOMES

ISSUES or
STRATEGIES

OPTIONS or
ACTIONS

Figure 4.7 Strategy development 'tear drop' model

searched individually. All information-retrieval systems have an index which helps to locate the full text records. Generally, they use an inverted file approach. The second process is solving a user's information needs in the form of a query through algorithms and ranking the results in some form of relevance to the user.

One recent trend has been the development of compression technology that allows direct indexing and searching on compressed text with high compression and decompression speeds. Text can be compressed to 30–35 per cent of its original size. This can be a critical consideration as text collections are increasingly becoming huge. A typical process of indexing a text database is shown in Figure 4.8 (p. 102).

Pause for thought

From your experience, what role has serendipity played when you've been trying to find information? Can you describe these experiences and see any patterns within them? How valuable have you found formal methods of information retrieval? What informal methods do you use to find information? If search engines or your traditional sources fail to provide you with your required information, what alternative strategies do you adopt?

Individual records such as full texts, news stories or market reports can be indexed using a structured taxonomy of terms generated from the text, with the indexed terms being attached to the record to enable retrieval. This approach has a long history in library sciences. An example of such indexing is the addition of SIC (standard industry classification) codes to documents. Another example of an index is the Dewey Decimal Classification, a bibliographic classification system that is used in many libraries to classify knowledge domains into 999 classes, each having a multitude of divisions to

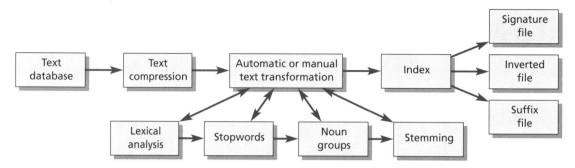

Figure 4.8 Indexing a text database

cater for the subtleties of any knowledge domain. The index terms are often a collection of selected keywords or concepts whose semantics helps us find the document's main themes. Indexing can be performed either manually by a specialist or automatically with text-classification tools. The accuracy of automatic text classification is improving and in some cases can be comparable to human indexers. The steps involved in the automatic classification process can utilise one or more of the following technologies (Baeza-Yates and Ribeiro-Neto 1999):

● Lexical analysis is used to identify the words in the text from a stream of characters including numerical digits, punctuation marks and hyphens.

● Stopwords that occur too frequently in a collection of documents are eliminated as they do not provide good discriminators for the purposes of retrieval. An advantage is that it results in compression of the index, though it may subsequently reduce the level of recall.

● As nouns tend to carry most of the semantics in a given sentence, they are often used as index terms rather than verbs, articles, adjectives, adverbs or connectives. Nouns that appear near to one another in the text can be clustered into a single indexing component called a noun group (e.g. human resource management). This can make retrieval much more efficient.

● Stemming is the removal of the affixes (prefixes and suffixes) of a word to improve retrieval performance. The premise is that a user may specify a variant of a word in a search that may not successfully retrieve the necessary document. For example, the word *construct* is a stem for the variants *constructing, construction, constructions* and *constructed*.

In lexical analysis and clustering of noun groups, there may be the additional association with terms not found in the document index but which act as alternative descriptors in the retrieval process. This can be done manually or automatically. Once the text classification, if any, has been conducted, the three most common index structures are as follows:

● **Inverted files**. These are currently the best choice for most applications. An inverted index is composed of the *vocabulary* or different words in the text and their occurences in terms of their precise storage location.

- **Suffix trees**. These form a tree data structure of the text rather than assuming the text is a sequence of words. These indices are particularly helpful for answering complex queries for non-word-based applications such as genetic databases.
- **Signature files**. These are index structures that divide text into blocks for analysis. They help reduce the size of documents to speed retrieval but impose a sequential mode of searching from one text block to another. The inverted file outperforms the signature file in most applications.

After the text database has been indexed, the retrieval process can commence. This comprises the user specifying their knowledge needs in the form of search terms on a user interface, as shown in Figure 4.9. The search terms may have the same 'text-classification' tools applied to form a query. Once a query is entered, this is processed to produce a representation such as terms and structures. These tend to involve co-occurence, frequency, position of terms and possibly semantic and syntactic processing. Similarly, documents in the database are processed and essentially the representation of the query is matched with the representation of the document. The query can be expressed in a variety of forms:

- Boolean operators (such as OR, AND and BUT) have precise semantics and are used most commonly by commercial systems. This is the most popular approach. The main drawback is that exact matching of Boolean expressions may result in too few or too many documents.
- Vector expressions assign weights to index terms according to their frequency in a document. The premise is that the lower frequency of an index term is likely to have much greater relevance in a search than a highly occurring index term.
- Probabilistic expressions try to assign probabilities to documents that it assumes users will find relevant. This approach is problematic as it is almost impossible to

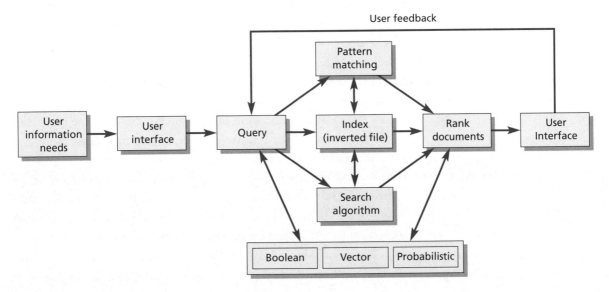

Figure 4.9 Information retrieval process

compute probabilities of relevance without the necessary feedback loops and learning from the user.

- Fuzzy expressions use a thesaurus to expand the query into related terms to allow additional documents to be retrieved.

The retrieved documents are subsequently ranked according to their likelihood of relevance based on a boolean, vector or probabilistic notion of the query. Following this, some systems enable the user to interact with the search process by specifying whether a certain text is relevant. The information-retrieval system redefines the search algorithm and, hopefully, retrieves similar texts. This is known as relevance feedback.

As databases grow at exponential levels in most organisations, there is a need to develop search technologies that will enable retrieval of information efficiently and speedily. One technique is to use parallel computing where several processors are used simultaneously in the retrieval process, with each processor focusing on a different aspect of the problem. An alternative is to use a distributed computing technique whereby different computers connected to a common network are used to tackle a search problem.

▶ Search engines

The above information-retrieval principles are applied in a wide range of environments and for a range of purposes. Search engines work on a similar process. You search an index and not the full text document. One of the main distinctions between traditional information retrieval techniques and the web is that queries do not have access geographically to the full text of documents. Simply, it would cost too much to have every page on the web stored locally and the retrieval times would be extremely slow, even with the most powerful networks. In addition, the web contains highly volatile and redundant data. It is estimated that 40 per cent of data on the web changes monthly and 30 per cent of web pages are almost duplicates (Baeza-Yates and Ribeiro-Neto 1999). An intrinsic characteristic of the web is the diverse variety of data types and the poor quality of the data as there are no editorial processes for publication. This can result in the problem of search precision where most documents retrieved are irrelevant to a user's needs (Marwick 2001).

Search engines are the most common form of retrieving material on the web. They are based predominantly on a crawler-indexer architecture, as shown in Figure 4.10 (p. 105). Crawlers are software programs using agent technology that send requests to remote web servers looking for new or updated pages. The results of the crawling are subsequently indexed centrally in the search engine. Most indices on the web use a variant of the inverted file. The second part of the search engine deals with user needs in the form of a query. The most common query on the web is two words and the average query length is 2.3 words (Marwick 2001). The search engine processes the index through a variety of algorithms and ranks the results. It is suggested that this crawler-

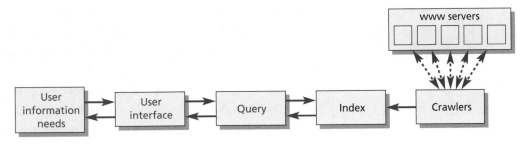

Figure 4.10 Search engine: crawler-indexer architecture

indexer architecture may not be able to cope with the exponential growth of the web in the future.

An alternative to the crawler-indexer architecture is a distributed approach using several networked web servers to act either as 'gatherers' (similar to crawlers) or 'brokers' (providing the query and index interface) in a distributed mode of operation. There are also 'metasearchers' on the web that work by sending a query to numerous search engines and collating and ranking the replies for a user.

▶ Agent technology

To the uninitiated, agent technology can appear like something from science fiction where certain computer systems act like robots (autonomously) to deliver the best solution in terms of their original design. In effect, agents are computer systems that are capable of *autonomous* action in a given enviroment in order to fulfil their design objective. These systems can act without intervention from humans and take control over their actions and internal state (Jennings and Wooldridge 1998). Agents are similar to crawlers that identify specific material in terms of semantic content, structure and properties. 'Tailored' crawlers can learn and mutate in terms of results and user feedback.

An advancement on agent technology is the development of intelligent agents. These computer systems are capable of *flexible* autonomous action where their *flexibility* derives from their responsiveness to the environment, their opportunistic and proactive behaviour, and their ability to interact with other agents or humans to optimise their problem-solving abilities.

Agents are particularly powerful tools for dealing with complex systems. They manage complex systems by making them *modular*. In essence agents take a large complex problem and divide it into smaller, simpler and more manageable components. This allows each agent to use the appropriate techniques to solve the smaller problem at hand. The other technique used by agents in complex systems is *abstraction*. This allows the complex system to be conceptualised as a series of cooperating autonomous agents. Agent technology has had a wide range of applications including the following:

● Electronic mail filtering agents observe every action a user performs and treats it as a lesson. After some time, the agents begin to predict the user's behaviour based on a history of patterns. As the agent becomes more successful in its predictions, it provides suggestions for the user to help manage their e-mail. This is particularly valuable for users experiencing information overload problems where they desire to focus clearly on their information needs rather than wasting time (Maes 1994).

- In business process management, agents negotiate for services on behalf of departments or divisions with other agents for a mutually acceptable price, time and degree of quality. This allows services in an organisation to be scheduled in a just-in-time manner (Jennings *et al.* 1996).
- In large organisations, 'agent wrappers' are built to enable critical organisational functions to be updated periodically by allowing software to interact with other parts of the system.
- Summarisation includes processing text in documents to identify key sentences.
- Business news feeds in organisations filter, cluster, summarise and deliver relevant news to users.

Nevertheless, agent technology does have its limitations which include (Jennings and Wooldridge 1998):

- no overall system controller;
- good optimal solutions locally but a lack of globally optimal decisions;
- quite a learning curve before people can feel comfortable trusting them and delegating some responsibility for decision making over to them;
- problem of relevance in terms of the changing profile of users.

▶ Personalisation

Agent technology has led to a more proactive push technology that can be personalised. The primary goal of all personalisation technology is to provide the needs and wants of every user perfectly. Without being asked, the technology tailors itself to fulfil the user's desire at any time. In information retrieval, personalisation technology may be used to restrict a search to particular categories most often sought by the user or to assign higher weights to documents from those categories. The technology can learn to refine the search specifications by examining keywords used in browsed documents or derived from profiles from communities of interest linked to the user. In addition, personalisation technology can analyse patterns of queries and query results in terms of relevance to the user (Mack *et al.* 2001).

Personalisation technology has been exploited by marketers to gain better knowledge of their customers' behaviours and preferences. The commonly adopted tools are called 'cookies'. These cookies are small data files that are planted on an end user's computer to allow websites to identify them. Cookies infringe a user's privacy and can allow retrieval of their preferences from a database. Typically cookies store an identification number and details of the last visit to a site. However, companies can associate personal information gained in different ways to the user's computer. There are privacy concerns that cookies may contain sensitive personal details as well as credit card information that could be exploited. It is possible to block cookies but this can be a difficult exercise for the average user. In many cases, users are unaware that their privacy has been infringed.

Evaluating knowledge

▶ Case-based reasoning (CBR)

One of the subfields of artificial intelligence is case-based reasoning (CBR). CBR offers a technique for acquiring and storing past problems, their solutions and the reasoning behind them in a retrieval system. Users can type various problem descriptors and check whether cases from the past can throw insights into their current problem. If the case is able to help, the new case is tagged outlining the current problems, evaluations and solutions with the original case for future retrieval. For example, the CBR framework developed to assist effective delivery on a construction project had the following case descriptors (Ribeiro 2001):

- problems – client requirements, client capabilities, project specifications, project environment, allocation of risk factors and relationships;
- project delivery solutions – procurement methods, contract structure, forms of contract and project management structure;
- project outcomes – schedule variance, budget variance, conformance with specifications, safety, servicing during operation, administrative burden, sustainability of facility and project return.

CBR applications have been particularly successful for help desk and call centre applications where users often face repetitive problems. The user can retrieve past solutions and learning and utilise or adapt them for their own problem solving and add their experiences and actions to the changing circumstances encountered.

Pause for thought

What do you consider to be the main strengths and limitations of case-based reasoning systems in organisations? How often do you use past lessons and experiences to solve current problems? What would you consider to be the time limits, if any, of past experience? Some managers may believe that past experiences hinder progress. How would you answer such managers on the benefits of CBR systems?

▶ Online analytical processing (OLAP)

Spreadsheets can become limited when an individual wants to analyse a large set of data from a variety of perspectives. They can be valuable for analysing data along two dimensions and provide tools to display the results as graphs or pie charts. However, let's explore an organisation that has thirty products in five regions and wishes to analyse all this data in terms of sales, expenses and profits. For such cases, online analytical processing (OLAP) comes into its own. It provides a multidimensional tool to analyse and manipulate the data into various categories. The OLAP Council defines OLAP as enabling the user:

> 'to gain insight into data through fast, consistent, interactive access to a wide variety of possible views of information that has been transformed from raw data to reflect the real dimensionality of the enterprise as understood by the user.'

OLAP uses the notion of a hypercube or a cube with more than three dimensions as a central aspect of this technique. The most common form of reporting multidimensional analysis is to rotate a cube by 90 degrees to show different analyses using the multidimensional variables. The technique of rotating the cube is sometimes called 'slice and dice'.

▶ Knowledge discovery in databases – data mining

The commonly used term 'data mining' can be misleading as the intention of the process is to produce knowledge from structured data. From a young age, we are used to observing and searching and discovering new things. The data mining or knowledge discovery process is similar, including an iterative progression of data cleaning, data analysis, model interpretation and integration of results. The development of knowledge discovery in databases (KDD) or data mining over the past twenty years can be charted in the following manner (Klösgen and Zytkow 2002):

- First generation (1980s): focused on single tasks such as building classifiers, finding clusters in data and visualising data using one approach.
- Second generation (around 1995): led to data mining 'suites' which supported data preprocessing and cleaning and performed multiple discovery tasks.
- Third generation: tightly integrated domain knowledge into discovery process to provide solutions in areas such as marketing, fraud detection, production control and the web.

Knowledge Discovery in databases is 'the non-trivial process of identifying valid, novel, useful and ultimately understandable patterns in the data' (Fayyad *et al.* 1996). It provides deeper insights than traditionally obtained from reports, queries, executive information systems and OLAP. However, investigations in organisations collecting large data sets such as NASA show that only 5–10 per cent of the data ever gets analysed.

Large organisations such as Walmart, the largest retailer in the US, have a strong urge to tap the hidden knowledge that may lie within their huge customer databases (43 tera-bytes at the time of writing). The resulting analysis may provide the key basis for improving their competitive advantage in their market.

Statisticians believe that every time the amount of data increases by a factor of ten we should rethink how we analyse it (Friedman 1997). This is a primary challenge in knowledge discovery where complexity has increased with the large number of cases and the high dimensionality or numbers of variables.

The tools used in knowledge discovery are simple, concise and easy-to-use algorithms that model non-random (statistically significant) relationships or patterns. These tools may include one or more ideas from the following models (Gargano and Raggad 1999):

- **Expert systems** tend to mimic the reasoning of experts whose knowledge is assumed to be deep in a narrow domain. The expert system consists of a knowledge base of rules and data and a logic inference engine that creates new rules and data based on accumulated knowledge. The weaknesses of expert systems are their narrow domain of application, their reliance on the knowledge of the expert, their poor clarity and internal inconsistencies. Attempts to resolve some of these problems have been made by using fuzzy expert systems where the truth or falsity of a fact can be captured on a scale from 0 to 1 rather than traditionally assuming a fact had to be either true or false.

- **Decision trees** are based on a simple tree model where every branch in the tree represents different classes and subclasses. Decision trees are effective when the user wants an exploratory understanding of the data to get a gut feel.

- **Rule induction** uses statistical techniques to discover rules which relate to the frequency of correlation, the rate of accuracy and the accuracy of prediction. Rules are most commonly developed using IF/THEN statements.

- **Genetic algorithms and genetic programming** evolve complex data structures and are based on biological mechanisms of natural selection. They are useful for finding solutions to hard optimisation problems. The main weakness is the nonexplanatory aspect of these models.

- **Neural networks or backpropagation** are tools designed to imitate the physical thought processes of a biological brain in the form of neurons or nerves. The model adapts weights for the interconnections among neurons to allow learning and memory creation to take place. These neural network problems are particularly suited to problems where a great deal of historic data exists for training purposes. Their strength is that they can handle multidimensional and 'noisy' data. However, neural network models do not provide much explanatory power and their training periods may be long.

- **Associative memories** are where pairs of associated data are memorised using a long-term memory network model. These associations can be retrieved at a later date and may provide creative data associations for creative solutions in response to novel stimuli.

- **Clustering techniques** are ideal for classification and category prediction problems. They tend to group together closely related data in a database. They can handle noisy multidimensional data sets but can suffer from long training times.

The knowledge discovery tasks to extract patterns from large datasets can be divided into the following taxonomy (Shaw *et al.* 2001):

● dependency analysis – looking at associations and sequences;
● class identification – examining the mathematical taxonomies and clustering of concepts;
● concept description – attempting to summarise, discriminate and compare different concepts;
● deviation detection – exploring anomalies and changes in the data;
● data visualisation – reporting the data analysis.

The key challenge in knowledge discovery is to provide intelligent systems that improve the selectivity of a search and the ability to understand and respond to a user's needs.

▶ Machine-based learning

Machine learning has been singled out as a vital tool in knowledge discovery in databases applications due to its ability to focus on complex representations, ill-defined problems and search-based methods (Domingos 2002). The flexibility of machine learning methods makes them well suited to problems where little is known about a particular domain. The theory in this area has produced highly successful algorithms such as 'boosting' (Littlestone 1997) and 'support vector machines' (Scholkopf *et al.* 1998). Machine learning has further developed into the realm of biases as biases are what remain in the absence of generalised assumptions in ill-defined problems. It is noteworthy that machine learning techniques are prolific and have found compelling applications in many large databases.

Sharing knowledge

▶ Internet, intranets and extranets

The start of the internet can be traced back to 1969 when the Advanced Research Projects Agency conducted research on networking to link scientists and academics around the world. These networks were configured either as local area networks (LANs) to connect computers via cables over short distances or as wide area networks (WANs) to connect computers over longer distances using transmission lines similar to phone systems. The internet was designed to connect these different networks (LANs and WANs) across the world and performed this task using special computers called routers. In essence, it became similar to a postal system and it needed a common system or set of rules whereby computers could transmit and receive data. This common system or *protocol* was called TCP/IP (transmission control protocol/internet protocol). The IP breaks any data or information into sizeable packets to be sent to a computer across the network and the TCP reassembles the packets of information when they reach their destination. Each computer on the internet has a unique IP address and allows each packet of information to know its sender's and destination address. A major application of the internet is using electronic mail (e-mail). This is the modern postal system of the internet. It also allows text, sound, video and image files to be sent with the e-mails as attachments.

All software used on the internet is based on client/server technology. This means that the software either acts as a server offering services to other computers on the network or acts as a client requesting a service from the server. All the data such as e-mails and web pages are stored on servers. Client software requests information from a server on a distant computer and server software sends the requested information to the client via the internet.

The basic document on the web is a page with its own particular location. This location or URL (uniform resource locator) is simply a web identifier starting with a string such as 'http' or 'ftp'. When you click on a link, your web browser (client) sends off a packet to that address asking for the URL and, subsequently, the server sends back the requested page to your computer. In the past, most pages have been written in a markup language called HTML (hypertext markup language). Each HTML page contains a number of tags or instructions on how text, video, graphics and sound are placed on the page and how links to other documents can be created.

A recent development to markup languages has been the introduction of XML (extensible markup language) to complement HTML and to improve the usefulness of the web. Whereas HTML has provided a predominantly formatting function for data on a page, XML provides valuable information on what the data means. For example, in HTML, we may only know whether a numerical integer has a certain textual attribute such as bold, body or title in the text. In contrast, XML will tell us what the integer means, whether it's a speed, a date or a sales figure. This extra information on a web page allows new computer software to automatically interpret, manipulate and perform operations without direct human intervention. This additional information is often termed metadata or data about data.

Metadata is directly linked to the resource and provides direct access to it. In bibliographic circles, a metadata standard or schema named 'Dublin Core' was developed in 1995 to allow greater bibliographic control over networked resources. The data elements include title, author, subject and keywords, description, publisher, other contributor, date, resource type, format, resource identifier, source, language, relation, coverage and rights management. Other standards are emerging across different industries and the standards are contained within an XML document type definition (DTD), often simply called a dictionary. To allow internationalisation of the web, XML has been firmly rooted in unicode which provides all kinds of text characters from different languages around the world. XML incorporates the direction in which text moves across a page (e.g. right to left in Arabic), hyphenation conventions and cultural assumptions on ways of addressing one another.

The beauty of XML is that it enables companies to provide access to their own data to customers and suppliers at relatively low developmental costs by addressing the schemas in the DTD for each party concerned. Another advantage of XML is that it provides output in many forms and on different platforms such as PCs and PDAs from one source document. As the information in XML documents is described so precisely, it also means that quality of information retrieval from search engines is likely to increase substantially. One casualty and potential danger may be the built-in bias on XML-driven search engines towards specific information, opinions, products and services based on future industry standards.

Pause for thought

Reflect on how the internet and your company's intranet have increased your knowledge base. What are the strengths and limitations of this new medium? How can the internet or extranet help your organisation share knowledge across your value chain? Do you foresee any dangers in using the internet as a knowledge-sharing medium? Are there any concerns over sharing ideas and intellectual property rights? Given the widespread nature of the internet, what are the implications for you and your future work using this medium?

The future direction of the web as described by Tim Berners-Lee, its inventor, is one moving more towards a semantic web. This would allow the user to access precise information for decision making immediately rather than having to browse through lots of documents to find the information. The goal is to make the web more intelligent. The language and schemas chosen for the semantic web are RDF rather than XML as information found in RDF (Resource Description Framework) maps links directly and unambiguously to a decentralised model and there are instruments known as parsers that can decipher this information more easily.

With the expanding bandwidths and processing power, multimedia technology is no longer an aspiration but a reality on the web. Image technology has advanced to an extent whereby images can be sent as scalable vector graphics in small abstract packets and reassembled on computers or small personal digital assistants in a style and resolution appropriate to the device. The quality of the image is much better than the traditional pixel graphics found in GIF or JPEG files. The independence of device and software has provided major advances in this area. Another standard called the synchronised multimedia integration language (SMIL) has offered a direction for integrating the different components of a multimedia experience into one. Increasingly, the disabled user is being brought to the forefront of web developments with an emphasis on supplying alternative mediums such as soundtracks with subtitles, images with descriptions and mouse movements with keyboard alternatives.

An intranet is a network that exists exclusively within an organisation and is based on internet technology. It can provide an e-mail system, remote access, group collaboration tools, an application sharing system and a company communications network (Laudon and Laudon 2000). It protects information from unauthorised use through a software mechanism called a firewall that blocks unwanted access from the outside but allows internal users to gain access to the internet. Some traditional applications of intranets are:

- access to databases;
- forum for discussion;
- distribution of electronic documentation;
- administering payroll and benefits packages;
- providing online training;
- frequently asked questions (FAQs) to provide answers to commonly raised questions.

When building intranets, organisations need to be mindful of the dangers of developing large and sophisticated solutions that nobody visits. The technology needs to be user led to meet explicit needs. Another danger is the use of intranets to develop 'electronic fences' in organisations contrary to the espoused principle of knowledge sharing (Swan *et al.* 1999).

▶ Security of intranets

Most organisations have adopted 'firewall' technologies to prevent intruders from gaining access to their sensitive organisational information. The most important goals of firewall systems are (Loew *et al.* 1999):

- access control at different levels;
- control at the application layer;
- user rights administration;
- isolation of certain services;
- proof back-up and analysis of the log;
- alarm facilities;
- concealment of internal network structure;
- confidentiality;
- resistance of firewall against attacks.

Firewalls examine every packet of information between networks (using packet filters) and analyse their characteristics to decide whether to deny any unauthorised messages or access attempts. A high-level security firewall can be constructed using two packet filters. The weakness of one packet filter is supported by the other. Attacks on these servers will not endanger the internal network. However, there can never be any guarantee of total security. In the future, it is likely that encryption technologies will be used to strengthen the security of firewalls.

▶ Text-based conferencing

There are a number of text-based conferencing channels through which individuals can share knowledge and information. Usenet newsgroups are worldwide discussion forums on a multitude of topics where discussions take place on an electronic bulletin board, with individuals posting messages for others to read. Another public forum for sharing knowledge within predefined groups is discussion lists that individuals can subscribe to. These lists are generally moderated, in comparison with newsgroups which are not. An individual subscribes and joins a discussion group and receives e-mail messages sent by others concerning the topic. The individual can reply to the group and their offerings are distributed to all subscribers to the group.

Various chat tools have been developed to allow two or more individuals on the internet to hold live interactive conversations. If the number of contributors increases substantially, chat groups can be divided into different themes and topic areas. Some enhancements are providing voice chat capabilities. Individuals can arrange to meet at predefined times to share their knowledge and ideas, particularly in cases where the phone may not be the appropriate medium. Discussion groups can also be set up on a variety of topics on an organisation's intranet to enable knowledge sharing. Sensitivities relating to the membership of these groups need to be considered so that full, frank and open discussions and dialogues can be promoted. For example, in a work context, people may be guarded in their contributions if they are aware that their boss or senior management may be party to the conference.

▶ Groupware tools

The raison d'être behind groupware is to encourage collaboration between people to enhance knowledge sharing. In commercial terms, the assumption is that greater collaboration will lead to increased productivity, lower costs and higher quality through better decision making. Groupware, as a concept, tends to be applied to information communication technologies (ICTs) that support collaboration, communication and coordination of activities over space and time as well as shared information spaces (Robertson *et al.* 2001). Two common technologies used in groupware are e-mail and Lotus Notes discussion databases. Lotus Notes is generally considered as the first groupware product to provide discussion databases, e-mail with attachments, shared databases, workflow automation and applications development. Other systems have included (Williams 1996):

- group decision support systems (GDSS) with brainstorming, ideas generation and voting systems;
- collaborative writing and whiteboards;
- computer-based conferencing;
- schedule meetings and diary organisers;
- e-mail systems used proactively.

▶ Videoconferencing

Desktop videoconferencing (DTVC) provides a means for two or more people to see and hear each other from their desktop computer, enabling them to collaborate and share knowledge without leaving their desk. A small camera and microphone are attached to the top of a PC and these relay the video information to a distant user. Using this technology, organisations can improve their workflows and save on travel time and costs. Most products provide a simple shared workspace or 'whiteboard' so that users can explain their ideas through drawings. More sophisticated applications allow users to work together on the same documents or spreadsheets. Poor picture quality issues of videoconferencing are normally associated with a lack of internet bandwidth.

▶ Skills directories: expertise yellow pages

To enable knowledge sharing in organisations, there is often a need to find the individual or groups with the necessary skills and expertise that may be required in another part of the organisation. Many firms now produce 'expert yellow pages' and directories of communities. Expert yellow pages comprise a listing of all the employees in an organisation, with a summary of their knowledge, skills and expertise. This is accessible to all employees who can access the 'expert' through keywords on an intranet-based search engine. A similar searchable listing may be developed for communities, groups and discussion lists within organisations.

▶ E-learning

E-learning is the generic term used to describe online learning, computer-based training and web-based training. It is the application of internet technologies to support the delivery and management of learning, skills and knowledge. E-learning does not have to occur exclusively on the internet. More reputable offerings tend to provide an integration of various learning technologies such as:

- mentoring;
- chat forums;
- expert-led discussions;
- web seminars;
- online meetings;
- virtual classroom sessions.

E-learning initiatives need to be considered as part of an organisation's portfolio of HRD interventions to meet training and development needs rather than being adopted as a panacea for cutting costs.

Storing and presenting knowledge

▶ Data warehouses

A data warehouse is a large physical database that holds a vast amount of information from a wide variety of sources. The data warehouse needs to serve as a neutral data storage area that can be used for a variety of analytical tools. The characteristics of a data warehouse are (Inmon 1992):

- subject orientation – data may be organised around business subjects;
- uniformity – common data elements related to multiple applications are treated consistently;
- time variant – data is updated as conditions change;
- non-volatile – data is loaded into the warehouse and retrieved easily from it.

Data warehouses can be structured to contain data at various levels (as shown in Figure 4.11) including current detail data, older detail data, lightly summarised data (often for middle management), highly summarised data (for top management) and meta data. The 'older level of detail' is often placed at the bottom of the data warehouse

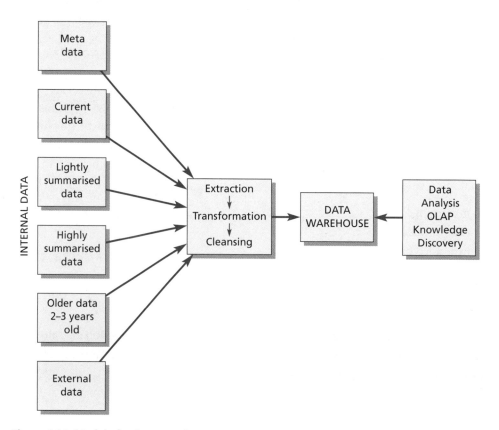

Figure 4.11 **Model of a data warehouse**

structure as it may be two or three years old and infrequently accessed (Ma *et al.* 2000). Meta data is used to describe the meaning and structure of the data as well as how it was created, accessed and used (Devlin 1997). The meta data can help the user locate the contents of the warehouse and map their elements. In addition, it may provide a guide to the algorithms used to summarise the data in different ways.

Relational database management systems (RDBMS) are widely used today as data warehouses to store, manipulate and query large data sets in a variety of applications. They are used in virtually every major organisation to manage tasks such as payroll, sales and marketing.

Pause for thought

Relational databases are very popular in organisations nowadays. What are your experiences of using these databases? How useful do you find them, particularly databases of customer records? Are there inherent limitations in using them for particularly large databases? How would you rate your statistical skills and ability to understand complex statistical analyses? Do you see any problems arising from managers misinterpreting complex analyses from OLAP or data mining tools? How could you overcome this potential problem?

▶ Visualisation

Visualisation is an emerging technology which allows users to understand the complexity of information through the use of rich computer graphics. This can be an invaluable tool, particularly for visualising analysis from data mining and information-retrieval techniques, as shown in Figure 4.12 (p. 118). For example, data in an information retrieval system can be represented and modelled in the following manner (Song 2000):

- 2-dimensional (2D) or 3-dimensional (3D) scatterplots;
- 2D or 3D vector field topology plots with geometric data points;
- tree or hierarchical visualisation techniques to simplify complex data by branching data into levels;
- network techniques to represent information structures as spatial networks;
- maps related to a domain's geography;
- bibliometric mapping techniques to represent authors and their writings on a landscape and clustering authors based on various commonalities.

More advanced visualisation techniques have adopted colour as well as a combination of rendering and photo-realism techniques (Cawkell 2001). Rendering is a technique to make computer-generated images appear as realistic as photographs. The emphasis is on modelling the way light creates shadows on surfaces, textures and objects and removing the transparency of obscuring objects. In the film industry, photo-realism techniques have been employed to create animation and special effects so that computer-generated graphics can blend seamlessly into the action in movies. These techniques have been used in films such as *Star Wars*, *Jurassic Park* and *Titanic*. It

Figure 4.12 **The Starlight Information Visualization System developed at the Pacific Northwest National Laboratory. The Starlight software displays complex relationships among large quantities of disparate information**

is notable that one of the greatest challenges in photo-realism is the ability to render human skin on animated objects. Many of these techniques are likely to enter knowledge management domains as the complexity of information and related analyses increases in the long term.

CASE STUDY

Technip-Coflexip

A glance through the 2001 annual report of Technip-Coflexip, the big global engineering and construction group, might create the impression that it was interested only in mega projects – massive ethylene steam crackers in Iran, refineries in Egypt, nickel-cobalt complexes in New Caledonia, or high-tech chemical plants in China and Taiwan.

'Our main target is big or medium-sized projects,' says Riccardo Mollo, chief executive of alliances at Technip Italy. 'But there is a significant level of mini- or micro jobs.' The problem, however, was how to take on these smaller jobs economically – the group was simply too expensive for executing projects at the doorstep of smaller customers, especially those in remote locations. 'We kept on hearing these clients saying, 'It's too bad, we can only use the local engineering companies.' These are cheap, but they are poor on project management, process competences and value-added services,' says Mr Mollo.

The company's solution was to use the internet. It set up an e-collaboration portal, TechniPlaNet, which aims to combine the group's global expertise with local cost advantages, and thus allows it to execute smaller projects in innovative ways. It is one of the most ambitious initiatives so far to exploit the web in an industry that has been relatively conservative in its adoption of new information technologies.

The TechniPlaNet portal is essentially a secure, permanent, interactive e-business club that allows T-C's operating centres, clients, subcontractors, vendors and others to design and construct small- to midsize projects more cost effectively and faster, without compromising quality. 'This tool networks all the actors in the development and construction of a project,' says Mr Mollo. 'It basically delocalises them. You need to be able to look at the job (without having to go to the site). With this tool you can relay information to local low-cost companies and they can send it back. We have been using e-mail but that is not really enough. Now the deliverables are sitting on a virtual desk accessible to all the people involved in the workflow process.'

One of the key IT vendors behind TechniPlaNet is Intergraph PPO (for Process, Power and Offshore), the Alabama-based company which is one of the two big names worldwide in engineering IT solutions for the process, power and energy industries. The other is Cambridge-based Aveva Engineering IT (formerly Cadcentre), part of the UK's Aveva Group.

Intergraph PPO sees the internet and web-enabled techniques as a key weapon in its assault on what it calls 'information erosion' in the industries it serves.

Plenty of attention is paid to efficiently creating and maintaining plant physical assets, but not enough, it says, to doing the same job with information assets. These can produce a return on investment, just as a physical asset can, but unfortunately information can be eroded if it is not looked after.

A few statistics and anecdotes from an Intergraph survey of owner/operators and engineering procurement contractors highlight the problems caused by inaccurate, poorly maintained information. One owner operator spent $12 million to ensure plant safety following a gas leak, when it was found that drawings and data did not reflect the actual plant. Another had to spend $1 million re-gathering 'as-built' information before it could redesign an existing plant. A third found that 85 per cent of information in more than 1,000 data sheets was inaccurate.

The solution, according to Intergraph, is an internet-enabled approach that manages plant information right through the lifecycle of the plant, from design and commissioning through to operations and maintenance. This lifecycle can be 30 years or more.

'The tools we are producing now are greatly speeding up, opening up and improving communication between different segments and groups in the industry,' says Ben Eazzetta, Intergraph PPO's executive vice-president for global sales, marketing and business development. Project engineers in remote locations and office workers can now look at the same piece of data on a live site, helping to reduce errors caused by looking at old data.

As engineering contractors increasingly outsource work to low-cost centres such as India, South-east Asia or Eastern Europe, and owners manage a wide range of facilities in remote places, the need for widespread access to live data will grow, he says. A web-based infrastructure, he adds, is very important, as it avoids the need for major reworking of data and also anticipates wider use in the future of wireless internet technology in the field.

According to figures from Intergraph and independent sources, using internet-enabled plant information management can save millions of dollars in the various stages of the project. For example, the savings in the concept development stage range from 10 to 30 per cent – typically $5 million – and in the commissioning stage from 30–60 per cent or, typically, $3 million-plus.

The biggest savings can be made in the 'handover' process between the contractor and the owner operator – 60 per cent savings or up to $10 million. Intergraph sees this point in the information lifecycle as critical – typically, owner operators have dumped all the project data into a variety of disparate databases, says Mr Eazzetta, so have not been able to derive much value from it.

A lot of the benefits of web-enabled plant information management (PIM) have been achieved in the construction and operation of Statoil's $4.4 billion Asgard project. Anchored in deep water 200 km off Norway's Atlantic coast, Asgard is the largest subsea development in the world. Statoil and Intergraph established an e-engineering business partnership, based around a web-enabled, industry standards-based PIM data warehouse to hold all the technical data for the project. Statoil's aim was to re-use this data throughout the plant's lifecycle, including the long commissioning, operations and maintenance stages. 'The data warehouse works as a single source for sharing and exchanging information,' says Adrian Park, Statoil's PIM product responsible manager. 'It gives much better control of plant configuration and change management.'

The traditional 'dump and run' scenario at the handover stage between contractor and operator was avoided by ensuring that data was automatically transferred each day from contractor Kvaerner Oil and Gas to the Statoil PIM. 'So we don't get problems at the end, when people are leaving the project,' says Mr Park. By focusing on maximising the quality and speed of the information transfer, the company says the handover was the best it had ever achieved.

In the operating phase, the web-based interface with the PIM system is bringing benefits because it is easy to use and very intuitive, says Mr Park, and training needs have been less than expected. 'No one is frightened by it. It's quite important during operations, when people might work for two weeks offshore, then have leave for three weeks, then work for another two weeks and have leave for four weeks – they can forget the application they are meant to be using.'

The web interface also gives universal access to contractors and suppliers, however geographically dispersed they are and however minimal the support they receive.

These are early days for such innovations in the process industry, however, and both Technip-Coflexip and Statoil are among the initial customers for such web-based systems. In the market for web-based tools, some standards issues remain to be resolved, but Mr Eazzetta says the market 'will set a standard. Something will emerge that people see a value in'. He sees the industry as being at the beginning of an adoption curve lasting 2–5 years.

But for the early adopters there is no turning back. The PIM programme has been so successful at the Asgard project that it is now part of corporate best practice, says Mr Park, and will be implemented in new offshore projects. As a result, Statoil is hoping to cut project development costs by 10–20 per cent, and operating costs by 5–10 per cent, on projects such as the $1.88 billion Kristin offshore development in the Norwegian Sea and the massive $5.1 billion Snohvit LNG development in the Barents Sea, northern Norway.

Meanwhile Technip-Coflexip, which deployed TechniPlaNet early last year, has realised that the system is not necessarily limited to small jobs. It is now migrating the tool to a much bigger IT platform and BP has agreed to use it for the worldwide strategic alliance that it has in place with Technip Italy for the development of purified terephthalic acid (PTA) production plants. These plants cost hundreds of million dollars apiece, and TechniPlaNet is being used as a standardised knowledge database for all the different users involved in building them.

The IT side of the process, power and offshore industry will always have a low external profile, given the sheer size and environmental impact of its physical assets. But within the industry the internet is unlocking the value of information and encouraging contractors, suppliers and operators to hold it in equal respect with their rigs, platform and pipework.

Source: Article by Andrew Baxter, *Financial Times*, 16 October 2002

Questions

1   Is the technology in this case another form of 'old wine in new bottles'? What innovative techniques have been used to create, organise, store, share and evaluate new knowledge?

2   Given the over-reliance on small subcontractors from low-cost countries in these industries, what are the likely consequences on training and effective use of these technologies?

3   How can new learning from past projects be stored in the data warehouse?

4   What are the difficulties of measuring and attributing cost savings to new technology for Technip-Coflexip rather than arising from improved work processes, worker incentives or project learning?

Summary

This chapter has elaborated five main technologies in the development of new knowledge in organisations:

1   Tools for organising knowledge emphasised the importance of ontology and taxonomy generation tools to categorise knowledge at an individual, organisational or knowledge domain level.

2   Tools for capturing knowledge examined cognitive mapping tools to help make tacit knowledge more explicit, information retrieval tools and the technology behind web-based search engines. Automation of knowledge capturing tasks was explored in relation to personalisation tools and agent technology.

3   Tools for evaluating knowledge considered the potential of case-based reasoning, OLAP, data mining and machine-based learning tools.

4   Tools for sharing knowledge focused on the power of the internet and intranets and how sharing could be facilitated through text-based conferencing tools, groupware tools, videoconferencing, expertise yellow pages and e-learning techniques.

5   Tools for storing and presenting knowledge highlighted data warehouses and the latest visualisation techniques.

QUESTIONS FOR FURTHER THOUGHT

1 Assuming high developmental costs, what can organisations do if they find their intranets and data warehouses are rarely visited by their employees?

2 How could second-generation semantic webs co-exist with first-generation HTML-based webs? Are there potential opportunities and challenges for knowledge sharing?

3 In group processes, how do you manage conflicting 'collective maps' of tacit routines?

4 A 2002 thesis proposed by Stephen Wolfram, chief executive of Mathematica, was that all knowledge could be described as an algorithm. How far do you agree with such a proposition and is the end goal of KM tools to discover these underlying algorithms?

5 What are the barriers facing human-computer interaction and the ability of humans to place greater trust in personalisation and agent technologies to meet their needs?

6 If knowledge discovery techniques can analyse only 5–10 per cent of data in large databases, what are the dangers of making decisions and building strategies on partial information?

7 What parameters are likely to encourage the adoption of certain tools and technologies over others in organisations?

8 Apart from saving travel costs, what are the likely advantages of using videoconferencing tools in an organisation?

9 What is the best way of managing two large data warehouses in a merger or acquisition situation?

10 When are traditional tools of knowledge creation and sharing such as a blank piece of paper or telephone more useful than more sophisticated tools outlined in this chapter?

Further reading

Laudon and Laudon 2000 is an easily accessible text on some of the tools outlined in this chapter. It also provides a good introduction to management information systems.

References

Ambrosini, V. and Bowman, C. (2002) 'Mapping successful organizational routines', *Mapping Strategic Knowledge*, A. S. Huff and M. Jenkins, eds, Sage, London.

Baeza-Yates, R. and Ribeiro-Neto, B. (1999) *Modern Information Retrieval*, Addison-Wesley Longman Limited, Harlow, Essex.

Barney, J. B. (1991) 'Firm resources and sustained competitive advantage', *Journal of Management*, 17(1), 99–120.

Cawkell, T. (2001) 'Progress in visualisation', *Journal of Information Science*, 27(6), 427–438.

Devlin, B. (1997) *Data Warehouse: From Architecture to Implementation*, Addison-Wesley, Reading, MA.

Ding, Y. and Foo, S. (2002) 'Ontology research and development. Part 1 – a review of ontology generation', *Journal of Information Science*, 28(2), 123–136.

Domingos, P. (2002). 'Machine learning', *Handbook of Data Mining and Knowledge Discovery*, W. Klösgen and J. M. Zytkow, eds, Oxford University Press, Oxford.

Eden, C. and Ackermann, F. (1998) *Making Strategy: The Journey of Strategic Management*, Sage, London.

Eden, C. and Ackermann, F. (2002) 'A mapping framework for strategy making', *Mapping Strategic Knowledge*, A. S. Huff and M. Jenkins, eds, Sage, London.

Fayyad, U., Piatetsky-Shapiro, G., Smyth, P. and Uthurusamy, R. (1996) *Advances in Knowledge Discovery and Data Mining*, MIT Press, Cambridge, MA.

Friedman, J. H. (1997) 'Data mining and statistics: what's the connection?', *Keynote Speech of the Proceeding of the 29th Symposium on the Interface Between Computer Science and Statistics*, Houston TX.

Gargano, M. L. and Raggad, B. G. (1999) 'Data mining – a powerful information creating tool', *OCLC Systems & Services*, 15(2), 81–90.

Gharajedaghi, J. and Ackoff, R. L. (1994) 'Mechanisms, organisms and social systems', *New Thinking in Organizational Behaviour*, H. Tsoukas, ed., Butterworth & Heinemann, Oxford, 25–39.

Grant, R. M. (1991) 'The resource-based theory of competitive advantage: implications for strategy formulation', *California Management Review*, 33(3), 114–135.

Grant, R. M. (1996) 'Toward a knowledge-based theory of the firm', *Strategic Management Journal*, 17, 109–22.

Gruber, T. R. (1993) 'A translation approach to portable ontology specifications', *Knowledge Acquisitions*, 5, 199–220.

Huff, A. S. and Jenkins, M. (2002) *'Mapping Strategic Knowledge'*, Sage, London.

Inmon, W. H. (1992) 'Data warehouse – a perspective of data over time', *Database Management*, February, 370–390.

Jennings, N. R., Faratin, P., Johnson, M. J., Norman, T. J., O'Brien, P. and Wiegand, M. E. (1996) 'Agent-based business process management', *International Journal of Cooperative Information Systems*, 5(2), 105–130.

Jennings, N. R. and Wooldridge, M. J. (1998) *Agent Technology: Foundations, Applications and Markets*, Springer-Verlag, Berlin.

Kelly, G. A. (1955) *The Psychology of Personal Constructs*, Norton, New York.

Klösgen, W. and Zytkow, J. M. (2002) *Handbook of Data Mining and Knowledge Discovery*, Oxford University Press, Oxford.

Laudon, K. C. and Laudon, J. P. (2000). *Management Information Systems: Organization and Technology in the Networked Enterprise*, Prentice-Hall, Upper Saddle River, NJ.

Littlestone, N. (1997) 'Learning quickly when irrelevant attributes abound: a new linear threshold algorithm', *Machine Learning*, 2, 285–318.

Loew, R., Stengel, I., Bleimann, U. and McDonald, A. (1999) 'Security aspects of an enterprise-wide network architecture', *Internet Research: Electronic Networking Applications and Policy*, 9(1), 8–15.

Ma, C., Chou, D. C. and Yen, D. C. (2000) 'Data warehousing, technology assessment and management', *Industrial Management & Data Systems*, 100(3), 125–134.

Mack, R., Ravin, Y. and Byrd, R. J. (2001) 'Knowledge portals and the emerging digital knowledge workplace', *IBM Systems Journal*, 40(4), 925–955.

Maes, P. (1994) 'Agents that reduce work and information overload', *Communications of the ACM*, 37(7), 31–40.

Marwick, A. D. (2001) 'Knowledge management technology', *IBM Systems Journal*, 40(4), 814–830.

Mertins, K., Heisig, P. and Vorbeck, J. (2000) *Knowledge Management: Best Practices in Europe*, Springer-Verlag, New York.

Nelson, R. and Winter, S. (1982) *An Evolutionary Theory of Economic Change*, Harvard University Press, Cambridge, MA.

O'Dell, C., Hasanali, F., Hunbert, C., Lopez, K. and Raybourn, C. (2000) *Stages of Implementation: A Guide for Your Journey to Knowledge Management*, American Productivity and Quality Centre, Houston, Tex.

Ribeiro, F. L. (2001) 'Project delivery system selection: a case-based reasoning framework', *Logistics Information Management*, 14(5/6), 367–375.

Robertson, M., Sørensen, C. and Swan, J. (2001) 'Survival of the leanest: intensive knowledge work and groupware adaption', *Information Technology & People*, 14(4), 334–352.

Ruggles, R. (1998) 'The state of the notion: knowledge management in practice', *California Management Review*, 40(3), 80–9.

Scholkopf, B., Burges, C. and Smola, A. (1998) *Advances in Kernel Methods: Support Vector Machines*, MIT Press, Cambridge, MA.

Shaw, M. J., Subramaniam, C., Tan, G. W. and Welge, M. E. (2001) 'Knowledge management and data mining for marketing', *Decision Support Systems*, 31, 127–137.

Smith, R. G. and Farquhar, A. (2000) 'The road ahead for knowledge management: an AI perspective', *American Association for Artificial Intelligence*, Winter, 17–40.

Sofia Pinto, H., Gomez-Perez, A. and Martins, J. P. (1999) 'Some issues on ontology integration', *Proceedings of IJCAI-99 Workshop on Ontologies and Problem-Solving Methods: Lessons Learned and Future Trends, in conjunction with the Sixteenth International Joint Conference on Articial Intelligence*, Stockholm, Sweden.

Song, M. (2000) 'Visualization in information retrieval: a three-level analysis', *Journal of Information Science*, 26(1), 3–19.

Spender, J. C. (1996) 'Making knowledge the basis of a dynamic theory of the firm', *Strategic Management Journal*, 17, 45–62.

Swan, J., Newell, S., Scarbrough, H. and Hislop, D. (1999) 'Knowledge management and innovation: networks and networking', *Journal of Knowledge Management*, 3(4), 262–275.

Uschold, M. and Gruninger, M. (1996) 'Ontologies: principles, methods and applications', *Knowledge Engineering Review*, 11(2), 93–155.

Weick, K. E. and Bougon, M. G. (1986) 'Organisations as cognitive maps', *The Thinking Organization*, H. P. J. Sims, ed., Jossey-Bass, San Francisco, 125–135.

Williams, A. (1996) 'Groupware: the next ware of office automation', *Industrial Management & Data Systems*, Vol. 96, No. 6, 11–13.

Wolfram, S. (2002) *A New Kind of Science*, Wolfram Media Inc., Champaign, IL.

PART 3

Evaluating knowledge

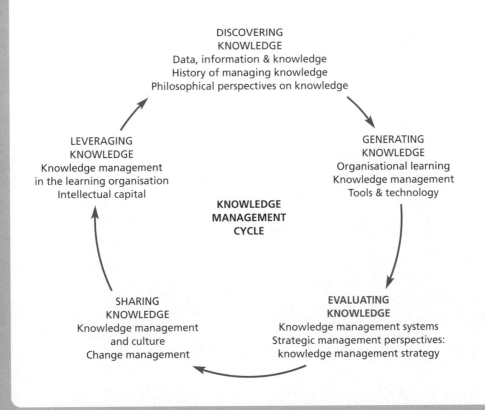

DISCOVERING
KNOWLEDGE
Data, information & knowledge
History of managing knowledge
Philosophical perspectives on knowledge

GENERATING
KNOWLEDGE
Organisational learning
Knowledge management
Tools & technology

LEVERAGING
KNOWLEDGE
Knowledge management
in the learning organisation
Intellectual capital

KNOWLEDGE
MANAGEMENT
CYCLE

EVALUATING
KNOWLEDGE
Knowledge management systems
Strategic management perspectives:
knowledge management strategy

SHARING
KNOWLEDGE
Knowledge management
and culture
Change management

Knowledge management systems

After completing this chapter the reader should be able to:

- explain the component technologies involved in different km systems;
- describe the different quality management processes driving km systems;
- outline a plan for the selection and effective implementation of km systems for any given business problem;
- construct a breakdown of overall costs for a KM system.

The use and application of knowledge management systems implies these questions for managers:

- How do you select an appropriate KM system to meet current and future business needs given the multitude of offerings in the marketplace?
- What are the key factors that lead to effective implementation and adoption of KM systems?
- Can higher quality information from new KM systems lead to poorer quality decisions?
- Do KM systems achieve the necessary return on investment and expectations for the end customer?

Links to other chapters

Chapter 4	describes the component tools and technologies found in KM systems.
Chapter 6	explores the role of KM systems in knowledge strategies.
Chapter 8	concerns change management and the effective implementation of KM systems in organisations.

New twists for old tricks

FT

Retailers have always devoted large parts of their customer relationship management (CRM) budget to technology, and now they are looking to new types of software to help them cross-sell and 'up-sell' – or encourage customers to buy a higher-grade product – and to ensure they are more loyal.

Many of these new developments are applying IT to activities which have long been common sense for retailers. An example is a technique known as 'clienteling'. Top retail sales staff have always kept a 'little black book' of customer contacts, says Monte Zweben, chief executive of Blue Martini Software, a US-based CRM vendor. This enables them to contact a customer if a new product lines comes in which they know might appeal to him or her. 'Clienteling' makes this more efficient; it allows customer information to be shared among sales staff and for a larger range of customers to benefit from this sort of personal service. It also helps with thank-you notes and follow-ups, allowing retailers to project a more professional image, while delivering the personal service that high-end tailors and boutiques have always been able to offer.

Nordstrom, the US fashion retailer, is installing clienteling applications developed by Blue Martini in its 137 stores. It involves point-of-sale terminals that will help the company manage customer preferences and product information. The software assists sales staff and marketing departments by building a picture of the customer's behaviour. Personalised marketing material can then be prepared for events such as a birthday or wedding. The software also allows marketing departments to create graphical workflow diagrams of any campaign and track events as they occur.

Gathering information through such techniques, and the now ubiquitous loyalty programmes, produces a huge amount of available data. The danger, however, is that the customer will be spammed with useless information, says Mike Muldoon, Europe business consulting services industry leader for retail at IBM. 'If technology companies, software companies and retailers don't work together to ensure (the CRM effort) can have mass appeal, it will be pointless,' he says.

Nevertheless, many retailers believe such initiatives will prove to be worthwhile. Sainsbury's, the UK supermarket chain, which has just launched a new loyalty scheme known as Nectar (with Debenhams, the department store group, BP and Barclaycard, the credit card company), says that by using a combination of the picture built up by the loyalty card as well as profiling the local population, it can ensure the right mix of products in store and make personalised mailings and offers to customers.

The Nectar scheme illustrates another risk of new CRM initiatives, however – technology that does not work. The Nectar website was overwhelmed by the initial response from consumers and online registration was suspended.

A further area of CRM investment involves the medium through which the dialogue between retailer and customer takes place. As technology progresses this can occur through a customer's PDA, in-store electronic kiosks or handheld devices.

All these CRM innovations require considerable investment, but the return could come in many ways. For one, it may reduce costs. Many retailers have staff churn of 30 per cent a year. Retraining is thus a major expense that 'clienteling' and similar technology may be able to minimise.

The cost of technology, although substantial, pales into insignificance in comparison to the marketing budgets of most large retailers, says Mr Muldoon. If even a tiny proportion of the marketing budget were diverted to IT investment, it would have a major impact, increasing sales. Even a 1 per cent increase in sales could cover the cost of the technology, agrees Pete Abell, director of research at AMR Research, referring to a pilot undertaken in Atlanta by Gap, the clothing chain.

Costs may be further controlled by avoiding big bang CRM and choosing an incremental approach. This is possible, for example, with store cards, according to GE Consumer Finance, which manages many such programmes. Because the data is held centrally and can be analysed on the company's database system, an incremental approach can be taken, controlling costs and measuring the success of each programme as it happens, says Seamus Smith, director of client services.

Investment in CRM technology is likely to continue increasing in the retail sector, mainly due to competitive pressures. The first-mover advantage is significant, says Mr Abell – if one retailer finds a technology that increases profitability, the others must follow.

Even so, the importance of technology in retailing, compared with human factors such as acknowledgement, respect and trust, can be overstated. 'CRM is about providing customers with what they need at every touch point and in retailing the majority of touch points are human,' says Rob Corrie, director at Spectra UK, a marketing analysis and data solutions company.

Source: Article by Paul Talacko, *Financial Times*, 6 November 2002

Introduction

A multitude of knowledge management systems have been developed by configuring different component technologies shown in Chapter 4 and integrating them in different ways. For certain business applications, generic and standard software has been developed for mass market appeal. A frequent dilemma for firms is whether to acquire off-the-shelf solutions or develop customised KM systems. A major issue concerning off-the-shelf solutions is whether organisations want to follow practices and ontologies embedded within the software. The underlying premise of KM systems is that they will meet expectations of senior management for return on investment or increased effectiveness. The current reality is that many KM systems have failed to deliver on these expectations due to their strong IT orientation and little regard to links with business strategy and the end customer.

In determining the appropriateness of KM solutions, one needs to be mindful of the five major concerns of senior executives related to IT investments in organisations (PriceWaterhouse 1995):

● integrating IT with corporate objectives;
● transforming through IT;
● infrastructure;
● uncertainty;
● cost control.

This chapter opens by exploring the notion of a system and examines the key contributors to systems thinking and methodologies. It argues that the dominant driver behind the development of KM systems is the improvement of quality management processes in organisations. In this regard, the chapter deliberates on the dominant contributors of the quality management movement starting with Deming and Juran and moving on to principles such as TQM (total quality management), BPR (business process re-engineering) and lean production. To reach these continuous improvement goals, a variety of KM systems are examined, including document management systems, decision support systems, group support systems, executive information systems, workflow management systems and customer relationship management systems. The emphasis throughout is to elaborate on the nature of these systems, their component technologies and shared good practice on their effective implementation. The economic and hidden costs of KM systems are also explored given the scaling back of IT spend in many organisations globally. In a study of 431 US and European firms conducted in 1997 exploring what firms are doing to manage knowledge, the following project priorities (in descending order) were discovered related to KM systems (Ruggles 1998):

- creating an intranet (47 per cent);
- creating data warehouses and knowledge repositories (33 per cent);
- implementing decision support tools (33 per cent);
- implementing groupware to support collaboration (33 per cent);
- creating networks of knowledge workers (24 per cent);
- mapping sources of internal expertise (18 per cent).

These figures are likely to have changed dramatically in the interim in response to changing organisational needs and market developments. The key question remains: can KM systems deliver individual and management expectations around knowledge creation and sharing? If not, what are the additional ingredients needed in the collective 'knowledge management' pot?

Systems thinking

Early management thinking tended to adopt a mechanistic view of reality and treat organisations and people more like machines. This mechanistic view is typified by Frederick Taylor's theory of scientific management (Taylor 1911) and Weber's notion of bureaucracies (Weber 1947). Scientific management stresses repetitive work cycles, detailed planning of work sequences and motivation based on economic rewards. Bureaucracies are characterised by top-down authority hierarchies, breakdown of jobs into routine and well-defined tasks, and a formal set of rules to ensure predictable behaviour. Despite numerous criticisms of this mechanistic conception of organisation, many commentators have argued that developments in information technology and virtual organisations have tended to refine this perspective.

Systems thinking emerged in the 1940s in the biological sciences as the traditional mechanistic view failed to explain the complexity of organisational phenomena. Soon this new perspective found its way into organisational thinking with an adoption of biological analogies such as survival, development and stability.

So what is a system? A system can be characterised as a series of elements connected by relationships or links surrounded by a clearly defined boundary to the external environment and with a role of transforming its inputs into desired outputs, as shown in Figure 5.1 (p. 131). Each element and relationship has an attribute depending on how they are measured, such as size, intensity and strength. The system is termed an open system if the boundary allows inputs from and outputs to the environment. A state of homeostasis is achieved when the system is able to control its internal environment and maintain a dynamic steady state with its changing external environment.

One early conception of organisations by Eric Trist was to view them as 'socio-technical' systems (Trist 1959). The goal of such systems was to find a 'best fit' between the social

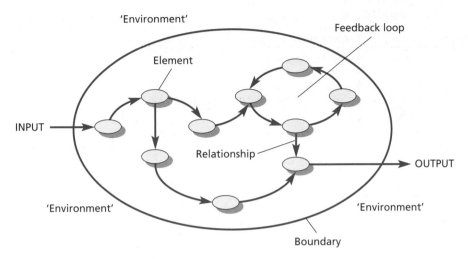

Figure 5.1 General characteristics of a system

(capabilities, needs, relationships) and the technical (material, apparatus, operational stages) aspects of the system. Such a conception still has some relevance in knowledge management with its preoccupations with technical or human resource aspects of knowledge creation and distribution. In the field of systems science, a wide range of other system methodologies has been forwarded, as shown in Table 5.1. There is currently no consensus on the best systems methodology for a given knowledge management situation but rather an understanding of the strengths and limitations of different systems methodologies as well as the advantages of combining methods to offer creative solutions to complex and ill-defined situations (Gao *et al.* 2002).

Table 5.1 Summary systems methodologies (adapted from Gao *et al.* (2002)

Author	Systems methodology and key points
Churchman (1970)	Social systems design (SSD) Uses dialectic process of thesis, antithesis and synthesis to better understand a situation.
Beer (1972)	Viable systems diagnosis (VSD) Belief that system is viable if capable of responding to environmental changes by achieving variety. Important role played by information flows and organisational structure. Subsystems labelled as implementation, coordination, control, development and policy.
Ackoff (1979)	Interactive planning (IP) Facilitates participation of all stakeholders in planning to generate consensus, commitment; mobilises creativity and eases implementation.
Checkland (1981)	Soft systems methodology (SSM) Emphasises systems as cyclical learning processes. 1 Enter unstructured problematic situation 2 Express problem situation 3 Formulate root definitions: CATWOE – Customers, Actors, Transformation process, *Weltanschauung* (view of the world), Owners, Environmental constraints

Table 5.1 **Summary systems methodologies (adapted from Gao *et al*. (2002) (continued)**

Author	Systems methodology and key points
	4 Build conceptual models 5 Compare models with real-world actions 6 Define feasible and desirable changes 7 Take action to improve problem situation.
Mason & Mitroff (1981)	Strategy assumption surfacing and testing (SAST) Useful for ill-structured problems with differences of opinion. Can be adversarial, participative, integrative and managerial mind supporting. Allows group formation, assumption surfacing, dialectic debate and synthesis of perspectives.
Ulrich (1983)	Critical systems heuristics (CSH) Attempts to link systems with practical reasons of a problem. Encourages debate in terms of practical relevance rather than theoretical justification. Contains twelve critical heuristic categories.
Flood and Jackson (1991)	Total systems intervention (TSI) Finds strengths and weaknesses of available systems and uses a range of systems to promote creativity. Supported by five pillars: 1 Critical awareness 2 Social awareness 3 Dedication to human emancipation 4 Complementarism at theoretical level 5 Complementarism at methodological level.
Linstone (1994)	Technical, organisational and personal perspectives (TOP) Views reality from multiple perspectives: scientific and technological, group or institutional, individual and self.

Drivers of KM systems: quality management processes

The raison d'être of most organisations is to provide products and services that meet the changing needs of their customers. For commercial organisations in highly competitive markets, this means developing systems and processes continually that produce higher quality services or products at a lower cost than competitors. The key driver of knowledge management systems in organisations is argued to centre around improving quality management processes linked to an organisation's ability to capture, share and apply new knowledge.

▶ Deming and Juran

The pioneers of quality management were Dr William Deming and Dr Joseph Juran. Both quality 'gurus' were influenced by the principles of statistical quality control (SQC) developed by Dr Walter Shewhart. Shewhart (1931) believed that every task had controlled and uncontrolled variations that could be understood through simple statistics, with the possibility of reducing or even eliminating the variations. In most cases, Deming believed that the uncontrolled (his term was 'special' – under operator control) variations accounted for around 15 per cent of the variations and the rest of the controlled ('common causes') variations were to do with the systems and processes and the responsibility of management. This emphasised the importance of leadership and the responsibility of senior management for initiating change.

It is noteworthy that the ideas of these two pioneers were almost ignored in their home country of America until the 1980s but found tremendous recognition in Japan. After defeat in the war, Japan was a country in ruins. In 1950, Deming met a group called the Union of Japanese Scientists and Engineers (JUSE), formed to promote revival of Japanese industry, and spoke to packed audiences across Japan. He became acquainted with the *Kei-dan-ren*, the association of Japan's chief executives, and proposed the importance of statistical process control (an adaption of Shewhart's ideas) to meet consumer demands for high-quality products. Having lost all in the war, the Japanese followed Deming's advice and his conviction that it would make them supremely competitive in global markets within five years. Japanese manufacturers went from strength to strength and by the 1980s had become a major economic threat to the US. Deming was a hero, with the national quality prize in Japan named after him, and was awarded the Second Order of the Sacred Treasure by Emperor Hirohito in 1960.

Deming's method of ensuring quality of every task was based on a form of learning cycle, the PDCA (plan, do, check, act) cycle that could be applied repetitively and continuously to every task (Deming 1986). His beliefs can be summarised into the following stages that lead from one to another:

- improve quality;
- costs decrease because of less rework, fewer mistakes, fewer delays, snags, better use of machine time and materials;
- productivity improves;
- capture the market with better quality and lower price;
- stay in business;
- provide jobs and more jobs.

After publication of his book (Juran 1950), Dr Joseph Juran was invited by JUSE to lecture in Japan. He developed the concept of company-wide quality management (CWQM) as a way of disseminating quality throughout an organisation. This was based on a trilogy linking together planning, control and improvement:

- planning – identify and ensure customer needs are easily understood by every person. Ensure that the process will produce something to meet customer needs. Produce a product for the customer;
- control – continuously monitor processes for variations. Management take responsibility for the majority (80 per cent) of controlled variations in processes;
- improvement – take all necessary steps to improve system including attitude and cultural change.

Juran's lectures were translated and sold in kiosks across Japan as well as being broadcast on radio. They were also used in 'reading circles' in organisations to help improve literacy. These reading circles were a precursor to 'quality circles' and were used to improve quality through joint problem solving in teams.

Reflect on your own organisation. How important is Deming and Juran's message to your organisation? Describe how quality is managed in your organisation. To ensure high and consistent levels of quality, what other factors do you think need to be taken into account apart from statistical quality controls? How important are customer perceptions of quality? One of the goals of modern-day marketing is to achieve one-to-one marketing rather than mass marketing. How do your organisational systems measure up to this goal in providing up-to-date knowledge of each customer?

▶ Total quality management (TQM)

Following the discovery in the west of Deming's work and in response to threats of Japanese imports, the concept of total quality management (TQM) was developed. TQM built on earlier concepts of quality control and quality assurance. Quality control was an extension of inspection to collect data and understand variations using statistical techniques. In contrast, quality assurance was about developing organisational structures, procedures, processes and resources to ensure that tasks were performed in a consistent manner. Some firms have opted to follow a quality standard such as ISO 9000, which defines different aspects of their quality system and the nature of third-party assessment. Verification in quality assurance is a major departure from quality control and allows an independent assessment of quality systems and procedures to be made.

TQM moves beyond the mechanistic orientation of quality assurance and emphasises the need to facilitate cultural change. It is linked with a commitment to total customer satisfaction achieved through continuous improvement and encourages the contribution and involvement of people in the process. It offers a multidisciplinary approach to empower employees at all levels and moves beyond the conformance needs to customer-driven needs. For example, in the automobile industry, TQM may focus more on what delights the customer, such as electric windows, rather than purely on the basic conformance needs such as the power of the engine. The key elements of TQM are:

- a total process involving all units in the organisation and led from the top;
- customer is king, with every strategy, action and process directed at satisfaction of customer needs;
- information is gathered and analysed rationally using ICT;
- all organisational processes that add to costs of poor quality are examined;
- greater involvement of people as an untapped resource;
- the use of multidiscipline and multilevel teams to solve problems related to meeting customer needs;
- the promotion of creative thinking to develop innovative solutions.

❱ Business process re-engineering (BPR)

In the mid 1990s, a controversial approach to quality and cost improvements was forwarded called business process re-engineering (BPR). The pioneers of BPR (Davenport 1993; Hammer and Champy 1993) defined BPR as:

> *The fundamental re-thinking and radical redesign of business processes to achieve dramatic improvements in critical, contemporary measures of performance, such as cost, quality, service and speed.*

BPR offered a fresh start to organisational redesign, with a blank sheet of paper ignoring past history or present structures and practices. It focused on the horizontal analysis of work along an activity chain and challenged the very foundations of traditional operations. As most organisations are structured vertically around functions, BPR represented a total shake-up of organisations into horizontal cross-functional processes. One result of the BPR approach was to flatten hierarchies and remove many middle managers with the necessary skills, knowledge and expertise. For some organisations, this lack of regard to 'context-specific' issues has had untoward consequences. Many senior executives have had to manage day-to-day operational issues for which their expertise has been clearly lacking.

A typical BPR project has four stages (Huczynski and Buchanan 2001):

- process mapping – drawing flowcharts of work activity sequences;
- identifying 'moments of truth' – deciding which steps are critical, add value and introduce errors;
- generating redesign proposals – streamlining processes and avoiding duplication and overlap;
- implementation – putting the redesign into effect.

Some commentators argue that TQM has been overtaken by BPR whereas others view each approach as complementary to another. Could TQM be seen as a form of single-loop learning (Argyris and Schon 1978) and the radical redesign of BPR as double-loop learning? The distinctions between the two methodologies are shown in Table 5.2 (Hammer and Champy 1993).

Table 5.2 Differences and similarities between TQM and BPR

TQM	BPR
Based on process flow to accomplish work	Same
Starts with the customer of the process	Same
Works within existing framework	Seeks to break from existing practices
Based on continuous incremental improvement	Seeks breakthrough
Focus on enhancing continually, facts, data, participation, teamwork, job design, based on technology application	Focus on entirely new information systems, a 'different approach to change management'

▶ Lean production

In 1990, a new concept of 'lean production' was forwarded to explain the increased performance and competitiveness of certain automobile manufacturers around the world (Womack *et al.* 1990). The goal of lean production was to achieve increased productivity, reduced lead times and costs, and improved quality across the organisation. The principles and techniques in lean production have focused on manufacturing firms and contain the following aspects (Sánchez and Pérez 2001):

- elimination of zero-value activities – anything that doesn't add value to the product or service (Womack and Jones 1996);
- search for continuous improvement in products and processes – involve production teams and management to develop creative solutions to the identification and adjustment of defective parts;
- multifunctional teams – to facilitate task rotation and flexibility to accommodate changes in production levels. Increased training effort on quality control and remuneration to compensate for new flexibility in workforce;
- just-in-time (JIT) production and delivery – integration of automation equipment with production information system to enable delivery of any part in the necessary quantity at the right time. This contributes to the reduction of inventories and lead times;
- integration of suppliers – with key departments to enhance buyer-supplier relationships such as R&D for new component prototypes;
- flexible information systems – to provide timely and useful strategic and operational information to all levels. Strategic information may contain organisation's production plans and sales forecasts whereas operational information may contain the factory's current productivity or quality performance.

Document management systems

Organisations tend to publish a variety of documents for internal consumption or for external sources such as suppliers, customers and shareholders. There is a growing tendency for the volume of these documents to increase substantially each year and an urgent need to manage them adequately for efficient storage and retrieval. Paper files can take up a lot of space in filing cabinets, with the likelihood that they are rarely retrieved for many years. Document management systems have developed to address these problems and have typically employed the intranet as an electronic medium rather than conventional document printing and circulation methods. The primary driving force has been the cost savings compared with conventional publication and distribution methods, together with the dynamic nature of intranets. Documents can be published and updated on the intranet when needed and become available instantly to all interested users (Frazee 1996). The types of documents may include policy and

procedure manuals, corporate phone directories, online help, human resource guidelines, sales and marketing literature, customer data, price lists and press releases.

Implementing a document management system constitutes an important stage in a
quality management strategy but may result in considerable resistance and even opposition within organisations. To overcome this resistance, many organisations have begun
with a pilot study using documents that were originally being delivered on paper and
where costs and results could be monitored and measured. Apart from emphasising the
reduced costs of intranet-based document management systems, the pilots have focused
on the value of enhanced access to information for users. Anecdotal statements focused
on value derived from the document management systems can help erode some of the
resistance to change. For example, value statements such as (Wen *et al*. 1998):

> *'I was able to win three new accounts over the telephone because I had the information
> at my fingertips, and I knew it was current. With the old system, I was always putting
> the customer on hold and asking the other reps for information.'*

Document management systems can be 'cheap and cheerful', operating on a limited
number of functions, or can be full-blown, expensive systems with a multitude of functions and potentially frightening in terms of their impact on organisational processes
and administrative practices. The 'value-adding' facilities of document management
systems may include (Raynes 2002):

- control to ensure only one user modifies a document at a time;
- audit trail to monitor changes in a document over time;
- security processes to control user access to documents;
- organisation of documents into related groups and folders;
- identification and retrieval of documents according to text they contain (free-text
  searching);
- recording information associated with the document as meta data such as author,
  creation date and title;
- ability to route documents from one user to another in a controlled fashion based
  on the workflow;
- converting paper documents into electronic format by scanning;
- organising documents into groups to enable them to be distributed to target audiences.

The choice of document management system is likely to influence the culture of the
organisation or, depending on its scale, may simply reflect the dominant culture. It is
important to consider clearly the current or future problems the system is likely to
solve and the advantages over traditional paper-based methods. The process of implementing a document management system can be divided into a number of phases, as
shown in Table 5.3 (p. 138) (Rowley 1999).

Table 5.3 **Phases of implementing a document management system**

Phase	Description	Initiated by
Identify content	Identify a subset of documents to be indexed and made available on the intranet	System administrator
Database set-up	Define a database template or framework for the text database, which will store the indices of the processed documents	System administrator
Populate database	Perform indexing and populate database with the indices of the processed documents	System administrator
Intranet enable/publish	Once the documents are processed and appropriate intranet/internet connections are made, an interface is created through which users can enter their search requests	User/client
Process search requests	Using the search criteria, the text-retrieval engine performs a search on the document repository	User/client
Present results	Displays search results in the form of a hit list. Users can make selections from hit list to view particular documents	User/client
View/download original	User can be presented document in a viewable format (such as PDF) or can download the required file	User/client

Some of the typical remaining organisational challenges presented by document management systems have included (Wen *et al.* 1998):

- privacy – the need to balance the desire to track visitors through site logs and the need for privacy. Also, the need to deliver sensitive information in a largely anonymous manner;
- currency of information – whether documents are updated regularly. This can be overcome by simply adding 'date of last change' to each page;
- performance – becomes an issue in high-volume, transaction–oriented applications. This can be overcome by increasing the bandwidth of the network but results in increased costs;
- security – to bar access to unauthorised personnel from sensitive financial, company or personnel records.

Decision support systems

Decision support systems (DSS) combine data analysis and sophisticated models to support non-routine decision making. They are particularly useful in helping managers make decisions on ill-defined problems in rapidly changing en vironments. They provide the user with an interactive interface and bring together analyses and models to make sense of existing internal and external data. The major capabilities of DSS are that they (Turban and Aronson 2001):

- provide support in semi-structured and unstructured situations;
- support several sequential and interdependent decisions;
- support intelligence, design, choice and implementation phases of decision making;
- support a variety of styles and processes;
- are adaptive and flexible over time;
- are user-friendly with strong graphical capabilities;
- improve accuracy, timeliness and quality of decision making;
- have substantial modelling capability to allow experimentation with different strategies under different scenarios.

There is a multitude of DSS on offer in the marketplace. A simplistic distinction would be to separate them into model-driven DSS and data-driven DSS, as shown in Figure 5.2. Model-driven DSS provide a range of statistical, financial, forecasting and management science models that may be applied at strategic, tactical or operational levels. They allow the user to conduct 'what if' analyses under a range of scenarios. Typically, they are end user-led such as the Bloomberg portal designed by a former financial trader to meet the information needs of other traders in the financial markets. The DSS may contain between a few and several hundred models encompassing strategic models, tactical models, operational models and analytical models. Strategic models tend to help high-level strategic planning processes within organisations. Tactical models assist in allocating and controlling organisational resources such as capital budgeting and human resource planning. Operational models help support day-to-day decision making, such as loans approval and quality control processes. Analytical models may cover methods of analysis such as statistical models or specific financial models.

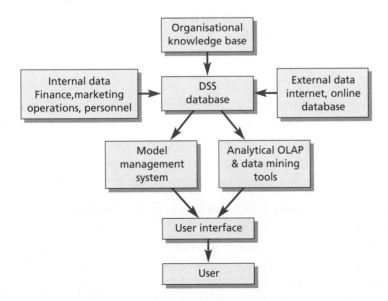

Figure 5.2 Typical configuration of decision support systems (DSS)

Imagine your ideal decision support system. What would you consider to be the optimal characteristics of a DSS that would allow you to solve organisational problems effectively? Given that the reality for most managers is incomplete information in decision making, how could a DSS be best employed? The quality of outputs in any system is based primarily on the quality of inputs. What measures could you take to ensure high quality of information was fed into a DSS in your organisation?

In contrast, data-driven DSS are more focused on examining patterns and relationships in large amounts of data. As described in Chapter 4, they use knowledge evaluation tools such as online analytical processing (OLAP) to provide multidimensional analyses and data mining techniques looking at associations, sequences, classifications, clustering and forecasting with the data (Laudon and Laudon 2000). Associations are occurrences linked to a single event. Sequences are events linked over time. Classification recognises patterns in certain groups such as loyal or fraudulent customers. Clustering techniques can help determine different groupings of certain customers where classifications don't necessarily exist. Forecasting techniques can help predict values for certain variables. Data mining techniques vary considerably in the variety of approaches adopted, from fuzzy logic to neural networks (see Chapter 4 for more details). The following uses in different industrial sectors illustrate typical analyses that data mining techniques may help to uncover:

● Banking industry – identify patterns of fraud, conduct risk analysis of customers who are habitually slow in mortgage payments, find hidden correlations between different financial indicators, identify loyal customers and predict customers likely to change credit card companies.

● Retail and marketing – discover buying patterns such as certain customers regularly buying wine and cheese together, uncover associations in buying habits linked to demographics, forecast customer responses to advertising and perform a market-basket analysis.

● Insurance – discover patterns of behaviour of risky customers, perform claims analyses and identify associations between claims.

In order to purchase a DSS, organisations need to decide between custom-made or off-the-shelf solutions. The advantage of off-the-shelf solutions are the lower costs, flexibility and applicability of many business problems in the same sectors. In contrast, custom-made solutions allow organisations to differentiate themselves from competitors and use a more sophisticated approach based on different configurations of the following seven classifications (Holsapple and Whinston 1996):

● Text-oriented DSS – using technologies such as web-based documents, hyperlinks and intelligent agents.

● Database-oriented DSS – featuring strong report generation and query searching capabilities.

● Spreadsheet-oriented DSS – such as Excel which uses statistical and financial models and techniques.

- Solver-oriented DSS – functions or procedures used for optimising certain variables such as the optimal ordering quantities of certain resources based on historical data.
- Rule-oriented DSS – often expert systems linked to procedural and inferential (reasoning) rules such as evacuation of a tall building in case of fire in certain parts of it.
- Compound DSS – containing two or more aspects of the above five classifications.
- Intelligent DSS – similar to rule-oriented DSS that can learn using agent technology and machine learning techniques.

Group support systems

Teamwork is part of most organisations in one form or another. It is relatively rare to find even freelance individuals purely working by themselves. In response to global and competitive pressures, organisations are increasingly having their activities geographically dispersed and using internet technologies to communicate over long distances. The growth of teleworking since its inception in the 1960s has given rise to virtual teams and virtual organisations. Distance and time differences globally are less of a barrier nowadays with a variety of technologies employed such as e-mail, videoconferencing, mobile phones and co-authoring systems. The important feature is the development of appropriate technologies to facilitate collaboration and cooperation in groups and teams. The five basic team processes supported by group support systems (GSS) and found in many commercial products such as Lotus Notes and Microsoft NetMeeting are (Andriessen 2003):

- communication – these include easy, fast and cheap technologies such as e-mail, voice-mail and video systems;
- knowledge sharing and learning – these include quick, reliable and inexpensive tools for knowledge storage and retrieval;
- cooperation – these include document sharing and co-authoring facilities as well as group decision support systems to support brainstorming, evaluating ideas and decision making;
- coordination – provided using synchronisers to synchronise work processes of a team using group calendars and workflow tools;
- social interaction – using cameras and monitors near coffee machines or other locations where people can meet each other unintentionally. An example of such a system is Media Space.

The term 'group decision support systems' can be misleading as teams may often convene in virtual environments for short periods of time without the opportunity for traditional face-to-face cohesion. They are designed to support simultaneous and anonymous idea generation with group displays, the evaluation and structuring of information, and the facilitation of agenda setting and group priorities. To meet social needs, advanced video systems have been developed to give group members the sense that they are sitting at the same table as colleagues. Further developments have moved

Table 5.4 Typology of group support systems (Andriessen 2003)

Group process systems	Support between encounters: asynchronous communication Different place/ different time	Support for synchronous electronic encounters Different place/ same time	Support for synchronous face-to-face meetings Same place/ same time
Communication	<ul><li>Fax</li><li>E-mail</li><li>Voice-mail</li><li>Video-mail</li></ul>	<ul><li>Telephone/ Mobile</li><li>Audio systems</li><li>Video systems</li><li>Chat system</li></ul>	
Knowledge sharing and learning	<ul><li>Document sharing systems</li><li>Message boards</li></ul>	<ul><li>Tele-consultation systems</li><li>Co-browser</li></ul>	<ul><li>Presentation systems</li></ul>
Cooperation	<ul><li>Document co-authoring</li></ul>	<ul><li>Shared CAD, whiteboard, word processor, spreadsheet</li></ul>	<ul><li>Group decision support systems</li></ul>
Coordination	<ul><li>Group calender</li><li>Shared planning</li><li>Shared workflow management systems</li><li>Event manager</li><li>Subgroup spaces</li></ul>	<ul><li>Notification systems, e.g. active batch</li></ul>	<ul><li>Command and control centre support systems</li></ul>
Social encounters		<ul><li>Media spaces</li><li>Virtual reality</li></ul>	

to virtual spaces where symbols of group members are depicted in virtual reality. A typology of group support systems is shown in Table 5.4 (Andriessen 2003).

Pause for thought

Think about the ways you communicate with people in your organisation. What would you say is your optimal approach? What role do face-to-face encounters play in your relationships with colleagues? What technological or collaborative tools do you use for communication and team working? If you use group support systems, how effective are they? For true collaborative working, how can you enhance trust in your dealings with colleagues using group support systems? Given the power of the internet to cover geographical boundaries, how important are face-to-face meetings?

Experience has shown that the success of group support systems relies on more than technology. Hence the development of future systems is likely to place the end user more centrally in the design process through a better understanding of socio-technical processes. Such group support systems are not a quick fix and may require a champion, a pilot and an effective communications process for their success. A few noteworthy guidelines to improve the effectiveness of group support systems include (Andriessen 2003):

- if possible, start group with face-to-face meetings;
- learn about each other's backgrounds through 'yellow pages' (expertise directory);

- prepare and structure synchronous meeting well, with minutes;
- use video links where possible to develop trust and cohesion;
- provide regular information on progress and milestones;
- pay attention to training and intercultural differences.

Even though group support systems provide a forum for knowledge sharing, learning and enhanced problem solving, they can pose certain challenges for groups. For example, there may be 'free-riders' relying on others to do all the work, a tendency to make riskier decisions, compromised solutions of low quality and information overload. However, improvements can be made through effective facilitation and by making these dangers explicit to group members. The results can lead to decreased costs, saved travel time and greater creativity through the anonymity of the systems. Group support systems have also been successfully used for distance learning programmes in universities to increase a student's learning experience through greater dialogue with peers and the faculty tutors.

Executive information systems

Executive information systems (EIS) were developed in the mid 1980s with a primary goal of enhancing the strategic planning and control processes of executives through the provision of quality, timely, accurate and accessible information (O'Brien 1991). In addition, to compensate for the computer illiteracy of many senior executives, they were designed intuitively so that even a ten-year-old child could use such systems. They provided a broad understanding of company information by summarising large quantities of data and allowed the user to drill down to different levels of data to gain insight into the detail of information. The challenges in EIS have been in understanding the rich and complex nature of executive decision making and especially the dynamic and fast-changing information needs of executives. As with many other systems, there has often been resistance to EIS from data owners in organisations who fear loss of control over data and the potential implications for changes in power structures. In addition, the high costs of EIS have been difficult to justify in comparison with opportunity costs of using the same resources for other activities.

One dilemma facing the high-quality information requirements of EIS is the fact that data is often input using unskilled and untrained operatives, which may lead to gross errors and misleading analyses. Careful consideration must be taken to avoid the dangers of 'garbage in, garbage out' syndrome and the potential risk of making the wrong decisions. Research on the effective implementation of EIS has found a number of factors linked with continuous improvement that increase the success of initiatives (Zairi *et al.* 1998):

- need for a committed executive sponsor to drive project and provide feedback on product quality and expectations for improvement;

- need for a pro-active operating sponsor (often in an IT/IS department) to act as market researcher with the executives, confidence builder, product designer and operational line manager;
- the bringing together of business knowledge and IT skills through teamwork;
- coordinating systems and processes lower in the organisation with EIS to ensure alignment of effort;
- visually attractive graphics.

The traditional alternative to EIS is having managers providing analyses of complex data at board meetings. The arguments in favour of EIS are that it provides a tool as a supplement to managerial knowledge and experience and allows decisions to be made in dynamically changing environments where the privileged recourse to managers may not always be available. The leading question is whether there is an alignment between a manager's decision-making patterns and the analyses generated from an EIS. The answer may lie more closely in the distinction between EIS providing rational modes of analyses and managers relying more on irrational information and political factors. A comparison of TQM and effective EIS practices is shown in Table 5.5 (Zairi *et al.* 1998).

Table 5.5 Impact of TQM factors on effective EIS practices

TQM	EIS practices
	Goal
Customer satisfaction	Meeting executives' information requirements
Quality product/service	Quality information
Cost effectiveness	Reducing cost of decision making and communication
	Concept
Customer–supplier chains	Operational level – managers – executives
Customer requirements	Identifying executives' information requirements
Performance measurement	Using key performance indicators (KPIs)
Failure prevention	Preventing wrong decision making and error in data input
	Implementation
Top management commitment	Strong support from an executive sponsor
Involvement of every employee	Everyone's information system
Cross-function teamwork	Teamwork including IT and business knowledge
Learning process	Executives' receptivity by learning
Benchmarking	Internal and external (competitor) information

Workflow management systems

One of the ideal tools in business process re-engineering has been the use of workflow management systems (WMS). WMS are a part of enterprise resource planning (ERP) and may be considered as the back-office integration processes in organisations. An important function of WMS is the modelling of workflows. WMS can be seen as repositories of an organisation's procedures and processes. They are predominantly suited to the efficient processing of a large number of 'cases' within a small number of predefined processes. Ad-hoc workflows with a separate workflow defined for each case is more likely to occur in future developments of WMS. Examples of cases include customer orders, insurance claims, university applications and tax returns. Each case (let's say a university applica-tion from Fred Bloggs) has a *unique identity* and a *limited finite lifetime*. The lifetime begins from the moment the university receives Fred Bloggs' application and ends when the uni-versity notifies Fred Bloggs of the outcome of his application. In the case of Fred Bloggs' application, the procedure may be broken down into a number of phases, each with a number of *conditions* that need to be fulfilled before certain other tasks are carried out. The conditions allows the user to see how far a case has progressed. The contents of the case may be held manually in a filing cabinet or electronically in a database.

Tasks in a WMS are logical units of work such as writing reports and assessing candi-dates, and can be manual, semi-automatic or automatic. The combination of a task and a case is termed a work item and the application of a task on a case is seen as an activity. There are a number of ways that a case can go through a process and this determines the nature and order of tasks to be performed. This *routing* of a case may be sequential (one task after another), parallel (tasks performed simultaneously) or selective (choice made between two or more tasks depending on the case attributes). The spark or trigger that initiates the work item may come from a resource such as an employee or an exter-nal event or a time signal (van der Aalst and van Hee 2002).

The traditional and formal analysis of processes is the use of '*Petri nets*' (see Figure 5.3) to ensure precise definitions of processes and prevent ambiguities. A petri net enables

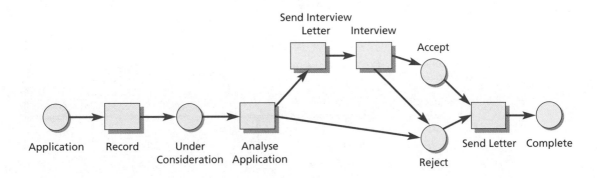

Figure 5.3 **Example of a Petri Net for a university application**

processes to be described graphically and is composed of places and transitions. Places indicate states within a process and are indicated with a circle whereas transitions may denote different activities between states and are shown by a rectangle. Places and transitions are often linked together using arcs shown by the arrows in the diagram.

Pause for thought

Imagine you were asked to manage workflows in a virtual organisation. How would you go about conducting this role? What KM systems would you employ to manage the changing knowledge base of your supply chain from customers to suppliers? On a practical level, what measures would you adopt to ensure that there weren't any blockages in your workflow particularly from staff illnesses or poorly performing sub-contract workers? How influential do you consider time differences when working in a global virtual environment?

In a quest to develop standards with the multitude of WMS offerings, the Workflow Management Coalition (WFMC) was set up to define terminology and provide standards for exchange of data between different systems. The WFMC has produced a workflow reference model as a general description of architecture in WMS, as shown in Figure 5.4 (p. 146).

The different aspects of WMS are as follows:

- Workflow enactment service – is at the heart of any WMS and creates new cases and work items and ensures that activities are conducted in the right order at the right time. It may be composed of several workflow engines that handle a certain number of cases and processes.
- Process definition tools – comprise tools for modelling process definitions (using Petri nets), resource classifications (such as qualifications and expertise of individuals, groups and departments) and analysis (such as semantic correctness of process definitions).
- Workflow client application – is the main contact employees often have with a WMS. Each employee has a worklist (in-tray) showing which work items need action. Work items can be locked to a user or passed on to another employee. Figures can be generated on individual or group performance.

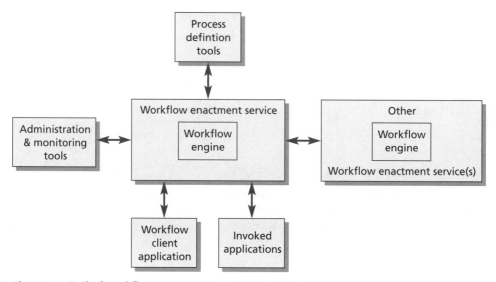

Figure 5.4 **Typical workflow systems architecture (WFMC)**

- Invoked applications – the performance of certain activities may require the starting and use of various applications such as different spreadsheets and databases. Applications are started by the workflow engine so that the activities may be completed satisfactorily. These applications may perform the tasks automatically, such as a mathematical analysis, or may be interactive and require human intervention.

- Administration and monitoring tools – contain day-to-day operational management tools as well as recording and reporting tools. Operational tools allow the user to examine bottlenecks and faults in the systems from a case perspective, such as reconfiguring the workflow system, or from a resource perspective, such as addition or removal of employees due to illness or holidays. Recording and reporting tools allow managers to analyse the performance of the WMS using indicators such as average completion rates for cases, average waiting times and average resource capacity utilisation. As the magnitude of recording increases substantially, OLAP and data, mining techniques can be employed to analyse the data, as shown in Chapter 4.

There are traditionally two methods of developing WMS using business process reengineering (BPR) or rapid application development (RAD). As shown earlier in this chapter, BPR aims to discover the most efficient and effective business processes without recourse to existing processes. The BPR lifecycle is traditionally initiated by senior management and contains the four phases:

- *diagnosis* – an analysis of existing working processes and their problems;
- *redesign* – starting with a clean slate, new processes are designed looking at the most efficient ways of converting inputs to desired outputs;
- *reconstruction* – the infrastructure to support the new processes are considered, such as IT systems and organisational structures;
- *operations* – performance of processes is measured, analysed and modified accordingly.

In contrast, RAD uses a more evolutionary method for developing WMS and has a strong emphasis on user participation. The RAD approach comprises four phases and there is less of a distinction between separate and consecutive design and construction phases:

- *requirements planning phase* – intended results and functionality of system defined;
- *user design phase* – user consultation results in designers making clear specifications in a CASE tool. Users can test specifications against prototypes of WMS;
- *construction phase* – WMS software is perfected and validated through testing by users;
- *delivery phase* – comprises acceptance testing by users and minor modifications as well as user training.

The future trends in WMS are towards modelling ad-hoc workflows with separate processes defined for each case (van der Aalst and van Hee 2002). More attention is likely to be paid to the scheduling of people using sophisticated timetabling systems and labour flexibility arrangements. The internet and corporate intranets provide future challenges for developing effective WMS to cater for the burgeoning e-business markets as well as providing easy access and protection to confidential information.

Customer relationship management systems

In contrast to the back-office aspects of WMS, customer relationship management systems are firmly rooted in front-office integration and revolve principally around marketing. The motivation is to integrate technology and business processes to meet customer requirements at any given moment. Customer relationship strategy is about cementing long-term, collaborative relationships with customers based on trust (Crosby 2002). Such strategies are not about short-term revenue gains from customers but more about enhancing the customers' lifetime value to the firm. In this sense, CRM technology needs to be aligned with business goals of maintaining and enhancing customer relationships.

In the 1980s, firms were preoccupied with a marketing orientation based around *customer segmentation*. This meant that firms tried to establish groups of customers with similar needs and wants around characteristics such as demographics and behavioural traits. This was a cost-effective method of satisfying many customer needs but by no means all them. As competition increased in the 1990s, market segmentation was seen as a starting point for many firms and the focus turned towards *customer-centric orientations*. This perspective was about relationships with customers and treating each customer individually and uniquely. It was one-to-one marketing. During this time advancements in technology meant that fast, low-cost storage and retrieval of individual customer preferences and needs became a reality. CRM emerged so that firms could concentrate on a share of each customer in the long term rather than a share of the overall market in the short term. The underlying premise was the difficulty and huge resources involved in gaining new customers rather than retaining existing ones. This resulted in a marked shift from mass marketing and communications towards focusing on successful interactions with existing customers at every turn.

Pause for thought

The ultimate goal in marketing is to achieve one-to-one marketing where each customer is treated individually in terms of their preferences and needs. How could you use CRM systems rather than purely segmentation marketing to achieve this goal? What incentives could you provide customers to gather regular, up-to-date knowledge on their changing needs? What ethical issues could such data collection present, particularly in connection with the internet?

Effective CRM systems are not confined to partnerships between marketing and IT departments but are likely to span divisional boundaries such as finance, operations and human resources. The component technologies involved with CRM systems are likely to include data warehousing, data mining techniques and world wide web integration through a website, intranet and phone support systems. The development and integration of a CRM system within an organisation can be painful and fraught with difficulties. There may be little user support and the user interfaces may not fit with users' working styles. There may be a tendency to focus on technology rather than process improvements. The scope of the project may change frequently and political infighting may result in lack of senior management commitment. Cost overruns and substantial time delays may result in firm and user disillusionment. Also, the CRM system may fail to integrate and support mobile communications (Corner and Hinton 2002). To overcome some of these problems, a CRM development plan based on a project lifecycle is outlined below (Bose 2002):

- *Planning* – identifying how managers will use customer information at various levels in the organisation and gaining senior management support. Identifying how, when and where employees will interact with customers such as help desks, website, sales person, mail or phone. Also, identifying decision interaction points on how managers and executives will use the knowledge to improve the quality of their decision making.
- *Research* – assessment of the firm's organisational structure, culture, hardware, software, vendors and suppliers.
- *Systems analysis* – identifying employee information needs to interact successfully with a customer. Exploring the need for automated interaction using web or automated phone systems. Implementing system in a number of stages. Integrating customer data across a firm, expanding customer data profile to include non-transactional information such as inquiries, management comments and complaints, integrating with legacy systems where data may be functionally based. Conducting a feasibility study.
- *Design* – to include a detailed specification of needs and core technologies. Any modifications required to link to existing KM systems.
- *Construction* – developing software to meet design plan.
- *Implementation* – including a solid training programme at all levels, including managers and executives, particularly in areas such as data mining and statistics. Erroneous conclusions may arise from managers confusing correlations with causation and using unreliable data.
- *Maintenance and documentation* – evaluation and modification of the system dependent on data quantity and quality.
- *Adaptation* – continuous improvement of CRM system from learning more about the customer.

There is a paradox with CRM systems. Even though CRM collects vast amounts of data to allow managers to make better quality decisions, the contrary may be true. Higher quality information may result in poorer decisions, especially where a decision maker fails to interpret and understand the true relationships between different variables (Raghunathan 1999). Future developments in CRM systems are likely to result in greater integration with decision support systems and executive information systems. In addition, as partnerships and alliances develop due to competitive pressures, CRM systems are likely to cross organisational boundaries and facilitate information sharing between different partners in the supply chain. Data mining techniques will also need to improve to cope with the needs of large data warehouses over and above the current performance limitations concerned with analysing only 5–10 per cent of data in these huge knowledge repositories.

Economics of KM systems

Early development considerations of KM systems by senior management need to take into account the overall costs of implementing and maintaining these systems. These can be divided into costs related to implementing a KM system including overheads, and the salary costs of employees with designated KM functions. The implementation costs of KM systems include (Maier 2001) the following:

- *Hardware* – networked PCs, high storage capacity databases, web servers running client-server applications, internet broadband connections and mobile technology such as mobile phones, palmtops, laptops and bluetooth (wireless) technology.
- *Software* – for KM systems to meet specific organisational needs. May use off-the-shelf solutions with significant customisation or develop own solutions.
- *Training and education* – continual communication about benefits of new system as well as structured training programme for all levels on use of KM system.
- *Literature, conferences, consulting and proactive participation in KM activities* – KM budget to spend on literature, funding (university) KM research programmes, attending conferences and employing consultants.
- *Organisation of KM events* – announcing and communicating KM initiative and facilitating 'communities of practice'.
- *KM overhead* – to coordinate KM initiative.
- *KM systems administration* – especially to protect system against hackers.
- *KM staff* – salaries, overheads and expenses of staff taking different KM roles.

In contrast, the benefits of KM systems can be determined using a variety of intellectual capital approaches outlined in Chapter 10.

CASE STUDY

E-business KM Systems

Portals are passé. Business-to-business online marketplaces have come and gone and the value of customer relationship management systems is being questioned. What has gone wrong with e-business software? What is next? And why should business managers still take note?

Back in 1999, e-business software was going to change the world. Online marketplaces were heralded as a way to find alternative suppliers and lower prices. There was much talk of 'disintermediation'. Traditional distributors and wholesalers would be out of the picture as businesses switched to buying and selling via the internet, many predicted. Entire industries would be restructured as even small businesses would have worldwide reach. Trade and competition laws would have to be rewritten.

Yet most online marketplaces are now history. The opportunities and threats they seemed to pose turned out to be hot air.

Customer relationship management was de rigueur. This created huge demand for CRM software that drew together all of the information regarding a customer's past and present interactions with a company. Tens of millions of dollars were spent implementing CRM, but software industry executives now say fewer than half the systems lived up to customers' expectations. One in five executives surveyed last year by Bain & Co, the consulting group, said CRM initiatives had damaged customer relationships.

It is tempting to write off e-business software as just another over-hyped technology bubble. Yet despite the failures – the software companies that have closed their doors and customer experiences that have gone sour – e-business lives on and some would say its prospects are improving.

Several important lessons have been learnt. The first is that the internet is a business tool but it does not alter business fundamentals. The second is that e-business applications evolved from enterprise software and they too are tools, not magic bullets. E-business automates or streamlines business processes but companies that attempt to map the software to their traditional operating practices make a grave error. It is entirely possible to customise the value out of e-business software by rigidly applying traditional approvals processes, for example, or limiting the ability of employees and business partners to access information.

To take full advantage of e-business, companies must be ready to embrace change, even if it is disruptive. The old 'command and control' management model is not compatible with e-business.

Another tough lesson that many have learnt is that systems integration is complex, time consuming and expensive – yet integration of legacy systems is essential to maximise value. However, it is not only e-business users who have learnt the hard way. Software vendors that focused on e-commerce have been humbled as the centre of gravity of e-business has shifted from transactions to information sharing.

Collaboration is the new e-business buzz word and this time it is not just a fad. Rather, the technology is mirroring and accelerating the changing shape of manufacturing and other industries. 'Outsourcing – whether it be of manufacturing or design or any other aspect of a company's operations – is driving demand for improved information sharing as the fortunes of a company become more closely intertwined with those of its suppliers and business partners,' says Mark O'Connell, chief executive of Matrix One, a supplier of collaboration software. 'Every company is under pressure to squeeze costs out of business processes and to speed new products to market. Our customers are looking for ways to get people to work together more effectively.'

The car industry is a good example. Big US carmakers have set goals to reduce the time it takes to bring a new vehicle to market, from three to four years to only one to two years. This involves radical changes in the structure of the industry. 'About 50 to 70 per cent of design work is now being done outside the big auto manufacturing companies,' says Bob Matulka, director of collaboration at Covisint, an online marketplace created by the car industry. 'There is a great need to tie globally dispersed teams together.'

Engineering design changes can play havoc with the product development schedule, he says. 'You can end up with weeks of wasted effort.' An internet-based collaboration environment in which information about design changes is rapidly disseminated can create big cost and time savings.

John Warniak, director, e-business speed, at Johnson Controls, is on the front lines. As a leading car industry supplier, his company must now deal with issues such as vendor-managed inventory and advanced quality planning. 'We have to be able to interface with our customers and our suppliers with a common interface. There has to be a single source of truth, of up-to-date information.'

Carmakers and their suppliers are not alone in adopting e-business collaboration. Hewlett-Packard and Compaq Computer are planning their merger in virtual online work spaces, using eRoom software, where documents and messages are shared and saved. François Gossieaux, chief executive of eRoom, expects his company's products will increasingly be used for such partnerships between businesses, rather than just internal communications.

Even CRM is finding a second wind. Bo Manning, chief executive of Pivotal, which supplies software to the mid-sized company CRM segment, is redefining his products to include 'partnership relationship management'. In other words, relationship management is shifting to include all the constituencies that are important to a business.

Now, B2B stands for 'back to business basics' and e-business is the confluence of best business practices, the internet and software. It is a potent mix, not to be ignored. Those 1999 predictions may yet prove prescient. E-business software is perhaps the most disruptive technology to emerge in the past five years. In the world of technology, that is a very long time.

Source: Article by Louise Kehoe, *Financial Times*, 6 March 2002

Questions

1 Why do CRM systems often fail to deliver customer expectations?
2 What are the differences between collaboration technologies in e-business and more traditional group support systems?
3 Strategic alliances and partnerships can become vulnerable over time due to differing organisational goals. What are the implications for knowledge sharing using aligned KM systems between a range of partners?

Summary

This chapter has argued that KM systems are primarily driven by an organisation's desire to improve quality management processes. Current trends in quality management are explored covering practices such as TQM, BPR and lean production. The intrinsic nature of systems and the development of systems thinking and methodologies are explored. Key KM systems are detailed, with an emphasis on their component technologies and their effective implementation. The financial implementation costs of KM systems are considered in greater depth. The KM systems elaborated in this chapter are:

1 *Document management systems* – getting the right information or knowledge to the right person at the right time.

2 *Decision support systems* – creating and evaluating knowledge through data analysis or using sophisticated models to support decision making.

3 *Group support systems* – systems designed to enhance communication, knowledge sharing, cooperation, coordination and social encounters within groups.

4 *Executive information systems* – providing high-quality information and knowledge to executives to aid strategic planning and control processes.

5 *Workflow management systems* – knowledge associated with workflows and aligning 'cases' with resources such as employees.

6 *Customer relationship management systems* – developing knowledge about customers' individual preferences and needs using knowledge repositories and knowledge discovery techniques.

QUESTIONS FOR FURTHER THOUGHT

1 Are there differences between information management systems and KM systems? Or is it a case of 'old wine in new bottles'?

2 The complexity of a system increases with the addition of different perspectives and subprocesses. How does one find a balance between simplicity and complexity of systems models in problem solving?

3 If conformance quality is a given starting point in today's competitive environment, how do organisations develop KM systems in order to delight their customers?

4 How would you advise a firm about the strengths and pitfalls of a business process re-engineering approach?

5 Decision support systems use a variety of models and analytical tools ranging from fuzzy logic to neural networks. How would you interpret the range of findings from different DSS using the same data warehouse? Are there lessons for designing the optimal DSS for structured and unstructured data?

6 If group support systems predominantly act to facilitate team meetings and coordination of tasks, how can the systems be developed to generate greater cohesion and build longer-term relationships?

7 Should a course in statistics be a pre-requisite for all managers and executives using KM systems for decision making?

8 How effective are workflow management systems for managing processes requiring high levels of skills and expertise? Do WMS encourage Frederick Taylor's view of scientific management with a disregard for the psychological and social needs and capabilities of workers?

9 The customer-centric orientation of CRM systems nowadays can lead to firm's holding sensitive information about customers. In the quest for understanding each customer uniquely, how can organisations prevent such information seen as private by some customers backfiring on them and destroying the very trust they were hoping to build?

10 How can firms develop faith in their KM systems investments when the speed of change in hardware and software may alter dramatically every 18 months?

Further reading

1 Flood and Jackson 1991 provides a good historical background on systems thinking and methodologies.

2 Laudon and Laudon 2000 is particularly good as an introduction and general overview of information and knowledge management systems.

3 Turban and Aronson 2001 is a more in-depth text on KM systems and focuses more on decision support systems including groupware.

4 van der Aalst and van Hee 2002 provides an accessible and detailed text on workflow management systems.

References

Ackoff, R. L. (1979) 'Resurrecting the future of operations research', *Journal of the Operational Research Society*, 30(3), 189–99.

Andriessen, J. H. E. (2003) *Working with Groupware: Understanding and Evaluating Collaboration Technology*, Springer-Verlag, London.

Argyris, C. and Schon, D. A. (1978) *Organizational Learning: A Theory of Action Perspective*, Addison-Wesley, Reading, MA.

Beer, S. (1972) *Brain of the Firm*, Allen Lane, London.

Bose, R. (2002) 'Customer relationship management: key components for IT success', *Industrial Management & Data Systems*, 102(2), 89–97.

Checkland, P. B. (1981) *Systems Thinking, Systems Practice*, Wiley, Chichester.

Churchman, C. W. (1970) 'Operations research as a profession', *Management Science*, 17(2), 37–53.

Corner, I. and Hinton, M. (2002) 'Customer relationship management systems: implementation risks and relationship dynamics', *Qualitative Market Research*, 5(4), 239–251.

Crosby, L. A. (2002) 'Exploding some myths about customer relationship management', *Managing Service Quality*, 12(5), 271–277.

Davenport, T. H. (1993) *Process Innovation: Re-engineering Work Through Information Technology*, Harvard Business School Press, Boston, MA.

Deming, W. E. (1986) *Out of the Crisis*, MIT Press, Boston, MA.

Flood, R. L. and Jackson, M. C. (1991) *Creative Problem Solving: Total Systems Intervention*, John Wiley & sons, Chichester.

Frazee, V. (1996) 'Six reasons for going paperless', *Personnel Journal*, 75(11), 70–1.

Gao, F., Li, M. and Nakamori, Y. (2002) 'Systems thinking on knowledge and its management: systems methodology for knowledge management', *Journal of Knowledge Management*, 6(1), 7–17.

Hammer, M. and Champy, J. (1993) *Re-engineering the Corporation: A Manifesto for Business Revolution*, Nicholas Brealey, London.

Holsapple, C. W. and Whinston, A. B. (1996) *Decision Support Systems: A Knowledge-Based Approach*, West Publishing, St. Paul, MN.

Huczynski, A. and Buchanan, D. (2001) *Organisational Behaviour*, Pearson Education Limited, Harlow, Essex.

Juran, J. M. (1950) *Quality Control Handbook*, McGraw-Hill, New York.

Laudon, K. C. and Laudon, J. P. (2000) *Management Information Systems: Organization and Technology in the Networked Enterprise*, Prentice-Hall, Upper Saddle River, NJ.

Linstone, H. A. (1994) *The Challenge of the 21st Century*, State University of New York, Albany, NY.

Maier, R. (2001) *Knowledge Management Systems: Information and Communication Technologies for Knowledge Management*, Springer-Verlag, Berlin.

Mason, R. O. and Mitroff, I. I. (1981) *Challenging Strategic Planning Assumptions*, Wiley, New York.

O'Brien, R. (1991) 'Brief case: EIS and strategic control', *Long Range Planning*, 24(5), 125–7.

PriceWaterhouse (1995) *Information Technology Review 1995/6*, PriceWaterhouse, London.

Raghunathan, S. (1999) 'Impact of information quality and decision-maker quality on decision quality: a theoretical model and simulation analysis', *Decision Support Systems*, 26(4), 275–286.

Raynes, M. (2002) 'Document management: is the time right now?', *Work Study*, 51(6), 303–308.

Rowley, J. (1999) 'Document publishing systems: a review of current issues', *Online & CD-ROM Review*, 23(1), 3–9.

Ruggles, R. (1998) 'The state of the notion: knowledge management in practice', *California Management Review*, 40(3), 80–9.

Sánchez, A. M. and Pérez, M. P. (2001) 'Lean indicators and manufacturing strategies', *International Journal of Operations & Production Management*, 21(11), 1433–1451.

Shewhart, W. (1931) *Economic Control of Quality of Manufactured Product*, Van Norstrand, New York.

Taylor, F. W. (1911) *Principles of Scientific Management*, Harper, New York.

Trist, E. L. (1959). 'Socio-technical systems', University of Cambridge: Department of Engineering & Psychology, Cambridge.

Turban, E. and Aronson, J. E. (2001) *Decision Support Systems and Intelligent Systems*, Prentice Hall, Upper Saddle River, NJ.

Ulrich, W. (1983) *Critical Heuristics of Social Planning*, Haupt, Berne.

van der Aalst, W. and van Hee, K. (2002) *Workflow Management: Models, Methods, and Systems*, MIT Press, Cambridge, MA.

Weber, M. (1947) *The Theory of Social and Economic Organization*, A. M. Henderson and T. Parsons, translators, Oxford University Press, Oxford.

Wen, H. J., Yen, D. C. and Lin, B. (1998) 'Intranet document management systems', *Internet Research: Electronic Networking Applications and Policy*, 8(4), 338–346.

Womack, J. P., and Jones, D. T. (1996) *Lean Thinking: Banish Waste and Create Wealth in Your Corporation*, Simon and Schuster, New York.

Womack, J. P. Jones, D. T. and Ros, D. (1990) *The Machine That Changed the World*, Rawson Associates, New York.

Zairi, M., Oakland, J. and Chang, S. (1998) 'Achieving a successful EIS: linking TQM and best practice', *Integrated Manufacturing Systems*, 9(1), 50–61.

Chapter 6

Strategic management perspectives

LEARNING OUTCOMES

After completing this chapter the reader should be able to:

- explain the differences between the industrial organisation tradition and the institutionalist perspective in strategic thinking;
- understand the contribution of the resource-based view and the knowledge-based view of the firm to strategic management;
- discuss the development of IS strategy and its influence on knowledge management strategies;
- apply different knowledge management strategies appropriately to different contexts.

MANAGEMENT ISSUES

The use and application of knowledge management systems implies these questions for managers:

- How far do you plan a knowledge management strategy or do you allow it to emerge through the everyday processes of organisational learning?
- What are the core competences of your organisation and how do you exploit them for competitive advantage?
- How do you manage the conflicting interests of the IS/IT department and HR department to develop a coherent knowledge management strategy?

Crucibles of innovation

FT

Every other article I read these days begins by trying to terrify its readers. Doom, gloom, uncertainty and the death of the company are popular themes. The perpetrators of this bleak economic outlook are amazingly certain. They know what causes the problem: globalisation, hyper-competition, technological change and a lack of innovation.

So, too, are they certain of what companies should do: transform themselves with radical innovations in products and/or services. Yet most companies continue to survive without such innovations. They plod on. They copy rather than invent new products. They rely on safe, incremental, 'me too' change.

In a recent paper*, three American academics report their findings from a six-year study of twelve radical innovations in ten large, mature companies. There are two forms of radical product innovation: new products or a service with unprecedented performance features; and existing products that break with the past to offer significant improvements in performance and/or cost. The innovations in research included a digital X-ray imaging system (General Electric), an ionic transport membrane (Air Products), a new material emitting light (Du Pont), decomposing polyester film (General Electric), a new generation of communication chips (International Business Machines) and vertical and horizontal lifts (Otis).

The true test of radical innovation is whether it will change existing markets or create new ones. To energise such change, four uncertainties are essential: technological uncertainty (will the product work?); market uncertainty (will they buy?); resource uncertainty (who will fund this project?); and internal uncertainty (can the goals of the innovators and the company be integrated?).

Radical innovation is not for the faint-hearted. The process is discontinuous. Work is sporadic, non-linear and stochastic, with unpredictable external events. Ten years from start to launch is not unusual. Nevertheless, the authors offer seven imperatives for lifting your performance.

First, build a radical-innovation hub. A hub is a group of people who encourage and oversee innovation. It includes idea-hunters, idea-gatherers, internal venture capitalists, members of project evaluation committees, members of overseeing boards, and experienced but corporate entrepreneurs.

Second, deploy hunters and gatherers. Work organisations have not been famous for generating ideas. The hub's prime function is to nurture idea-hunters and idea-gatherers from all over the company.

Third, monitor and redirect projects. Projects like these are notorious for apparent mismanagement because high levels of uncertainty make control almost impossible. Further, radical innovators are not like the rest of us. Controlling the four sources of uncertainty is impossible. Monitoring them is feasible.

Fourth, develop a resource acquisition skill set. Long-term projects are difficult to resource. The innovators are swimming in uncharted waters. Sharks are an ever-present threat to survival. Withdrawal of funds can kill a project quickly. What aggravates this uncertainty is the arrival and departure of vital players. Only the hub, as overseer, can ensure that the necessary skills are available when and where they are needed.

Fifth, accelerate project transition. Projects cannot remain buried in research indefinitely. Their destination is development. To the creative scientists, handing over their baby can be tantamount to kidnapping by second-rate scientists. It is probably unrealistic to assume either researchers or developers are capable of handling this transition amicably. In the successful cases in the study, a transition team moved projects on. Members of this temporary team included people from the project team, people from the receiving and operating units, transition management experts, market development specialists and members of the project supervision board.

Sixth, use people who drive radical innovation. A vital player is the champion who takes risks, breaks the rules, energises and rescues and re-energises the project. Once identified, he or she blossoms and becomes a performer with a market value. Turnover is high. Loyalty to the company is low. They are idealists. The project, not the company, is their focus. None of the ten American companies had developed human resource strategies for coping systematically with the personnel dimensions of radical innovation.

Seventh, mobilise the multiple roles of leaders. In 90 per cent of the companies, those at the top recognised the importance of patronage. They were seen to be supporting specific projects. In turn, this reinforced positive values within the corporate culture about innovation. Consistency in patronage proved to be vital. Where a patron left a company, 50 per cent of successors either slowed down his projects or killed them.

However, we learn little about the people who had the bright ideas. After six years, what 'imperatives' emerged about them? Only that they differ from idea-gatherers? Without them, no systems or hubs will result in radical innovation.

* Leifer R., O'Connor G. C. and Rice, M., 'Implementing radical innovation in mature firms: the role of hubs', *Academy of Management Executive*, 2001, Vol. 15, No. 3.

Source: Article by John Hunt, *Financial Times*, 18 January 2002

Questions

1 Given its radical nature, how can you effectively foster innovation? Do the seven lessons provide a useful template for planning innovation strategies in organisations?

2 If none of the American companies developed human resource strategies to cope with radical innovation, can one deduce that such innovations are unmanageable and are more luck than design?

3 What lessons can we learn for knowledge management strategies focused on innovation?

Introduction

The underlying assumption within the knowledge management literature is that actions arising from KM practices will result in some form of competitive advantage. But how is this likely to happen? One of the implications is that firms may need some form of knowledge management strategy to achieve these goals. But what is the nature of a KM strategy and how does it change over time? The two dominant pillars of knowledge management are technology and human resource considerations. What are the likely configurations of technology and human aspects to make such strategies effective? The current situation is unclear as the literature on KM strategy is relatively young and has been developing in the last few years.

An important starting point is to explore how KM strategies may relate to a firm's business strategy. Similar to philosophical perspectives, there is a diverse range of viewpoints and schools of thought on the nature of strategy and competitive change. This chapters begins by exploring the meaning of strategy in terms of deliberate and emergent strategies as our goals and plans may not be realised as expected. Then three dominant schools of strategic thought are examined showing their theoretical and economic foundations. These schools are the industrial organisation tradition, excellence and turnaround literature, and the institutionalist perspective. In the last decade, this perspective has developed greater prominence as scholars have explored the resource-based view (RBV) and knowledge-based view of the firm. A number of recent publications have explored the notion of a 'knowledge management strategy' and the resulting debates and arguments are considered towards the end of the chapter. There is a distinction between codification strategies which are technology led and innovation strategies that are people led. It is not surprising that this can give rise to confusion in the KM literatures where articles are either technology oriented or human resource oriented. Both types of literature are important in our understanding of the interplay between them in KM strategies.

Strategic management: schools of thought

What is a strategy? Many people may say it is a plan of action linked to achieving one's goals. The assumption is that in any given situation, be it a football match, a war between nations or a product launch, the strategy or plan will deliver the desired outcomes. However, it does not often happen that the intended or deliberate strategy becomes the realised strategy. There may be some aspects of the strategy or plan that are unrealised and get overlooked (or swept under the carpet!). The notion of strategy as a plan gives much greater power to those in authority such as managers and executives to determine the effective plan/strategy for the organisation. But how often do strategies achieve corporate goals and visions? The problem is that we live in dynamic environments prone to change where sudden economic forces, competitor behaviour and maybe even loss of key players can require a response from organisations that is at odds with the intended strategy.

On the other hand, if you ask a group of people about their firm's strategy in the past year or five years, they will tend to describe a pattern of actions and behaviours which have converged over time into a certain consistency. This is referred to as an 'emergent strategy' and is likely to have arisen through the firm's learning over time (Mintzberg and Waters 1985). The notion of strategy as a plan is more about control whereas a pattern is more about learning. In reality, it is likely that executives will respond to changing circumstances with a mixture of these two notions, as shown in Figure 6.1 (p. 159).

The dominant school of thought in strategic management treats strategy as a plan and is known as the 'industrial organisation' or microeconomic tradition. In contrast, an alternative school of thought is concerned with the dynamics of competitive processes and the contribution of learning and uncertainty in strategy. This school is referred to as the institutionalist perspective. A new strategy literature developed in the 1980s in response to the Japanese threat to the west (see Chapter 5 on drivers of KM systems) became known as the 'excellence and turnaround' school of thought in strategy. This school was high on generic recipes and prescriptions but relatively low on empirical foundations. Nevertheless, the excellence and turnaround movement has had considerable influence on senior management thinking on strategy.

Pause for thought

Reflect on the strategy in your organisation. Describe how you perceive the corporate strategy of your organisation. To what extent were you consulted in the preparation of it? In relation to your organisation, what do words such as 'mission', 'vision' and 'strategy' mean to you? How alive are those words in informing your everyday actions? How typical are your views compared with those of colleagues in the organisation? Is there any advice you would give to senior managers in the preparation of annual strategies?

Industrial organisation tradition

In the industrial organisation (IO) tradition, the relationship between the firm and industry is central. The performance of a firm is determined by the structure of the industry and its market structures. Many of the principal models about market

Figure 6.1 Strategy as a plan and pattern (adapted from Mintzberg and Waters 1985)

structure and competition come from rational microeconomic theory. At its most basic level, the market is concerned with the supply and demand of goods and services and the elasticity or inelasticity of the demand curve. Ideally, firms want elastic demand curves where price falls can still lead to revenue increases. Without labouring over the intricacies of microeconomics, the market structure can lead to perfect competition (large number of buyers and sellers), a monopoly (allowing the firm with the monopoly to earn abnormal profits) or an oligopoly (competition among a few firms). The dominant form of market structure in many countries is an oligopoly where firms tend to fluctuate between intensely competitive and often unstable collusive behaviours.

The nature of competition in this school is determined by the number and relative size of firms and the barriers to entry to that market (Bain 1956). From this perspective, the raison d'être of the firm is to reduce the level of competition either by collusion, creating higher barriers to entry, greater differentiation of their products and services, or lowering costs. The intended consequence is to reduce the number of firms in the market and lead to greater profits. The notion of differentiation has its roots in Chamberlinian economics which recognises the unique capabilities of a firm, such as its know-how and reputation, and tries to exploit the firm's uniqueness through its strategies (Chamberlin 1933; Pettigrew and Whipp 1991).

The industrial organisation tradition has been influenced by a design model and a planning model of strategy (Ansoff 1965; Chandler 1962; Porter 1980). In the design model, the central technique is to use a SWOT (strengths, weaknesses, opportunities and threats) analysis in order to design a unique response following the dictum that structure follows strategy (Chandler 1962). In the planning model, different generic strategies are forwarded to respond to certain market conditions (Porter 1980):

- cost leadership – reducing the cost of product and services relative to competitors with a drop in quality;
- differentiation – providing products or services which are unique or different and valued by customers;
- focus – providing high perceived value justifying higher prices in certain market segments such as traditional corner shops compared with supermarkets.

In the planning model, adopted by most MBA students and executives, the traditional approach to strategy is along the following rather mechanical lines (Johnson and Scholes 2002):

- Conduct a PESTEL (political, economic, social, technological, environmental and legal) analysis at a macro level within the external environment and its likely effect on the firm.
- Conduct a SWOT (internal – strengths, weaknesses; external – opportunities and threats) analysis and look at half a dozen critical success factors in a particular industry.
- Analyse the competitive environment using Porter's (1980) five force framework exploring the threat of entry of new players, the power of buyers and suppliers, the threat of substitutes and the extent of competitive rivalry.
- Analyse the impact of the industry lifecycle such as growth markets that require strategies to fight to increase market share compared with mature markets that require strategies to maintain market share.
- Use scenario planning techniques to determine how different scenarios may affect your strategy.
- Analyse resources in terms of Porter's 'value chain analysis' where activities are isolated that have a perceived value to the customer. Linkages between different activities are seen as competitive, particularly where competitors cannot imitate them.
- Examine strategic options such as generic strategies and whether to follow different directions for strategy development such as withdrawal, consolidation, market penetration, market development, product development or diversification.
- Evaluate the strategic options and check for their suitability in terms of organisational structure and cultural fit. Use a BCG matrix (cash cows, stars, question marks and dogs linked to a plot of market share and market growth) to determine which products or services to divest or invest. Consider a strategic planning or financial control style of operation.
- Manage strategic change through forcefield analysis to identify forces for and against change and adopt suitable management styles to circumstances.

Despite the popularity of the industrial organisation tradition, it does have its shortcomings. The drawbacks of this approach include the following (Mintzberg *et al.* 1998; Pettigrew and Whipp 1991):

- Only 10 per cent of formulated strategies get implemented.
- Separating thought from action by isolating the formulation and implementation processes.
- Assuming that firms and individuals have perfect knowledge of market changes when in reality there may be considerable ignorance leading to questioning of the rationalist tenets of the microeconomic tradition.
- No real conception of competition as a process over time.
- Environments assumed to be predominantly stable.

- Detachment of management from everyday actions and processes.
- Focused more on large businesses.
- Denial of internal social and political influences on strategy.

Excellence and turnaround

With the Japanese beating US competition in terms of design features, price, reliability, speed to market and quality in the 1980s, there was an enormous need to show managers how to respond effectively to these threats. This gave rise to an extensive literature in excellence and turnaround based on a wide range of managerial remedies and recipes of successful companies (Grinyer *et al.* 1988; Peters and Waterman 1982). Many of these publications became bestsellers in airport lounges and made a considerable impact on management strategy.

In Search of Excellence (Peters and Waterman 1982) prescribed eight attributes that characterised excellent and innovative companies: 'a bias for action, close to the customer, autonomy and entrepreneurship, productivity through people, hands-on/value driven, stick to the knitting, simple form/lean staff, simultaneous loose-tight properties.' Many similar books defined half a dozen or so prescriptions for success, with amusing anecdotes to support them, and offered glib platitudes and panaceas in easy-to-read form (Newstrom 2002). They confirmed the beliefs and attitudes of the typical managers, providing them with simple lists for success where they were in control and promoting universal application of their prescriptions across different sectors and environments (Huczynski 1992). The effective management of cultural change often plays an important role in these prescriptions. In order to win hearts and minds, ordinary people are espoused to do extraordinary things thanks to the strength of corporate cultures (Peters and Waterman 1982):

> *'The top performers create a broad, uplifting, shared culture, a coherent framework within which charged-up people search for appropriate adaptations. Their ability to extract extraordinary contributions from very large numbers of people turns on the ability to create a highly valued sense of purpose. Such purpose invariably emanates from love of product, providing top-quality services, and honouring innovation and contribution from all.'*

This literature continues to play a role in strategic development, particularly where managers require ideas for quick-fix solutions. For example, a recent remedy to turnaround situations suggests the following prescription for managers (Reisner 2002):

- Don't miss your moment – the importance of timing in strategic initiatives.
- Connect change initiatives to your core business.
- Don't mistake incremental improvements for strategic transformation (a call for double-loop learning?).
- Be realistic about your limits and the pace of change.

The shortcoming of this school of thought is the overemphasis on the firm and internal processes rather than on competitive changes in the external environment. There is also often a lack of empirical evidence to support the remedies prescribed. In fact, it is hard to see how the excellence and turnaround literature has contributed to further theory development in strategic thinking. In the face of objective scientific inquiry, the remedies offer little evidence of reliability, validity, practicability and integrating with a firm's existing knowledge base (Argyris 2001). Ultimately, many of the successful companies cited as following many of these bestseller prescriptions have often declined in performance or in some cases ceased trading.

Institutionalist perspective

The institutionalist perspective draws heavily on Schumpeter's (1934; 1950) stream of microeconomics which argues against the rational and stable notions of competitive forces and the external environment. Instead, this perspective suggests that competitive forces are inherently unstable and in a continual process of 'creative destruction' (Schumpeter 1950). As one can imagine, this perspective does not sit comfortably with strategic planners following the industrial organisation form of analysis.

Institutional economics places greater emphasis on agents (individuals) and suggests that their economic relations are determined through their experience and learning over time rather than through some form of rational maximisation behaviour. In this explanation, economic activity is dynamic and is informed by social institutions that interact with agents. In turn, competition is viewed as dynamic, impermanent and a continual process informed by people's day-to-day learning. This uncertainty in competition contrasts directly with the industrial organisation tradition that treats it as a steady state affair. For strategic planners, their rational conjectures of competition led to considerable shock waves in the 1970s when their assumptions of incremental change were severely challenged as a result of an oil crisis. Subsequently, the notion of discontinuous (uncertain) change has come into mainstream thinking and many strategic planners have tried to rationalise it through the process of scenario planning. This attempts to create a number of plausible scenarios and considers effective management responses to them. However, one wonders how many scenario planners predicted the consequences of discontinuous changes, such as the September 11 attacks in America, the fall of the Berlin Wall in Germany and the end of apartheid in South Africa.

In the case of September 11, the events leading to it may be considered wholly unpredictable in terms of location and timing, even though some may argue that conceptually this was not the case. In this instance, we can deal only with the consequences of the event. However, with the fall of the Berlin Wall and the end of state socialism in Eastern Europe, a wide range of scenarios had been predicted with reasonable accuracy. Similarly, the end of apartheid was not entirely unexpected, though few scenario planners would have envisaged the peaceful transition to democracy and multiculturalism.

Strategy from an institutionalist perspective is seen as a process over time and considered synonymous with strategic change. Strategic change is informed by the managers' (or other agents) understanding and learning of a situation over time. This includes their subjective and objective understandings of the competitive environment in relation to their firm as well as the political dimensions pertaining to both. In this respect, competition and strategic change are viewed as intimately linked (Pettigrew and Whipp 1991). A contrast between the industrial school tradition and the institutionalist perspective in terms of their approach to thought and action is shown in Figure 6.2.

Mintzberg (1991) has provided a major strategic framework from an institutionalist perspective that examines the dynamics of competitive forces in an organisation. This framework doesn't provide a blueprint for organisations but rather an understanding of the interplay between competitive forces, as shown in Figure 6.3 (p. 164). The underlying assumption of this model is that there is the potential for one or more of seven forces to dominate an organisation at any given time:

- the force for *direction* is concerned with strategic vision and may relate to organisations in startup or turnaround situations;
- the force for *efficiency* is concerned with standardisation and formalisation of processes and may relate to bureaucratic organisations where rationalisation and restructuring are a major focus;

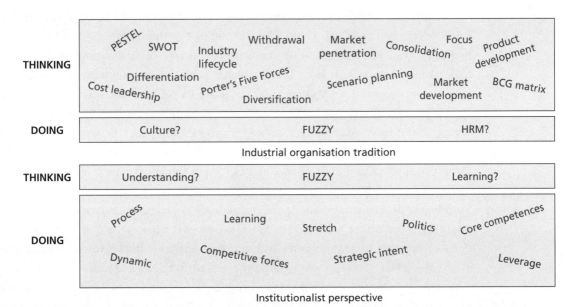

Figure 6.2 Strategic thought and action: industrial organisation tradition and the institutionalist perspective

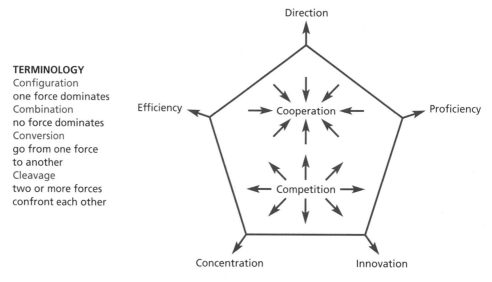

TERMINOLOGY
Configuration
one force dominates
Combination
no force dominates
Conversion
go from one force
to another
Cleavage
two or more forces
confront each other

Figure 6.3 Dynamic forces in organisations (adapted from Mintzberg 1991)

- the force for proficiency is concerned with tasks requiring high levels of knowledge and skills and may relate more to professional organisations;
- the force for concentration is concerned with concentrating efforts on serving certain markets, particularly in large diversified firms;
- the force for innovation is concerned with discovering new things for the customer and may relate to adhocracies comprising skilled experts or multidisciplinary projects.

The internal catalytic forces comprise forces of cooperation and competition. The force for cooperation is concerned with the pulling together of ideology such as norms, beliefs and values. At one extreme, dominant forces of cooperation may result in ideological organisations such as an Israeli kibbutz. The force for competition is concerned with the pulling apart of politics and may relate to political organisations where in-fighting is rife. There may be limits to levels of cooperation as ideology discourages change and if individuals perceive a need for change, they may be forced to challenge the ideology which breeds politics. From the industrial organisation perspective, the force for efficiency and innovation could be seen as similar to generic strategies of 'cost leadership' and 'differentiation' respectively.

In line with an institutionalist perspective, there is a recognition that these forces are rarely static but rather tend to vary continuously over time. A state of 'configuration' occurs when one force dominates and the organisation is drawn towards a coherent established form. However, configuration can lead to the problem of 'contamination' where the dominant force undermines other equally valid forces. For instance, a firm dominated by the force of efficiency may be hindered from following the force for innovation in response to critical changes in the marketplace.

In some periods, an organisation may go through states of 'combination' of different forces where no single force dominates. This may result in periods of 'conversion' from one form to another. For example, an adhocracy may develop a highly successful product or service and settle down into a bureaucracy to exploit it. The state of 'combination' may result in problems of 'cleavage' where two or more forces may confront each other and eventually paralyse the organisation. One can imagine only too well the consequences of boardroom battles where different factions try to pull the organisation in different directions based on their understanding of competitive changes. The internal forces of competition and cooperation can act as useful catalysts to manage the problems of 'contamination' and 'cleavage'. Is this continual flux of forces a 'dialectical interplay between actions (practices and structures), meanings, and actors' (Zilber 2002)?

Two important concepts within this perspective are core competences and strategic intent (Hamel and Prahalad 1989; Prahalad and Hamel 1990). The premise is that strategy is based on learning and learning depends on capabilities (dynamic? See Chapter 3). The core capabilities or competences arise from collective learning in organisations, especially from the coordination of skills and the integration of technologies. By nature, core competences do not diminish in value but need to be nurtured as knowledge and skills are lost over time. They are identified as roots of competitive advantage and the idea of core competence is developed using the analogy of a tree (Prahalad and Hamel 1990):

> 'The diversified corporation is a large tree. The trunk and major limbs are core products, the smaller branches are business units; the leaves, flowers and fruit are end-products. The root system that provides nourishment, sustenance and stability is the core competence. You can miss the strength of competitors by looking only at their end-products, in the same way you miss the strength of a tree if you look only at its leaves.'

As firms respond to competitive pressure, there may be an anomaly between their resources and their aspirations. If a firm has considerable resources but low aspirations, this could be considered as a low 'stretch' circumstance (Hamel and Prahalad 1993). On the other hand, a firm may have very low resources but very high 'stretch' aspirations driven by high ambitions. Such high aspirations or 'stretch' are insufficient to gain competitive advantage and firms require leverage. Leverage entails (Hamel and Prahalad 1993):

- concentrating resources effectively around a strategic focal point;
- accumulating resources more efficiently by extracting knowledge from experience and grafting knowledge from other sources;
- complementing one resource with another to create synergy and higher value;
- conserving resources by recycling and partnering resources from other firms;
- resources from the market in the shortest possible time.

An additional drive to stretch and leverage is 'strategic intent' (Hamel and Prahalad 1989). Strategy is seen as revolution and strategic intent is a firm's obsession with winning in the short or long term. It is stable over time and provides the major driver for organisational commitment and motivation from employees. Strategic intent requires the following demands of senior management (Hamel and Prahalad 1989):

- create a sense of urgency;
- develop a competitor focus at every level through widespread use of competitive intelligence;
- provide employees with the skills they need to work effectively;
- give the organisation time to digest one challenge before launching another;
- establish clear milestones and review mechanisms.

Resource-based view of the firm

In situations of perfect competition, there is a competitive price for products and services. However, in reality, firms may generate 'superprofits' or 'rents' for a variety of reasons. The difference between the actual price of a product or service and its competitive price is known as an 'economic rent'. Rents are payments to assets that exceed their competitive price (Ricardo 1817). This provides firms with their source of competitive advantage. The key question in strategic management is how firms can do this and sustain the competitive advantage over time.

One institutionalist response to increasing rents in firms is to suggest that it is the firm's resources that lead to competitive advantage, arising from a 'resource-based theory of the firm' (Barney 1991; Wernerfelt 1984). Resources are the tangible and intangible assets a firm uses to choose and implement its strategies (Barney 2001). One of the historic tools used in strategic management has been the SWOT analysis where attempts are made to give equal attention to the internal (strengths and weaknesses) and external (opportunities and threats) factors affecting a firm. One could argue that the industrial organisation has shifted the balance in this analysis more towards the external industrial, market-based perspective (Porter 1980). The resource-based view of the firm is an attempt by institutionalists to shift the balance back to the internal aspects of the firm. A seminal paper in this area suggests a number of characteristics of resources to achieve competitive advantage (Barney 1991):

- Resources are distributed heterogeneously across firms.
- Resources have a 'stickiness' and cannot be transferred from firm to firm without a cost.
- Resources are rare – not widely held.
- Resources are valuable – they promote efficiency and effectiveness.
- Resources are not imitable and cannot be replicated easily by competitors.
- Resources are not substitutable – other resources cannot fulfil the same functions.
- Resources are not transferable and cannot be bought in resource markets.

A wide variety of resources that follow the above conditions has been suggested to lead to sustainable competitive advantage in the current literature. These include information technology, strategic planning, human resource management, top management skills, trust and organisational culture (Priem and Butler 2001). One of the highly influential concepts arising from the resource-based view is the notion of core competence described earlier (Prahalad and Hamel 1990).

Many companies adopt the rhetoric that 'people are our greatest assets'. What is your experience of the difference between rhetoric and reality in your organisation? If knowledge was considered the most critical resource in organisations, how would you suggest that it was developed among colleagues and work teams? What role do social networks play in your organisation for developing and sharing your knowledge base?

An outcome of the resource-based view of the firm is the development of the 'knowledge-based view' of the firm which assumes that knowledge (know how and know what) is the firm's most important resource (Grant 1996; Spender 1996). This view revisits many of the tenets of individual knowledge (Polanyi 1967; Ryle 1949), organisational learning (Huber 1991), conversion of one form of knowledge to another (Nonaka 1991) and organisational routines (Levitt and March 1988) as potential sources of competitive advantage. Knowledge sharing is seen as vital to this perspective and there is a recognition of the difficulty of sharing tacit knowledge which may be primary to competitive advantage. The principal role of the firm is to integrate the knowledge resident in individuals into their goods and services (Grant 1991). Hence, the primary task of management is to coordinate the process of knowledge integration. One potential aid in this integration process is to treat the firm as a dynamic sociotechnical and self-regulating system (Spender 1996).

There are a number of criticisms aimed at the resource-based view of the firm (Priem and Butler 2001):

- How can resources be obtained?
- How and in which contexts do resources contribute to competitive advantage?
- How do resources interact and compare with other resources?
- How can a firm operate successfully through the denial of market context?

Information systems strategy

In our quest to develop knowledge management strategies, one can learn a great deal from the more mature literature on information systems (IS). It is important at this stage to make a distinction between information systems (IS) and information technology (IT). IT is purely about technology such as hardware and software. In contrast, IS is concerned with the effective interaction between technology and social phenomena (people). It is possible for some IS to have no technology (where information is exchanged verbally between people) whereas other IS may be totally reliant on technology. The importance of the IS is how they can aid effective action and decision making (Checkland and Holwell 1998).

Organisations can become overwhelmed by technology where IT and IS become synonymous terms. IT is not a strategy on its own and the purchase of hardware and software without recourse to organisational issues and activities is unlikely to lead to competitive advantage. It is easy to be seduced by applications (software designed to meet certain business processes or activities) rather than examining whether they will address key business problems in an effective manner and taking into account the competence of the existing workforce.

The past decade has seen the dominance of e-commerce – conducting business electronically using internet technologies. This gave rise to the boom (and subsequent collapse) of dotcom companies and there was a stage a few years ago where the mere announcement of a firm's name change to a dotcom company sent its share price soaring without necessarily any other change in its business. E-commerce did exist in the 1980s when electronic data interchange (EDI) was used to exchange documents between firms at a much reduced cost. Subsequently, financial EDI allowed the customer into the loop by enabling them to issue electronic payment instructions to the supplier directly. More recently the appearance of WAP (wireless application protocol) has allowed individuals to use mobile devices (such as mobile phones and personal digital assistants) to browse the net and make purchases directly while on the move (Ward and Peppard 2002). The use of mobile devices for conducting business transactions has been termed m-commerce.

In the 1960s, the dominant IS/IT strategy was focused on 'data processing' (DP) where the emphasis was to use technology to automate tasks. The rationale was to produce twice as many products in half as much time through automation leading to greater efficiency and profits. This data-processing approach did not change the business processes or alter the overall corporate strategy. Modern-day examples of the data-processing approach are the computerised reservation systems (CRS) used among airlines and the electronic point of sale (EPOS) systems used in retailing. The aim of both these systems is to increase the overall efficiency in the business process through efficient transaction handling and resource control. The users of the data-processing approach tend to be operators, clerical staff or first-line supervisors (Ward and Peppard 2002).

In the 1970s and 1980s there was a development in IS/IT towards management information systems (MIS). The objective was to provide middle and senior managers with information for monitoring and controlling business processes and to aid decision making. The focus became the information needs of the users and there was a development of information centres in many organisations to meet this need. The linkages between MIS and organisational performance became much harder to justify than the data-processing approach. The development of large databases characterised this approach but they were not necessarily integrated between different parts of the firm.

The contributions of DP and MIS are (Strassman 1985):

- IS/IT has increased the efficiency of information-based activities;
- returns on investment likely to be around 5–10 per cent;
- in terms of managerial effectiveness, good managers get even better, bad managers get worse!
- IS/IT can speed up the mess if used inappropriately.

A further development of information systems and one that builds on DP and MIS is known as strategic information systems (SIS) (Galliers and Somogyi 1987). The aim of SIS is to improve the firm's competitiveness through the effective deployment of IS/IT. SIS is business driven in terms of competitors, suppliers and customers and links directly to the firm's corporate strategy. The four main types of strategic systems (Ward and Peppard 2002) are those that:

- change the nature of the relationship with customers and suppliers by sharing information through technology-based systems. This may include e-procurement, web-based ordering systems and customers tracking their orders online through workflow management systems;
- produce effective integration of information linked to a firm's value-adding processes. This has often been achieved through customer relationship management systems or enterprise resource planning systems;
- enable a firm to develop and market new products or services based on information. These have included online banking, online support and order-tracking initiatives;
- provide executive management with information (internal and external) to support development and implementation of strategy. An example of this is the use of executive information systems for tracking market, customer and industry changes through external databases as well as key internal indicators of performance.

Pause for thought

Imagine you were given the position of IS manager in your organisation. What would be your approach to strategy? Think of data processing, management information systems, strategic information systems and information systems capability as potential options for IS strategy. Given the nature of your organisation, which option or combination of options would you adopt and why? How would you integrate and justify your approach with your company's strategy?

The most recent development in the IS/IT strategy literature is the notion of 'IS capability' (Bharadwaj 2000) that is likely to enhance a firm's competitiveness. Instead of a fixation on external changes, the focus of IS strategy becomes more internal. The suggestion is the desire to embed IS capability into all the various practices and processes within the organisation. IS capability takes on a resource-based theory of the firm and appears to be reminiscent of the notions of dynamic capabilities and double-loop learning (Argyris and Schon 1978; Zollo and Winter 2002). Similar to March's (1991) distinction between exploitation and exploration, there may be a tidal swing in the direction of exploration and looking at things differently. As Hamel (2000) asserts about the key factor affecting the competitiveness of e-commerce:

> *'The real story of Silicon Valley is not "e" but "i", not electronic commerce but innovation and imagination…It is the power of "i" rather than "e" that separates the winners from the losers in the twenty-first century economy.'*

Developing a knowledge management strategy

As industrialised economies have moved from natural resources to intellectual assets, it has been argued that the most important asset that a firm possesses is its knowledge. In terms of economic theory, we are looking for strategies that will produce Ricardian rents (or super profits) (Ricardo 1817) where the effective use of knowledge will enable firms to sustain competitive advantage. There are other forms of rent, such as luck, chance and history, but these rents cannot be managed (Liebeskind 1996). It is assumed that knowledge in its tacit and explicit manifestations can be managed. But how do we develop knowledge management strategies to effectively utilise this valuable resource? Also, how do we protect the valuable knowledge from expropriation and imitation?

The KM strategy literature is relatively young and the forms of strategy proposed can be characterised as a dialectic between the forces of efficiency and innovation (Mintzberg 1991), as shown in Figure 6.4 (p. 171). Firms are never static and are moving in one or another direction towards efficiency or innovation given a certain set of market conditions. In this manner the firm's KM strategy becomes aligned with the overall business strategy. It is likely that a crisis or discontinuity will trigger the firm to move from one force, say, efficiency to innovation. Discontinuities may arise from sudden deregulation of markets, economic downturns or aggressive competitor behaviour resulting in drastic loss of market share.

Among management consultants, the most common forms of knowledge management strategies are codification strategies and personalisation strategies (Hansen *et al.* 1999) as shown in Figure 6.5 (p. 171). For example, Andersen Consulting and Ernst & Young have pursued codification strategies. Codification strategies are heavily based on technology and use large databases to codify and store knowledge. The rationale of a codification strategy is to achieve 'scale in knowledge reuse'. After completion of a project, consultants will retrieve key pieces of knowledge from the assignment and create 'knowledge objects' to store valuable knowledge such as key industry information, market segmentation analyses, presentations, interview guides, programming documents and change management programmes. This knowledge is stored in a knowledge repository so that others in the firm can use the same material for their assignments. Put crudely, consultancy reports for clients become little more than a 'cut and paste' affair from knowledge and templates found in the repository. Of course, there is signifi-

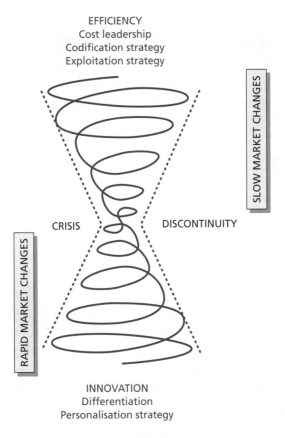

EFFICIENCY
Cost leadership
Codification strategy
Exploitation strategy

SLOW MARKET CHANGES

CRISIS   DISCONTINUITY

RAPID MARKET CHANGES

INNOVATION
Differentiation
Personalisation strategy

Figure 6.4 The dialectic of knowledge management strategies

cant input from consultants about the specifics of the case, but the tools, techniques and background knowledge come from the knowledge repositories. There is little room for creativity and innovation in this approach and they are likely to be discouraged. Instead, the tried and tested methods of consultancy are promoted. This is what the clients are paying them for: a solid consultancy approach based on previous knowledge without the potential risks of innovation. In this case, codification strategies are clearly

CODIFICATION STRATEGY	PERSONALISATION STRATEGY
Technology-led Explicit knowldege orientation Codify knowledge Use databases High turnover	People-led Tacit knowldege orientation Engage in dialogue Channel expertise High profits

Figure 6.5 Codification and personalisation strategies

Pause for thought

Think of the way knowledge is managed in your organisation. How would you assess the level of personalisation or codification strategies involved? Has the emphasis towards one or the other strategy changed over the past few years? What is your involvement with strategy development? On a theoretical level, which one of these strategies do you consider most appropriate for small organisations? Do you consider personalisation strategies as the ultimate knowledge management strategy if companies can afford them?

aligned with the consultancy firm's business strategy focused on efficiency, cost savings and cost leadership. What the clients value from such consultants is their reduced fees (half or a third) compared with other consultants in the field.

Other consultants such as Bain or McKinsey tend to favour knowledge management strategies focused on 'personalisation' strategies. These strategies are less about technology and more about people. Bain and McKinsey are more interested in developing people through brainstorming exercises and face-to-face communication and gaining deeper insights into problems. They place considerable emphasis on knowledge sharing, either face to face, over the phone, by e-mail or via videoconferences (Hansen *et al.* 1999). In terms of KM technology, they tend to use expertise databases or internal 'yellow pages' to find consultants with the right set of knowledge and skills for their problem. The focus is on networking within the organisation and through dialogue developing creative solutions for unique problems in their assignments. Knowledge sharing, mentoring and the use of creative and analytical skills are key to this approach. As certain clients value this approach, they are prepared to pay substantially higher fees for this personalised and unique service. In this sense, a personalisation strategy is in alignment with the business strategy focused on differentiation through innovative solutions.

Similar knowledge management strategies have been found in other industries where firms have followed a codification strategy if they were led by efficiency or cost leadership concerns and personalisation strategies where innovation forces and differentiation concerns were foremost. In the US pharmaceutical industry, the knowledge management strategies firms followed a similar pattern of codification strategies ('exploiters' and 'loners') and personalisation strategies ('explorers' and 'innovators') (Bierly and Chakrabarti 1996). Codification strategies rely on large investments in knowledge repositories and proprietary search engines and use incentives to encourage people to codify and store their knowledge in these large databases. On the contrary, personalisation strategies require low levels of technology such as expertise databases but high levels of reward for knowledge sharing and dialogue with their colleagues. Firms that try to pursue both strategies simultaneously tend to fail, as with the problems of 'cleavage' in business strategy where the forces of efficiency and innovation confront each other in the boardroom and can paralyse the firm if there are major divisions in competitive response (Hansen *et al.* 1999; Mintzberg 1991).

Given the dominance of codifying knowledge, what is the best way of codifying explicit knowledge that can be useful and valuable? For example, Ernst & Young has a three-level hierarchy in its knowledge repositories. There is an 'elite' database that has its best knowledge on a topic. In the next level there are specific 'knowledge objects' containing consultancy reports, templates, market analyses and so on from previous assignments. Finally, there are 'holding tanks' for a variety of materials (Hansen *et al.* 1999). A similar framework for mapping knowledge is to classify it under three levels of core knowledge, advanced knowledge and innovative knowledge (Zack 1999):

- Core knowledge is the minimum knowledge required to function in any business or public arena.
- Advanced knowledge is knowledge in process, cost or quality that enables a firm to compete in a particular market and allows some knowledge differentiation between firms.
- Innovative knowledge is knowledge that is substantially differentiated and allows the firm to lead the industry through doing things differently.

An alternative codification of strategic knowledge distinguishes between four types of business knowledge and the tools associated with them (Drew 1999):

- What we know we know: knowledge sharing, access and inventory. Tools include benchmarking and communities of practice.
- What we know we don't know: knowledge seeking and creation. Tools include R&D, market research and competitive intelligence.
- What we don't know we know: uncovering hidden or tacit knowledge. Tools include knowledge maps, audits, training and networks.
- What we don't know we don't know: discovering key risks, exposures and opportunities. Tools include creative tension, audits, dilemmas and complexity science.

Once we have codified knowledge in an appropriate manner, how do we acquire, integrate, store, share and apply the knowledge to achieve competitive advantage? It has been argued that the key drivers and creative tension for strategic action arise from a knowledge gap and strategic gap (Zack 1999). A knowledge gap is the difference between what a firm must know and what it actually knows. Similarly a strategic gap is the difference between what a firm must do and what a firm can do given its resource base. From this gap analysis, there are two potential orientations to knowledge strategy (Zack 1999):

- pursue a conservative knowledge strategy of exploiting past internal knowledge (similar to a codification strategy);
- pursue an aggressive knowledge strategy that integrates exploration and exploitation of internal and external knowledge (a combination of a codification and personalisation strategy). Whereas personalisation or exploration strategies may provide a useful alternative in their own right, firms need to be mindful of the dangers of pursuing both strategies at the same time (Hansen *et al.* 1999). This has often resulted in failure.

A knowledge management strategy needs to contribute to a firm's bottom-line performance. But who takes responsibility for knowledge management in an organisation?

If the firm pursues a codification strategy, should the IS/IT department take the lead? Alternatively, if a personalisation strategy is pursued, should the human resource department provide the necessary direction? Our argument is that knowledge management strategies need to be developed in consultation and partnership with both IS/IT and human resource departments. We would go further to include the finance department in these consultations as the benefits of a knowledge management strategy will affect the firm's financial performance and its intellectual capital. The relationship between KM strategy and performance is shown in Figure 6.6.

Innovation and personalisation strategies

It appears that in times of crisis – rapid market changes or economic decline – many firms may need to reconsider their position and move more towards personalisation or innovation strategies. Their traditional codification or efficiency-related strategies may not be enough. But how do we innovate, particularly if we are used to a totally different way of working? This could be a wake-up call for many firms to change their ways and look more closely at their processes of innovation.

Most people think of innovation as starting with an idea, an 'aha' feeling in the bath, or as an invention. But ideas are not enough in themselves. They need to be nurtured to prevent them from decay and need to be implemented in an organisational context. A useful definition of innovation is as follows (Van de Van 1986):

> 'The process of innovation is defined as the development and implementation of new ideas by people who over time engage in transactions with others within an institutional context.'

Research in organisational innovation shows that the results from different studies are inherently inconsistent and do not provide us with a clear road map of the best way to proceed (Wolfe 1994). Ideas come from people and need champions to take them forward. People carry, develop and marshal their ideas in a socio-political process of

Figure 6.6 **KM strategy and performance**

dialogue and discussion with other people before they gain legitimacy and currency. Ideas may go through a number of stages over time (Van de Van 1986):

- appreciation – a threatening, disruptive event leading to the idea;
- articulation – ideas may surface as solutions;
- adoption – ideas may galvanise through networks and political debate;
- institutionalisation – ideas gain legitimacy and are taken for granted;
- decay – ideas become outmoded.

This research has focused predominantly on what are the determinants of organisational innovation. Effectively the determinants fall into a variety of organisational, innovation, managerial and environmental characteristics. The studies have followed quantitative regression models where innovation is measured in terms of its magnitude and speed of adoption. Parallel studies have focused on diffusion of innovation in organisations. These studies have explored the pattern, extent and rate of diffusion of innovation across an organisation. Again these studies have used cross-sectional surveys looking at organisational, innovation and managerial characteristics of the promoter of the innovation. Lastly, research has looked at innovation as a process to see how it emerges, develops, grows and terminates over time. This has been done in a qualitative manner by conceptualising innovation as a series of stages over time. The common stages in the innovation cycle among many studies are (Wolfe 1994):

- idea conception;
- awareness;
- matching;
- appraisal;
- persuasion;
- adoption decision;
- implementation;
- confirmation;
- routinisation;
- infusion.

These processual innovations have had a profound effect on many organisations and have occurred in forms such as business process re-engineering, lean production and customer requirements management. They are affected considerably by cognitive, social and organisational factors. The political dynamics, interests and power bases can also considerably influence the innovation. By their nature, innovations can be irrational, unpredictable and uncertain and fail to follow rationalised management processes. These can lead to frustrations among managers about how to effectively manage innovation. An alternative conceptualisation to the stages of innovation shown above is the notion of innovation as four 'episodes', as shown in Figure 6.7 (p. 176). The four episodes emphasise that the different stages are overlapping and may not occur in a linear manner.

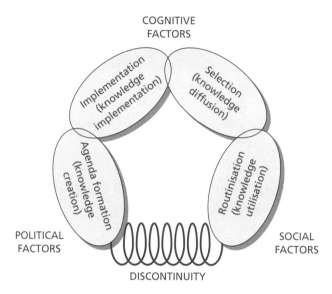

Figure 6.7 Episodes in the innovation process (Clark and Fujimoto 1992; Newell *et al*. 2002)

The agenda formation episode is principally about knowledge creation and acquisition. Firms can acquire knowledge internally through congenital or experiential learning or externally through vicarious learning, grafting, searching and noticing (Huber 1991). Given that many new ideas come from external sources, the firm's ability to acquire new ideas from external sources becomes critical. This is normally achieved through individuals engaging in external networks, acquiring new ideas and sharing them across the firm (knowledge diffusion). It is argued that weak ties in these networks provide the most productive source of ideas as they are more likely to challenge conventional thinking rather than conform to it (Hansen 1999; Newell *et al*. 2002). The strength of networking is measured as a form of social capital (Adler and Kwon 2002) and determines the level and quality of new ideas coming into the organisation from external sources.

New ideas on their own do not create innovation. They need to be developed and merged into local conditions through organisational processes, practices and political environments. The culture of the organisation can significantly influence whether these ideas are accepted or rejected. Strong ties between organisational members are important as they allow greater facility to engage in discussion and dialogue leading to a greater opportunity for the idea to be implemented in a practice or process as an innovation (Hansen 1999). These phases are part of the implementation and selection episodes. The last episode in the innovation cycle is the routinisation episode concerned with the utilisation of knowledge and its efficient reuse. This episode has parallels with the codification strategy where knowledge codification, storage and retrieval mechanisms are developed. To be successful, an innovation that starts as an irrational idea but turns into a codified, constrained and routinised form of knowledge. Exploration leads back to exploitation. It needs a discontinuity to kick start the innovation process again.

Exploitation strategies require 'discipline' in collecting knowledge for any given situation, developing alternatives and evaluating the one most likely to increase the value of the firm. A form of convergent thinking towards a problem. In contrast, exploration strategies require 'imagination' to go beyond the conventional methods of thinking and promote divergent thinking towards a problem. The primacy of imagination in the long term is illustrated by Einstein (Szulanski and Amin 2001):

> *'Imagination is more important than knowledge. For knowledge is limited, whereas imagination embraces the entire world, stimulating progress, giving birth to evolution.'*

CASE STUDY

Knowledge management strategy at BG

'A lot of businesses are like caterpillars, wanting to be sleeker, fitter and more sustainable,' says David Varney, the chief executive of BG, the oil, gas and pipeline company formed from the upstream half of the old British Gas. 'The trouble is that the caterpillars often don't realise they are blind, so when the opportunity to become a butterfly comes along, they say "this is not for me".'

Mr Varney may be unusual in his use of metaphor, but his quandary is shared by many executives at the head of large privatised companies. At BG, he found that the company carried a lot of baggage from its state-owned days. 'Change' was not a word everyone in the group recognised. He thought BG needed an outside influence to counter the 'dominant logic', or fixed ideas, that had developed within the company.

So when the Performance Group, a Norwegian-owned management consultancy, approached him to chair a global learning consortium, he eagerly took up the offer. Two years on, the results are in. And BG has in the past few weeks made a series of announcements that suggest the company is learning to be radical.

Mr Varney's consortium searched Europe for other companies that were facing similar challenges. It assembled a collection that included ABB, the Swiss engineering group; SJ, the Swedish State Railways cargo division; Posten, the Swedish postal service; Wallenius Wilhelmsen Lines, the Nordic cargo shipping group; and Unitor, the Norwegian shipping-services group.

'People got involved because they had a need-driven appetite,' explains David Oliver of the Performance Group. Unitor, for instance, was facing the challenge of global purchasing in the ship-maintenance industry. BG, for its part, was pondering how to increase growth and value for shareholders. In addition, the regulator that oversees BG's gas-pipeline

business was becoming tougher, and the scope for further performance improvements appeared limited.

The aim of the consortium was to visit international companies that were recognised as either having gone through a lot of change or being leaders in their industries. The companies were a mixture of large and rapidly growing businesses. They included FedEx, International Business Machines, Sears, Cisco Systems and 3M, and all agreed to be interviewed on a confidential basis, provided that they would receive the conclusions of the consortium's research. 'We were amazed that all of the companies we approached wanted to see us and took the exercise very seriously,' says Mr Varney.

The findings from the visits were shared at a two-day conference in Chicago, and then filtered back to the participating organisations through further internal meetings. They have been compiled in CD-Rom format and made available to all of the companies involved.

The consortium discovered that in order to increase the odds of successfully changing their business, companies had first to conduct an honest appraisal of themselves and be ruthlessly blunt about where they stood in the market. They then had to develop their ability to look ahead. Only that way could the companies determine what threats and opportunities were coming along, and create the energy and focus within the organisation to implement the appropriate response.

The last main conclusion was that companies too often played to their traditional strengths and failed to recognise new ideas. The consortium advocated that companies create a 'question everything' culture and a 'hothouse', where ideas could develop without being judged too early in the process.

Mr Varney says that, in all, his company spent about two man-years on the exercise. Yet at first

▶

glance the conclusions appear to be fairly obvious and none of the findings particularly new. So why spend so much time and money, when the spade work could have been done by a management consultancy, and the lessons could have been gleaned from any one of hundreds of management manuals?

Mr Varney says the real value of the programme lies partly in having the weight of real-life examples behind him when he reported back to his own board, and partly in seeing first-hand how BG was analysed by a cross-section of companies. 'People listen a lot more if you can say "this is what IBM did in that situation". Consortium exercises like this catalyse activity and help to make the process of changing the company's culture more transparent,' he says.

There were surprises, too. The most helpful company for BG to learn from was FedEx – a company it 'would never have dreamed of looking at', says Mr Varney. 'They were going from an asset-rich company to an information-systems company which told its customers where their parcels were.'

In the past few weeks BG has also embarked on an information-systems strategy. It has announced that it will develop a network of fibre-optic cables and communications towers around its pipeline to take advantage of the growing need for high-quality data transmission capacity. The group is also demerging Transco, its regulated pipelines company,

from the international oil and gas exploration and production arm of the business. And it has created a 'venture laboratory' to work on a few good ideas, including natural-gas vehicles and small-scale combined heat and power plants.

In business, as in anything else, it helps to see things for yourself.

It remains to be seen how successful the consortium members will be in implementing their change programmes, but Mr Varney is hopeful that it will help BG to succeed in becoming a top-quartile FTSE 100 performer.

Source: Article by Matthew Jones, *Financial Times*, 12 May 2000

Questions

1 Is organisational transformation from a 'chrysalis to a butterfly' about a journey and learning rather than a planned process? What is the value of the consortium exercises rather than employing a cheaper management consultant?

2 As BG is constrained considerably by its regulator, is the most appropriate KM strategy likely to be a codification strategy focused on efficiency and cost savings?

3 What are the drawbacks of a strategy based on adding knowledge or information to your products or services?

Summary

This chapter has elaborated five areas that need to be considered when developing a knowledge management strategy:

1 Realised strategies may emerge from the way a firm develops through experience rather than as an outcome of a deliberate plan or strategy. Many deliberate strategies may be unrealised.

2 A clear understanding of strategy needs awareness of the different schools of thought and their underlying assumptions. The dominant schools of thought in the knowledge management literature are the industrial organisation tradition, the excellence and turnaround literature, and the institutionalist perspective.

3 The resource-based and knowledge-based view of the firm place greater emphasis on the firm's resources (tangible and intangible assets) to achieve competitive advantage.

4 Information systems and information technology strategies have developed from operational data-processing approaches to management information systems and

strategic information systems. More recently, IS/IT strategies have adopted a resource-based view of the firm and suggest that IS capabilities are the primary source of competitive advantage.

5 Knowledge management strategies occur as a dialectic between codification (exploitation) strategies and personalisation (exploration) strategies. Firms that follow both strategies simultaneously are likely to fail. The dialectic or change between strategies is likely to occur following a crisis or discontinuity.

QUESTIONS FOR FURTHER THOUGHT

1   At the extremes of KM strategy, is a codification strategy purely an IS/IT strategy and a personalisation strategy a human resource (HR) strategy? What is the importance of the IS/IT department and HR departments talking to one another for the development of a KM strategy?

2   Given the institutionalist perspective's preoccupation with learning, how do we know that the organisation is learning about the right things and responding to market changes in the appropriate manner?

3   If only 10 per cent of formulated strategies ever get implemented, why do firms bother with elaborate planning processes?

4   Why do people knock books and publications from the excellence and turnaround literature when they have probably had more impact and influence on managers than literature from the industrial organisation and institutionalist perspective put together?

5   Core competences are described using the analogy of the roots of a tree. How effective are these core competences in times of discontinuity when the environment changes the soil nourishing the roots of competence into sand?

6   Is there potential in development of strategic thinking by a synthesis of the best ideas from the industrial organisation and institutionalist perspective?

7   What lessons can managers take from the innovation literature when the results of several studies are inconsistent? Could literature hinder the very creative and innovative processes it is trying to describe?

8   If we cannot predict the future, what is the point of codifying strategic knowledge into 'what we don't know we know' and 'what we don't know we don't know' (Drew 1999)? Is this the same as the use of scenario planning in the industrial organisation tradition?

9   Is KM strategy development the domain of the finance director, the IS/IT director or the HR director? If you propose a joint body, how do you overcome the communication difficulties between the different areas, their interests and different languages?

10   What is the likelihood of codification strategies developing superficial learning and personalisation strategies developing a deeper insight on any subject?

Further reading

1 Mintzberg *et al.* 1998 is an excellent exploration of the different strategy schools and their underlying assumptions. The authors distinguish ten schools of strategic thought rather than the three described in this chapter.

2 Johnson and Scholes 2002 is a classic strategy text for MBA students. The main caution is that it comes from a predominant industrial organisation background and needs to be read in this context.

References

Adler, P. S. and Kwon, S. (2002) 'Social Capital: Prospects for a new concept', *Academy of Management Review*, 27(1), 17–40.

Ansoff, H. I. (1965) *Corporate Strategy*, McGraw Hill, New York.

Argyris, C. (2001) *Flawed Advice and the Management Trap*, Oxford University Press, New York.

Argyris, C. and Schon, D. A. (1978) *Organizational Learning: A Theory of Action Perspective*, Addison-Wesley, Reading, MA.

Bain, J. S. (1956) *Barriers to New Competition*, Harvard University Press, Cambridge, MA.

Barney, J. B. (1991) 'Firm resources and sustained competitive advantage', *Journal of Management*, 17(1), 99–120.

Barney, J. B. (2001). 'Is the resource-based 'view' a useful perspective for strategic management research? Yes', *Academy of Management Review*, 26(1), 41–56.

Bharadwaj, A. (2000) 'A resource-based perspective on information technology and firm performance: an empirical investigation', *MIS Quarterly*, 24(1), 169–196.

Bierly, P. and Chakrabarti, A. (1996) 'Generic knowledge strategies in the U.S. pharmaceutical industry', *Strategic Management Journal*, 17(Winter Special Issue).

Chamberlin, E. H. (1933) *The Theory of Monopolistic Competition*, Harvard University Press, Cambridge, MA.

Chandler, A. D. (1962) *Strategy and Structure. Chapters in the History of the Industrial Enterprise*, The MIT Press, Cambridge, MA.

Checkland, P. B. and Holwell, S. (1998) *Information, Systems and Information Systems: Making Sense of the Field*, John Wiley & Sons, Chichester.

Clark, K. and Fujimoto, T. (1992) *Product Development Performance*, Harvard Business School Press, Boston, MA.

Drew, S. (1999) 'Building knowledge management into strategy: making sense of a new perspective', *Long Range Planning*, 32(1), 130–136.

Galliers, R. D. and Somogyi, E. K. (1987) 'From data processing to strategic information systems: a historical perspective', *Towards Strategic Information Systems*, R. D. Galliers and E. K. Somogyi, eds, Gordon & Breach Publishing Group, Reading, 5–25.

Grant, R. M. (1991) 'The resource-based theory of competitive advantage: implications for strategy formulation', *California Management Review*, 33(3), 114–135.

Grant, R. M. (1996) 'Toward a knowledge-based theory of the firm', *Strategic Management Journal*, 17, 109–22.

Grinyer, P., Mayes, D. and McKiernan, P. (1988) *Sharpbenders: The Secrets of Unleashing Corporate Potential*, Basil Blackwell, Oxford.

Hamel, G. (2000) *Leading the Revolution*, Harvard Business School, Boston, MA.

Hamel, G. and Prahalad, C. K. (1989) 'Strategic intent', *Harvard Business Review*, May–June, 63–76.

Hamel, G. and Prahalad, C. K. (1993). 'Strategy as stretch and leverage', *Harvard Business Review*, 71(2), 75–84.

Hansen, M., Nohria, N. and Tierney, T. (1999) 'What's your strategy for managing knowledge?' *Harvard Business Review*, March–April, 106–16.

Hansen, M. T. (1999) 'The search-transfer problem: the role of weak ties in sharing knowledge across organization subunits', *Administrative Science Quarterly*, 44, 82–111.

Huber, G. P. (1991) 'Organizational learning: the contributing processes and the literatures', *Organization Science*, 2, 88–115.

Huczynski, A. (1992) 'Management guru ideas and the 12 secrets of their success', *Leadership & Organization Development Journal*, 13(5), 15–20.

Johnson, G. and Scholes, K. (2002) *Exploring Corporate Strategy: Text and Cases*, Prentice Hall, Harlow, Essex.

Levitt, B. and March, J. G. (1988) 'Organizational learning', *Annual Review of Sociology*, 14.

Liebeskind, J. P. (1996) 'Knowledge, strategy, and the theory of the firm', *Strategic Management Journal*, 17 (Winter Special Issue), 93–107.

March, J. G. (1991) 'Exploration and exploitation in organizational learning', *Organization Science*, 2(1), 71–87.

Mintzberg, H. (1991) 'The effective organization: forces and forms', *Sloan Management Review*, Winter edition, 54–67.

Mintzberg, H., Ahlstrand, B. and Lampel, J. (1998) *Strategy Safari*, Pearson Education Limited, Harlow, Essex.

Mintzberg, H. and Waters, J. A. (1985) 'Of strategies, deliberate and emergent', *Strategic Management Journal*, 6(3), 257–72.

Newell, S., Robertson, M., Scarbrough, H. and Swan, J. (2002) *Managing Knowledge Work*, Palgrave, Basingstoke, Hampshire.

Newstrom, J. W. (2002) 'In search of excellence: its importance and effects', *Academy of Management Executive*, 16(1), 53–56.

Nonaka, I. (1991) 'The knowledge-creating company', *Harvard Business Review*, 69(November–December), 96–104.

Peters, T. J. and Waterman, R. H. (1982) *In Search of Excellence: Lessons from America's Best Run Companies*, Harper & Row, New York.

Pettigrew, A. and Whipp, R. (1991) *Managing Change for Competitive Success*, Blackwell Publishers, Oxford.

Polanyi, M. (1967) *The Tacit Dimension*, Doubleday, New York.

Porter, M. (1980) *Competitive Strategy*, Free Press, New York.

Prahalad, C. K. and Hamel, G. (1990) 'The core competence of the corporation', *Harvard Business Review*, 68(3), 79–91.

Priem, R. L. and Butler, J. E. (2001) 'Is resource-based "view" a useful perspective for strategic management research?', *Academy of Management Review*, 26(1), 22–40.

Reisner, R. A. F. (2002) 'When a turnaround stalls', *Harvard Business Review*, 80(2), 45–52.

Ricardo, D. (1817) *Principles of Political Economy and Taxation*, Murray, London.

Ryle, G. (1949) *The Concept of Mind*, Hutcheson, London.

Schumpeter, J. (1934) *The Theory of Economic Development*, Harvard University Press, Cambridge, MA.

Schumpeter, J. A. (1950) *Capitalism, Socialism, and Democracy*, Harper, New York.

Spender, J. C. (1996) 'Making knowledge the basis of a dynamic theory of the firm', *Strategic Management Journal*, 17, 45–62.

Strassman, P. A. (1985) *The Information Payoff*, Free Press, New York.

Szulanski, G. and Amin, K. (2001) 'Learning to make strategy: balancing discipline and imagination', *Long Range Planning*, 34, 537–556.

Van de Van, A. H. (1986) 'Central problems in the management of innovation', *Management Science*, 32(5), 590–607.

Ward, J. and Peppard, J. (2002) *Strategic Planning for Information Systems*, John Wiley & Sons Ltd, Chichester.

Wernerfelt, B. (1984) 'A resource-based view of the firm', *Strategic Management Journal*, 5, 171–180.

Wolfe, R. A. (1994) 'Organizational innovation: review, critique and suggested research directions', *Journal of Management Studies*, 31(3), 427–453.

Zack, M. (1999) 'Developing a knowledge strategy', *California Management Review*, 41(3), 125–145.

Zilber, T. (2002) 'Institutionalization as an interplay between actions, meanings and actors: the case of a rape crisis center in Israel', *Academy of Management Journal*, 45, 234–254.

Zollo, M. and Winter, S. G. (2002) 'Deliberate learning and the evolution of dynamic capabilities', *Organization Science*, 13(3), 339–351.

PART 4

Sharing knowledge

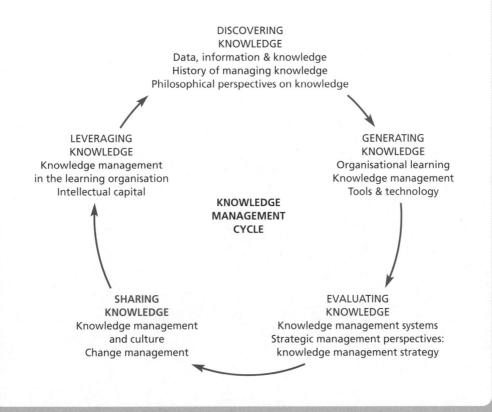

DISCOVERING
KNOWLEDGE
Data, information & knowledge
History of managing knowledge
Philosophical perspectives on knowledge

LEVERAGING
KNOWLEDGE
Knowledge management
in the learning organisation
Intellectual capital

**KNOWLEDGE
MANAGEMENT
CYCLE**

GENERATING
KNOWLEDGE
Organisational learning
Knowledge management
Tools & technology

SHARING
KNOWLEDGE
Knowledge management
and culture
Change management

EVALUATING
KNOWLEDGE
Knowledge management systems
Strategic management perspectives:
knowledge management strategy

Chapter 7

Knowledge management and culture

LEARNING OUTCOMES

After completing this chapter the reader should be able to:

- explain the distinctions between organisational culture and organisational climate;
- understand the surface manifestations and deeper aspects of organisational culture;
- discuss different approaches to developing knowledge-sharing cultures;
- apply the notion of 'communities of practice' to organisations.

MANAGEMENT ISSUES

An understanding of cultural issues and the development of knowledge sharing-cultures and communities of practice implies these questions for managers:

- How do you embed knowledge management technologies to a given culture?
- What types of cultures are likely to facilitate knowledge sharing and how do you achieve them?
- What is the role of the manager in cultivating communities of practice?

Links to other chapters

Chapter 6   examines knowledge management strategies where cultural factors and communities of practice may play a central role.

Chapter 8   explores implementation of knowledge management initiatives and the role of cultural management of the change process.

Chapter 10   concerns intellectual capital which is clearly an intended outcome of knowledge-sharing cultures and communities of practice.

Tough-guy, macho culture

Of all the ideas propagated by Jack Welch, this must be the most dangerous. Every year, the former General Electric boss says, you should fire the weakest 10 per cent of your staff. It will get harder to do as the years go by and you have got rid of the obvious incompetents. But you must carry on weeding out that bottom tenth all the same.

Many do not have the heart. 'Managers will play every game in the book to avoid identifying their bottom ten,' Mr Welch writes in his autobiography. 'Sometimes they'll sneak in people who were planning to retire that year, or others who have already been told to leave the organisation.' One GE executive included an employee who had died two months previously. If you are that queasy a manager, Mr Welch says, it is time for you to go too.

It is hard to argue with either GE's success or Mr Welch's. But what works at GE does not always work elsewhere. GE, for example, has been a successful conglomerate. Other multibusiness groups, such as Tyco in the US and Hanson in the UK, have proved less sustainable. The perennial rout of the Cs may have served GE well; I suspect that most companies would make a mess of identifying their worst performers.

Marks and Spencer, the once-great UK retailer, was last month defeated at an industrial tribunal by Michael Davies, a senior manager it had dismissed. Several newspapers reported that Mr Davies was sacked because he had been too modest in a self-assessment exercise. M&S insisted this was untrue; his self-assessment scores were in line with those of his colleagues. It was his line manager, Paul Nursaw, who had given him low scores. Mr Nursaw told the tribunal he had placed Mr Davies in, wait for it, 'the bottom ten'. M&S said it conceded the case because it accepted it had failed to follow proper procedures, although Mr Davies had agreed not to demand compensation beyond the £140,000 pay-off he had already received.

What a murky tale. The McKinsey consultants say it is vital to get the legal details right when you nail your bottom tenth. That is certainly true. If '10 per cent out' becomes a worldwide trend, no one will benefit more than the lawyers. Nor will the annual search for the Cs do much for those other corporate must-haves: trust and teamwork. How much knowledge sharing will there be in a team whose members spend their year calculating how to escape being one of the terminated tenth?

There is another danger: that fear of being in the bottom 10 per cent will encourage reluctance to stand out from the crowd. Company recruitment advertisements incessantly demand 'out of the box thinking'. But who is more likely to come up with innovative ideas? Is it the raucous group that discusses the same television programmes every morning, drinks together every night and heads off en masse to play in the chairman's golf challenge each spring? Or are new ideas more likely to come from Joe in the corner, who does not say much, does not know a birdie from a bunker but can sort out all his software glitches without bothering the help desk? And who is more likely to be labelled a C?

Source: Article by Michael Skapinker, *Financial Times*, 13 February 2002

Questions

1 How would you describe the cultural values at General Electric?

2 What are the implications for knowledge sharing in a culture that fires the weakest 10 per cent of staff each year?

3 What are the advantages and drawbacks of a 'tough-guy, macho culture' described in this article?

Introduction

The failure of many information or knowledge management systems is often as a result of cultural factors rather than technological oversights. Culture, by its nature, is a nebulous subject with a variety of perspectives and interpretations. In practice, we may be left with expressions such as 'We don't do it that way around here!'. To the puzzled inquirer, this chapter is about gaining some clarity about the notion of culture and its historic roots in the organisational climate literature. We explore the variety of surface manifestations of culture in organisations as well as its deeper expressions in values, beliefs, attitudes and assumptions. We follow this path so as to better understand the emerging literature in knowledge-sharing cultures. The current literature suggests that such cultures can be cultivated through the deployment of certain artefacts, the promotion of certain values such as 'care' and a healthy dialectic between cooperative and competitive cultures. We proceed to understand the nature of informal groupings called 'communities of practice' in organisations and how they differ from more formal groupings such as project teams. The importance of storytelling and narratives for embedding tacit knowledge cognitively and socially is investigated in detail. The organisational benefits of communities of practice are explored and a blueprint for their development is provided.

Understanding organisational culture and climate

In an attempt to understand social environments and their effects or interactions with individuals, there have been two distinct concepts that have developed in the literature: organisational climate and organisational culture. Organisational climate has much older roots in psychology and was strongly influenced by field theory (Lewin 1948; Lewin 1951). In the Lewinian understanding of social environments, the individual is assumed to be separate from the environment, acting either as a subject or an agent, and the underlying framework for field theory can be expressed simply as:

$$B = f(P,E)$$

where the social processes equate to B=behaviour, P=person and E=environment. In its early conception, climate could be created through leadership styles which produced dependable social situations in three categories, namely autocratic, democratic and laissez-faire (Lewin *et al.* 1939). The climate literature comes from a positivist, functionalist paradigm and measurement of this concept has been strongly influenced by the quantitative measurement of attitudes using the Likert scale (Likert 1967). The use of surveys has been predominant in this approach. One early example is a study of the impact of organisational climate on individual motivation (Litwin and Stringer 1961) which classifies organisational climate along nine dimensions: structure, responsibility, reward, risk, warmth, support, standards, conflict and identity. Most research in this area has focused on measuring either the individual's perception of individual attributes (the 'psychological climate') or the perceptions of organisational attributes (the 'organisational climate'). Hence, debate has continued on whether climate is a 'shared perception' or a 'shared set of conditions' (Denison 1996).

The weakness in the organisational climate literature has been the lack of agreement on metrics, the poor contingent relationships and the lack of clear categorisations of climate that could be used by managers. In response to these weaknesses and a critique of the dominant positivist paradigm of the climate literature, the study of organisational culture developed from strong anthropological and sociological roots. The literature on organisational climate has been relatively neglected recently. Cultural researchers have taken a more qualitative approach and become more interested in inductive accounts to understand the complexity of social phenomena.

One of the most influential anthropologists in cultural studies has been Geertz's (1973) interpretative theory of culture. Geertz's approach is 'semiotic' and focuses on language and symbols to discern what ordinary people consider to be significant in the 'organisational glue' or social contexts that develop through interaction. Other anthropological roots of cultural studies come from symbolic interaction (Mead 1934) and questioning values and practices in western societies. The other main intellectual tradition of cultural research is sociology, looking at social reality from a variety of social construction perspectives (Berger and Luckmann 1966; Durkheim 1984; Weber 1947) such as myths, rituals, symbols, norms and ambiguity. An interesting development of cultural scholarship has been the promotion of culture from a postmodern and critical theory perspective (Alvesson 2002). Culture is not inside people's head but exists in the interactions and material objects where symbols and meanings are publicly expressed.

Pause for thought

Culture is often described as the way we do things around here. How would you describe the culture of your organisation? How homogeneous would you describe this culture? Are you aware of subcultures that exist within your organisation? How prevalent are they? Have you observed any changes in your organisational culture over the past few years? What were the driving forces for these changes and how effective were these changes in your opinion?

As ontological and epistemological assumptions of climate and culture begin to merge, it is clear that these two concepts become less differentiated (Ashkanasy et al. 2000b). Quantitative survey-based research is seen in climate research (O'Reilly et al. 1991) and interpretivist dimensions can be found in cultural studies. A realist perspective that tries to integrate these two concepts and builds on the popular three-level model of culture (Schein 1985b) is shown in Figure 7.1 (p. 189). Organisational climate is the static or temporary phenomenon found in norms and organisational artefacts that can be determined through traditional survey-based approaches. In contrast, organisational culture is the result of processes that arise from dynamic interactions between individuals or members of a social system. The 'cultural soup' or structures that underlie organisational cultures are the deeply held values, beliefs, attitudes and assumptions in the organisation.

There are a multivariate number of definitions on organisational culture and climate which are based on the ontological and epistemological positions of the researchers. One definition that tends to contrast the widely accepted distinctions between the two phenomena is (Denison 1996):

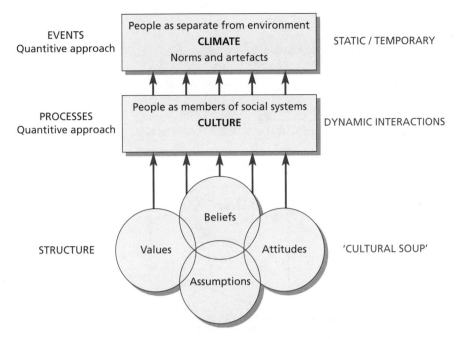

Figure 7.1 Distinction between culture and climate in organisational environments

'Culture refers to the deep structure of organizations, which is rooted in the values, beliefs and assumptions held by organizational members. Meaning is established through socialization to a variety of identity groups that converge in the workplace. Interaction reproduces a symbolic world that gives culture both a great stability and a certain precarious and fragile nature rooted in the dependence of the system on individual cognition and action.

Climate, in contrast, portrays organisational environments as being rooted in the organisation's value system, but tends to present these social environments in relatively static terms, describing them in terms of a fixed (and broadly applicable) set of dimensions. Thus, climate is often considered as temporary, subject to direct control, and largely limited to those aspects of the social environment that are consciously perceived by organisational members.'

Norms, artefacts and symbols

At a more surface or superficial level, we have the manifestation of culture as norms, artefacts and symbols, as shown in Figure 7.2 (p. 190). Norms are expectations of appropriate and inappropriate behaviour. This may be norms about dress code or issues such as expectations surrounding performance and handling conflict (bottling it up or confronting it). Norms attach approval or disapproval to holding certain beliefs and attitudes and acting in particular ways. They can vary along two dimensions (O'Reilly 1989):

- intensity of approval or disapproval attached to an expectation;
- degree of consistency with which a norm is shared.

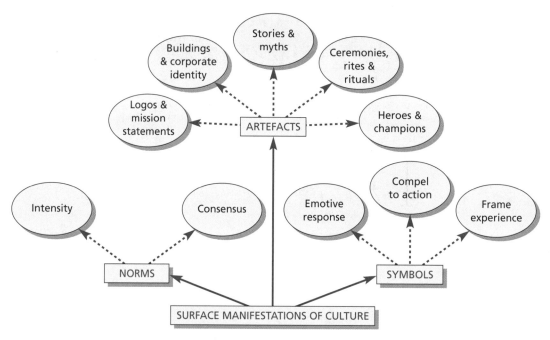

Figure 7.2 Surface manifestations of organisational culture

For example, there may be consensus over senior management values such as respect and integrity but little intensity one way or the other. Or there may be strong approval and disapproval for the same value such as excellence in the organisation leading to great intensity but little consensus. When great intensity and consensus exists in an organisation, this leads to a strong culture where organisational members share a common set of expectations. If there is a weak culture in the organisation (low intensity and consensus), there is a greater likelihood of sub-cultures forming. An example of norms for promoting innovation in organisations is provided in Table 7.1. These collective norms are based on a study of over 500 managers from diverse industries sharing very similar expectations on what they saw as necessary for innovation in organisations. A useful tool in a change management program would be to conduct a survey of existing and desired norms and base organisational interventions on assisting a convergence between these two norms.

Table 7.1 Examples of Norms that Promote Innovation (O'Reilly 1989)

Norms to Promote Creativity	Norms to Promote Implementation
Risk Taking	**Common Goals**
Acceptance of mistakes	Eliminate mixed messages
No punishment for failure	Build consensus
Rewards for Change	**Autonomy**
Ideas are valued	Freedom to act
Top management support and attention	Minimise bureaucracy
Openness	**Belief in Action**
Listen better	Anxiety about timeliness
Encourage lateral thinking	Eagerness to get things done

Artefacts also provide us with shared systems of meaning that construct organisational life. They can exist as material objects, physical layouts, technology, language and behaviour patterns as well as procedures and practices in organisations (Brown 1998).

Material artefacts can exist as company logos and mission statements. Company logos give us clear signals of the meaning and values behind them. Mission statements inform the reader about company aspirations in terms of its principal aims, beliefs and values. However, there may be a serious gap between the senior management rhetoric glossed over in these mission statements and the reality at ground level.

The corporate architecture and identity in terms of appearance and uniform also provide clues about an organisation's culture. The nature of the building, its external appearance, its internal layout and furniture can provide signals to organisational members about how the company values them and their interactions with others. For example, the organisation may provide open-plan offices, water fountains and subsidised restaurant facilities to encourage interaction and dialogue with different levels of the organisation. Or the corporate building may be compartmentalised to prevent dialogue and reinforce divisional or operational boundaries. In each case, we learn a bit more about the organisational culture. Many large organisations commission buildings by renowned architects to reinforce their identity and show clear signs of opulence.

Stories are powerful artefacts that tell us about problems and solutions, disasters and triumphs. They also tell us about informal rules and procedures; how things are done around here. War stories encourage an understanding of what happened and why in a particular circumstance. They also convey indicators of status and the norms of compliance and deviation from rules. Stories enable organisations to develop their own unique identity. A common deviant of stories are myths. They are based on unjustified beliefs and recounted as stories. They serve the purpose of influencing action in particular contexts. For example, there may be myths about super-human characteristics of certain individuals or groups and derogatory characteristics of some others. These may be perpetuated as part of the organisational culture even though they bear little resemblance to reality.

Recurrent patterns of behaviour such as ceremonies, rites and rituals remind and reinforce organisational members of cultural values (Brown 1998). Ceremonies may include presentations and prizes for high achievers. Corporate heroes or champions may be celebrated in order to share their success stories and the values communicated through them. Rites may be planned activities such as rites of passage from one role or status to another. Rituals may include company retreats and away days. In each case, these cultural artefacts help individuals develop a deeper sense of company values.

Organisational culture can be construed as a network of meanings or shared experiences that provide members with a shared and accepted reality (Pettigrew 1979). This shared reality can derive from certain symbols that may stand for a multiplicity of meanings that serve to link emotions and interpretations and compel people to action. For example, working late at night above one's contracted hours may symbolise loyalty to an organisation. Hence, symbols can act to reflect aspects of organisational culture, frame experiences that may be vague or controversial, and mobilise members to action through their emotional response to a symbol (Ashkanasy *et al.* 2000b). Symbols are rich in meaning and can occur as a word, a statement, an action or a material phenomenon. There are private symbols and collective symbols which stand ambiguously for something else or more than the object itself (Alvesson 2002).

Values, beliefs, attitudes and assumptions

All too often, senior managers and chief executives place considerable effort in formulating their corporate values statement. However, why is it that many of these values statements can be bland, hollow and meaningless? They may lack credibility and have the undesired effect of generating cynicism, alienation and insincerity. The corporate values may stand for nothing with organisational members and a gulf emerges between organisational rhetoric and reality. Instead of differentiating a company by clarifying its identity and motivating employees, they may actually have the opposite effect of being destructive to the organisation. For example, the relatively meaningless corporate values of Enron are: Communication, Respect, Integrity and Excellence.

Pause for thought
What do you see as potential problems in a values led organisation or a values led society? How would you describe your own values? From your experience, have you had encounters where your values have differed dramatically from your organisation's values? If so, please describe the nature of disparity in values and how you managed the situation? Given that many organisations work in multicultural environments, what would you consider to be some pitfalls in organisational values?

In contrast, real values are far from being bland and can be painful for organisations as they constrain strategic and operational freedom as well as individual behaviour. They demand constant monitoring and may leave executives open to criticism for minor breaches. Organisational values fall into four categories and it is important to avoid confusion between them (Lencioni 2002):

- Core values are deeply ingrained principles that guide a company's actions. They are never compromised for convenience or economic gain and often reflect the values of the company founders.
- Aspirational values are values to support a new strategy. They are values that the company needs to compete in the future but currently lacks.
- Permission-to-play values are the minimum behavioural and social standards required of employees in the organisation.
- Accidental values are values that arise spontaneously over time. They reflect the common interests or personalities of employees. They may be positive, such as inclusivity of employees, or negative, such as an ingrained mistrust of management.

But what is the best way of developing a corporate values statement? The traditional method of the HR departments conducting numerous surveys and focus groups to build consensus is to be avoided because such consensus may integrate values that do not belong to the organisation and give an equal weighting to all employee contributions. For example, senior managers may feel that certain values espoused by certain employees may better belong to other organisations than their own. Hence, a more appropriate response to values statement development is to form a small team of executives including the chief executive to discuss values over a long time frame and provide enough time for reflection of the consequences of these values in the workplace (Lencioni 2002). Core values guide every action and decision that a company makes. They form the fabric underlying every recruitment, selection, appraisal and rewards policy. If the core values are poorly implemented, they can lead to the mistrust and cynicism of senior management motives. Core values require constant vigilance to make explicit what a firm stands for and to act as a rallying call to employees to guide their action. They can reinforce individual commitment and willingness to give energy and loyalty to an organisation. Individuals may make sacrifices and investments based on corporate values.

Values have considerable potency as they tend to link the social, cognitive and behavioural dimensions of an organisation. The social aspects characterise the history of experiences and understandings of groups within the organisation. The cognitive aspects draw on the history and experiences of individuals within these groups and the behavioural aspects show how these values affect individual actions and interactions (Ashkanasy *et al.* 2000b).

Beliefs are another core manifestation of culture and concern what people think is true. For example, some executives may believe that focusing organisational efforts on efficiency is more likely to lead to greater organisational performance whereas others may believe it is an innovation strategy. Sometimes values and beliefs may be hard to distinguish, especially where the belief and value such as innovation are closely related. Values could be considered as enduring beliefs where certain actions are considered socially more appropriate than others (Rokeach 1973).

Our attitudes connect our beliefs and values with feelings (Brown 1998). They are a learnt predisposition to act in a favourable or unfavourable manner to a given circumstance and involve evaluations based on our feelings. Attitudes are more enduring than opinions and have an impact on an individual's motivation. They can result in prejudices and stereotypes, such as the negative attitudes towards quality circles in the United States as workers did not feel that sitting down in groups and talking about quality was beneficial.

Basic assumptions are the taken-for-granted solutions to particular problems (Brown 1998). They are the 'theories-in-use' (Argyris and Schon 1978) that perpetuate organisational routines and single-loop learning. Assumptions are unconsciously held, making them difficult to confront or make explicit. They are highly complex interpretations based on our beliefs, values and emotions. One typology of basic assumptions considers five dimensions (Schein 1985a):

● whether an organisation dominates the external environment or is dominated by it;
● whether truth and reality are received dogma, rules and procedures, a consequence of debate or what works;
● whether people are inherently lazy or self-motivated;
● whether 'doing' and work are more primary than 'being' and valuing employees' private lives;
● whether human interaction is based on individualism or collectivism.

Typologies of organisational culture

In the language of organisational culture, it may be useful to provide classifications for different configurations of culture found in organisations. It is not expected that organisations will necessarily fall into these idealised types, but their characteristics may help organisations understand their social environments. Two popular typologies of organisational culture are provided below (Brown 1998; Deal and Kennedy 1982; Handy 1985; Scholz 1987). The Handy typology has been very influential among cultural scholars and suggests four types of culture (Handy 1985), as shown in Figure 7.3:

- Power cultures are characterised as a web with a person or small group of people at the centre. There are few rules and people tend to act politically and are more concerned about ends rather than means. Such organisations can react quickly to environmental changes but may suffer from high turnover rates if suitable people are not recruited.
- Role cultures are characterised by bureaucracies where rules, procedures and job descriptions tend to predominate. They are successful in stable environments but may have difficulties adapting to more turbulent environments.
- Task cultures are characterised by project or matrix organisations that bring together the appropriate resources and competence required for effective team functioning. Mutual respect is based on ability rather than status or age. These cultures can be highly effective for innovative projects but are less successful where there is an emphasis on cost rationalisation and economies of scale.
- Person cultures are characterised by individual autonomy and collective action based on fulfilling individual self-interests. Individuals decide on their work allocations rather than it being a function of a central body. Examples of person cultures may be found in academia, among architects or barristers.

Another popular cultural typology is based on the degree of risk in company activities and the speed of feedback on actions and decisions, as shown in Figure 7.4 (p. 195, Brown 1998; Deal and Kennedy 1982). In this framework, the four idealised cultural typologies are:

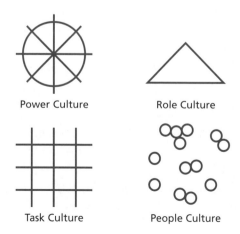

Figure 7.3 **Handy's typology of culture (Handy 1985)**

- tough-guy, macho culture characterised by high risks and fast feedback on actions. This culture focuses on speed and can lead to internal competition and tensions as individuals take high risks. These cultures are predominantly uncooperative and can lead to high staff turnover. Similarities with the power culture?;

- work-hard, play-hard culture characterised by low-risk but quick-feedback environments. These cultures can be fun and action oriented but may suffer from 'quick-fix' solutions and lack of reflection in crisis situations. Similar to a task culture?;

- bet-your-company culture characterised by high-risk but low-feedback environments. There is a greater tendency towards cooperative endeavours and producing innovations in such cultures. Similarities with a people culture?;

- process cultures exist in low-risk and slow feedback environments. Due to the low levels of feedback, the organisations are characterised by procedures, rules and hierarchies. They can be threatening in highly changeable environments as they are unable to respond quickly. Similarities with a role culture?

Measuring organisational culture

Despite the strong anthropological and sociological roots of cultural research, there have been numerous attempts to conceptualise and quantify the construct of 'organisational culture'. In this sense, the quantification of culture as an instrument has adopted the traditional methodologies found in climate research. This relates to the more observable and accessible levels of culture, the surface manifestations. If one accepts the realist notion of organisational culture as a process (see Figure 7.1), is it feasible or meaningful to quantify this process?

Currently, there is little consensus about the nature of the 'organisational culture' construct and its various subconstructs. Hence, a number of instruments have been developed with a varying level of homage to existing theory. The types of surveys can be classified into two categories (Ashkanasy *et al.* 2000a):

- *Typing surveys* classify organisations into particular typologies such as the Handy or Deal and Kennedy ones shown above. Such instruments attempt to generate a number of organisational culture 'types' that have certain behaviours and values

Figure 7.4 **Deal and Kennedy's typology of culture**

Figure 7.5 The typing and profiling nature of the organisational culture inventory

linked with them. These surveys can provide senior managers with snapshots on their current positions and their desired outcomes from a cultural change management programme. The drawbacks with these typing surveys is that they assume that organisations fit neatly into strictly defined categories rather than conforming to a number of different types that demonstrate their uniqueness. The different types do not assume a continuity between the different typologies.

● *Profiling surveys* aim to develop a profile of the organisation on multiple categories of norms, behaviours and values. There are three types of profiling surveys, namely effectiveness surveys, descriptive surveys and fit profiles. *Effectiveness surveys* tend to assess organisational values associated with high levels of performance. *Descriptive surveys* purely measure organisational values. *Fit profiles* tend to assess the level of fit between an individual and an organisation.

Organisational culture instruments can be used in a variety of contexts: to monitor and evaluate organisational change, to identify cultures of high-performing teams and to facilitate mergers and acquisitions. There are numerous culture instruments available but few that meet the acid test of high levels of reliability and show clear evidence of validity (convergent, discriminant, nomological and known groups). One such instrument that meets these rigours of instrument development and is widely used is the 'organisational culture inventory' (OCI) (Cooke and Lafferty 1987). The instrument is based on two subconstructs of 'concern for people or tasks' and 'behaviour driven by security of self-actualisation needs', as shown in Figure 7.5. The instrument provides a typing survey in terms of three categories of culture as well as a profile survey of the organisation against a variety of norms. The twelve norms for any organisation can be plotted on an OCI circumplex, as shown in Figure 7.6 (p. 197), and the descriptions of each norm are given below.

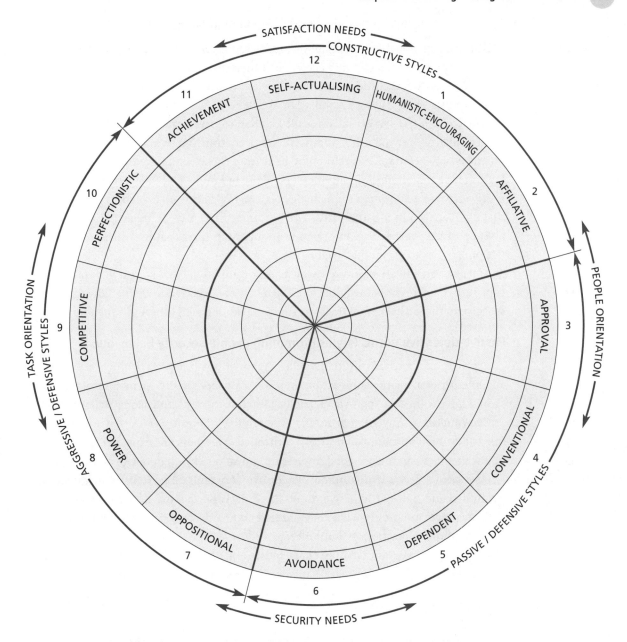

Figure 7.6 Organizational culture inventory circumplex.
Copyright 1987, 1994 by Human Synergistics, Inc. All Rights Reserved.
Reproduced by permission

◗ Description of the twelve OCI styles

The following text is from *Organizational Culture Inventory* by R.A. Cooke and J.C. Lafferty, 1983, 1986, 1987, 1989, Plymouth, Michigan, USA: Human Synergistics. Copyright 1989 by Human Synergistics, Inc. Adapted by permission.

Constructive norms (styles promoting satisfaction behaviours)

Achievement: an achievement culture characterises organisations that do things well and value members who set and accomplish their own goals. Members are expected to set challenging but realistic goals, establish plans to reach those goals, and pursue them with enthusiasm. (Pursuing a standard of excellence)

Self-actualising: a self-actualising culture characterises organisations that value creativity, quality over quantity, and both task accomplishment and individual growth. Members are encouraged to gain enjoyment from their work, develop themselves, and take on new and interesting activities. (Thinking in unique and independent ways)

Humanistic-encouraging: a humanistic-encouraging culture characterises organisations that are managed in a participative and person-centred way. Members are expected to be supportive, constructive and open to influence in their dealings with one another. (Helping others to grow and develop)

Affiliative: an affiliative culture characterises organisations that place a high priority on constructive interpersonal relationships. Members are expected to be friendly, open, and sensitive to the satisfaction of their work group. (Dealing with others in a friendly way)

Passive-defensive norms (styles promoting people-security behaviours)

Approval: an approval culture describes organisations in which conflicts are avoided and interpersonal relationships are pleasant – at least superficially. Members feel that they should agree with, gain approval of, and be liked by others. ('Going along' with others)

Conventional: a conventional culture is descriptive of organisations that are conservative, traditional and bureaucratically controlled. Members are expected to conform, follow the rules and make a good impression. (Always following policies and practices)

Dependent: a dependent culture is descriptive of organisations that are hierarchically controlled and non-participative. Centralised decision making in such organisations leads members to do only what they are told and to clear all decisions with superiors. (Pleasing those in positions of authority)

Avoidance: an avoidance culture characterises organisations that fail to reward success but nevertheless punish mistakes. This negative reward system leads members to shift responsibilities to others and avoid any possibility of being blamed for a mistake. (Waiting for others to act first)

Aggressive-defensive norms (styles promoting task-security behaviours)

Oppositional: an oppositional culture describes organisations in which confrontation and negativism are rewarded. Members gain status and influence by being critical and thus are reinforced to oppose the ideas of others. (Pointing out flaws)

Power: a power culture is descriptive of non-participative organisations structured on the basis of authority inherent in members' positions. Members believe they will be rewarded for taking charge, controlling subordinates and, at the same time, being responsive to the demands of superiors. (Building up one's power base)

Competitive: a competitive culture is one in which winning is valued and members are rewarded for outperforming one another. Members operate in a 'win–lose' framework and believe they must work against (rather than with) their peers to be noticed. (Turning the job into a contest)

Perfectionistic: a perfectionistic culture characterises organisations in which perfectionism, persistence and hard work are valued. Members feel they must avoid any mistake, keep track of everything and work long hours to attain narrowly defined objectives. (Doing things perfectly)

In international contexts and particularly among multinational corporations, there has been considerable interest in the role of national cultures on organisational cultures. For example, do 'American organisational cultures' or 'Japanese organisational cultures' lead to greater effectiveness? One seminal study in this area conducted a descriptive survey of national culture across 40 nations and derived distinctions between national cultures along four value dimensions (Hofstede 1980). The theoretical basis for this study arises from a psychological, anthropological and sociological review of national character (Inkeles and Levinson 1969). The four value dimensions that differentiate national character are (Hofstede 1980):

- *power distance* – the extent to which the less powerful members of organisations and institutions accept and expect that power is distributed unequally. (Example: high power distance – Malaysia and Venezuela; low power distance – Sweden, New Zealand);
- *individualism versus collectivism* – the extent to which individuals are integrated into groups. (Example: individualist – USA and Netherlands; collectivist – Ecuador and Indonesia);
- *masculinity versus femininity* – assertiveness and competitiveness versus modesty and caring. (Example: Masculine – Japan and Mexico; feminine – Norway and Costa Rica);
- *uncertainty avoidance* – intolerance for uncertainty and ambiguity. (Example: high uncertainty avoidance – Greece and Guatemala; low uncertainty avoidance – Singapore and Denmark).

Pause for thought

Reflect on situations where you have had cultural misunderstandings among friends or colleagues at work. How did you manage those situations and what lessons did you learn? How could some of those misunderstandings have been avoided and better cultural understanding be promoted in your organisation?

Creating knowledge-sharing cultures

Many executives aspire to develop knowledge-sharing cultures where knowledge is shared easily among organisational members through social and electronic networks. This aspiration is also a primary assumption behind the knowledge management literature that knowledge-sharing cultures are more conducive to knowledge creation and enhanced performance. But how do we turn this aspirational value of knowledge sharing into a core value? Let's assume that the culture in many organisations may be hostile to knowledge sharing and more conducive to knowledge hoarding. For example, 'power' or 'tough-guy' cultures may be highly political and uncooperative environments. What interventions are likely to help senior managers in these circumstances steer a clear path in managing cultural

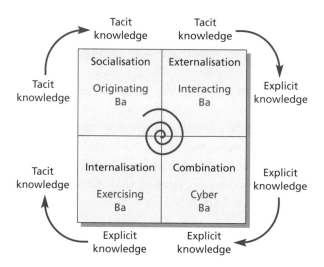

Figure 7.7 Knowledge conversion and characteristics of 'Ba' (Nonaka and Konno 1998)

change? (See next chapter.) If the interventions are successful, have we unintentionally changed strong effective cultures with little consideration of their strategic impact?

Are there dangers in assuming that knowledge-sharing cultures are effective in all situations? If we follow this line of reasoning, one could argue that ultimately organisations need to move towards idealised forms of cultures such as task or person cultures that promote knowledge sharing. However, we know that there is a diversity of cultures that are equally effective in different industries. The reality is that cultural research in this area is limited and has not begun to address the complexity of managing aspirational values of knowledge sharing and their likely impact on the organisation. If such values are managed wrongly, they may appear hollow, lack credibility and generate widespread cynicism. Organisational members will pay lip-service to these perceived management fads and the interventions will fail to win over 'hearts and minds'.

Our current understanding of developing cultures for knowledge creation is based on the deployment of artefacts (Nonaka and Konno 1998), the promotion of certain values (von Krough 1999), a healthy cultural dialectic (Jashapara 2003) and certain prescriptions based on a few case studies (McDermott and O'Dell 2001; Newell *et al.* 2002). The deployment of artefacts, 'Ba' or spaces builds on an earlier 'SECI' model of knowledge conversion between different forms of tacit and explicit knowledge (Nonaka 1991), as shown in Figure 7.7.

The concept of 'Ba' is new to many western palettes and translates to a place or space in Japanese. This artefact of space or 'Ba' can be physical, virtual or mental. On first impressions, this model is examining the surface manifestations of culture in terms of artefacts. The model does not suggest whether the 'mental spaces' of 'Ba' go more deeply and manifest as attitudes, beliefs and values. There are four types of 'Ba' which tend to facilitate the different aspects of the knowledge conversion process (Nonaka and Konno 1998):

● Socialisation involves sharing tacit knowledge between individuals. Tacit knowledge is considered as more than 'know how' and can include intuitions, hunches and insights. It is deeply embedded in a person's values and beliefs. The space that contributes to socialisation is 'Originating Ba' where individuals share feelings, emotions, experiences and mental models. The values that support the transfer of this tacit knowledge are care, love, trust and commitment.

- Externalisation involves the articulation of tacit into explicit knowledge. This conversion normally occurs through dialogue and the use of figurative language, metaphors, narratives, images and creative inference. The space required to facilitate this knowledge conversion is 'Interacting Ba'. The main characteristic of this artefact is dialogue where individuals share their mental models and reflect and analyse their own understandings.

- Combination involves conversion of explicit knowledge into more complex explicit forms. This may arise from capturing, collecting, sorting, editing and integrating new explicit knowledge. Such conversions are promoted through 'Cyber Ba'. These cyber spaces encourage the documentation of knowledge and the use of databases and groupware tools.

- Internalisation relies on converting explicit into tacit knowledge. This usually occurs through experience (learning-by-doing) and training. The spaces that encourage such conversions are 'Exercising Ba', characterised by reflection through learning, training and mentoring.

A development of the 'Originating Ba' artefact promoting socialisation is the suggestion that the primary value in knowledge creation is 'care' (von Krough 1998). Care is characterised by considerable mutual trust, active empathy, access to help, lenience in judgement and courage. Sounds like love but without the organisational embarrassment! The emphasis is on organisations to cherish the value of care/love at all costs. If this value is not nurtured, the likely consequences are the emergence of greater levels of fear where members reinforce routines and scare stories, abandon good ideas and stunt any transformations. The ways to cultivate care are:

- incentive schemes that encourage care-related behaviour;
- mentoring programmes to encourage senior members to transfer their knowledge;
- training programmes in care behaviour;
- project debriefings with sufficient time for reflection;
- social events to improve organisational relationships.

The assumption from the 'care' perspective is that supportive or cooperative cultures are more likely to result in knowledge creation. This view is challenged as highly cooperative or supportive environments (such as a kibbutz) can discourage change and if organisational members perceive a need for change, they may be forced to challenge the dominant ideology which breeds politics and fear. Instead, research shows that effective organisations tend to operate in a 'zone of knowledge creation' in a dialectic between the internal forces of cooperation and competition (Jashapara 2003), as shown in Figure 7.8 (p. 202). Extreme forms of these idealised cultures are likely to suppress the very knowledge they are trying to create. In this conception, the dialectic of knowl-

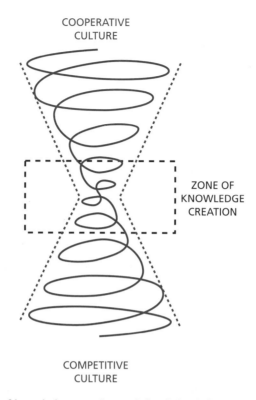

COOPERATIVE
CULTURE

ZONE OF
KNOWLEDGE
CREATION

COMPETITIVE
CULTURE

Figure 7.8 The zone of knowledge creation and the dialectic between cooperative and competitive cultures

edge-sharing cultures can be viewed as a continual struggle by groups of organisational members to impose their values and identities on the role of others (Carroll 1995).

Efforts in cultural engineering are often doomed to fail if they do not support the

Pause for thought   Reflect on your experiences of knowledge sharing. What social environments have made you feel more comfortable about sharing your knowledge? Do you think that incentives would help you share knowledge more easily in your organisation? If so, what form do you think these incentives should take? Are there aspects of your knowledge base that you would be unwilling to share under any circumstance? If so, can you elaborate on the unique quality of this prized knowledge asset?

more deeply held organisational values and assumptions. An alternative approach adopted by many effective companies is to build knowledge management interventions that fit the embedded culture. In some organisations, such as PricewaterhouseCoopers (PwC) and American Management Systems (AMS), knowledge sharing was explicit and directly informed corporate strategy. Clear knowledge-sharing programmes were developed including reward and recognition initiatives, and distinct roles and responsibilities related to knowledge sharing, such as the appointment of a chief knowledge officer. In other organisations like Ford and Lotus Development, knowledge sharing was more implicitly embedded into everyday routines and projects. There were different degrees of formal, informal and electronic networks to promote knowledge sharing. A number of lessons arise from different attempts to create a knowledge-sharing culture (McDermott and O'Dell 2001; Newell *et al.* 2002):

- make a visible connection between sharing knowledge and practical business goals;
- match the style of the organisation to the intervention (e.g. developing artefacts such as social events, language and websites);
- promote appropriate reward and recognition interventions;
- provide adequate resources to encourage human networks of knowledge sharing such as time to share ideas and information in communities of practice;
- try to link knowledge sharing with widely and deeply held core values rather than aspirational values;
- encourage 'boundary-spanning' individuals who can translate knowledge and experiences from one group to another;
- support a committed project champion who can enthuse and motivate others with the knowledge-sharing initiative. Bring together people in the organisation who already share ideas and knowledge.

Cultural stickiness: developing communities of practice

Explicit knowledge is relatively easy to codify, store and retrieve as knowledge objects using traditional technologies. However, how do we tackle the externalisation, sharing and integration of tacit knowledge that may be embedded within the minds of organisational members? The holy grail of competitive advantage may be closely related to exploiting the cognitive and social aspects of tacit knowledge. It is often through dialogue and interaction with others that we are able to contact the inner depths of our tacit knowledge and generate new ideas and insights. Many organisations have recognised the intrinsic value of water coolers, coffee machines, subsidised canteens and common rooms as being instrumental in facilitating this creative process.

Another approach to cultivating tacit knowledge that moves beyond organisational artefacts is the notion of 'communities of practice' (Brown and Duguid 1991; Lave and Wenger 1991). Communities of practice are informal, self-selecting groups that are open ended, without any deadlines or deliverables. They exist to serve a number of cognitive and social interests, set their own agendas and elect their own leadership. Communities of practice can be defined as follows (Wenger *et al.* 2002):

> *'Communities of practice are groups of people who share a concern, a set of problems, or a passion about a topic, and who deepen their knowledge and expertise in this area by interacting on an ongoing basis.'*

The World Bank sees communities of practice as the main component of its knowledge management strategy in its attempts to become a 'knowledge bank'. In this context, tacit knowledge is acknowledged as embedded in organisational practice and interactions rather than simply in the domain of an individual's head. Communities of practice can also exist online as communities of transaction (buying and selling), communities of interest (related to a topic), role-playing communities and communities of relationships (around a shared life experience) (Newell *et al.* 2002). But what are the characteristics of communities of practice that distinguish them from other organisational groupings? A comparison of different groupings in organisations is shown in Table 7.2.

In formal groupings, the common approach to team learning is to adopt tools such

Table 7.2 Characteristics of formal and informal groupings in organisations (Wenger and Snyder 2000)

	FORMAL GROUPINGS 'CANONICAL PRACTICE'		INFORMAL GROUPINGS 'NON-CANONICAL PRACTICE'	
	Work group	Project team	Informal network	Community of practice
What is their purpose?	To deliver a product or service	To accomplish a specific task	To collect and pass on business information	To develop members' capabilities; to build and exchange knowledge
Who belongs?	Everyone who reports to group's manager	Employees assigned by senior management	Friends and business acquaintances	Members who select themselves
What holds it together?	Job requirements and common goals	Project's milestones and goals	Mutual needs	Passion, commitment and identification with the group's expertise
How long does it last?	Until the next reorganisation	Until the project is completed	As long as people have a reason to connect	As long as there is interest in maintaining the group

as brainstorming or cognitive mapping to encourage dialogue and discussion. However, the success of such approaches may often depend on the motivations (or lack of) of team members, their composition and power relations underlying the team and organisational culture. For example, the use of 'quality circles' was highly successful in Japan where team members got together regularly to share problems and discuss ways of improving work practices. However, the same concept failed to gain acceptance in the US or the UK due to major cultural reservations about discussing problems.

The major interest in communities of practice is that they provide significant benefits to organisations than do more formalised forms of activity. On the social side, they provide individuals with a sense of identity, confidence and trust through meeting like-minded individuals who share similar problems and outlooks. In terms of tacit knowledge, they provide a forum to facilitate knowledge creation through externalisation of tacit knowledge, the sharing of knowledge and increasing knowledge flows, enhanced creativity and integration of collective knowledge. Some direct benefits of communities of practice in organisations are (Wenger and Snyder 2000):

- they help drive strategy;
- they start new lines of business;
- they solve problems quickly;
- they transfer best practices;
- they develop professional skills;
- they help companies recruit and retain talent.

The informal interactions of organisational members in communities of practice are considered to encourage reflection of practice rather than simply reworking everyday processes. People come together from similar backgrounds from around the organisation with a passion and interest in improving practice. Communities of practice can allow organisational members to think outside the box and to question organisational routines where appropriate. This does not necessarily mean that such questioning will always lead to radical innovation, dynamic capabilities or double-loop learning (Swan *et al.* 2002; Zollo and Winter 2002).

The commonly cited example of communities of practice is a network of technical reps at Xerox who got together regularly over breakfast, lunch and coffee breaks to share their 'war stories' about problems in servicing photocopiers (Orr 1996). Stories were central to sharing such tacit knowledge and making sense of the collective knowledge. A repertoire of stories formed the collective knowledge over time which was greater than anything one could find in organisational repair manuals. In fact, repair manuals on their own would be incapable of solving many of the problems encountered by these reps. There was banter in their dialogue, laughing at mistakes and frequent questioning of the storyteller to test their own understanding. One story recounted two highly competent reps addressing a near impossible situation that defied all standard procedures. A dialogue pursued between these two reps all afternoon where they went through their reasoning associated with the collective knowledge and stories until they were able to narrow down the potential causes and solve the problem through trial and error. This story of course went back into the collective knowledge and psyche of the reps.

Pause for thought

Reflect on different stories you may have heard in your organisation over the past few months. Describe some of the stories that are foremost in your mind. What role do these stories play in your working life? For example, do they help you to work much better? If so, what aspects of stories have you found useful? How important is the storyteller and can you describe their role in your organisation? How far do these stories make you feel like a communal part of the organisation?

The role of storytelling and narratives for embedding tacit knowledge socially in a community of practice is shown in Figure 7.9 (p. 206). Each story has a connection with certain ideas, lessons and best practice. These ideas relate to different actors in the community of practice who are joined together by strong and weak ties. It is these linkages that provide the embedding of collective tacit knowledge and make it 'sticky' (von Hippel 1994) as it is difficult for other organisations to imitate the complexity of the social and cognitive linkages. This can become a potential source of competitive advantage as it

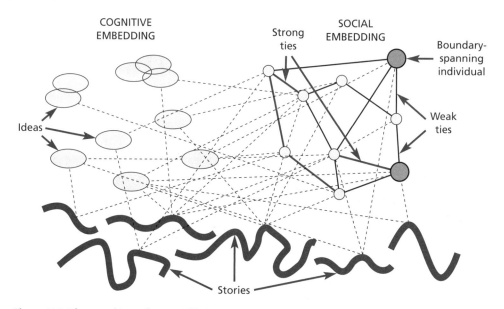

Figure 7.9 The ontology of storytelling

is difficult to commodify the 'sticky' knowledge. Stories are self-perpetuating, creating knowledge that reinforces and renews itself through these connections embedded in work practice. Stories are a powerful way of understanding what happened in a sequence of events and the causes of why they happened (Brown and Duguid 2000). They allow preservation of knowledge and its subsequent diagnosis (Brown and Duguid 1991).

The use of stories and narratives for embedding knowledge in work practice may be considered as a 'perspective making' (Boland and Tenkasi 1995). This is the process by which a community of practice develops and strengthens its knowledge domain and practices. But how do communities of practice facilitate radical innovation or double-loop learning? Many commentators suggest a need for some interaction between different communities of practice as isolated communities can become self-reinforcing and self-deluding, turning core competencies into core rigidities (Blacker 1995; Swan *et al.* 2002). Communication that improves a community's ability to take the knowledge of another community into account is known as 'perspective taking' (Boland and Tenkasi 1995). Radical innovation may require embedding new knowledge and work practices and, at the same time, discarding obsolete practices and routines. The sharing of this new knowledge between communities can be promoted in a number of ways (Brown and Duguid 1998):

- Organisational translators can frame the interests of one community in terms of another's perspective. They may be external mediators or consultants.
- Knowledge brokers or boundary-spanning individuals can participate in several communities. The strength of their 'weak ties' may help facilitate knowledge flows between communities.
- Boundary objects such as documents, contracts and architectural plans may coordinate links between communities who may view the boundary objects from many different perspectives. These boundary objects may also include the use of powerful metaphors.

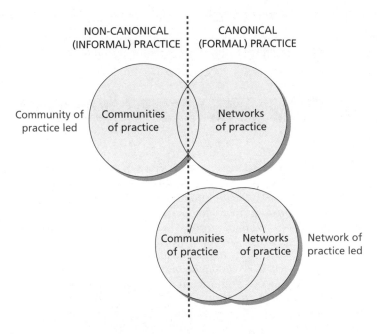

NON-CANONICAL
(INFORMAL) PRACTICE

CANONICAL
(FORMAL) PRACTICE

Community of
practice led

Communities
of practice

Networks
of practice

Communities
of practice

Networks
of practice

Network of
practice led

Figure 7.10 Communities of practice and networks of practice

In many organisations, some members may be engaged in professional or occupational networks outside the organisation. Such communities or 'networks of practice' are different from traditional communities of practice as they are not self-selecting but rely on formal institutional arrangements such as examinations to control membership. They engender shared identity between professionals or occupational groups and could be characterised as an intermediate form between canonical and non-canonical practice (see Table 7.1). When communities of practice are composed more of professional networks or networks of practice as shown in Figure 7.10, the issue of power relations between network members and managers becomes more prominent. Communities of practice cease to fulfil many of the emancipatory needs of members as they pursue a greater managerial or professional agenda (Swan *et al.* 2002). This breeds organisational politics due to competing interests and power struggles requiring more conventional interventions such as negotiation and persuasion of community members.

There are a number of measures that organisations can actively take to cultivate rather than constrain communities of practice. Too much control and intervention may have adverse consequences on their development. The following design features are recommended as enhancing communities of practice (Wenger 2000):

● events to bring the community together and tuned to its sense of purpose;
● leadership – use of multiple leaders such as 'community coordinator', thought leaders and pioneers;
● connectivity – brokering relationships between people to enhance trust and generate dialogue;

- membership – critical mass of members but not too large to dilute participation or interest;
- learning projects – taking responsibility for learning agenda;
- artefacts – producing documents, tools, stories, symbols and websites.

Knowledge ecology at Xerox

It is refreshing to find someone in Silicon Valley who thinks that most information technology sucks. But John Seely Brown, chief scientist at Xerox Corporation and former director of its Palo Alto Research Centre (Parc), is not your archetypal techie.

Mr Brown has spent the best part of 30 years thinking about how technology works and how it is used. He has little time for the trendy 'knowledge management' initiatives inflicted by many companies on their employees. 'Most knowledge management is information management relabelled,' he says. 'Usually there is no attempt to gain a deep understanding of how tacit knowledge works within an organisation, how the social practices compare with the professional practices, or what communities of practice exist within the enterprise. These questions have to do with how people really do work.'

This comment contains the marrow of the very large bone that Mr Brown has to pick with how technology is deployed. Myopic focus on business processes, how they can be streamlined and automated using computers, means managers have lost sight of much messy, informal, value-creating work. 'CEOs talk a lot about value when most of them don't see the value being created in their own workplace. They see the movement of matter, not the creation of ideas,' he says.

Conversation with Mr Brown is like riding on a supercharged Ferris wheel. You see a long way from many perspectives, and end up feeling exhilarated and giddy. It is the sheer range of references that leaves his interlocutors dizzy. Who else would pack the Toyota production system, Claude Levi-Strauss and instant messaging software into a single train of thought?

The breadth is not just for show. From its foundation in the early 1970s, researchers at Xerox Parc were encouraged to apply pioneering technology to how people think, work and learn. This brought to Palo Alto not only hardcore electronic engineers but also, in 1978, the young Mr Brown, who had a background in artificial intelligence and psychology.

This mix of talents produced some important breakthroughs. The modern graphical user interface, ethernet networking and the laser printer were developed in the modernist glass-and-concrete building at 3333 Coyote Hill Road. Less recognised is the work done by Mr Brown and others on learning, cognition and innovation. He notes, for example, that modern working practices often fragment the 'communities of practice' that develop in companies. Professionals end up working in an endless stream of project teams with a lifespan of a few weeks or months. Or process re-engineering demands that field engineers work from home rather than in a central office or depot. 'Formal processes may structure the work but it is communities of practice that do the work,' says Mr Brown. 'So how do we work as part of a cross-functional taskforce while maintaining a sense of presence to our specialist community?'

Thankfully, he comes equipped with answers to such teasers. New technologies such as instant messaging, videoconferencing and workgroup software can help companies repair the technologically inspired vandalism done to their social fabric over the past decade. But, as ever, the technology will help only if the executive mindset is correct. Executives who continue to think of their organisations as machines to be controlled and directed will miss the point. 'What you really want is an organisation with a different metaphor – a knowledge ecology. Think of your organisation as an ecology and you start to think about diversity, cross-pollination of ideas, how social capital is created,' he says, crossing the room to draw another diagram on the whiteboard.

The bigger technological change Mr Brown sees on the near-horizon is the emergence of a new, modular method of building software known as web services. The impact, he says, could be as profound as anything since the dawn of commercial computing in the 1950s. 'The 21st century will bring about the reinvention of Adam Smith,' he says. 'In the industrial age he talked about the power of specialisation. Now we have a platform to bring together specialised services from all over. We have a chance to look for radical specialisation and all the productivity enhancements that flow from that.'

The logic behind this is that computers have imposed a kind of tyranny on companies. First, getting systems to talk with one another within corporations has proved so difficult that giant 'enterprise resource planning' systems have been imposed to tie everything together. Yet these systems are so cumbersome and difficult to change that the structure of the enterprise is, in effect, set in stone. Second, getting systems to talk to one another across corporate boundaries is so difficult that companies have become highly selective about which suppliers they deal with.

Web services, it is claimed, will break this tyranny by providing a lingua franca for computers, no matter which programming language, operating system or microprocessor architecture provides the motive force. Mr Brown enthuses: 'We've been in a position where IT systems are like monolithic blocks of concrete and are used as the reason for not changing anything. Now here is a technology that can get you out of monolithic thinking. You can start to think about just-in-time outsourcing. You don't have to buy from just one provider because the systems integration is so difficult. You can start to pick whatever provider is best for the particular subservice you need. Think about risk assessment in a financial services company. The best provider for large buildings in New York is probably not the best for small buildings in the Midwest. Web services will let you discover and integrate with specialist service providers.'

It is a beguiling vision. The doubt is that business people have been burnt before by promises of flexibility, interoperability and plug-and-play computing. This time, however, the whole software industry appears to be drinking the same alphabet soup of protocols that underlie web services. Moreover, progress can be made via small steps, pilot projects, trial and error.

Source: Article by Simon London and John Seely Brown, *Financial Times*, 6 September 2002

Questions

1 If a manager is contributing scarce resources such as people's time or web services to a community of practice, how can these resources be evaluated and effectively managed? When does a manger draw a line under these informal approaches?

2 Knowledge ecologies may suffer from lack of participation. How can organisations engage members to participate and share their knowledge in communities of practice?

3 How can communities of practice provide 'just-in-time' knowledge?

Summary

This chapter has elaborated five areas that need to be considered when developing a knowledge-sharing culture and communities of practice:

1 The importance of norms, artefacts and symbols in providing explicit clues to a given culture and how knowledge management interventions can be aligned to the prevailing culture.

2 The development of core values that guide every action and decision in a company to prevent them from becoming meaningless and generating cynicism with senior management.

3 The different approaches to measuring culture fall into typing surveys or profiling surveys such as effectiveness surveys, descriptive surveys and fit profiles.

4 The debates related to knowledge-sharing cultures arising from the promotion of different forms of 'Ba' (space) in the knowledge-conversion process or the development of cooperative cultures through the values of 'care' or the result of an interplay or dialectic between cooperative and competitive cultures.

5 Communities of practice as informal, self-selecting groups that are open ended, without any deliverables. They play an important role in embedding tacit knowledge cognitively and socially through storytelling and narratives shared regularly between actors.

QUESTIONS FOR FURTHER THOUGHT

1 If culture is so difficult to change let alone understand, why should managers concern themselves with such a construct?

2 Communities of practice place considerable emphasis on stories and narratives for embedding tacit knowledge. What are the dangers in the current literature for not considering other surface manifestations of culture in communities of practice?

3 What issues need to be considered when the culture of different communities of practice may differ significantly from the dominant organisational culture?

4 Is radical innovation or double-loop learning asking for cultural change when its tenets are to question the underlying assumptions and values in an organisations?

5 What is the relevance of measuring organisational or group cultures?

6 How does the concept of 'Ba' add to the SECI model of knowledge conversion?

7 In what ways could the development of values of 'care' be detrimental to an organisation?

8 If communities of practice are the main component of a firm's knowledge management strategy, how do you evaluate them?

9 What are the advantages and disadvantages of online communities of practice or threaded discussion groups?

10 How do you discard obsolete practices and routines that are embedded in a community of practice?

Further reading

1 Brown 1998 is an excellent book providing a grounding and elaboration of the organisational culture literature. It has a clear and easily accessible style.

2 Ashkanasy, Wilderom and Peterson 2000b provides a more heavyweight elicitation of the current debates in the organisational culture and climate literature. This may be useful if you wish to conduct a more in-depth study of this area.

3 Wenger, McDermott, and Snyder 2002 provides an erudite background to the different approaches related to communities of practice.

References

Alvesson, M. (2002) *Understanding Organizational Culture*, Sage Publications, London.

Argyris, C. and Schon, D. A. (1978) *Organizational Learning: A Theory of Action Perspective*, Addison-Wesley, Reading, MA.

Ashkanasy, N. M., Broadfoot, L. E. and Falkus, S. (2000a) 'Questionnaire measures of organizational culture', *Handbook of Organizational Culture and Climate*, N. M. Ashkanasy, C. P. M. Wilderom and M. F. Peterson, eds, Sage Publications, Thousand Oaks, CA.

Ashkanasy, N. M., Wilderom, C. P. M. and Peterson, M. F. (2000b) *Handbook of Organizational Culture and Climate'*, Sage, Thousand Oaks, CA.

Berger, P. L. and Luckmann, T. (1966) *The Social Construction of Reality: A Treatise in the Sociology of Knowledge*, Penguin, New York.

Blacker, F. (1995) 'Knowledge, knowledge work and organizations: an overview and interpretation', *Organization Studies*, 16, 1021–46.

Boland, R. J. and Tenkasi, R. V. (1995) 'Perspective making and perspective taking: in communities', *Organization Science*, 6, 350–372.

Brown, A. D. (1998) *Organisational Culture*, Pearson Education Ltd, London.

Brown, J. S. and Duguid, P. (1991) 'Organizational learning and communities-of-practice: towards a unified view of working, learning and innovation', *Organization Science*, 2, 40–57.

Brown, J. S. and Duguid, P. (1998) 'Organizing knowledge', *California Management Review*, 40(3), 90–111.

Brown, J. S. and Duguid, P. (2000) 'Balancing act: how to capture knowledge without killing it', *Harvard Business Review*, May–June, 73–80.

Carroll, C. (1995) 'Rearticulating organizational identity: exploring corporate images and employee identification', *Management Learning*, 26(4), 463–82.

Cooke, R. A. and Lafferty, J. C. (1987) *Organizational Culture Inventory*, Human Synergistics, Plymouth, MI.

Deal, T. E. and Kennedy, A. A. (1982) *Corporate Cultures: The Rites and Rituals of Corporate Life*, Addison-Wesley, Reading, MA.

Denison, D. R. (1996) 'What is the difference between organizational culture and organizational climate? A native's point of view on a decade of paradigm wars', *Academy of Management Review*, 21(3), 619–654.

Durkheim, E. (1984) *The Division of Labour in Society*, W. D. Halls, translator, Free Press, New York.

Geertz, C. (1973) *The Interpretation of Cultures*, Basic Books, New York.

Handy, C. B. (1985) *Understanding Organizations*, Penguin, Harmondsworth.

Hofstede, G. (1980) *Culture's Consequences: International Differences in Work-related Values*, Sage Publications, Beverly Hills, CA.

Inkeles, A. and Levinson, D. J. (1969) 'National character: the study of modal personality and sociocultural systems', *The Handbook of Social Psychology*, G. Lindzey and E. Aronson, eds, Addison-Wesley, Reading, MA, 418–506.

Jashapara, A. (2003) 'Cognition, culture and competition: an empirical test of the learning organization', *The Learning Organization*, 10(1), 31–50.

Lave, J. and Wenger, E. (1991) *Situated Learning: Legitimate Peripheral Participation*, Cambridge University Press, Cambridge.

Lencioni, P. M. (2002) 'Make your values mean something', *Harvard Business Review*, July, 113–117.

Lewin, K. (1948) *Resolving Social Conflicts*, Harper & Row, New York.

Lewin, K. (1951) *Field Theory in Social Science*, Harper & Row, New York.

Lewin, K., Lippitt, R. and White, R. K. (1939) 'Patterns of aggressive behavior in experimentally created "social climates"', *Journal of Social Psychology*, 10, 271–299.

Likert, R. (1967) *The Human Organization*, McGraw-Hill, New York.

Litwin, G. H. and Stringer, R. A. (1961) *Motivation and Organizational Climate*, Harvard Business School Press, Boston, MA.

McDermott, R. and O'Dell, C. (2001) 'Overcoming cultural barriers to sharing knowledge', *Journal of Knowledge Management*, 5(1), 76–85.

Mead, G. (1934) *Mind, Self, and Society*, University of Chicago Press, Chicago.

Newell, S., Robertson, M., Scarbrough, H. and Swan, J. (2002) *Managing Knowledge Work*, Palgrave, Basingstoke, Hampshire.

Nonaka, I. (1991) 'The knowledge-creating company', *Harvard Business Review*, 69(November–December), 96–104.

Nonaka, I. and Konno, N. (1998) 'The concept of 'Ba': building a foundation for knowledge creation', *California Management Review*, 40(3), 40–54.

O'Reilly, C. A. (1989) 'Corporations, culture and commitment: motivation and social control in organizations', *California Management Review*, Summer, 9–25.

O'Reilly, C. A., Chatman, J. and Caldwell, D. F. (1991) 'People and organizational culture: a profile comparison approach to assessing person–organization fit', *Academy of Management Journal*, 34(3), 487–516.

Orr, J. (1996) *Talking About Machines: An Ethnography of a Modern Job*, IRL Press, Ithaca, NY.

Pettigrew, A. M. (1979) 'On studying organizational cultures', *Administrative Science Quarterly*, 24, 570–581.

Rokeach, M. (1973) *The Nature of Human Values*, Free Press, New York.

Schein, E. H. (1985a) 'How culture forms, develops and changes', *Gaining Control of the Corporate Culture*, R. H. Kilmann, M. J. Saxton and R. Serpa, eds, Jossey Bass, San Francisco, CA.

Schein, E. H. (1985b) *Organizational Culture and Leadership: A Dynamic View*, Jossey-Bass, San Francisco, CA.

Scholz, C. (1987) 'Corporate culture and strategy – the problem of strategic fit', *Long Range Planning*, 20(4), 78–87.

Swan, J., Scarbrough, H. and Robertson, M. (2002) 'The construction of "communities of practice" in the management of innovation', *Management Learning*, 33(4), 477–496.

von Hippel, E. (1994). '"Sticky information" and the locus of problem solving: implications for innovation', *Management Science*, 40, 429–439.

von Krough, G. (1998) 'Care in knowledge creation', *California Management Review*, 40(3), 136–7.

von Krough, G. (1999) 'Care in knowledge creation', *California Management Review*, 40(3), 136–7.

Weber, M. (1947) *The Theory of Social and Economic Organization*, A. M. Henderson and T. Parsons, translators, Oxford University Press, Oxford.

Wenger, E. C. (2000) 'Communities of practice and social learning systems', *Organization*, 7(2), 225–246.

Wenger, E. C., McDermott, R. and Snyder, W. M. (2002). *Cultivating Communities of Practice: A Guide to Managing Knowledge*, Harvard Business School Press, Boston, MA.

Wenger, E. C. and Snyder, W. M. (2000) 'Communities of practice: the organizational frontier', *Harvard Business Review*, January–February, 139–145.

Zollo, M. and Winter, S. G. (2002) 'Deliberate learning and the evolution of dynamic capabilities', *Organization Science*, 13(3), 339–351.

Change management

After completing this chapter the reader should be able to:

- understand the different dimensions and interventions that contribute to successful change management;
- successfully apply the different leadership and human resource interventions to a knowledge management initiative;
- analyse the training and development needs at individual and job level in a change management process;
- explain the critical factors that will lead to the successful implementation of knowledge management practices.

MANAGEMENT ISSUES

The use and application of knowledge management systems implies these questions for managers:

- What are the most effective ways of implementing a knowledge management initiative?
- How can knowledge management programmes be managed with moderate levels of support from senior managers?
- How can resistance to change be minimised?

Links to other chapters

Chapter 3   examines the different forms of learning linked with the change process resulting in organisational routines and dynamic capabilities.

Chapter 6   concerns strategic management of knowledge management and institutional practices linked with change and everyday learning.

Chapter 7   explores the nature of culture and climate rather than the effective management of cultural change programmes.

War for talent

Do you hear the guns? How many casualties have you sustained and how many have you inflicted? There is a corporate war on. It is a battle for talent and if you do not know how to fight, telephone security downstairs and tell them to run up the white flag.

The military metaphor is several years old. In 1998, a group of McKinsey consultants sounded 'a call to arms'. They said: 'Companies are about to be engaged in a war for senior executive talent that will remain a defining characteristic of their competitive landscape for decades to come.'

The latest word from the front is that the smoke of battle has grown thicker. A dispatch in the most recent issue of the *McKinsey Quarterly* says: 'The war for management talent is intensifying dramatically.' We can laugh but it's all true, isn't it? There is a shortage of talented staff and if you want to survive, you had better go out and recruit the best quickly. As the magazine *Fast Company* said last year: 'It's hard to argue with the idea that the company with the best talent wins.'

In fact, it is easy to argue with the idea, says Jeffrey Pfeffer, professor of organisational behaviour at Stanford Business School. The idea of a war for talent is dangerous nonsense. It is not only that the military analogy is inappropriate. 'Even fighting the war for talent may be hazardous to an organisation's health and detrimental to doing the things that will make it successful,' Prof Pfeffer argues in a recent paper.

To understand what is wrong with the 'war for talent', think about Xerox, a company fallen on hard times. Is Xerox's problem that it lacks talent? Of course not. Xerox invented many of the tools of the digital age. What Xerox lacks is not talent but the management, systems and culture to exploit it.

The search for talent inevitably focuses on individuals, Prof Pfeffer says. And they are usually individuals who work for someone else. When you recruit allegedly talented individuals, you set them apart from the people you already employ. You have to pay the new recruits more than the rest of your staff; you have already told them how much more talented they are. And you send a message to your own staff that they are not quite talented enough.

But talented people cannot on their own achieve success in business, any more than they can in football or basketball. They have to be part of a team, and a system, that works. That is less likely to happen if the new recruits are seen as a group apart.

The rest of the organisation will feel demoralised and will make even less effort than before.

The thinking behind the 'war for talent' is at odds with another prevailing management fashion: knowledge management. Stripped of the verbiage that invariably accompanies it, knowledge management means spreading best practice throughout the organisation. It recognises that knowledge is found in all parts of the company. Employees who deal directly with customers and machines may be low in the hierarchy but they often know more than anyone else. Prof Pfeffer particularly admires Toyota's ability to use the knowledge of all its people. He argues that the Japanese manufacturer's achievements cannot be replicated by companies that are preoccupied with the war for talent. 'If you hire the best people who think (or even know) they are the best, how likely are they to be willing to listen and learn? How likely are they to treat others not as "smart" as they are with respect, as opposed to the contempt more often seen? One of the geniuses of Toyota was recognising that the people on the assembly line really knew something about automobile assembly, regardless of the formal degrees and their ability to talk smoothly.'

The 'war for talent' is a distraction from companies' real task: devising systems that get the most out of everyone. 'As W. Edwards Deming and the quality movement pointed out a long time ago – a lesson that we clearly need to relearn – what is important is not so much individual motivation or ability but the attributes of the system in which the person works,' Prof Pfeffer says.

Is he right? Of course he is. The real difficulty is finding the managers who can make that system work. There are not many of them around. But they are just as likely to be lurking in your own company as in someone else's. If you can find them, they will already know your own organisation inside out and will probably have spent years brooding on how to make it better. And they will be a lot cheaper than outsiders.

Source: Article by Michael Skapiner, *Financial Times*, 6 June 2001

Questions

1 How important are talented people in a change process or KM initiative?
2 What are the dangers and drawbacks of talented people?
3 What are the other factors required for the successful management of a change process?

Introduction

Change is an ephemeral word and its nature is increasingly uncertain and unpredictable. It affects people in different ways and the traditional emotional response can provide considerable resistance to change. All knowledge management initiatives such as implementing new technical solutions or promoting knowledge-sharing cultures can provide considerable challenges to their effective implementation. The reasoning adopted in this chapter is that a contingency approach using different interventions depending on context is more likely to be successful than a single solution. A KM framework showing the different dimensions and interventions likely to lead to successful implementation of KM initiatives is shown in Figure 8.1 (p. 216).

This chapter begins by examining the nature of change and the personal response to it. Leadership is considered vital in any change programme and the nature of situational skills is explored for developing a vision and goal commitment towards the new initiative. The change management strategy adopted follows a cycle of three phases of unfreezing, moving and refreezing (Lewin 1951) and using a variety of interventions to reduce the resistance to change (Kotter and Schlesinger 1979). The chapter then proceeds to explore in detail the variety of human resource interventions that can be used in the change process. Of particular interest are the variety of employee involvement practices, the diversity of training and development interventions, and the role reward and recognition schemes can play to smooth the implementation of KM initiatives. Finally, the chapter explores the politics of change and how they can undermine and cause failure in a rationally determined change programme.

The nature of change

Change in organisations can occur at almost any time internally or externally. There may be periods of 'incremental change' followed by periods of increased turbulence or complexity as well as periods of major disequilibrium or 'discontinuous change'. Such patterns are often referred to as 'punctuated equilibrium,' as shown in Figure 8.2 (p. 217). Prior to the 1970s, the dominant form of change experienced by many organisations was 'incremental change', characterised by stable markets, the past repeating itself in the future and predictable organisational challenges (Ansoff and McDonnell 1990). The common tool adopted to meet these challenges was forecasting by extrapolating from past experiences and figures and forecasting into the future. This worked well for annual budgeting purposes but soon many organisations started to experience strategic drift where they found their incremental change strategies were no longer moving at the same pace as forces in the environment.

Change was no longer slow and predictable but showed much greater flux due to increased internal complexity and turbulence in the external environment. Such 'bumpy incremental change' (Grundy 1993) or flux can often result in periodic reor-

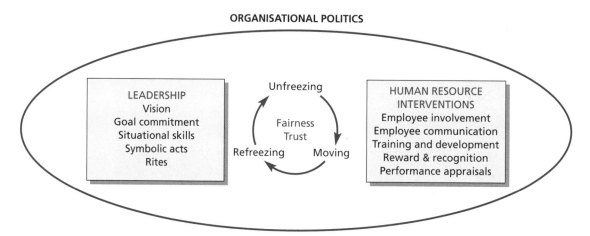

Figure 8.1 KM initiatives and change management

ganisations to increase the organisation's ability to respond to the quickening pace of daily problems and perceptions of work overload (Senior 1997). The organisational focus in periods of incremental change tends more towards 'doing things better' or single-loop learning (Argyris and Schon 1978).

The logic of organisations responding incrementally to changes can also lead to serious consequences. For example, using the 'boiled-frog' analogy (Handy 1993) shows that if a frog is placed in cold water and slowly heated, the frog will let itself be boiled to death. Like the organisation, the frog attempts to respond slowly to the changing environment until it is too late. In contrast, if a frog is placed in boiling water it will jump straight out in order to survive.

In the 1970s, the consequence of the oil price shock forced many companies such as Shell to reappraise how they conducted business. Such unpredictable surprises or discontinuous changes led to major periods of disequilibrium where unexpected events occurred at a faster rate than the ability of organisations to respond to them. The old ways of prediction and forecasting were no longer valid and new tools and techniques were needed to manage such transformational change. One such tool developed by Shell during this period was 'scenario planning' to obtain a number of plausible futures against which to test organisational responses. The organisational focus in periods of discontinuous change tends more towards 'doing things differently' or double-loop learning (Argyris and Schon 1978).

Personal response to change

Organisations are about people. In order to manage change effectively, we need to understand how change affects people at an emotional and cognitive level. There are a number of relatively predictable transition phases that people encounter linked with

Figure 8.2 **The nature of change**

their ability to exercise control over a new situation, as shown in Figure 8.3 (p. 218). These transition phases in the cycle of change include (Hayes 2002):

● shock from an individual feeling overwhelmed and paralysed by the new situation or event. This can lead to rejection of the change process and an assertion that the change won't happen;

● denial as the individual clings to the past and their everyday routines. Resistance to change is at its highest level at this stage, leading to a defensive reaction. If the individual panics, this may also lead to sabotage of the change process. This is characterised by the individual response of 'I'm not going to let this happen';

● depression as the individual feels that the situation is beyond their control, resulting in sadness, anger, confusion and withdrawal from the change process;

● letting go by the individual. The individual acknowledges and accepts the change but does not necessarily like it. This represents a turning point in the change process;

● testing as the individual tries out new behaviours and ways of working;

● consolidation of new experiences and ways of behaving to develop new norms and routines;

● internalisation, reflection and learning leading to effective adaptation of change process. The individual response tends to be 'things are changing, let's work with it'.

Pause for thought

Reflect on a time of major change in your life. Describe the nature of your feelings at this time. What did you find helped or hindered you through this change process? What lessons have you learnt from this personal introspection? How do you feel that your experiences could help you in future change processes or if you were tasked with leading a major change initiative?

This emotional response to change can lead to considerable resistance to change for four primary reasons (Kotter and Schlesinger 1979):

● parochial self-interest as people feel that they will lose something of value through the change such as resource allocation, career prospects and power imbalances;

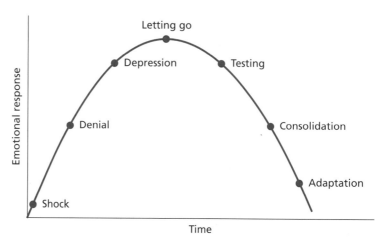

Figure 8.3 **Emotional response to change (Hayes 2002)**

- misunderstanding and lack of trust arising from poor communication of the change process and how it will affect individuals. Trust also depends on the background of employee relations between senior management and staff;
- different assessments as conflicting views and interpretations arise about the nature and benefits of the change process;
- low tolerance for change, especially when it means job losses, reskilling or relocation.

Leadership and change

It is clear that outstanding leaders can play a vital role in the change process and particularly in enabling effective transformations to occur. But what are the leadership skills and abilities that are required? Firstly, leaders offer a vision of what is possible that mobilises, energises and empowers people to reach that vision. Secondly, they play a role in goal setting connected with building and articulating clearly accepted goals and expectations. Lastly, they play a role in gaining commitment to the goals in the change process. This is not purely an awareness of the goals ('I know') or a knowledge of the goals ('I understand') or a belief in the goals ('I can') but a commitment to the goals ('I will'). This requires an active involvement of people in the development of goals. It is noteworthy that there are no conclusive studies showing that certain leadership styles, such as a participative style or an autocratic style, are more effective than others.

There is much debate about the distinctions between a leader and a manager. One distinction is that managers 'do things right' whereas leaders 'do the right thing' (Bennis and Nanus 1985). Managers are more concerned with the activities related to the formal structure and goals of the organisation whereas leaders are more concerned with establishing a direction, aligning, motivating and inspiring people (Senior 1997). The two main skills for managing people in the change process are:

- creating energy through motivation by getting the right people in the right places in the change programme. Selecting the right person is about more than purely their skills and abilities. It is about their motivation and attitudes about the role. Does the person enjoy their role and do they feel proud of their work? Choosing the right person frees up energy for leadership as the leader isn't sidetracked purely managing resistance to change;

- channelling energy through leadership and goal commitment.

One common practice in the leadership of change is to adopt a three-phase approach over roughly a three-month period. The first consultative phase is where the leader asks questions and actively listens to managers, employees, customers, suppliers and other stakeholders. This phase serves as a business analysis to understand problems and opportunities. The leader also builds relationships and conducts a human resource analysis to find out what managers are good at, what makes them tick, what they would fight for or against and what turns them on. The second phase is testing out reactions to a goal or a plan. The aim of this phase is to test for commitment to the change process by simulating the benefits and challenges of the change. The third phase is the announcement of the change process through conferences, meetings, newsletters and other media. The aim of this phase is to encourage concrete action and commitment to the change rather than further discussion and argument.

As we do not live in a perfect world, the leader may not be able to gain the perfect commitment to a vision or goal as desired. In this case, leaders often rely on situational skills. In order to influence people, the leader needs to understand the readiness of people along two dimensions: job readiness (their knowledge, skills and experience) and psychological readiness (their confidence, commitment and motivation). Once the person or group's readiness is understood as well as their level of supportive behaviour, the leader can choose the appropriate situational skill as shown in Figure 8.4 (Hersey et al. 2000). In cases of low levels of job and psychological readiness, the leader may use 'telling' or 'selling' styles depending on the level of support required. In contrast with high levels of job and psychological readiness, the leader is more likely to use follower directed styles of 'participating' and 'delegating'. In high trust styles of delegation, the person or group are given full responsibility for their work and the leader is kept informed if they run into any problems.

The second situational skill used by many leaders is 'reading the traffic lights' to provide appropriate direction and control, as shown in Figure 8.4 (p. 220). If the lights are 'green' where things are running smoothly towards agreed goals, the leader recognises that it would best not to intervene in these circumstances. If the lights are 'red', where major problems are gathering, the leader is best informed to stop, change their agenda and pay close attention to the problems. If not, the problems could mushroom out of all proportion. The real challenge for leaders is reading the amber/orange lights on whether or not to intervene: are the amber lights in a given situation on their way to green or on their way to red? This is part of the armour of an outstanding leader.

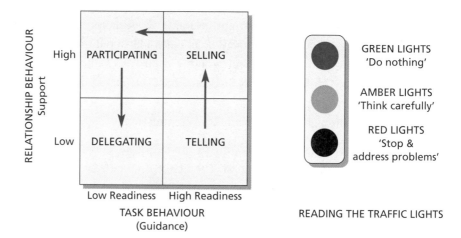

Figure 8.4 **Leadership situational skills in change management (Hersey et al. 2000)**

Change management strategies

The underlying assumption of the change management process among many managers is that it follows a three-phase process. The three phases assume that there is a need for some permanency or stability within organisations, even if this happens to be temporary. The three phases advocated for helping individuals, groups and organisations manage change are (Lewin 1951):

- unfreezing and loosening current sets of behaviours, mental models and ways of looking at a problem;
- moving by making changes in the way people do things, new structures, new strategies and different types of behaviours and attitudes;
- refreezing by stabilising and establishing new patterns and organisational routines.

Even though this model is predominant in many organisations, it has been criticised for its emphasis on stability, particularly when organisations are faced with turbulent environments and discontinuous change. Such cycles may perpetuate single-loop learning in the refreezing process rather than double-loop learning through continual adaptation to the external environment.

An important tool used by managers to understand the dynamics of change in any given situation is a forcefield analysis (Lewin 1951), as shown in Figure 8.5 (p. 221). This uses a military metaphor of examining the driving forces and restraining forces that create a 'quasi-stationary equilibrium' at any given moment. The intention of any manager is to strengthen the driving forces while reducing the influence of restraining forces. Such an analysis will provide the manager with a number of problems to be tackled to help drive the change process in the desired direction.

Figure 8.5 Forcefield analysis

Once a manager has understood the restraining forces and the change management problems, there are a number of approaches and options for managing resistance to change (Kotter and Schlesinger 1979):

- *Education and persuasion.* This involves explaining the problems and issues concerned with current working practices and how the change management programme can benefit individuals, groups and the organisation as a whole. Persuasion is about convincing people about the benefits of changing practices and the costs of continuing with current practices. Managers need to guard against defensive reactions from overcritical analysis of current practices and the problems of misinformation or, at worst, no information at all.
- *Participation and involvement.* This is an important approach to engage people and get 'buy-in' for the change process. It involves relinquishing some control and involving organisational members in diagnosing the problems, addressing options, finding solutions and implementing the change process. The result is that champions are created with much greater motivation and shared understanding for the change programme. It empowers individuals and reduces the victim mentality often associated with change. The drawback is that the consultative process can be very time consuming and the people may not have the necessary technical expertise to conduct an effective analysis of the current situation. The threat is that a suboptimal solution may result from the consultation process (Hayes 2002).
- *Facilitation and support.* Resistance to change often results from the loss of something that is valued by organisational members. Some of this can be overcome by offering individual opportunities for training and development in new skills. However, loss also implies grief and staff may need emotional support and a listening ear in the change process.
- *Negotiation and agreement.* If an individual or a group such as the unions has significant power to resist change, one approach is to engage in negotiations to secure an agreement. In this case, the negotiations are about reaching a compromise so that both parties can gain some benefits from the new situation. However, negotiations can be time consuming and add costs to the change management programme.

- *Manipulation and cooption*. The common term used for this approach nowadays is 'spin'. This involves a covert operation to bias information and communications in an organisation in order to gain support. However, this can result in coopted members feeling deceived in the long term and can act as a restraining agent.
- *Coercion*. This approach is used in more extreme cases where a manager has the ability to exercise power over granting or withholding a valued outcome, such as promotion or pay, from an organisational member (Hayes 2002). Such threats tend to be used when commitment to the change process is very low within a workforce. The dangers of this approach are that it can lead to resentment and loss of goodwill from organisational members.

Pause for thought

Some managers adopt bullying tactics in order to manage change. As a manager, what do you think could be some of the benefits or limitations of this approach? What do you envisage could be some of the short-term and long-term consequences of bullying behaviour? If one of your colleagues was being bullied, what would you advise them as their best course of action?

Gaining commitment for change

For successful implementation of knowledge management practices and encouraging knowledge-sharing behaviour, organisational commitment is a major asset to be nurtured. But what is the nature of commitment and its root causes? Commitment affects how employees behave and their attitudes towards their workplace. Commitment can be seen as an attitudinal consequence of the psychological contract (Guest and Conway 1997; Hislop 2002), as shown in Figure 8.6. The psychological contract is the perceptions that the individual and organisation bring to the employment relationship. The core components of a psychological contract are fairness, trust and 'delivering the deal' by meeting expectations of key obligations and promises on both sides. Fairness in daily practices relates to the level of equity in the way people are valued and rewarded for their contributions. Trust concerns the level of confidence in an organisation to meet expectations of future outcomes. Much depends on the mutual expectations within a psychological contract.

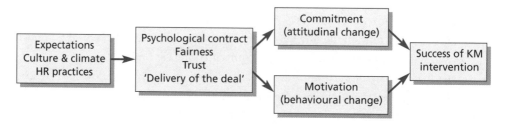

Figure 8.6 **Psychological contract and commitment (Guest and Conway 1997; Hislop 2002)**

There are criticisms of this model of commitment as it doesn't take into account the complexity of this construct. There may be different types of commitment and individuals may be committed to certain parts of the organisation rather than the organisation as a whole. Similarly, employees may develop psychological contracts with key individuals or groups rather than with the organisation (Hayes 2002).

As knowledge-based organisations are dependent on the commitment and ideas of their employees, the role of a fair process becomes crucial as it affects attitudes and behaviours of individuals to achieve superior performance. Employees will commit to a manager's decision even though they may disagree with it as long as they feel that the process has been fair (Kim and Mauborgne 2003). They will cooperate freely with a situation even though they may not benefit from its consequences. However, if employees feel that there is something deceitful in a manager's actions and a general lack of respect, the level of trust and commitment is likely to deteriorate. This will probably result in employees hoarding their knowledge rather than sharing it. Being valued is a basic human need in all employees; people like to contribute their ideas and have them taken seriously. There are three basic principles underlying a fair process (Kim and Mauborgne 2003):

- *Engagement* is about involving and consulting people in the decision-making processes. Such engagement makes people feel valued and conflicting views help sharpen understanding and gain commitment. There is ownership of the process.
- *Explanation* allows employees to understand the rationale behind certain decisions and gain trust in a manager's intention even though their own ideas may be ignored.
- *Expectation* clarity is about managers defining the new behaviours expected of employees and the rewards and penalties for achieving certain standards. This allows new rules and policies to be understood and minimises allegations of favouritism.

Average performance often occurs in organisations due to 'distributive justice'. This arises when employees receive outcomes they deserve (such as compensation) and feel compelled towards a compulsory form of cooperation. However, superior performance and strong knowledge-sharing behaviours are more likely to occur through 'procedural justice'. This involves a fair process building trust and commitment and leading to voluntary cooperation and behaviours where individuals go beyond their call of duty. It affects people's everyday attitudes and behaviours. There are often three stages in achieving employee commitment (O'Reilly 1989):

- *compliance*, where an individual accepts the rules of the game in expectation of some reward such as pay;
- *identification*, when an employee accepts influence to maintain a satisfying relationships with individuals and groups;
- *internalisation*, when an employee finds the organisational values intrinsically rewarding and aligned with their personal values.

Cults and religious groups exhibit high levels of commitment marked by the internalisation of group values with personal values.

Pause for thought As a manager, what strategies could you use to make your staff feel valued at work? Think of your own experiences of being valued at work. What were effective interventions that made you feel valued? One of the pitfalls of valuing some staff over others is described as favouritism. How could you avoid this pitfall? What are the likely consequences if you are unable to do so?

Employee involvement

In many organisations, there is an increasing shift away from control towards commitment. As we have seen, an important factor in gaining this commitment is engagement or employee involvement. But what is the nature of employee involvement and what impact does it have on the power relations between a manager and their teams? Employee involvement implies a certain loss of management prerogative in decision-making processes. However, the spectrum of employee involvement practices can span from one-way communication of management decisions to full-blown democratic systems in decision making. Employee involvement is time consuming and many senior managers may feel that it detracts from their focus on tight cost control or other strategic directions and leave themselves open to criticisms about lack of investment in human resources such as training and development.

The history of involving the workforce in the decision-making process can be traced back to the Second World War. In response to the strong demand for products and services during the war, works committees or joint consultative committees were set up across many organisations. These committees lost favour with unions and employers alike soon after the war. Instead, direct collective bargaining between unions and employers was preferred. In the 1960s and 1970s, there was a greater focus on 'industrial democracy', with union members fulfilling consultative roles in organisations. The extent of power delegated to them was unclear. In the 1980s, industrial democracy interventions became tarnished by left-wing ideologies and 'employee involvement' schemes became much more popular. Power relations between management and the workforce still play an important role in the nature of employee involvement. It has been argued that there may be waves of participation, especially linked to the perceived threat or loss of control of labour in some manner (Beardwell and Holden 2001).

A spectrum of different employee involvement practices linked to the level of management or worker control is shown in Figure 8.7 (p. 225). In reality, the nature of employee involvement practices in organisations is likely to have significant overlaps and behave more dynamically than shown due to environmental pressures. The nature of employee involvement schemes can be divided into four groupings (Beardwell and Holden 2001; Marchington *et al.* 1992):

- *downward communication* or one-way communication from management using company newsletters, the intranet and regular team briefings. Newsletters are a popular form of communication but can be seen as a medium to convey management rather than

MANAGEMENT CONTROL – WORKER CONTROL

| INFORMATION E-mail, intranet, newsletter | COMMUNICATION Team briefings, mass meetings, intranet, e-mails | CONSULTATION Quality circles, attitudes surveys, videoconference | CO-DETERMINATION Union representation, works council, JCC, negotiations | WORKER CONTROL Cooperatives, worker self-management |

Figure 8.7 Spectrum of employee involvement

worker views. Team briefings are an effective face-to-face medium to allow management goals to be addressed and any misunderstandings to be clarified. They involve small numbers of people in short meetings with a question and answer session at the end;

- *upwards, problem-solving forms* which aim to capture employee knowledge and expertise. These may include attitude surveys, quality circles, TQM and suggestion schemes. Quality circles are about teams getting together focusing on problems, using statistical techniques and presenting managers with potential solutions. They have declined in popularity in many countries for cultural reasons (they originated in Japan) and the fact that they may undermine union authority;

- *financial participation* which aims to link employee effort with performance of the organisation. This may include organisation-wide rewards such as profit-sharing schemes, share ownership or bonus schemes. The aim is to achieve greater identification with the organisation among employees with the assumption that this will lead to greater levels of commitment;

- *representative participation* of employees through their representatives such as union members. These may include joint consultative committees (JCC), works councils, co-determination and collective bargaining.

Even though there has been a decline in union membership in many countries, there are still examples of industrial democracy such as co-determination practices, particularly in countries with a strong union presence. In Sweden, there is the Co-determination at Work Act (MBL) which places an obligation on organisations to extend their collective bargaining to areas of strategic management and operational changes. Hence, the emergence of any new practices or organisational direction has to be negotiated with the workforce, often through the unions.

In Germany, the co-determination law places similar obligations on employers to consult and consider the views of their workforce through works councils, supervisory boards and management boards. Employees and their representatives have a right to participate in any personnel matters and planned changes in a company likely to affect employees. The different committees can make suggestions to employers but they are not obliged to necessarily accept them. The impact of co-determination schemes often varies with economic cycles and the change in power relations between the government, employers and the workforce. For instance, the power of unions during times of recession may be weak and the role of works councils may be weakened.

Training and development

For change management strategies to be successful, one core element is the use of training and development to provide the necessary education, facilitation and support in the change process. Training is a planned process to help modify the attitude, knowledge or skill behaviour of an individual through a learning experience. Development is more long term and can be associated with an individual's maturity. Development can be described as a journey starting with some level of confusion and leading to highs and lows towards a new understanding. Nothing is changed at the end of the journey but the individual is transformed internally (Daloz 1986).

Many organisations have a propensity to send their employees on courses as the mainstay of their training programmes. However, this can result in the common problem of 'Del the Delegate'. He returns from a course full of new ideas only to be faced with scepticism and cynicism from colleagues and bosses. His enthusiasm is undermined and he reverts to old patterns of behaviour and routines. If this is to be avoided, organisations need to adopt formalised or focused approaches to training and development (Barham *et al.* 1987):

- formalised approach is linking the planned training and development programme with performance appraisal and career planning processes;
- focused approach is linking training and development activities to organisational goals and continuous learning.

The common approach to human resource policy and practice as well as individual performance reviews is to adopt a systematic training cycle, as shown in Figure 8.8 (p. 227). The human resource development plan is based on establishing training needs from business objectives as well as training needs of employees and determining the gap between these two entities. Appropriate training methods are decided and the human resource development plan contains material on responsibilities and how the plan will be implemented, monitored and evaluated.

Training needs need to be linked closely to organisational objectives and exist at organisation, job and individual levels. At the job level, it is the body of knowledge, the range of skills and the necessary attitudes required to perform a certain job. At the individual level, it is the gap between the knowledge, skills and attitudes (KSA) held by the individual and those required for a job. At the organisational level, the training needs are the summation of all the individual training needs or gaps in order to deliver performance objectives. There are a number of analytical techniques that can be adopted in a change management programme to identify training needs at individual or job level (Reid and Barrington 2000):

- *comprehensive analysis* of all job tasks. This is useful for repetitive tasks that are difficult to learn and in which the potential cost of error is unacceptable;

Figure 8.8 Systematic training cycle (Stewart 1999)

- *key task analysis focusing on core tasks*. This form of analysis is useful when a job is changing and the focus is on the tasks critical for performance;
- *problem-centred analysis*. Here the need for training is urgent and resources are unavailable to conduct an extensive analysis;
- *stage and key points analysis*. This provides a breakdown of training needs at stages and key points;
- *manual skills analysis*. Isolates the knowledge and skills required by experienced workers performing tasks requiring high levels of manual dexterity;
- *faults analysis*. Where certain faults are costly and keep recurring. A fault specification is produced to help the trainee understand the nature of faults, what causes them, who is responsible for them and how to best act when a fault occurs;
- *critical incident analysis*. Examines the training needs related to critical incidents in problem situations;
- *job-learning analysis*. Looks at the processes in performing a job and the generic learning skills required.

Once the training needs have been identified, the training solution can be designed by considering a number of strategies and interventions. The appropriateness of the training interventions will depend on how they meet organisational objectives, the likelihood of learning transfer in terms of the organisational climate ('Del the Delegate' syndrome), the available resources and learner-related factors such as their learning style. The common training and development strategies found in organisations include (Reid and Barrington 2000):

- *on-the-job training*. This may involve learning by doing or 'sitting next to Nellie'. There is a potential danger that *Nellie* may not have the necessary skills to transfer knowledge and skills effectively. Work shadowing can be another useful training intervention. However, if poorly planned, trainees can feel unwelcome and be seen by other workers as a hindrance to their everyday routines. Job rotation can provide a good learning experience for workers, equipping them with new skills and providing greater flexibility for managers in times of crisis or change;

- *planned organisation experience*. This can involve mentoring or coaching. In mentoring, a senior or experienced employee acts as an adviser to a trainee in terms of professional and emotional support. The role is similar to a master-apprentice one. Coaching has parallels to mentoring as they are both learning processes that support and encourage learning to occur. The distinction is one of contextual roles. A mentor seeks to develop a special relationship with an employee and is rarely a learner's line manager. In contrast a coach is more concerned with immediate performance results and is more likely to be a person's line manager (Parsloe and Wray 2000);

- *In-house programmes*. These may include part-time courses leading to externally validated qualifications. There is also a rise in using the intranet as a medium for e-learning, particularly for developing technical knowledge and skills. Interactive computer learning packages are also used for developing IT skills;

- *planned experiences outside the organisation*. These may include secondments to other divisions or other companies. In addition, study tours and visits to competitors and suppliers can provide fruitful learning experiences;

- *external courses*. These may comprise short full-time courses or more longer (usually part-time) courses, often leading to a qualification. In both cases, it is important to examine how well the courses meet the person's training needs and link to the organisational objectives;

- *self-managed learning*. This is an ultimate goal of employees rather than human resource departments taking full responsibility for their learning. Logbooks and records of progress are often used and provide a stimulus for further learning.

Pause for thought

A common situation in many organisations is that training and development budgets are insufficient to cover all training needs. How would you decide on the most effective ways to prioritise these limited budgets? Can you suggest any internal low-cost training alternatives that could be adopted? What could be some of the dangers of relying too heavily on internally driven training solutions?

The staff appraisal process has become an important method for evaluating training interventions. The trainee and line manager can discuss the effectiveness of certain interventions and how they affected the individual's performance. There are a variety of other approaches used to evaluate training and often a combination of these is used (Beardwell and Holden 2001; Harrison 2000):

- questionnaires or feedback sheets often known as 'happy sheets' on training courses;
- tests leading to qualifications help identify a trainee's progress;

- interviews with trainees and tutors to gain feedback on training;
- observation of training provision can provide additional valuable feedback;
- participation and discussion with participants at the end of a training intervention.

The change process may also need to address the management development needs in the organisation. Without engaging in the debates about the precise nature of management, there are numerous interventions to meet a manager's development needs. Even though each manager has unique needs, some organisations have adopted a portfolio approach to management development (Odiorne 1984), as shown in Figure 8.9 (p. 230). The portfolio approach allows resources to be targeted cost effectively to particular groups of managers where there is a higher likelihood of immediate or long-term benefit to the organisation. At the same time, resources may be withheld from poorly performing managers described as 'deadwood' in this model. The danger with this approach is that certain managers may become stigmatised with certain labels and their efforts to change perceptions through their performance may go unheeded. Such an approach also has implications for the individual manager's career progression.

A management development needs analysis can be conducted using the same tools described above for training and development of employees. The traditional forms of management development interventions are (Beardwell and Holden 2001):

- management education and training interventions such as MBA programmes;
- action learning through tackling problems that have defied solutions in the organisation;
- mentoring using a personal development plan. Checking that goals are 'SMART' (specific, measurable, achievable, relevant and timescaled). Mentor encourages learner to solve problems and acts as a sounding board (Parsloe and Wray 2000);
- coaching, which can be hands-on for inexperienced learners or hands-off for more experienced learners relying on questioning and feedback skills (Parsloe and Wray 2000);
- secondments;
- outdoor management development to develop team and leadership skills by giving managers physical, mental and emotional challenges in an unfamiliar outdoor environment;
- management team development involving workshop and game playing at informal residential venues;
- self-development through self-learning groups, psychometrics, books, distance learning materials and e-learning.

Reward and recognition

Reward and recognition schemes are an important tool in the change management process to increase employee motivation and gain commitment. For example, some organisations have adopted 'Miles for Knowledge Sharing' schemes similar to Airmiles used by travel companies and retail outlets. Each employee is given a notional number of miles, say 500, and is able to give away different numbers of miles to others in the organisation

Figure 8.9 Portfolio approach to management development (Odiorne 1984)

for their helpful knowledge-sharing behaviours. Individual totals are added up at the end of the year and prizes are awarded annually at an awards ceremony to those exhibiting exceptional knowledge-sharing behaviours. Other companies, such as Buckman Laboratories, have held one-off events at a fashionable resort with 150 employees attending who had exhibited the greatest knowledge-sharing behaviours. Each employee was given a new laptop and participated in a workshop on how to improve knowledge management practices in the organisation. Such initiatives found that participation in knowledge management practices rose dramatically (Newell *et al.* 2002).

The assumption behind reward and recognition schemes is that employee engagement and effort will lead to greater performance. This performance will be rewarded, leading to greater employee satisfaction and commitment, as shown in Figure 8.10.

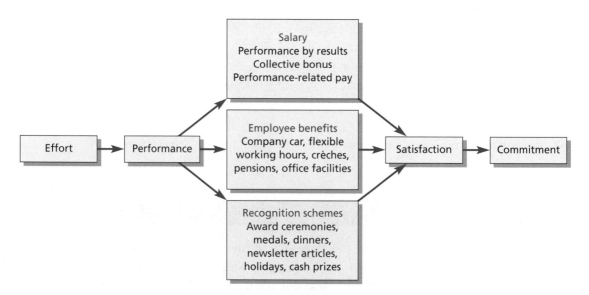

Figure 8.10 Commitment through reward and recognition schemes (Beardwell and Holden 2001; Porter and Lawler 1968)

The rewards may be a combination of employee salary incentive schemes, employee benefits and recognition schemes.

There are four broad types of incentive-based schemes (Casey *et al.* 1992):

- *Individual payment by results (PBR)*. This depends on the relationship with incremental pay and incremental output, the threshold output for receiving PBR over and above an employee's salary and the capping level of PBR. Such schemes can give employees greater freedom and opportunities to achieve high earnings. However, they can ignore the fact that many effective change processes are a result of team effort.
- *Collective payment by results*. This is similar to individual PBR but more focused on a group, division and department. It acknowledges that individual PBR can be divisive for group working and long-term knowledge sharing. Instead, it rewards cooperative behaviours.
- *Collective bonus schemes*. The aim of these schemes is to foster greater cooperation between departments to achieve corporate objectives and to attract and retain the right staff. They may include profit-sharing schemes in the form of company shares or allow staff to buy company shares at a discount. A critical factor is the proportion of bonuses to an employee's total compensation. If it is small, it is unlikely to persuade individuals to change their behaviours.
- *Performance-related pay (PRP)*. This is an incentive scheme based on an assessment of performance, often conducted through a staff appraisal process. This can allow managers to identify high-achieving employees as well as the 'deadwood'. The aim of PRP is to increase employee motivation and encourage certain behaviours and attitudes in the change process through performance norms. Institutionalising knowledge-sharing behaviours as part of these performance norms brings knowledge management practices clearly on to the everyday agenda. However, PRP can undermine the cooperation and cohesiveness of a work group. Employee performance cannot be judged in isolation but is often a result of group effort. Also, there is a danger that the psychological contract is changed from relational to transactional. Employees are more concerned with their performance (transactional) rather than all the altruistic or helpful behaviours (relational) that allow an organisation to meet its objectives (Beardwell and Holden 2001).

Pause for thought

Reflect on your role as a knowledge worker. What reward and recognition schemes do you feel are most appropriate for knowledge workers? Do you believe that PRP schemes related to knowledge-sharing behaviours could work in your organisation? What are the likely problems with this approach? How would you devise a scheme to measure knowledge-sharing behaviours? As 'game playing' behaviours could distort the results, how would you attempt to prevent game playing among staff?

Another aspect of the rewards package is the employee benefits for increasing employee motivation and commitment to a change process. These are benefits that the employee values and can be linked to performance and achievement of targets. The benefits may be flexible, known as 'cafeteria benefits', where the employee chooses from a selection of rewards and constructs their own benefits package. The types of potential employee benefits include:

- company cars;
- flexible working practices;
- pensions;
- upgraded office accommodation and facilities;
- private healthcare;
- sports facilities;
- assistance with educational fees;
- assistance with crèches.

Lastly, organisations use recognition schemes to acknowledge and recognise the efforts of high-performing individuals in the direction of the change process. This is more than an everyday 'pat on the back' and may include:

- article or story in company newsletter;
- annual awards ceremony;
- medals, plaques and certificates for exceptional performance;
- paid luxury holidays;
- business accessories such as laptops;
- cash prizes.

Cultural change management

Organisational culture concerns the underlying values and assumptions that define prevailing norms and behaviours. But what if the norms are not compatible with organisational goals and objectives? What if the prevailing norms are knowledge-hoarding behaviours rather than the desired knowledge-sharing behaviours? How do organisations effect and manage a cultural change process? A widely accepted framework for managing the cultural change process involves five stages (Kilmann 1984):

- surfacing actual cultural norms;
- articulating new directions;
- establishing new cultural norms;
- identifying gaps in cultural norms;
- closing gaps in cultural norms.

As shown earlier in this chapter, there are predominantly two drivers for cultural change management: leadership and human resource interventions. Leadership and commitment from senior managers is vital to the success of cultural change programmes. Leaders have tremendous power to influence employees through personal enactment. They can resort to symbolic actions frequently and consistently to reinforce certain beliefs values and assumptions. Symbolic acts can include the way they use their time, such as visiting operational sites and customers to show what they consider to be important. The way a chief executive announces new directions or ways of working with stories and anecdotes can shape individual understandings. Placing certain topics continually at the top of the agenda in meetings informs employees about what is important to a leader (Brown 1998).

Leaders can also employ rites to facilitate cultural change. Rites are organised and planned activities. Existing rites can be modified to include new values and assumptions in an organisation. Certain rites can be eliminated if they are no longer desirable and maintain the status quo. A more risky approach is to develop new rites which express the desirable beliefs and values in an organisation. For example, rites of passage involving recruitment, selection and induction procedures may shift from a legislation-led, equal opportunities emphasis more towards valuing diversity in the organisation. Rites of enhancement may reward employees for exhibiting behaviours associated with new values and beliefs through various reward and recognition schemes as described above. Leaders can use rites of degradation for demoting or removing employees resistant to the change process. Other rites include rites of conflict reduction through committees between warring factions and more informally using sporting contest or humour. Lastly, the leader can use rites of integration to develop greater social cohesion through recreational activities such as drinking, dancing and picnics.

Apart from clear leadership in the cultural change process, there are a number of human resource interventions that can be employed to reinforce the desired norms, beliefs and values. The ultimate goal is to have all aspects of the human resource programme using a 'consistent cues' approach (Brown 1998) to ensure that consistent signals are sent to achieve the desired cultural end state. The spectrum of human resource interventions to manage culture includes:

- changes in recruitment and selection norms;
- changes in induction, socialisation and training norms;
- changes in performance appraisal norms;
- changes in reward and recognition norms.

Politics of change

Many organisational change programmes fail due to resistance to the change process. People use organisational politics to resist and influence the change process particularly if it is not going in their intended direction. The majority of managers find that politics becomes more intense when change is radical, complex and wide ranging (Buchanan *et al.* 1997). In fact, many managers feel that change programmes are likely to fail unless managers and leaders are adept in political skills. A common approach in the politics of organisational change is to focus on the 'dominant coalition'. Such coalitions of senior executives have considerable influence over decisions and resources. They decide organisational direction and what is important. Coalitions are dynamic and can become unstable depending on the nature of external market changes, social ties and internal politics.

Major changes such as delayering in organisations, use of teamwork and business process re-engineering practices recently have meant that the prevalence of political behaviour is a norm rather than an exception (Browning 2003). People are responding less to rational reasons and more to egotistical motives such as personal security and career advancement (Stone 1997). Research in this area can be a minefield as managers are reluctant to discuss the subject in case it lowers their image, and managers often fail to legitimise the power and influence of organisational politics (Paton and McCalman 2001). The political tactics often employed in organisations include (Carnall 1990):

- selective use of performance criteria to manage credibility;
- use of external consultants to validate their views;
- control of agenda in formal meetings;
- building internal alliances and coalitions;
- use of promotions;
- control of access to information and key decision-makers;
- group pressure for employee conformity.

CASE STUDY

Clifford Chance

The most poignant line in the now-notorious memo from junior lawyers at Clifford Chance in New York was this plea to the firm's partners: 'At least say 'hello' in the hallways. It sounds like a small thing, but simply talk to us.'

Much comment about the memo has, understandably, focused on the allegation that the firm was encouraging 'padding' – or charging for time not spent on customer business – by insisting each lawyer bill clients for an enormous 2,420 hours a year. (The firm denies that padding occurred.) But for students of organisational pathology, the memo reveals more than shabby behaviour towards clients. It demonstrates nearly everything that can go wrong in a knowledge-based business.

Clifford Chance's New York office is, on the evidence of the memo, a horrible place. Not only did the partners not greet their juniors, the associate lawyers, in the hallways. They often deleted their e-mails without replying. Most significant was the

associates' feeling that the firm had lost its moral way. Padding was one example. Another was the firm's attitude to pro bono work. One partner is alleged to have said: 'If you want to do pro bono, that's fine, but I don't want to know about it.' The memo said the 'animosity to pro bono is deplorable and violates the ethical principles of our profession'.

With an admirable American belief that even the grubbiest glass can be topped up, the associates pleaded: 'Let us help you construct the ideal firm.'

What is the ideal firm? Few people know. In 1988, the management expert Peter Drucker called dealing with knowledge workers the 'managerial challenge of the future'. It still is. Writing in the *MIT Sloan Management Review*, Thomas Davenport, director of the Accenture Institute for Strategic Change, and two colleagues bemoan how little we know about increasing knowledge workers' productivity. 'Knowledge work thus far has no Frederick Taylor or Henry Ford,' they say.

Long may that last. Taylor measured every aspect of a manual worker's job. Ford developed the assembly line. Their idea was to create uniform tasks, carried out with as little variation as possible. Knowledge work is the opposite. It involves independent judgement, creativity and varying work to suit the circumstances.

Prof Drucker defined knowledge workers as people who knew more about their jobs than their bosses did. Law, advertising, consulting, software and architectural practices are knowledge-based organisations. So are newspapers, orchestras, hospitals, universities and the research, design and marketing departments of large companies.

Prof Davenport and his colleagues devote much of their article to discussing seating arrangements in knowledge-based organisations. One large open-plan office for everyone or different layouts for different jobs? At Merrill Lynch, brokers and portfolio managers get private offices. Traders sit in vast open-plan spaces so that they can shout at each other. Information technology professionals have 'semi-open offices with plenty of team spaces'.

One of the many things that upset the Clifford Chance associates was a rumour that the partners had voted to move office without telling them. Offices matter in knowledge organisations. So does IT, although Prof Davenport wisely steers clear of the many who think knowledge management is all about e-mail, webcasts and databases.

But neither office layout nor information systems will, in themselves, make organisations work. Many videoconferencing suites stand empty. Knowledge workers, dizzy from open-plan babble, stay home to get things done.

So what is managing knowledge workers about? I believe it is about three things: trust, measuring the right outcomes, and common purpose. Knowledge workers have to be left to get on with it. There is no point hiring people with specialist knowledge if you are going to monitor their every move. That is where trust comes in. People not only have to be trusted to do their jobs. They have to be able to trust each other. Successful knowledge work requires collaboration. The most senior managers set the tone. Openness and honesty are contagious; so are secrecy and deceit.

How do you know whether knowledge workers are working? You don't. That person staring out of the window could be dreaming up an advertising campaign or just staring out of the window. You will soon find out. The work either gets done or it doesn't. You measure the outcome, not the input.

How do you know what the right outcome is? Prof Drucker wrote that a conductor can trust members of an orchestra to play their instruments because they all have the same score. All organisations need one of those – a common purpose, an understanding of what they are trying to achieve. It is what the Clifford Chance lawyers were crying out for: 'Associates felt unsure of what the firm expected of them that year or over the course of their careers, or what the firm even expected of itself.'

It is a question every organisation should ask when deciding what outcomes to measure: what do we expect of ourselves? Let us hope the Clifford Chance partners are asking what they expect of themselves and, after reading their colleagues' memo, have concluded: not this.

Source: Article by Michael Skapinker, *Financial Times*, 13 November 2002

Questions

1 Critically analyse the leadership at Clifford Chance.

2 As a consultant to the partners, discuss how you would develop a successful change management programme to energise, mobilise and empower the associates at Clifford Chance.

3 What special considerations, if any, need to be taken into account to gain commitment from knowledge workers rather than ordinary workers at Clifford Chance?

Summary

This chapter has elaborated five key areas that need to be considered when developing a change management plan or the successful implementation of a knowledge management initiative:

1 The importance of leadership to develop a vision and goal commitment towards the change process. This is done through getting the right people in the right place and

using situational skills. Additional leadership skills are the use of symbolic acts and rites, especially in cultural change programmes.

2 Change is most effectively managed in a three-phase process of unfreezing, moving and refreezing. A number of options can be used to overcome resistance to change including education and persuasion, participation and involvement, facilitation and support, negotiation and agreement, manipulation and cooption and coercion.

3 Fairness, trust and 'delivering the deal' are important components for generating high levels of commitment towards a change programme.

4 Successful human resource interventions in a change process include the use of different levels of employee involvement, the use of training and development and management development practices and a mixture of reward and recognition schemes.

5 The importance of politics in the change process cannot be underestimated.

QUESTIONS FOR FURTHER THOUGHT

1 As many of the interventions suggested in this chapter are time consuming, how can organisations manage effectively in times of discontinuous change?

2 How would you manage redundancies as part of a KM initiative?

3 What are the dangers of the three-phase change management strategy of unfreezing, moving and refreezing (Lewin 1951)?

4 What determines the nature and level of consultation given that a manager could lose control in the change process?

5 What is the most effective approach to training and development if the organisation has limited resources?

6 What are the ethical issues associated with a portfolio approach to management development?

7 Discuss the advantages and disadvantages of individual and collective incentive schemes.

8 What type of recognition schemes are likely to be most effective in knowledge management initiatives?

9 Some commentators believe that cultural change programmes do not deliver their goals. How feasible is it for human resource interventions to influence the deeper values, beliefs and attitudes rather than purely affect surface level norms?

10 What is the best way of developing political skills in the change process?

Further reading

1 Senior (1997) is an excellent book covering the different approaches and challenges in the change management process and explores the hard systems and soft systems approach to change.

2 Brown (1998) is strong on cultural change management.

3 Beardwell and Holden (2001) provides a contemporary text on different human resource interventions in the change process.

References

Ansoff, I. H. and McDonnell, E. J. (1990) *Implementing Strategic Management*, Prentice-Hall, Englewood Cliffs: NJ.

Argyris, C. and Schon, D. A. (1978) *Organizational Learning: A Theory of Action Perspective*, Addison-Wesley, Reading, MA.

Barham, K., Fraser, J. and Heath, I. (1987) *Management for the Future*, Ashridge Management College, Ashridge.

Beardwell, I. and Holden, L. (2001) *Human Resource Management: A Contemporary Approach*, Pearson Education, Harlow, Essex.

Bennis, W. and Nanus, B. (1985) *Leadership: The Strategies for Taking Charge*, Harper and Row, New York.

Brown, A. D. (1998) *Organisational Culture*, Pearson Education Ltd, London.

Browning, G. (2003) 'Office politics: the new game.' *Management Today*, May, 54–59.

Buchanan, D. A., Claydon, T. and Doyle, M. (1997) 'Organization development and change: the legacy of the nineties', *Leicester Business School Occasional Paper, De Montford University*, 43.

Carnall, C. A. (1990) *Managing Change in Organizations*, Prentice Hall, Hemel Hempstead, Hertfordshire.

Casey, B., Lakey, J. and White, M. (1992) *Payment Systems: A Look at Current Practice*, Policy Studies Institute, Department of Employment, London.

Daloz, L. A. (1986) *Effective Mentoring and Teaching*, Jossey-Bass, San Francisco.

Grundy, T. (1993) *Managing Strategic Change*, Kogan Page, London.

Guest, D. and Conway, N. (1997) *Employee Motivation and the Psychological Contract*, IPD, London.

Handy, C. B. (1993) *The Age of Unreason*, Century Business, Chatham, Kent.

Harrison, R. (2000) *Employee Development*, Chartered Institute of Personnel and Development, London.

Hayes, J. (2002) *The Theory and Practice of Change Management*, Palgrave, Basingstoke.

Hersey, P., Blanchard, K. H. and Johnson, D.E. (2000). *Management of Organizational Behaviour: Leading Human Resources*, Prentice-Hall, Upper Saddle River, NJ.

Hislop, D. (2002) 'Linking human resource management and knowledge management via commitment: A review and research agenda', *Employee Relations*, 25(2), 182–202.

Kilmann, R. H. (1984) *Beyond the Quick Fix: Managing Five Tracks to Organizational Success*, Jossey-Bass, San Fransico, CA.

Kim, W. C., and Mauborgne, R. (2003) 'Fair Process: Managing in the Knowledge Economy', *Harvard Business Review*, January, 127–136.

Kotter, J. P. and Schlesinger, L. A. (1979) 'Choosing Strategies for Change', *Harvard Business Review*, March/April(2), 106–114.

Lewin, K. (1951) *Field theory in social science*, Harper & Row, New York.

Marchington, M., Goodman, J. P., Wilkinson, A. and Ackers, P. (1992) *New Developments in Employee Involvement*, Manchester School of Management, Manchester.

Newell, S., Robertson, M., Scarbrough, H. and Swan, J. (2002) *Managing Knowledge Work*, Palgrave, Basingstoke, Hampshire.

Odiorne, G. S. (1984) *Strategic Management of Human Resources: A Portfolio Approach*, Jossey-Bass, San Francisco.

O'Reilly, C. A. (1989) 'Corporations, Culture and Commitment: Motivation and Social Control in Organizations', *California Management Review*, Summer, 9–25.

Parsloe, E. and Wray, M. (2000) *Coaching and Mentoring: Practical methods to improve learning*, Kogan Page, London.

Paton, R. A. and McCalman, J. (2001) *Change Management: A guide to effective implementation*, Sage, London.

Pfeffer, J. (2001) 'Fighting the war for talent is hazardous to your organization's health', *Organizational Dynamics*, Vol. 29, No. 4, 248–259.

Porter, L. W. and Lawler, E. E. (1968) *Management Attitudes and Performance*, Irwin, Homewood, Ill.

Reid, M. A. and Barrington, H. (2000) *Training Interventions: Promoting learning opportunities*, Chartered Institute of Personnel and Development, London.

Senior, B. (1997) *Organisational Change*, Pearson Education Ltd, Harlow, Essex.

Stewart, J. (1999) *Employee Development Practice*, Pitman Publishing, London.

Stone, B. (1997) *Confronting Company Politics*, Macmillan, Basingstoke.

PART 5

Leveraging knowledge

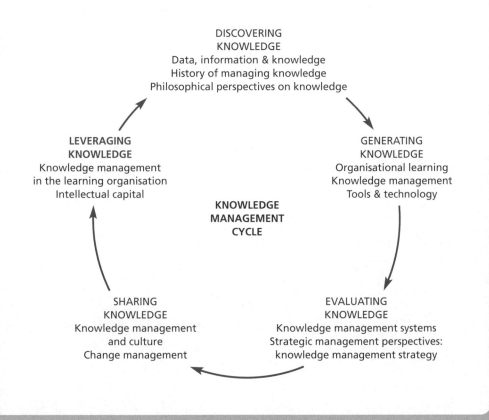

DISCOVERING
KNOWLEDGE
Data, information & knowledge
History of managing knowledge
Philosophical perspectives on knowledge

GENERATING
KNOWLEDGE
Organisational learning
Knowledge management
Tools & technology

**LEVERAGING
KNOWLEDGE**
Knowledge management
in the learning organisation
Intellectual capital

**KNOWLEDGE
MANAGEMENT
CYCLE**

SHARING
KNOWLEDGE
Knowledge management
and culture
Change management

EVALUATING
KNOWLEDGE
Knowledge management systems
Strategic management perspectives:
knowledge management strategy

Chapter 9

Knowledge management and the learning organisation

After completing this chapter the reader should be able to:

- contrast the differences between organisational learning and the learning organisation;
- explain the characteristics of the dominant conceptual models in the field;
- describe the differences between a static, teaching and learning organisation;
- outline the different strategic dimensions of a learning organisation.

The use and application of the learning organisation implies these questions for managers:

- What is the most appropriate model of a learning organisation to adopt in your organisation?
- How can a shared vision of a learning organisation be developed?
- How can trust and commitment be developed to promote a true learning organisation rather than a teaching organisation?

Chapter 3   explores the similarities and distinctions between the learning organisation.
Chapter 6   expands on institutionalist perspectives of the competitive learning organisation.

The growing pains of business

The world's biggest companies are facing a growth crisis. So says a chorus of consultants-turned-Cassandras who, unlike the mythical prophetess of Troy, are selling solutions as well as portents of doom.

Take Adrian Slywotzky, a big wheel in strategy practice at Mercer Management Consulting. His new book, *How To Grow When Markets Don't*, notes that in the 1990s only 7 per cent of US public companies achieved eight or more years of double-digit growth in revenue and operating profits. 'As the growth crisis worsens in the coming decade you can expect this percentage to shrink significantly,' he warns, 'unless companies rethink their approach to growth.'

Dramatic stuff. But also familiar. Strategy wonks may recall *Creative Destruction* (2001) by Dick Foster, an erudite senior partner at McKinsey, which presented data showing 'a steel link between survival and underperformance' among large companies. Then came *Profit From the Core* (also 2001) by Chris Zook, head of the strategy practice at Bain, a consulting rival to both Mercer and McKinsey. Mr Zook's numbers demonstrated that throughout the 1990s fewer than one in five public companies managed to increase revenues and profits at an average real rate of 5.5 per cent or above.

There is no reason to doubt these statistics and every reason to take them seriously – with an important caveat. The fact that individual companies find it hard to improve revenue and profits at above-average rates over long periods is not, in itself, surprising. Any company earning supra-normal returns on capital can expect to attract competitors. The effect will be to reduce returns. Such is capitalism.

That said, growing fast is difficult, not impossible. So which strategies do our gurus suggest are likely to reignite the growth engines? The trick, says Mr Foster, is for companies to learn how to 'change at the pace and scale of the (stock) market' – developing new businesses, selling old ones and cultivating a corporate culture that is ready to embrace change. The biggest enemy of sustained growth is 'cultural lock-in', the phenomenon by which managers get attached to existing products and processes.

Mr Zook's prescription is conservative by comparison: focus first on your core business. Only when the core is well defined and purring along should managers start to think about diversification. Even then, they should focus on 'adjacencies' – products sharing customers, costs, channels, competitors or technologies with the core. The further companies travel from the core, argues Mr Zook, the less likely they are to succeed. Thus Gillette glided smoothly from male shaving products into female shaving and toiletries but got a nasty shock when it went further afield into batteries (Duracell) and pens (Parker and Waterman).

Salvation, Slywotzky-style, lies elsewhere. In *Value Migration* (1996) and *The Profit Zone* (1998), the donnish Mr Slywotzky argued that the rules of corporate strategy had changed. It was no longer enough to design great products, build market share and wait for profits to flow. A new breed of competitors – Dell, Southwest Airlines, Wal-Mart – were developing business models that could turn the economics of an industry on its head. The buzz-phrase was 'business model innovation'. In his new book, Mr Slywotzky argues that competition is now so intense that even having a nifty business model is no guarantee of success. The next strategic wave, he says, is 'demand innovation' – that is, 'using your product position as the starting-point from which to do new things for customers that solve their biggest problems and improve their overall performance'.

Such as? Take Cardinal Health, quite possibly the biggest US company you have never heard of. This $50 billion-a-year distributor of medicines used its relationships with drugs companies and hospitals to expand into everything from manufacturing automated drug-dispensing machines to providing outsourced product development for pharmaceuticals companies. An even better example, although not cited in the book, is International Business Machines, which in the 1990s leveraged its position as a trusted supplier of computers to sell information technology services, outsourcing and consulting. IBM Global Services is now Big Blue's biggest business.

So far, so convincing. Just do not be lulled into thinking that 'demand innovation', 'profiting from the core' or 'learning to change at the pace and scale of the market' will, in isolation, solve your company's growth problems. The uncomfortable truth is that the best growth strategies are much too complex to be captured in single volumes of the Cassandra kind.

In his excellent 1998 book *Strategy Safari*, Henry Mintzberg identifies no fewer than ten schools of thought about what makes corporate strategy. These fall broadly into two categories. First are the rationalists who believe that strategy formulation is a discipline that requires an elaborate process, lots of all-day meetings and tools ranging from Swot (strengths, weaknesses, opportunities and threats) analysis to game theory. This is the realm of Bruce Henderson, the late founder of Boston Consulting Group, and Michael Porter, the Harvard Business School superstar who 20 years ago wrote *Competitive Strategy*, the definitive (if unreadable) work on industry analysis. It is also the tradition that Messrs Zlywotsky and Zook represent.

Second are the humanists, who believe that far from being handed down by senior executives, strategy arises from within organisations through a messy process of experimentation, failure and feedback. Big names here include Peter Senge, author of *The Fifth Discipline*, the 1990 book that popularised the idea of 'learning organisations', and Gary Hamel and C.K. Prahalad, arguably the most influential strategy writers of the 1990s, who argued that companies need to focus on developing 'core competencies', strategic flexibility and a vibrant company-wide market for ideas.

Mr Foster, at least in Creative Destruction mode, with his emphasis on the dangers of cultural lock-in, also lives on this side of the intellectual tracks.

Needless to say, the best real-world strategies combine both rationalist and humanist elements, put together in an original way. In the 1990s, for example, General Electric combined an elaborate formal planning process with a strong emphasis on cultural change and a vibrant market for new ideas

focused on its Crotonville management centre. GE also broke many of the rules in *Profit From the Core* on its way to becoming the most admired US company of the decade.

'Managers love these menu-driven books because it relieves them of the burden of having to think very hard,' observes Prof Hamel with customary pith. 'The only thing that really matters about any strategy is how it is different from every other strategy.'

Preston McAffee, an economics professor at Texas University, is even more blunt in the preface to *Competitive Solutions*, his own guide to the real-world nuances of strategic thinking: 'A book that promises to provide a single vision, or even three visions, for all firms in all circumstances should be discarded, or should be read only to identify the activities uninspired competitors might choose.'

Harsh, but fair.

Source: Article by Simon London, *Financial Times*, 5 May 2003

Questions

1 As chief executive of a large private organisation, which one of these Cassandra offerings would you use and why?
2 Are concepts such as 'business model innovation' synonymous with the 'learning organisation'? If not, what are the differences?
3 What is the best mix of a rationalist and humanist perspective for a high-growth company

Introduction

The external environment for many organisations nowadays is characterised by turbulence associated with globalisation, deregulation of markets, changing customer and investor demands and increasing product-market competition (Jashapara 2003; Mitroff *et al.* 1994). There is a growing need in organisations to move beyond solving existing problems to improving continuously in the face of changing conditions (Hamel and Prahalad 1994). Knowledge has emerged as the most strategically significant resource of the firm (Grant 1996) and the ability of a firm to learn faster than its competitors as the only sustainable form of competitive advantage (de Geus 1988).

These assumptions have given rise to the notion of a *learning organisation*. Much of the literature tends to be conceptually based and prescriptive in nature with little empirical work to support its assertions. There is also confusion between the terms 'learning organisation' and 'organisational learning' as some authors use the terms synonymously and interchangeably. A useful distinction is to consider organisational

Table 9.1 Distinctions between organisational learning and the learning organisation

Organisational learning	Learning organisation
Means	End
Process or activity	Idealised form
Attainable	Easily lost due to changes
Descriptive research	Prescriptive research
Inductive	Deductive (normative)
Academic and scholarly orientation	Practitioner and consultancy orientation
Predominantly qualitative research	Predominantly quantitative research (little empirical evidence so far)
Theoretical orientation	Action orientation

learning as the processes or activities in an organisation whereas a learning organisation can be considered as the end state. Some authors suggest that the learning organisation exists only in an ideal form, creating an unattainable tension; a holy grail (Jashapara 1993). Some major distinctions between organisational learning and the learning organisation are shown in Table 9.1.

The learning organisation literature gained in popularity in the mid 1990s but interest has declined as the concept of knowledge management has taken over (Swan *et al.* 1999). Despite the fact that knowledge is often the output of the learning process, many key contributors in knowledge management fail to acknowledge the processes of organisational learning or the learning organisation in their considerations (Davenport and Prusak 1998; Svieby 1997). In the same way, exponents of the learning organisation literature say relatively little about the pervasive use of information systems and technology to achieve competitive advantage in contemporary organisations. There currently exists an opportunity to synthesise these two emerging literatures and bring together the technological and human dimensions into a coherent whole (Loermans 2002).

This chapter shall attempt to forward the major conceptual and empirical advances in the learning organisation literature. It begins by examining the major US contribution of *The Fifth Discipline* by Peter Senge that popularised the notion of the 'learning organisation' in the early 1990s. It continues to explore some of the British contributions to the concept in the early 1990s (Garratt 1990; Honey 1991; Pedler *et al.* 1991). The Japanese contribution of Nonaka (1991) is recognised for its elucidation of transformation processes involved in converting tacit and explicit knowledge from one form to another. None of these idealised forms of learning organisations shows explicitly how they will lead to competitive advantage. Instead a model of a 'competitive learning organisation' (Jashapara 1993; Jashapara 2003) is forwarded showing how learning can be aligned to changes in the competitive environment. The problems of ideology, power and politics in learning organisations and the potential exploitation of the workforce are highlighted towards the end of the chapter to show how the concept could be misused by organisations. As empirical research on the learning organisation is limited and has suffered from widespread anecdotes and assertions, the current position of empirical research is examined (Jashapara 2003; Örtenblad 2002).

US contribution: the fifth discipline

Peter Senge was instrumental in popularising the concept of the 'learning organisation', especially among consultancy and business school circles, and placing it firmly on the academic agenda. He saw organisations as a product of how we think and how we interact. His definition of a learning organisation was (Senge 1990):

> 'Learning organizations [are] organizations where people continually expand their capacity to create the results they truly desire, where new and expansive patterns of thinking are nurtured, where collective aspiration is set free, and where people are continually learning to see the whole together.'

He considered the quality movement as the first wave of the true learning organisation and believed that the building blocks for such organisations revolve around practising five distinct disciplines, as shown in Figure 9.1: personal mastery, team learning, systems thinking, mental models and shared vision.

Personal mastery is seen as developing our capacity to clarify what is important to us in terms of our personal vision and purpose. This helps to develop a 'creative tension' between our current reality and our future vision. The qualities of perseverance and patience become guiding principles. This assumes that individual commitment to one's own growth and a supportive environment are prevalent in the organisation. Cynics often opposed to personal mastery are recognised as 'frustrated idealists' disappointed when reality falls short of their high ideals.

Team learning is deemed to develop our capacity for conversation and balancing dialogue and discussion. In many decision-making processes there can be a tendency towards engaging in 'discussion' where different views are presented and defended.

Figure 9.1 The learning organisation (Garvin 1993; Senge 1990)

This is useful in instances of convergent thinking where a quick decision needs to be made and the best argument prevails. However, in many other instances that require divergent thinking, engaging people in 'dialogue' is considered primary where different views are presented as a means to discovering a new view. People are more receptive to new and different views and willing to change their own views.

Systems thinking is seen as developing our capacity for putting the pieces together and seeing wholes rather than disparate parts. This is the conceptual cornerstone of the fifth discipline as it provides the incentive and means to integrate disciplines and recognise the whole. This is seen as the major drawback with traditional management approaches to problems that produce simplistic frameworks to understand complex and dynamic systems and processes.

Mental models is our capacity to reflect on our internal pictures. This discipline involves balancing our skills of inquiry and advocacy as well as understanding how our mental models influence our actions. An example of mental models is the increasing use of scenario planning which forces managers to examine how they would manage under different conditions in the future.

Shared vision is concerned with building a sense of commitment in a group based on what they would really like to create. In this respect, leaders and managers play an important role in developing learning organisations through building shared visions rooted firmly in personal visions.

There are a number of questions and reservations that arise from this notion of the learning organisation. These are predominantly linked to the prescriptive nature of the model. How did these disciplines arise? What empirical or theoretical background underpins this model? Why not have another five equally valid disciplines such as training, mentoring, participation, partnerships and feedback? How realistic is the development of a shared vision given the inherent difficulty of aligning individual goals and organisational goals? Also, many organisations are unlikely to want to relinquish management control to the extent suggested by this model in the quest for employee empowerment. The internal political environments have been ignored. Instead, the lasting contribution of this model has been the promotion of 'dialogue' in team learning and recognising the importance of systems thinking for understanding complex and dynamic situations.

In response to the prescriptive and idealistic nature of the five disciplines, the significant other US contribution (Garvin 1993) took the notion of a learning organisation back to various aspects of organisational learning. Hence, it is not surprising that confusion has persisted between these two related concepts to this day. The definition of a learning organisation from this perspective is (Garvin 1993, pp. 80):

> *'A learning organization is an organisation skilled at creating, acquiring, and transferring knowledge, and at modifying its behavior to reflect new knowledge and insights.'*

Here we have an operational perspective of the learning organisation where learning can be measured, is actionable and provides guidelines for practice. Given the fact that often what gets measured gets managed in organisations, are the right forms of learning being measured? Are there dangers that measures may show high levels of learning that are misdirected? As shown in Figure 9.1, the five forms of organisational learning or activities construed as important in this model are (Garvin 1993):

- systematic problem solving;
- experimentation;
- learning from past experiences and mistakes;
- learning from others – including vicarious learning and benchmarking;
- transferring and sharing knowledge across the organisation.

UK contribution: the learning company

Apart from the above US contributions, much of the activity in the learning organisation literature has occurred in the UK. This began with Bob Garratt (1987) who proposed a model based on a three-level hierarchy, as shown in Figure 9.2. Garratt was influenced by the principles of action learning (Revans 1977) and was critical of the 'action-fixated non-learning cycle' found in many organisations. He argued that there was a tendency to ignore the reflection phase in this action orientation with a consequence of people trying harder rather than thinking smarter on problems.

There are also important cultural dimensions related to a reflection orientation. For example, in Japan, a manager sitting on his own in his office is less likely to be interrupted due to the assumption that he is reflecting on important organisational problems and matters. The fact that he may be thinking about lunch is immaterial! This valuing of reflection is less common in the west.

This model of the learning organisation is based on a three-level hierarchy of policy, strategy and operations. Organisational learning occurs at these three levels in the form of double-loop learning with multiple feedback loops from information flows, direction giving and monitoring environmental changes. The model provides a means of processing and integrating these information flows by positioning the direction givers (business brain) at the centre of organisational learning. This places a large responsibility

Figure 9.2 A three-level hierarchy for the learning organisation (Garratt 1987)

for learning on direction givers, even though senior executives can often exhibit major defences to learning (Argyris 1991). This model suggests that organisational learning is highly dependent on executive learning but fails to consider the political dimensions of learning at this level.

Similar to Garvin's model, another UK model was more focused on organisational learning and valued experimentation highly (Easterby-Smith 1990). This central quality of experimentation was promoted in a number of ways. The proposed model suggested experimenting in people to generate creativity and innovation, experimenting in organisational structures to introduce flexibility, experimenting in reward systems so that risk takers were not disadvantaged, and experimenting in information systems by focusing on unusual variations. The difficulty is that experimentation can be costly, especially when it does not lead to any clear signs of creativity or innovation and lessons learnt from mistakes are not passed around the organisation.

Another UK perspective on the learning organisation saw the concept much more simply as encouraging wanted behaviours in organisations and suppressing unwanted behaviours. The role of managers from this behaviourist perspective was to discover the triggers and reinforcers for wanted behaviours and suitable mechanisms to discourage unwanted behaviours. Examples of potential wanted and unwanted behaviours in a learning organisation are shown in Table 9.2 (Honey 1991).

Table 9.2 **Potential wanted and unwanted behaviours in a learning organisation**

Wanted behaviour	Unwanted behaviour
Asking questions	Acquiesing
Suggesting ideas	Rubbishing ideas
Exploring alternatives	Going for expedient, quick fixes
Taking risks/experimenting	Being cautious
Being open about the way it is	Telling people what they want to hear/ filtering bad news
Converting mistakes into learning	Repeating the same mistakes
Reflecting and reviewing	Rushing around keeping active
Talking about learning	Talking anecdotes (i.e. what happened, not what was learnt)
Taking responsibility for own learning and development	Waiting for other people to do it
Admitting inadequacies and mistakes	Justifying actions/blaming other people or events

Pause for thought

Imagine you were tasked with initiating a company-wide programme for surfacing people's mistakes and learning from them. How would you instigate such an 'error harvesting' programme where mistakes were surfaced and errors were discussed? What do you see as the primary difficulties in implementing such a programme? What cultural factors would you need to consider and how could they be overcome?

The most telling UK contribution has come from two conceptual models of a 'learning company' (Pedler *et al.* 1991). The definition of a learning organisation from this perspective is:

> *'The Learning Company is a vision of what might be possible. It is not brought about simply by training individuals; it can only happen as a result of learning at the whole organization level. A Learning Company is an organization that facilitates the learning of all its members and continuously transforms itself.'*

The first proposed blueprint of a learning company was composed of five components, as shown in Figure 9.3. The authors were highly influenced by action learning, double-loop learning and the quality movement (Argyris 1999; Deming 1986; Revans 1977) in their proposed model. They suggested that the five key clusters in a learning organisation are:

- *strategy* includes a learning approach to strategy with small-scale experiments and feedback loops to enable continuous improvement and participative policy making;
- *looking in* includes using IT to help individuals understand what's going on and using formative accounting and control to assist learning and delighting internal customers. In addition, this cluster includes developing an environment of collaboration between internal departments and exploring assumptions and values behind the reward systems;
- *structures* implies the need for roles and careers to be flexibly orientated to allow for experimentation, growth and adaptation;
- *looking out* includes regularly scanning and reviewing the external environment and developing joint learning with competitors and other stakeholders for 'win:win' learning;
- *learning opportunities* includes a climate of continuous improvement where mistakes are allowed and encouraged together with self-development opportunities for all.

The original model above can appear somewhat mechanical and lifeless. In order to convey a greater dynamic to this model, Pedler, Burgoyne and Boydell went further to

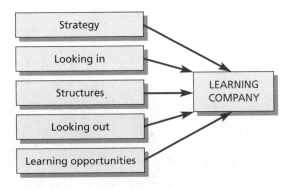

Figure 9.3 The learning company (Pedler *et al.* 1991)

Source: Pedler, M., Burgoyne, J. and Boydell, T. (1991) *The Learning Company: A Strategy for Sustainable Development*, McGraw-Hill, London. Reproduced with the kind permission of the McGraw-Hill Publishing Company.

propose an energy flow model based on four components: ideas and actions at the individual level and policy and operations at the collective level. All of these four components are connected through four figures of eight to represent double-loop learning. There is little elaboration of the potential drivers and retarders of this energy flow in organisations or recommendations if the energy becomes stuck in organisations.

Japanese contribution: the knowledge-creating company

Instead of learning being the critical success factor in organisations, Nonaka (1991) argues that it is knowledge that is more primary and the lasting source of competitive advantage. He forwards the notion of a knowledge-creating company based on continuous innovation through knowledge creation. Despite the fact that knowledge is the output of learning, the major contribution in this model is the transformation process of tacit knowledge to explicit knowledge and vice versa to create new knowledge, as shown in Figure 9.4. He looks at six successful Japanese companies to discern the different dimensions of innovative processes. He uses the distinction of tacit and explicit knowledge (Polanyi 1967) and incorporates an individual's mental models and beliefs into the difficult-to-articulate concept of tacit knowledge.

Pause for thought

Imagine that you have been asked to manage the development of a new product or service in your organisation. Describe how you could use metaphors, slogans, symbols and other figurative forms of language to fire the imagination of your team. What interventions could you make if your initial approaches were not well received? Can you think of any alternative approaches that could spark the creative spirit of your team?

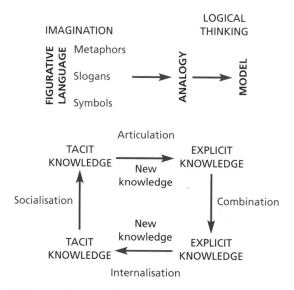

Figure 9.4 **The knowledge-creating company (Nonaka 1991)**

The knowledge-creating company uses four processes for creating knowledge. However, it is only when one form of knowledge is transformed into another, such as tacit to explicit or vice versa, that new knowledge is created. The four processes as shown in Figure 9.4 are as follows:

- *Socialisation* allows tacit knowledge from one person to be passed to the other. For example, this is traditionally how knowledge is passed in a master–apprentice relationship. Such knowledge does not become explicit and, hence, cannot be leveraged and used by the whole organisation.
- *Combination* is about combining discrete pieces of explicit knowledge held by individuals. Such explicit to explicit knowledge transfer does not expand the organisation's knowledge base.
- *Articulation* is the conversion of tacit knowledge to explicit knowledge. Here new knowledge is formed and made explicit in a form that can be shared around the organisation.
- *Internalisation* allows individuals to broaden their knowledge base and create knowledge by converting explicit knowledge to tacit knowledge.

In all the companies studied, articulation was a primary process for successful innovation. This involved using people's imagination, playing with abstract ideas and moving them towards a model of logical thinking that could be exploited by the organisation. To get the tacit knowledge and ideas moving in a group, there was considerable recourse to figurative language. This allowed hunches, intuitions and insights in the group to surface. For the development of a new car, Honda used the slogan 'Theory of Automobile Evolution' with its design team. Such creative tension allowed the design team to consider a car as a living organism and explore how it would evolve. Metaphors were also used to express the inexpressible, even though they might have multiple meanings and appear contradictory. The tension in meanings was seen as a valuable resource in the creative process. Once the knowledge creation process was triggered through figurative language and the use of imagination, there were two additional steps to get those ideas into a workable solution. The first was the use of analogy to reconcile differences and make clear distinctions between ideas. The second was to create a model of the ideas to give them a logical coherency.

Nonaka sees the continual challenge of knowledge-creating companies as re-examining what they take for granted. In terms of organisational design, he promotes a 'redundant organisation' to encourage knowledge sharing and dissemination. By redundancy, he means the conscious overlapping of company information, business activities and responsibilities. This can be achieved by individuals and groups overlapping information and responsibilities to allow greater dialogue and communication to occur. Another approach is to promote job rotation so that employees can see the business from a wide range of perspectives. In addition, internal competition between groups on the same project is encouraged so that the merits and shortcomings of different approaches and perspectives are aired and the most effective solution is chosen.

The primary assumption behind the knowledge-creating company is that innovation is vital to a company's survival. Hence, one can see why the use of figurative language in the articulation process can become so important. However, if the dominant competitive force in the external environment is efficiency, the model says little on how the same knowledge-creating spiral could be used to these ends. Also, as an individual's tacit knowledge is intrinsically linked to a person's mental models and beliefs, the model does not explore how disparities between individual values and organisational values would be managed. There are implications in employee commitment to the knowledge-creating process.

The competitive learning organisation

The major shortfall in many models of the learning organisation is the lack of emphasis on the competitive performance of the organisation. This remains implicit in the models and there is little discourse on how such learning organisations would lead to sustainable competitive advantage. The organisational learning and operational aspects are articulated but the strategic dimensions appear to be missing.

One dynamic model that pursues the strategic nature of organisational learning is the 'competitive learning organisation' (Jashapara 2003), as shown in Figure 9.5 (p. 253). The model adopts an institutionalist perspective where competition and strategic change are seen as intimately linked (Pettigrew and Whipp 1991). This means that organisational learning cannot be viewed separately from competition and the key to success is alignment between an organisation and its environment (Fiol and Lyles 1985). Competition is regarded as a process through people's day-to-day learning rather than as a steady state of affairs. The model rejects the planning school approach to competition as the dynamic processes of competition are never explored. Instead, it assumes that strategy formation is adaptive, incremental and a complex learning process where ends and means are either specified simultaneously or are intertwined (Jashapara 2003). A competitive learning organisation is defined as:

> 'a continuously adaptive enterprise that aligns itself to the environment by focusing its learning on the major competitive forces at a given time.'

This model comprises two aspects: an organisational learning one and a strategic one. Organisational learning can be considered as a distinction between cognitive and behavioural development. Behavioural development can be seen as new responses or actions based on existing interpretations. In contrast, cognitive development can be regarded as organisational changes that affect the interpretation of events and development of shared understanding among organisational members. The behavioural learning is referred to as 'single-loop learning' in the model and the cognitive level as 'double-loop learning' (Argyris and Schon 1978). Another way of looking at single-loop

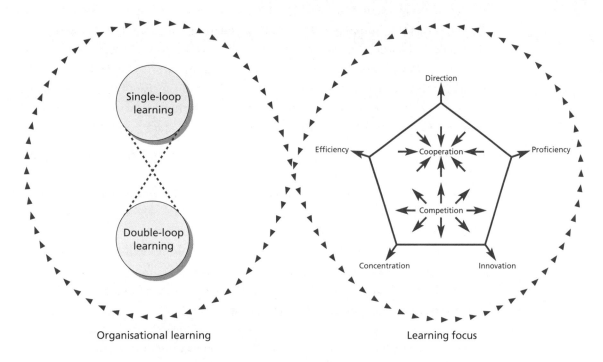

Figure 9.5 Competitive learning organisation (Jashapara 2003)

learning is 'doing things better' in organisations whereas double-loop learning is 'doing things differently or doing different things' (Hayes and Allinson 1998).

The model of a 'competitive learning organisation' argues that learning by itself is not enough to achieve competitive advantage. What if the learning is misdirected? Instead, the emphasis in the model is on how best to focus the learning. Would sending senior executives on Japanese flower-arranging courses be suitable? Is sending all prospective senior managers on MBA programmes the best way forward? The problem with any pre-scriptive approach is that the external environment and competitive changes tend to be left out of the equation. Instead, this model argues that any learning needs to be focused on the predominant competitive force acting on an organisation at any given moment. Undoubtedly, these forces are dynamic and change over time.

> **Pause for thought**
>
> As a manager, how can you ensure that the collective learning of your team is responding to changes in the competitive environment? How would you manage your team learning in an uncertain and turbulent environment? What time frames do you consider most workable for managing learning in your teams? How would you influence your team to be more proactive and take greater responsibility for their learning?

The learning focus for a competitive learning organisation is based on a system of seven forces identified in effective organisations (Mintzberg 1991), as shown in Figure

9.5. There are five generic forces that act externally on an organisation and two diametrically opposite internal forces. At any given time, one of these forces tends to dominate and learning is focused on responding to this force as best as possible. For example, if innovation is the dominant force, learning efforts may be driven towards creativity through articulation of tacit knowledge and the use of figurative language (Nonaka 1991). The dominant external forces impacting on an organisation due to changes in the competitive environment are as follows:

- *The force for direction* is concerned with strategic vision and may relate to organisations in start-up or turnaround situations.
- *The force for efficiency* is concerned with standardisation and formalisation of processes and may relate to bureaucratic organisations where rationalisation and restructuring are a major focus.
- *The force for proficiency* is concerned with tasks requiring high levels of knowledge and skills and may relate to professional organisations.
- *The force for concentration* is concerned with concentrating efforts on serving certain markets, particularly in large diversified firms.
- *The force for innovation* is concerned with discovering new things for the customer and may relate to adhocracies comprising skilled experts or multidisciplinary projects.

There are also two internal cultural forces that have an impact on a firm's learning and effectiveness: the forces of cooperation and competition. In this conception, organisational culture is viewed as a product of continual struggles by groups of organisational members to impose values and identities on the role of others (Carroll 1995). If the forces of cooperation are dominant in an organisation, this may result in an ideological organisation such as a kibbutz. In contrast, if the forces of competition are dominant, this may result in the pulling apart of politics and a highly political organisation where conflicting in-fighting takes over. There may be limits to the levels of cooperation in an organisation as ideology discourages change and if individuals perceive a need for change, they may be forced to challenge the ideology which breeds politics.

As competitive forces are rarely static and vary continuously over time, a state of 'configuration' may occur where one of the external forces described above dominates and the organisation is drawn towards a coherent form (Mintzberg 1991). However, configuration may lead to the problem of 'contamination' where the dominant force undermines equally valid forces. For example, a firm may be so fixed on improving its efficiency over five years that it fails to recognise that it needs to focus on innovation given the market changes with new products and services.

In some periods, organisations may go through states of 'combination' where no single force dominates. This may result in periods of 'conversion' from one form to another. The state of 'combination' may result in problems of 'cleavage' where two or more forces may confront each other and eventually paralyse the organisation. For instance, half the management board of an organisation may wish to focus organisational energies and learning on efficiency whereas the other half may see innovation as a much greater priority. The internal forces of competition and cooperation can be important catalysts for managing these problems of 'contamination' and 'cleavage'.

The competitive learning organisation is seen as an ideal rather than an end state. Metaphorically, such organisations can be seen as in a 'continual quest for the Holy Grail' (Jashapara 1993). The Holy Grail represents a search for improved methods of learning at all levels and an understanding of the changing nature of competitive bases which act as a focus for organisational learning. The fluctuating nature of the competitive environment and the fragility of competitive bases means that organisations are likely to maintain their 'competitive learning' phase for very limited periods before they slip into either a 'teaching' phase, or a 'static' phase as shown in Table 9.3.

Table 9.3 Development of a competitive learning organisation (Jashapara 1993)

	Static organisation	Teaching organisation	Competitive learning organisation
Level of organisational learning	Poor	Fair	High
Rate of learning	Poor	Fair	High
Learning focus	None	Limited	High
Level of communication	Poor	Fair	High
Flow of communication	None	One way	Two-way
Organisational performance	Poor	Fair	High

The static organisation is characterised by a lack of learning. Such organisations may view their workforces as costs to be minimised rather than assets to be developed. It is inevitable that such organisations will face an internal crisis through lack of responsiveness to the external environment. This crisis may act to inhibit learning or result in a transformation into a 'competitive learning' phase. Such crises can be seen as opportunities for growth or can herald the beginning of the eventual decline of an organisation.

The competitive learning organisation places high value on the learning of all its employees at individual, group and organisational levels. Double-loop learning is encouraged, with an emphasis on questioning underlying assumptions. The distribution of learning is facilitated through open channels of two-way communication throughout the organisation. Each employee is committed to focused learning that responds to forces in the external environment.

However, the problems of contamination and cleavage may become more evident or major cultural changes (fluctuation in forces of cooperation or competition) may dominate an organisation, forcing it to slip towards a 'teaching organisation' where the overarching role of senior managers as teachers becomes important. Learning can become prescriptive and the domain of human resource departments rather than the responsibility of each learner. As these organisations are characterised by one-way communication from senior managers to employees, there is little scope for an equal exchange of ideas and knowledge. The role of learning focus is left solely to organisational strategists and human resource departments. Learning becomes parochial and employees may feel blocked due to a lack of challenge and responsibility for their learning. In such circumstances, firms may slip into static organisations. This model promotes the nature of adaptive enterprises responding to the ideal of continuous improvement similar to the quest for the Holy Grail. Each time they feel they have arrived at this elusive destination, the goal posts change due to the dynamics of the competitive environment.

Power, politics and the learning organisation

The concept of a learning organisation conveyed in this chapter has been conceived as a Utopian ideal, but could it be a Foucauldian nightmare instead (Coopey 1998)? Is the concept of the learning organisation prone to exploitation of workers by managers in more devious ways to attain their own goals? Let's explore the nature of reality in many organisations nowadays. Directors are under increasing pressure to satisfy short-term profit goals of shareholders and more concerned about potential underperformance which may lead to predatory action. This nervousness often results in tight organisational controls where employees can be reduced to mechanical objects in a performance-driven system. Employees don't have the same voice through their representatives (traditionally the trade unions) as the balance of power has moved more towards employers in many western countries through successive government interventions and diminishing trade union membership.

There are two perspectives of the learning organisation. One is of a Utopian sunshine forwarded by practitioners and consultants, the other a Foucauldian gloom promoted by academics (Denton 1998; Driver 2002). From the Foucauldian gloom perspective, human resource management can be seen as a device to organise and control the work process. Any deviation from the norm is a cause for concern. Individuals lose their personal identity in the workplace as they are subsumed in an overarching ideology of enterprise and competition. People are disempowered and maintain the 'them and us' attitude. This hides the crucial element of trust as employees have little confidence that their personal interests and goals will be honoured by their line managers. If trust is in short supply, this will have a direct influence on employee commitment to organisational learning or the Utopian goal of a learning organisation. Under the Foucauldian gloom perspective, we have a teaching organisation where senior managers learn and win. This contrasts with a Utopian sunshine perspective where everyone learns and wins along the lines espoused in a competitive learning organisation.

Reflect on any organisational situation where you feel power has been misused by your line manager. Describe your general feelings and impressions over the situation. What impact did the incident have on your performance and commitment to learning? How could the incident have been handled differently? What lessons have you learnt in the use of power as a manager?

The dangers of the learning organisation concept is that organisations can use it as an ideology to disguise control but phrased in an emancipatory rhetoric. The consequences are that employees may be manipulated through coercive controls or outright exploitation (Driver 2002). In these teaching organisations, dominant coalitions may form and decide on the nature and form of learning. True learning is discouraged as it could disrupt established norms and become harder to control. Learning becomes radical and a challenge to those in power. There is little room for dissent or questioning organisational values and assumptions. The power dynamics of such a scenario mean that the organisation is caught in a perpetual single-loop learning cycle leading to its eventual decline. Double-loop learning is considered too disruptive to the balance of power in such organisations.

Group norms can also play a negative role on indoctrination and coercive persuasion (Schein 1999). This can result in a suppression of conflict and diversity and greater conformity to the rhetoric of the dominant powerful coalitions in an organisation. In its extreme form, there may be participatory control through group surveillance of an individual's behaviour. There is little room for dissent and personal identity is reduced to a psychic prison from which employees may be unable to escape due to fear of job losses or impact on career progression (Driver 2002).

Are there ways out of this Foucauldian nightmare scenario of the teaching organisation? How can diversity and conflict be managed effectively in learning organisations? One suggestion is to move from an adversarial to an inclusive approach with stakeholders (Coopey 1998). This implies greater employee involvement and a loss of management control which may be unpalatable to some parties comprising the dominant coalitions in organisations. In 1995, British Airways created a post of a 'court jester' reminiscent of the medieval courts with kings (chief executive) and senior courtiers (executives). The jester's role was to provide unorthodox criticism couched as harmless jest in an environment where questioning was not the norm. Being a fool allows the jester to play with ideas and ask basic questions about buried assumptions and ways of thinking.

A more challenging suggestion is to use theatre to explore roles, discourses and power dynamics in organisations (Coopey 1998). This is about getting people to take different roles that allow them to play out various perspectives, including their own, and to explore different ways of approaching everyday scenarios. It is about giving 'oppressed' employees a voice and reducing their sense of powerlessness. An influential form of this radical theatre is the 'Theatre of the Oppressed' or 'Forum Theatre' (Boal

1979). This has been used to elicit employee views by commissioning live theatre by a British local authority to solve communication difficulties. Drama stimulates the power of imagination and allows people to play different roles from everyday scenarios and explore different options and solutions to their problems. Such theatre celebrates diversity and difference in social groups, though it can be seen to challenge hierarchy and established norms. The central political problem is how organisations can explore issues of power imbalances and their negative impacts on organisational learning. If they succeed, they become a Utopian sunshine learning organisation. Otherwise, the Foucauldian gloom of a teaching or static organisation beckons.

Empirical research and the learning organisation

Empirical research on the learning organisation and the role of knowledge within the firm and links with a firm's strategy has suffered from widespread reliance on anecdotes and assertion rather than statistical evidence. Apart from small-scale, in-depth studies of a few organisations, there is virtually no empirical work in this area. Even the related discipline of organisational learning is characterised by qualitative research with a few handful of studies involved with hypotheses development and testing. These tend to be around earlier research on learning curves in organisations.

A recent inductive study with a small sample of ten Swedish people showed that their understanding of a learning organisation arose from four perspectives, as shown in Figure 9.6 (Örtenblad 2002). The first perspective is that the learning organisation is synonymous with organisational learning and is purely 'old wine in new bottles'. The second perspective is that the learning organisation is learning at work and connected with experiential and action learning. The third perspective is an association with a learning climate. This is concerned with positive attitudes and beliefs towards learning. The last perspective is that a learning organisation is a learning structure where the ideal is an organic, flatter structure.

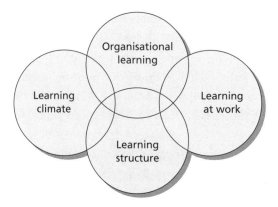

Figure 9.6 **Inductive typology of a learning organisation (Örtenblad 2002)**

Apart from this small-scale inductive study, there is currently only one empirical study that has engaged in hypothesis testing of the concept of a learning organisation (Jashapara 2003). This study used a large stratified random sample of 180 construction executives in the UK and developed an instrument of a 'competitive learning organisation' and organisational performance. Much of this research was developmental as no scales of the learning organisation existed. The questionnaire was composed of ten constructs comprising 125 items with at least eight items per construct. As individuals may be prone to give socially desirable answers of their learning, this was controlled using a shortened form of the Marlowe–Crowne social desirability scale (Ballard 1992).

Each construct in this study demonstrated high levels of reliability and there was considerable evidence for convergent, discriminant, nomological and known groups validity. The results showed that organisational learning in the form of double-loop learning does lead to competitive advantage and provides support to the assumptions underlying the learning organisation literature (de Geus 1988). The results also showed that cooperative cultures are more likely to achieve competitive advantage. However, an anomaly arose in the results showing that competitive or political cultures are more likely to lead to double-loop learning. Hence, successful organisations are more likely to have a flux between cooperative and competitive cultures rather than either extreme. At the time of the study, the competitive dynamics showed that learning focused on efficiency and proficiency led to increased performance in the UK construction industry.

The results of the stratified sample in this study could be developed into benchmarks related to company size. However, this is to be discouraged as benchmarking can lead to organisations developing imitative strategies more akin to single-loop learning rather than strategies to align themselves to changing environments. Also, it is unlikely that executives would engage in benchmarking exercises on a regular basis due to the strategic and sensitive nature of the information supplied. In addition, the information gathered in benchmarking exercises can have a very short shelf life if the competitive environments are highly volatile. The greatest challenge in future quantitative studies is to provide sufficiently large representative samples from within an organisation as well as large representative samples across organisations. This may be a pipe dream and it is not surprising that most studies in this area are of a qualitative nature. In current studies, the assumption is that executives can accurately assess levels of organisational learning given that they have a 'helicopter view' of their organisations. From our discussions of power and politics in organisations, this may prove to be insufficient.

CASE STUDY

Carley Fiorina, CEO, Hewlett-Packard

I tell people inside HP that leadership requires a strong internal compass. A company can get thrown off course if it isn't clear about its goals. It can get thrown off its moorings in terms of ethics and standards if it is tempted by the wrong things. A person can get buffeted by conventional wisdom that is frequently wrong. Remember, at the time of the proxy battle, AOL Time Warner was a 'brilliant' deal and HP Compaq was a 'stupid' deal. Both are examples of conventional wisdom being dead wrong.

So you have to learn to ignore a lot of conventional wisdom and a lot of talk that isn't core to the purpose of what you're doing. I knew what we were doing was the right thing for the company. Therefore I had no alternative but to keep doing it. Sure, [there were dark moments]. It is very hard on some days not to take criticism personally and not to have moments of self-doubt. Those are moments when having a tremendously strong and supportive board, who brought *me* in, not the other way round, helped; when having tremendously supportive customers and partners helped; when having a management team and employees who would buck me up helped, and I could go home and talk to a wonderfully supportive family.

I would think back to my mother and father and what they would say: 'You have to be who you are and do what you think is right.' They never pointed me in a particular direction because I was a girl. They were very demanding in a positive way, because of what they thought I was capable of.

My mother had a lot of zest for life. She was very positive. From her I get fundamental optimism. Both my parents [had] very high standards of integrity. Watching them I learnt that authenticity is everything.

I have never thought about the next job. That's probably because most of the time when I started in the business world, I was scared to death. I was scared I was going to fail. I didn't think I knew enough. Until I was in my early 40s, and opportunities started to come along, I had never really thought about [being a chief executive].

One of the things that I was very naive about when I first came to HP was that I was totally unprepared for and quite caught off-guard by the amount of publicity and scrutiny, in particular around my gender. It remains one of the most difficult parts of the job. I am disappointed to have to say: Yes, [I am treated differently as a woman]. I would not have said that four years ago. I thought we had gone beyond that. But I think it did make a difference

during the proxy battle and it does make a difference still. In the end it's irrelevant to the job I have to do. I don't spend a lot of time worrying about it. But I think there is a real difference in media treatment. I think in some ways the media is behind the reality of the business world.

I don't think there is a particularly male or female way to lead. I think there are common elements of leadership and common stresses and strains of being a CEO that both men and women can understand. One of the reasons organisations like the Business Roundtable and the Business Council work is that not only do CEOs talk about issues that are common to them, or form public policy positions, but it is also lonely in these jobs and there are some things – dilemmas, or pressures, or choices – that only other CEOs understand.

Certainly, there's an opportunity to commiserate with other female CEOs. Marjorie Scardino [chief executive of Pearson, the FT's owner] and I have laughed about press coverage of the two of us. I have never felt the need to act like a man or look like a man. I'm proud of being a woman. I don't believe in trying to be someone I'm not. But I also think that you have to speak to people in language they understand.

In the case of the Lucent acquisition of a company called Ascend [when she went on stage with three socks stuffed down the front of her trousers], these were guys who, to be direct, thought a lot about the size of their balls. They were sales guys. It was a very macho kind of culture. They thought they'd been taken over by a bunch of wimps and that they were going to run the place, and I needed to tell them who was in charge. I was trying to make a point and I made it extremely effectively and in a way that made them laugh. You've got to have a little humour sometimes too. I found a way to laugh throughout the proxy battle. Humour, and humanity, are part of being able to keep going, and part of life.

No change programme is unanimously supported. The proxy battle in many ways became not about a merger. It became about: 'Are we standing still or are we moving ahead?' HP was such a great company, but it was almost frozen in time. That is to take nothing away from the legacy of my predecessors. However, this was a company that in some ways had lost its ambition. Its rate of innovation had declined dramatically. It was growing in single digits in the middle of the biggest technology boom in history. There were real danger signs. But this was a company that had not *ever* brought in an outsider at the top. When I arrived, 50 per cent of our employees had been there less than five years, but not in the senior ranks, which were generally built from within.

We had to find a common language. One of the first things I did was not *tell* people what we were going to do, but *ask* our customers, our leaders and our people what we needed to do. I was reasonably certain that people did know what needed to be done. I was also reasonably certain that without real leadership, and alignment around purpose and goal, we weren't going to get it done.

Because I was an outsider I couldn't dictate, knowing this was a strong and deep culture and I was only one person. I know that big companies can thwart a CEO. The organisation had to decide its vision, its goal and its willingness to change. Then I could lead.

If you looked at our company values today, you would find they are the exact same values that have guided HP for 60 years, except that we have added 'speed and agility'. We don't want to change the fact that trust and respect are part of our value system, that contribution is important and that passion for customers is important. Those basic values originally were referred to as 'the HP way'. Over time, the phrase came to mean any defence against any change. I would go into meetings where somebody would bring up a new idea and someone would say: 'We don't do it that way, that's not the HP way.' Especially for a technology company, it is death if you stop trying new things.

HP tended to be very process-intensive, which is really important when you're dealing with big, complex systems and problems. The downside is that sometimes HP processed endlessly and never decided. Compaq tended to be fast and aggressive, which is good in a fast-moving market. The downside was [that] sometimes Compaq lacked

judgement. Sometimes they had to do things over and over because they hadn't thought it through.

We said: 'The goal is to be fast and thorough.' That's how we got through the integration. I don't think the timing was luck, I think it was choice. People asked me: 'Why would you do this in a downturn?' We chose a downturn because it gives us time. Customers and competitors aren't moving as fast. We will spend our time doing the tough things we have to do, so when the economy begins to recover we will be ready.

I do believe in learning by mistakes. We did our first lay-off in HP before the merger was announced. I knew it was going to be very traumatic. I was concerned the organisation didn't have the skills, experience or stomach to do what needed to be done and so we moved very fast. We provided a lot of outside support and we didn't involve middle and first-line supervisors in the process enough. I learnt two things from that: I learnt that I had underestimated in many ways the people of the company, their appetite for change and their ability to do hard things. And I learnt that sometimes you have to go slow to go fast.

Source: Article by Alison Maitland, *Financial Times*, 20 November 2003

Questions

1 In what ways would you describe Hewlett-Packard as a learning organisation?

2 What role did culture play in aiding or hindering effective learning at Hewlett-Packard?

3 Describe the importance attributed to action and reflection at Hewlett-Packard. How would you know whether you had got the balance right?

4 Given the process-intensive nature of its operations, how can Hewlett-Packard learn effectively from its mistakes? In short, how can Hewlett Packard promote double-loop learning?

Summary

This chapter has explored the latest thinking around the concept of a learning organisation and elaborated five key themes:

1 The distinction between organisational learning and a learning organisation. Organisational learning is seen as a process and means in an organisation whereas a learning organisation is an end and an idealised state.

2 The popular conception of a learning organisation by Peter Senge as five disciplines of personal mastery, team learning, systems thinking, mental models and shared vision.

3 Different models of a learning organisation were articulated, some emphasising organisational learning, some knowledge creation, some structures and others strategy.

4 The problems of the learning organisation ideology were highlighted where the concept could be used for management manipulation and control. Various approaches such as the use of 'court jesters' and radical theatre were suggested as ways of overcoming power imbalances and generating trust and commitment to learning in organisations.

5 The paucity of empirical research to test various assumptions in the conceptual frameworks. Apart from some small sample inductive studies, there is little statistical evidence to support the assertions of the various models of learning organisations.

QUESTIONS FOR FURTHER THOUGHT

1 What are the main differences between organisational learning and the learning organisation? Is the notion of a learning organisation little more than 'old wine in new bottles'?

2 How can an idealised notion of a learning organisation help organisations succeed?

3 What are the problems of high-stretch goals?

4 What are the advantages and drawbacks of a prescriptive approach to a learning organisation?

5 How can a shared vision be achieved in organisations?

6 What are the dangers of clusters of learning and equal clusters of non-learning in organisations?

7 In what ways can imagination be mobilised in organisations?

8 How can cooperative cultures be a liability for organisations?

9 What are the dangers of a Foucauldian nightmare conception of a learning organisation?

10 What are the advantages and limitations of quantitative empirical research on the notion of a learning organisation?

Further reading

1 Senge 1990 is a must-read if only because it placed the concept of the learning organisation firmly on the academic and consultancy agenda.

2 Pedler *et al.* 1991 is the dominant UK contribution in this field and contains many useful organisational development exercises to complement the conceptual models developed.

3 Nonaka and Takeuchi 1995 is useful from a knowledge management perspective as the book elaborates on the whole knowledge-creation process.

References

Argyris, C. (1991) 'Teaching smart people how to learn', *Harvard Business Review*, 69(3), 99–109.

Argyris, C. (1999) *On Organizational Learning*, Blackwell, Oxford.

Argyris, C. and Schon, D. A. (1978) *Organizational Learning: A Theory of Action Perspective*, Addison-Wesley, Reading, MA.

Ballard, R. (1992) 'Short forms of the Marlowe–Crowne social desirability scale', *Psychological Reports*, 71, 1155–60.

Boal, A. (1979) *Theatre of the Oppressed*, Pluto Press, London.

Carroll, C. (1995) 'Rearticulating organizational identity: exploring corporate images and employee identification', *Management Learning*, 26(4), 463–82.

Coopey, J. (1998) 'Learning to trust and trusting to learn: a role of radical theatre', *Management Learning*, 29(3), 365–82.

Davenport, T. H. and Prusak, L. (1998) *Working Knowledge: How Organizations Manage What They Know*, Harvard Business School Press, Boston, MA.

de Geus, A. (1988) 'Planning as learning', *Harvard Business Review*, 66(March/April), 70–4.

Deming, W. E. (1986) *Out of the Crisis*, MIT Press, Boston, MA.

Denton, J. (1998) *Organizational Learning and Effectiveness*, Routledge, London.

Driver, M. (2002) 'The learning organization: Foucauldian gloom or Utopian sunshine', *Human Relations*, 55(1), 33–53.

Easterby-Smith, M. (1990) 'Creating a learning organisation', *Personnel Review*, 19(5), 24–28.

Fiol, C. and Lyles, M. (1985) 'Organizational learning', *Academy of Management Review*, 10(4), 803–13.

Garratt, B. (1987) *The Learning Organization*, Gower, Aldershot.

Garratt, B. (1990) *Creating a Learning Organization: A Guide to Leadership, Learning & Development*, Director Books, Cambridge.

Garvin, D. A. (1993) 'Building a learning organization', *Harvard Business Review*, 71(4), 78–91.

Grant, R. M. (1996) 'Toward a knowledge-based theory of the firm', *Strategic Management Journal*, 17, 109–22.

Hamel, G. and Prahalad, C. K. (1994) *Competing for the Future*, Harvard Business School Press, Boston, MA.

Hayes, J. and Allinson, C. W. (1998) 'Cognitive style and the theory and practice of individual and collective learning in organizations', *Human Relations*, 51(7), 847–71.

Honey, P. (1991) 'The learning organisation simplified', *Training and Development*, July, 30–33.

Jashapara, A. (1993) 'The competitive learning organization: a quest for the Holy Grail', *Management Decision*, 31(8), 52–62.

Jashapara, A. (2003) 'Cognition, culture and competition: an empirical test of the learning organization', *The Learning Organization*, 10(1), 31–50.

Loermans, J. (2002) 'Synergizing the learning organization and knowledge management', *Journal of Knowledge Management*, 6(3), 285–294.

Mintzberg, H. (1991) 'The effective organization: forces and forms', *Sloan Management Review*, Winter edition, 54–67.

Mitroff, I. I., Mason, R. O. and Pearson, C. M. (1994). 'Radical surgey: what will tomorrow's organizations look like?', *Academy of Management Executive*, 8, 11–22.

Nonaka, I. (1991) 'The knowledge-creating company', *Harvard Business Review*, 69(November–December), 96–104.

Nonaka, I. and Takeuchi, H. (1995) *The Knowledge-Creating Company: How Japanese Companies Create the Dynamics of Innovation*, Oxford University Press, New York.

Örtenblad, A. (2002) 'A typology of the idea of learning organization', *Management Learning*, 33(2), 213–230.

Pedler, M., Burgoyne, J. and Boydell, T. (1991) *The Learning Company: A Strategy for Sustainable Development*, McGraw-Hill, London.

Pettigrew, A. and Whipp, R. (1991) *Managing Change for Competitive Success*, Blackwell Publishers, Oxford.

Polanyi, M. (1967) *The Tacit Dimension*, Doubleday, New York.

Revans, R. W. (1977) *The ABC of Action Learning*, Action Learning Trust, Luton.

Schein, E. H. (1999) 'Empowerment, coercive persuasion and organizational learning: do they connect?', *The Learning Organization*, 6(4), 163–72.

Senge, P. M. (1990) *The Fifth Discipline: The Art and Practice of the Learning Organisation*, Doubleday Currency, New York.

Svieby, K. (1997) *The New Organizational Wealth: Managing and Measuring Knowledge-Based Assets*, Berrett-Koehler, San Francisco.

Swan, J., Scarborough, H. and Preston, J. (1999) 'Knowledge management – the next fad to forget people?', *Proceedings of the 7th European Conference on Information Systems*, Copenhagen.

Intellectual capital

After completing this chapter the reader should be able to:

- understand the differing conceptions and frameworks of intellectual capital;
- evaluate the need to have non-financial measures of intellectual capital to supplement traditional financial measures;
- apply concepts of intellectual capital in practice;
- appreciate the different aspects of intellectual property such as patents and copyrights.

MANAGEMENT ISSUES

The measurement and management of intellectual capital implies these questions for managers:

- Are intellectual capital accounts likely to help a firm gain competitive advantage and how can they enable a firm to critically review its practices and processes?
- What aspects of 'knowing how' and 'knowing that' can be reliably measured to be meaningful for an organisation and its external stakeholders?
- How can intellectual capital accounts be produced using existing organisational processes. If new processes are needed, what form should they take?
- How can a firm strategically manage its intellectual property?

Links to other chapters

Chapter 4	helps to understand the implications of intellectual capital measurement and reporting on strategic development.
Chapters 7 and 9	recognise the implications of knowledge management systems and communities of practice on organisational and human capital.

Value added scorecard

Which companies are best at creating wealth? And how do they go about it? These questions – of vital interest to managers across industry – are addressed in an analysis of European businesses, published today. *The Value Added Scoreboard*, produced by the UK's Department of Trade and Industry, focuses on a measure of company output frequently neglected by investors, managers and other business observers.

A company's 'value added' is calculated by taking its sales and subtracting the cost of buying in materials, components and services. When divided by the number of employees, or the time they spend working, it is the commonest definition of productivity – of interest to economists and politicians around the world. Put simply, value added depicts in one of the purest possible ways how good a company is at turning ideas and physical goods into products and services that customers want to buy.

The DTI set out to measure value added across Europe's 300 top value-creating companies, using published data for either the 2000 or 2000/01 financial years. The businesses – in 34 sectors – created a total of £1,081 billion (sterling) in value added over the period, equivalent to about a fifth of western Europe's gross domestic product.

The finished report provides useful benchmarks for individual businesses in almost any sector to measure how well they are performing in relation to their peers. The document also sheds light on why companies perform better or worse than others. At its most basic level, the report details which European companies are biggest in terms of value added. DaimlerChrysler, the German/US car company, is at the top of the tree, with an annual value added of £27 billion. Other well-known names including BP, the oil company, Siemens, the electrical goods supplier, and Deutsche Telekom are also in the top 10.

But value added by itself indicates only the scale of a company's operations. A manufacturer that makes most of its own parts has higher value added than a company of similar size that leaves this to suppliers. To provide a clearer insight into how well companies are performing, the scoreboard focuses on two key ratios. These are value added divided by the number of employees, which reflects companies' skills in using workers to produce high-value goods and services; and value added divided by employee and equipment costs, which is a measure of underlying profitability.

Almost all companies – and the governments of the countries where they are based – would like these two ratios to be as high as possible. High value added per worker indicates the employees are skilled at what they are doing, perhaps because they work in 'knowledge industries' where intellectual property is highly important. Workers in such sectors will almost certainly be rewarded with high wages – a good thing for the community as a whole.

An above-average figure for value added divided by costs is also positive, because it indicates the company is making profits that can be reinvested. A key finding from the report is that value added ratios differ widely between different sectors, depending on the inherent characteristics of the sector.

The 300 businesses in the report have an average annual value added per employee of £49,900. The comparable figure for value added/costs is 153.2 per cent. However, certain sectors – the 'elite' group, including the oil and gas, banking and pharmaceuticals industries – generally have both ratios above the average. Then there are the middle rankers, where typically (as in car making, diversified industrials and food processing) one ratio is above average and one below average. The low scorers – including general retailing and support services – typically have both ratios well below the average.

Why some sectors have higher scores for these ratios than others is, in many cases, fairly easy to understand. The oil and gas sector, for instance, buys in cheap raw materials and uses more capital equipment than human labour. Those workers it does use tend to be highly skilled and paid above average. The sector also has tight control over the distribution mechanisms needed to channel products to the market – which is why it can charge high prices. For all these reasons, both ratios for oil and gas are among the highest figures for any sector in the analysis, at £191,500 and 264 per cent.

At the opposite end of the spectrum is retailing, where virtually all the goods sold are bought in from suppliers, employees are fairly numerous but low-skilled and – apart from areas such as marketing and logistics – companies have little intellectual capital to exploit to push up margins. General retailing, therefore, has an average value added per person of just £21,300, with a value added/cost figure of 131 per cent.

The main lesson from the report is that within individual sectors, the performance of specific companies varies widely. Thus Svenska Handelsbanken of Sweden and Dexia of Belgium – neither of them generally considered to be in the top league of

European banks – score well on both ratios, while the main UK clearers such as Barclays are in the middle ranks of the sector. In the support services category, Adecco, the Swiss recruitment agency, scores well for its sector on both counts, while TNT Post of the Netherlands does poorly.

But what does this mean for managers? The report comes up with some tentative conclusions that companies that have invested more in research and development and capital equipment tend to have better scores for both key ratios. Thus in engineering – a generally low-scoring sector – Heidelberger Druckmaschinen, a large German maker of printing equipment and a big investor, has some of the highest ratios of its peers.

Broader conclusions from the report are that to some degree managers in individual industries are trapped by the limitations of their sector. It is futile, for instance, for someone managing a run-of-the-mill catering business to aim for the productivity

and profits performance of a top drugs company. But within individual businesses, managers may be able to do quite a lot – through tighter cost control and closer relations with suppliers or by moving into new market niches – to improve their companies' performance. By studying the wealth of data in the report, managers should be able to make up their own minds about which specific companies they can pick up lessons from – and which ones they would do better to ignore.

Source: Article by Peter Marsh, *Financial Times*, 16 May 2002

Questions

1 What are the advantages and drawbacks of using the value added scorecard for measuring a company's ability to create wealth?
2 What is the difference between intellectual capital and the value added scorecard?
3 Why could an analysis of value added benchmarks be misleading?

Introduction

In an international survey conducted in 1998, 82.3 per cent of the 1,300 firms questioned named intellectual capital as the critical factor for their future business success (Bertels and Savage 1998). National governments have also recognised intellectual capital as a major factor in their country's future prosperity. For example, the UK government's White Paper, *Our Competitive Future: Building the Knowledge Driven Economy*, clearly recognises the power of knowledge to transform economic growth and performance. An interesting trend of the so-called 'knowledge-driven economy' is that shareholders are becoming better informed from a variety of financial and non-financial sources (often from the internet) and becoming more critical in their analyses of companies. Jean-Claude Paye, Secretary General of the OECD, reinforced the importance of knowledge for economic performance (Skyrme and Amidon 1997):

> 'Knowledge is now a critical factor underpinning economic growth. Producing goods and services with high value-added is at the core of improving economic performance and international competitiveness [...] Increasing investment [...] has become a major issue for enterprises and governments.'

A great deal of the current literature on intellectual capital is about how we measure this elusive entity. Measurement of any entity needs to consider its overriding purpose and its likely market of recipients. This can raise a number of key questions:

- Is measurement purely for internal consumption to improve management practices?
- Is measurement for external consumption by analysts, brokers, banks, customers or any other stakeholders?
- Are there dangers in predominantly measuring the more easily accessible explicit knowledge base of the firm at the expense of the potentially more valuable tacit knowledge or 'know how'?
- What is the time frame for such measures to be meaningful? Are snapshots annually likely to be meaningful in highly fluctuating capital markets?
- Commonly accepted frameworks of intellectual capital are likely to lend themselves to benchmarking among organisations. Are there likely dangers of benchmarking? Are firms likely to reveal their sensitive knowledge assets for external monitoring purposes?

We start this chapter by considering the nature of intellectual capital from a variety of perspectives as well as its historical background. The dangers of adopting a purely financial approach to intellectual capital are highlighted and the need to build in non-financial measures is explored. A multitude of intellectual capital frameworks is presented and the notions of human capital and organisational capital are examined in greater depth. We illustrate how intellectual property can be managed, especially through the use of smart patents. An interesting recent development of intellectual capital as a narrative is forwarded as well as a practical approach to the process of knowledge auditing.

What is intellectual capital?

'Intellectual capital' is a relatively new academic endeavour that is grounded in practice and has its origins in consultancy and industry. There are currently no universally accepted definitions of this term. A simplistic definition would be: 'The difference between the market value of a publicly held company and its official net book value is the value of its intangible assets' (Svieby 1997). One argument for existence of intellectual capital is the marked way in which stock prices change in response to changes in management of an enterprise. A general characteristic of knowledge-intensive organisations such as Microsoft, Oracle and SAP is that their market-to-book-value ratio is often several times higher than that of traditional organisations. From a financial perspective of intellectual capital, one recognises that intellectual capital can be a highly volatile entity and dependent on daily fluctuations of capital markets. The inherent potential of rapidly changing values of intellectual capital may create tangible risks for investors and other stakeholders, such as witnessed by the collapse of some dotcom companies with high market-to-book values.

Stewart (1997) has proposed that intellectual capital is the 'intellectual material – knowledge, information, intellectual property, experience – that can be put to create wealth'. Some authors have used the term expressively 'to refer to the knowledge and knowing capability of a social collectivity, such as an organisation, intellectual community, or professional practice' (Nahapiet and Ghoshal 1998). Other scholars have associated the term more closely with human resources (Boudreau and Ramstad 1997) or with information technology (Davenport and Prusak 1998). A workable definition of intellectual capital has been offered by the Organisation for Economic Co-operation and Development (OECD 1999):

> 'The economic value of two categories of intangible assets of a company: organisational ('structural') capital and human capital.'

There can be some confusion between intellectual capital and intangible assets. The OECD definition treats intellectual capital as a subset of the overall intangible base of an organisation such as its reputation. Structural capital refers to the tangible elements within an organisation such as software and supply chains that remain after employees go home at night. Human capital is what remains in employees' heads when they go home at night, such as customer relationships, know how and their creativity. A useful map of the intellectual capital terrain is proposed by Roos *et al.* (1997) who make a distinction between efforts focused on a strategic perspective or a measurement perspective, as shown in Figure 10.1. A strategic perspective is interested in the management of intellectual capital to increase value of the organisation whereas a measurement perspective focuses on reporting mechanisms of a quantitative or qualitative nature.

A critical aspect of these definitions is that intellectual capital is not an object or a stable entity (such as knowing that) but rather a consequence of certain elements of collectivity. In this conception, intellectual capital is a dynamic entity and closely linked with the processes and practices of knowledge management.

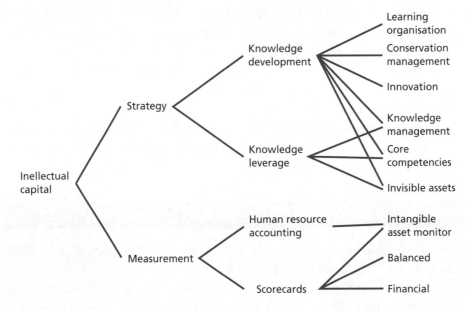

Figure 10.1 **Conceptual roots of intellectual capital (Roos *et al.* 1997)**

Reflect on your personal knowledge assets. How would you describe your personal intellectual capital? Do you believe this is a function of your academic or professional qualifications or more concerned with your general skills and experience? How far would you factor the strength of your contacts and relationships into your intellectual capital? How would you ascribe a market value to your intellectual capital?

There have been considerable efforts to capture the concept of intellectual capital with a number of frameworks forwarded to encapsulate the term. In its current stage of development, it is important to recognise the shortcomings of the different schemas proposed by asking the 'so what?' questions (Andriessen 2002): For example:

- As an employee, what does it mean to be told that the share of employees with higher degrees has gone up and line manager satisfaction rating has gone down?
- As a senior manager, how would an instrument of intellectual capital assist you in your change management programmes or strategic development plans?
- As an investor, how would the notion of an intellectual capital account help you to decide whether or not to invest in a company?

History of intellectual capital

Intellectual capital has emerged from the accounting discipline in a quest to find more comprehensive measures of organisational performance. The roots of the accounting profession can be traced back to its father, Luca Pacioli, whose starting point in 1494 was to measure tangible assets linked to factors of production. However, the interest in intellectual capital is much more recent. In the 1980s, James Tobin's q ratio highlighted the major differences between the market value and book value of firms as they entered the information age. During this time, there was a recognition of the inadequacy of traditional financial measures and a search began to incorporate non-financial measures into the analysis. The first major turning point in intellectual capital came from Skandia, the Swedish financial services firm, which in 1990 appointed Leif Edvinsson as 'Director of Intellectual Capital' and published an intellectual capital supplement to its annual accounts in 1994. A rough history of intellectual capital is depicted in Table 10.1 (p. 271) with a number of milestones presented.

Problems of measuring organisational performance

Conventional measures of organisational performance tend to favour the more widely available financial information. This has arisen due to requirements in law where companies must disclose specific financial information annually. For instance in the UK, a public limited company has to disclose a profit and loss account, a balance sheet and a funds flow statement. From these accounts, analysts can calculate a number of financial performance ratios such as return on capital employed (ROCE), return on investment (ROI) and so on.

Table 10.1 History of intellectual capital

Period	Milestones
1969	Tobin's q ratio established to compare a firm's market to book ratio.
1969	John Kenneth Galbraith first coined phrase 'intellectual capital' in a letter to economist Michael Kalecki: '*I wonder if you realise how much those of us in the world around have owed to the intellectual capital you have provided over these past decades.*'
Early 1980s	Accounting profession uses the term intangible assets predominantly in the form of goodwill.
Mid 1980s	Gap between market and book values widens for many IT-related firms.
1988	Establishment of the European Foundation for Quality Management promoting non-financial indicators of excellence.
1989	Attempts by Svieby to measure intellectual capital in the form of an 'invisible balance sheet'.
1990	Leif Edvinsson is appointed 'Director of Intellectual Capital' at Skandia AFS.
1992	Kaplan and Norton introduce concept of 'balanced scorecard'.
1994	Skandia and Rambøll publish a supplement on intellectual capital to their company's annual accounts. Went on to develop an instrument for measuring intellectual capital called 'Skandia Navigator'. Dow Chemical collaborates with Skandia and pursues an intellectual capital framework forwarded by Petrash.
1995	World Trade Organisation (WTO) negotiates agreement on Trade Related Aspects of Intellectual Propert Rights (TRIPS). Celemi uses a 'knowledge audit' to provide a detailed assessment of its intellectual capital.
1997	Roos *et al.* propose a single 'intellectual capital' index to group the different indicators. Stewart develops an instrument called the 'Intellectual Capital Navigator'.
1998	'Method of doing business' (MDB) is given right to be patented under US case law. Danish Agency for Trade and Industry sponsors a report on the preparation of 'intellectual capital accounts' based on the experience of ten companies. UK government publishes White Paper entitled *Our Competitive Future: Building the Knowledge Driven Economy*. In Spain, 23 companies form 'Club Intellect' to promote measurement of intellectual capital.
1999	OECD co-sponsors an international symposium on intellectual capital in Amsterdam. Danish Confederation of Trade Unions proposes a framework for intellectual capital. European Union funds research project 'MERITUM' to examine intellectual assets.
2000	Launch of academic *Journal of Intellectual Capital* dedicated to an international exchange of research and best practice on all aspects of managing intellectual capital in organisations.
2002	Mouritsen *et al.* propose the addition of a narrative to intellectual capital accounts.

However, these conventional measures are not free from accounting manipulations, as witnessed by the collapse of the US giant Enron. For example, Smith (1992) identified 45 leading UK companies that used five or more debatable 'financial engineering' techniques to massage financial figures and present a spurious reflection of the firm's performance. These financial engineering techniques included questionable approaches to undervaluation of assets, provisions, capitalisation of costs, depreciation, goodwill, brands and off-balance-sheet finance. For instance, BAA increased the economic life of its terminals and runways from 16 and 23.5 years respectively to 50 and 100 years. This resulted in the reduction of annual depreciation costs and a subsequent major increase in profits with comparatively little change in its organisational practices.

Despite the potential for accounting manipulations, one financial method for evaluating intellectual capital from an external perspective is Tobin's q derived from the Nobel Prize winner and economist James Tobin (1969). The Tobin q ratio compares the market value of an asset with its replacement cost (book value). If the quotient q (known as the 'market-to-book value') is less than 1, the market value of the product or service is lower than its cost of reproduction. If the firm enjoys a high q, it is likely to generate higher profits and income. Assuming that similar sized firms have comparable tangible assets, the difference in competitive performance can be said to arise from intellectual capital.

There are hazards of measuring intellectual capital from the market-to-book value. In high-growth markets, the intellectual capital may become inflated purely due to speculations of investors. For instance, Bill Gates lost $5 billion during the 'Russia crises' between August and September 1998 even though the 'intellectual capital' of Microsoft remained relatively unchanged (Reinhardt et al. 2001). Additional external influences that can affect Tobin's q are the interest rates, inflation rates, money supply and cyclical shifts from bonds and shares. The book value of a firm can be distorted and is not entirely free of accounting manipulations. Hence, even though knowledge management practices and processes may increase within a firm, they may not be supported by external perceptions of the firm through such ratios.

There has been an increasing call to supplement the small set of traditional financial performance measures with non-financial indicators that provide an understanding of the processes behind them (Eccles and Nohria 1992). In addition, there has been a recognition that a new paradigm of performance measurement is required that regards it as an ongoing evolving process. The European Foundation for Quality Management (EFQM), formed by 14 leading European companies in 1988, has established an annual European Quality Award for the most successful exponent of Total Quality Management (TQM) in Europe. It is revealing that the performance categories deemed critical for excellence in organisational performance are rather sparse of financial measures, as shown in Figure 10.2 (p. 273).

The measurement of intellectual capital can be viewed as a continuation of the historical approaches used to measure human resource performance. Morgan (1992) identified three dominant approaches to measuring human resource performance. The first approach attempts to identify meaningful and reliable human resource measures of greatest concern to the organisation. This approach can be costly, time-consuming and may result in no clear guidelines for action. There is also the danger of creeping numeration as every measure deemed relevant is turned into the official measurement system (Eccles and Nohria 1992).

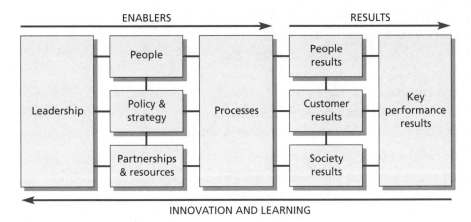

Figure 10.2 EFQM excellence model

The second approach is to develop measures whose potential benefit outweigh the expense or difficulty of data collection. The rationale is to keep things simple and to avoid information overload by developing a few measures to help managers gauge the state of affairs. This approach runs the risk of being too superficial as it does not tell a manager why an outcome may have occurred and how to incorporate the lessons learnt into the system.

The third approach to human resource performance is the use of benchmarking. This involves a comparison of selected performance indicators with other firms in the same industry. It can help managers to establish whether certain human resource practices are within or outside a given norm in a particular sector and to take appropriate action. The most common form of human resource benchmarking is salary surveys. Benchmarking does have its limitations. There can be a difficulty in finding standard and acceptable indicators and a reluctance within companies to divulge sensitive information. It can be a time-consuming and expensive process and promote a culture of imitating competitors' practices rather than encouraging innovative 'leading-edge' practices. Also, the data collected does not provide the highly prized (qualitative) information of the processes that enabled certain outcomes to occur. Clearly the same issues are likely to be apparent if a common benchmarking framework for intellectual capital is developed. At the current time, a number of frameworks for intellectual capital have been forwarded but none has been universally accepted.

Frameworks of intellectual capital

When considering various frameworks and indices to measure intellectual capital, one has to be mindful of the old adage that what gets measured gets managed but what is not understood is ignored. Some key questions in determining the effectiveness of various frameworks and indices includes:

- Does it add value to the customers?
- Can it offer potential for the future?
- How can one interpret it during a recession?
- Does it provide a unique competitive advantage?
- Is it sustainable over some years?
- Is it firmly anchored within the organisation?
- Does it engender a proactive transformative approach?

In 1992, Robert Kaplan and David Norton (1992) developed the first approach to intellectual capital that took into account a number of perspectives apart from the traditional financial one. They suggested that a 'balanced scorecard' that included a customer perspective, a financial perspective, an internal business perspective and an innovation and learning perspective was likely to provide senior managers with a fast single report on organisational performance. This approach has become popular, as shown in Figure 10.3, as it provides management with extra internal indicators to establish cause-and-effect relationships and examine performance drivers. However, it is less appropriate for external reporting.

Pause for thought

Using the balanced scorecard approach, how would you go about measuring the less tangible dimensions such as the 'internal business process' perspective in your organisation? What do you see as potential difficulties in comparing these measures historically? In your opinion, how realistic is the use of the balanced scorecard to report performance across an industry? What are the pitfalls of an industry benchmarking exercise in this area?

In 1993, Leif Edvinsson reported the 'hidden' intellectual assets of Skandia AFS as a supplement to the annual report. It was the first time that the term 'intellectual capital' was used rather than the accounting term 'intangible assets' (Edvinsson and Malone 1997). Using the intellectual capital framework shown in Figure 10.4 (p. 276), Skandia

Figure 10.3 The balanced scorecard (from Kaplan and Norton 1992)

went on to develop the 'Skandia Navigator' for managing intellectual capital. The aim of managing these invisible assets was to create further sustainable value for the organisation. The intellectual capital reports published subsequently in the accounts provided concrete display of different indicators of intellectual capital:

- financial focus;
- customer focus;
- human focus;
- process focus;
- renewal and development focus.

Dow Chemical was another pioneering company to measure intellectual capital at this time and its efforts were based on a similar framework forwarded by Petrash (1996). The dotted lines between the three major forms of intellectual capital (see Figure 10.4) depict the dynamic management of these assets. Dow Chemical collaborated with Skandia and based its definition of intellectual capital on this simple formula:

Intellectual Capital = Human Capital + Organisation Capital + Customer Capital

There has been a growing trend towards developing a single index for intellectual capital rather than reporting a multitude of differing indicators. Roos *et al.* (1997) found Skandia used 24 different indicators to measure intellectual capital. They proposed grouping the different indicators together into an 'intellectual capital' index. Such an index would encourage managers to discuss any areas that were uncertain and enable benchmarking to occur.

Lowendahl (1997) provides an alternative perspective of intangible assets based on competence and relational resources, as shown in Figure 10.4. He further divides these entities into individual or collective resources depending on their specific focus. Competence is the ability of the individual or firm to do things. In contrast, relational resources are based on the reputation, client loyalty and reputation of the firm or individual.

As shown in Figure 10.4, Sullivan (1998) develops a model primarily based on human capital. He defines human capital as the capabilities of employees, contractors and suppliers to solve customer problems. This capability is based on collective experience, know how and skills of employees. The human capital is supported by structural capital such as computers, information systems and physical buildings. Effective management of the human capital is likely to lead to increased intellectual assets and intellectual property. Another similar framework is proposed by Annie Brooking (1996) based on four aspects of intellectual capital: market assets (such as brands, customers, distribution channels and backlog), human-centred assets (problem-solving abilities), intellectual property assets (such as patents, trademarks and copyrights) and infrastructure assets (such as culture, processes, databases and communication systems).

In comparing the different frameworks forwarded, one needs to be mindful of the assumptions underlying them. For instance, is the goal of the measurement framework (such as Sullivan) to enable managers to extract value from the know how of human

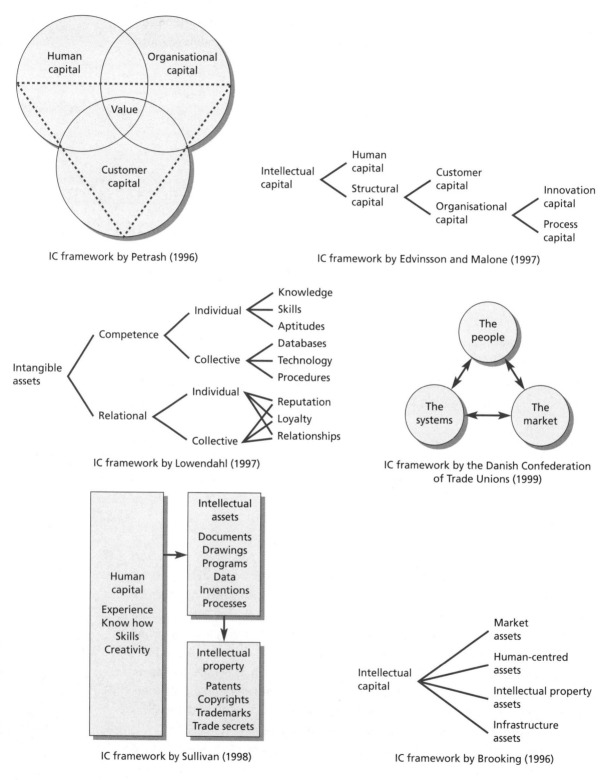

IC framework by Petrash (1996)

IC framework by Edvinsson and Malone (1997)

IC framework by Lowendahl (1997)

IC framework by the Danish Confederation of Trade Unions (1999)

IC framework by Sullivan (1998)

IC framework by Brooking (1996)

Figure 10.4 Sample of varying intellectual capital frameworks

capital and possibly lead to higher profits? Or is the goal focused on value creation which is concerned with the creation of knowledge through managing training and development, developing relationships and managing organisational culture?

Human and social capital

Human capital theory has its roots in the 1960s (Becker 1964; Schultz 1961). The preoccupation at the time was the levels of investment required in education and the likely returns on this investment in the form of economic growth and profitability. Becker defined the development of human capital as:

'activities that influence monetary and psychic income by increasing the resources in people.'

The 'black box' notion of human capital with certain inputs leading to prescribed outputs has lingered, with more recent attempts to link individual competences with organisational competencies. In their theory of core competencies, Hamel and Prahalad (1994) argue that the success of any company lies in the optimal utilisation and development of its core competencies rather than its products or services or current markets. The core competencies consist of a combination of intangible assets which flourish in a given culture. The problem of considering core competences as intangible assets is that they do not fit the traditional accounting transaction-based model. Intangible assets can increase or decrease without a transaction taking place. Intangible assets are difficult to identify and do not lend themselves to simple addition of their separate values. The benefits of intangible assets are uncertain and their competitive advantage can be lost almost overnight (Andriessen 2002).

A human capital approach to intellectual capital needs to take into account three considerations (Reinhardt *et al.* 2001). First, that economic theory has not dealt adequately with the problem of knowledge creation (Machlup 1984). Secondly, human capital flows and their transformations are predominantly discussed from an individual or organisational learning perspective. Lastly, there is a distinction between human embodied knowledge (human capital) and non-embodied knowledge (organisational capital).

A closely related aspect of human capital is social capital. This concept has its roots in community studies examining functioning of city neighbourhoods and the relationships inherent in the development of young children. In an organisational context, this concept is based on the premise that a firm's capabilities are best developed through cooperating individuals. It has its organisational origin in Barnard's (1956) conception of an organisation as a cooperative entity made up predominantly of relationships. This view has resulted in the notion of organisations as social communities (Kogut and Zander 1996; Nahapiet and Ghoshal 1998). There are intrinsically three dimensions to social capital:

- structural dimension showing the linkages and connections between actors such as the density and hierarchy of networks;

- relational dimension that provides the history of interactions between individuals resulting in certain levels of trust, norms and expectations;
- cognitive dimension that leads to shared meanings, interpretations, mental models and alignment of views.

Pause for thought

Given the diversity of individual personalities in a team, what measures could you take to maintain or increase your team's social capital? For example, how would you get more introverted colleagues to develop social networks across and outside your organisation? In addition, how could you promote shared understanding of problems and alignment of views? How would you gauge whether the level of your team's social capital has risen or decreased from one year to the next?

Organisational capital

The roots of the concept of organisational capital come from research exploring ways of increasing efficiencies in organisations where employee effort was considered to be suboptimal (Tomer 1987). Hence, organisational capital has been seen as an extension of human capital as it contains both organisational and behavioural variables (Reinhardt *et al.* 2001). It is based on the level of knowledge sharing, cooperative effort and conflict resolution within organisations.

Tomer (1998) identified two types of organisational capital: a pure form (such as its organisational structure) and a hybrid form (embodied in individuals through investment in activities such as socialisation). The assumption underlying this concept is that investment in organisational capital will lead to a range of benefits in terms of worker productivity. The types of intervention may include (Tomer 1987):

- changing formal and informal relationships and patterns of activity within the organisation;
- changing certain attributes key to organisational effectiveness;
- developing information to match the optimal worker to a given situation.

It is clear that the literature on organisational capital is closely linked with the concept of structural capital within the intellectual capital literature. However, there is a danger of the hybrid conception of organisational capital creeping into intellectual capital frameworks and resulting in confusion between human and organisational capital.

Intellectual property and smart patents

The collective experience, skills and general know how of a firm lead to the development of intellectual assets. These intellectual assets may be in the form of documents, drawings, software programs, data, inventions and processes (Sullivan 1998). As these explicit assets are codified, tangible or contain physical descriptions of a firm's knowledge and processes, a firm has the right to claim ownership to this intellectual property in the form of patents, copyrights, trademarks and trade secrets. In an increasingly knowledge-based economy, strategic management of intellectual property may well lead to competitive advantage where value is generated from protecting the knowledge, skills, processes and ideas of a firm. It can no longer be left purely as a technical or legal imperative in successful organisations.

Patents are a common form of intellectual property and provide a high level of protection. They can enable firms to gather valuable sources of revenue through licensing agreements. In the US, there has been a marked growth in software patents and, since 1998, a 'method of doing business (MDB)' has been given the right to be patented under case law. Hence, a firm can provide an effective barrier to entry if it owns a software patent and an MDB patent for at least the twenty-year life of the patent (Lang 2001). However, the real life of patents is typically 15–17 years from the original date of application. MDB patents can include information systems, investment systems, e-commerce systems, insurance systems and training methods. Maxwell (2002) shows that the life of the patent can be extended almost indefinitely by using a smart patent in the form of a continuation patent, as shown in Table 10.2. This has the benefit of rewarding honest innovation and discouraging competitors that may try to exploit a patent's weakness.

Table 10.2 Characteristics of patents and continuation patents

Patent	Continuation patent
Description of invention	Allows changes to original patent
Citations of 'prior art'	Can add new 'claims'
Related publications and patents	Can add newly discovered 'prior art'
'Claims' – descriptions of exclusive rights of patent holder	Can be modified taking into account competitor's product

The process of securing a patent involves filing a patent application at a Patent Office. The proposed patent undergoes an 'examination period' often lasting a few years where the examiner enters into a dialogue with the inventor about the precise language to be used in the patent. Once the patent is issued, it has a life of twenty years. However, if the inventor files an application for a continuation patent (child of the original patent) before the original patent (parent) issues, the examination period for the patent is extended to allow the inventor to make changes that may take into account competitor offerings. This process can be continued for generations, creating grandchildren patents and so on where each continuation patent is filed just before its parent issues (Maxwell 2002), as shown in Figure 10.5 (p. 280).

Copyright is primarily rights to the owner in the distribution medium to prevent infringements on copying, distributing, performing or displaying material. It protects the original works for a longer period of 100 years. In the case of the creator's death, copyright lasts for 70 years. However, in our age of digital networks, because of the ease of distribution and the minimal cost of making perfect copies on digital printers, there is a pertinent threat to copyright unless digital information can be encrypted.

Ignoring or mismanaging intellectual property rights can have disastrous results for firms. One example illustrating the minefield of intellectual property rights is the case

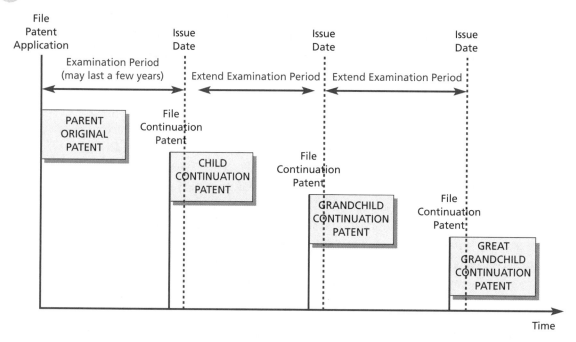

Figure 10.5 Smart patents: using patents and continuation patents

of Kodak in 1975. Polaroid had erected vast patent barriers in the high-growth instant camera market. Kodak was well aware of these patents but it was advised by its lawyers that they were invalid. Kodak took a calculated risk but was found to have infringed Polaroid's patents soon after it launched a line of instant cameras and films. Kodak was ordered to pay $925 million in damages to Polaroid, shut down its manufacturing plant and retrieve the 16 million cameras sold to consumers between 1976 and 1985 (Rivette and Kline 2000). This example illustrates the strategic importance of intellectual capital and how it can result in the potential demise of a company.

There can be considerable differences in laws on intellectual property and their enforcement in countries worldwide. There have been attempts by the World Trade Organisation to promote harmonisation of intellectual property laws. In 1995, the WTO negotiated an agreement on Trade Related Aspects of Intellectual Property Rights. This agreement establishes the right of member states to impose sanctions on TRIP signatories that do not fulfil their obligations under TRIPS. It is interesting to note that TRIPS protects computer programs as literary works under the Berne Convention.

Pause for thought

What might you consider patenting in your organisation? How would you decide on the strategic importance of a patent? How would you scan the competitive environment to ensure that your intellectual property rights were not being infringed? From your experience, how effective do you find patents as a barrier to entry for competitors?

Financial reporting of intellectual capital

The basic problem for international accounting bodies has been how one captures the present value of a highly volatile asset, namely, intellectual capital. Conventional reporting methods are not sufficiently responsive and may lead to risky investments from unreliable reports. This risk has the potential to lead to reduced economic growth from the increased cost of capital and reduced liquidity in the markets. The Financial Accounting Standards Board (FASB) has got together with a number of international accounting bodies to take action. They have concluded that the measurement of financial instruments such as intangible assets needs to be tackled with the notion of fair value (Kossovsky 2002). The FASB (1999) describes fair value as:

> 'an estimate of the price an entity would have realized if it had sold an asset or paid if it had been relieved of a liability on the reporting date in an arm's-length exchange motivated by normal business conditions.'

The European Commission (2000) describes fair value as:

1. *a market value, for those items for which a reliable market can readily be identified. Where a market value is not readily identifiable for an item but can be identified for its components, the market value of that item may be derived from that of its components; or*

2. *the value resulting from establishing valuation models and techniques, for those items for which a reliable market cannot be readily identified. Such valuation models and techniques should ensure a reasonable approximation of the market value.*

It is worthy to note that traditional intangibles such as brand equity, patents and goodwill could not be reported in financial statements until recently unless they met strict recognition criteria (International Accounting Standards Committee (IASC) 1998; International Federation of Accountants (IFAC) 1998). In these circumstances, it is not surprising that more novel forms of intangibles such as customer loyalty, staff competences and computer systems have not received the recognition they merit. There may be a sea change in the pipeline as the Securities and Exchange Commission in the US has indicated that it would like to see an intellectual capital supplement to companies' annual accounts.

Intellectual capital as a narrative

If one accepts that the aim of measurement of intellectual capital is to grasp the knowledge management processes that underlie this unstable entity, our focus needs to be directed to a qualitative understanding of this term. Roos *et al.* (1997) suggest the notion of 'intellectual capital as a language for thinking, talking and doing something about the drivers of companies' future earnings'. Intellectual capital comprises relationships with customers and partners, innovation efforts, company infrastructure and the knowledge skills of organisational members. In this sense, knowledge may be usefully presented and interpreted in the form of a narrative (Mouritsen *et al.* 2002). This insight was gained from the experience of Danish firms working to develop intellectual capital statements. They found the notion of knowledge as a narrative most useful when it was centred around the 'value to a user'.

A narrative is seen as a plot of a certain phenomenon that leads one through a sequence of events and highlights the linkages between the events. The narrative may highlight 'positive' things that happen along the way as well as 'problems and pitfalls' to allow the narrative to succeed (Boland and Schultze 1996; Czarniawska 1997). A narrative is more than a story and provides a real-life example of the trials and tribulations of an organisation. It is deeply embedded in the culture and identity of the firm and presents the raison d'être of its decisions, processes and activities (Mouritsen *et al.* 2002). To complement the notion of knowledge as 'value to the user', the strategy for managing knowledge is organised around a knowledge narrative that explains the relevance of a firm's knowledge to a group of users. Mouritsen *et al.* (2002) suggest three elements to a narrative as:

- a product/service;
- an account of value to user;
- presentation of firm's 'intellectual production function'.

In each of the cases examined, a simplistic map is provided of the intellectual capital statement containing the knowledge narrative or value proposition, management challenges, efforts and indicators, as shown in the example in Figure 10.6.

The difficulty in this approach arises where one may have multiple potentially conflicting value propositions in a large organisation engaged in a highly turbulent environment where the simplicity of these maps may not fulfil the necessary value to user nor aid investors in their decision making. Also, how much would the knowledge

Figure 10.6 Example illustrating framework for key components of an intellectual capital statement (adapted from Mouritsen *et al.* 2002)

narrative reveal about the firm's potential with new and challenging environments rather than a historical review of the past year? Are there likely to be biases in this approach where the positive aspects of the narrative are embellished and the negative aspects are curtailed or even not reported? Who would take on the role of the independent storyteller and narrator of the firm's knowledge narrative? How could one determine the reliability of the narrative?

Knowledge auditing in practice

It has been argued that traditional tools of financial reporting are losing relevance in a world where the most valuable assets are information, expertise, technology and skill (Svieby 1997). The problem for companies is how they can identify these elusive knowledge assets when they often don't know what they know. There has been a tendency in earlier attempts at mapping knowledge assets to concentrate on the explicit knowledge and produce long inventories that are difficult to use. An important characteristic of any knowledge audit is that it needs to capture the explicit as well as the more dynamic tacit knowledge within organisations.

From consultancy experience in knowledge management, Truch (2001) has proposed a 'value-based knowledge management' approach to auditing a firm's intellectual capital based primarily on an information-processing perspective. He suggests that the evaluation of knowledge assets is most effective when linked to a firm's key processes and aligned to its strategic development. This approach comprises three stages, as shown in Figure 10.7:

Figure 10.7 Process of knowledge auditing (adapted from Truch 2001)

1 *Strategic review*. This comprises a top-down review of business strategy including the critical success factors as well as the core competences required for success in the business. The stage may include capturing the strategic intent of the senior managers and developing potential scenarios for the future.

2 *Process review*. This comprises a bottom-up identification of key business processes and the knowledge assets they produce in terms of tacit and explicit knowledge. Existing process maps formed as part of a quality assurance system such as ISO 9000 can be used to map key business processes. Each knowledge asset is analysed further in terms of the 'knowledge value chain', as shown in Figure 6.7. This allows a better understanding of the tacit and explicit assets which may follow different but interlinked value chains. A knowledge inventory of tacit and explicit knowledge is developed at this stage.

3 *Synthesis*. This comprises of an evaluation of the knowledge inventory (Stage 2) in the context of the core competencies and critical success factors (Stage 1) and conducting a cost-benefit analysis of current and potential knowledge assets.

Pause for thought

Imagine you were asked to produce an intellectual capital account for your organisation. How would you go about reporting such an account in practice? What forms of data collection would you adopt? How cost intensive is your approach? How far could your intellectual capital accounts be used for external reporting? How valuable do you think shareholders would assess these accounts over and above conventional financial reporting and material available through other sources such as the internet? How could you guard against potential filtering of bad news from senior executives in such accounts?

During the synthesis stage, Truch (2001) suggests that a cost-benefit analysis can be conducted on each knowledge asset by identifying the additional value or leverage they provide to key business processes. The value may be derived from new synergies in areas such as revenue from new business opportunities, new markets and efficiency gains. In contrast, the cost of each knowledge asset needs to consider factors such as training people, IT infrastructure, special software, external data, expert consultants and any other resources. Each knowledge asset can then be plotted on a 2×2 grid of value of knowledge asset (or benefit) against cost of knowledge asset (high or low). This would allow decisions to be made about future knowledge investments or divestments from a company's knowledge portfolio.

CASE STUDY

Eti

You have just finished a meeting with Marzio Basile, chief executive of Eti, Italy's state-owned tobacco groups. He has appointed your firm to conduct an 'intellectual capital account' of Eti for publication in three weeks' time. The Italian treasury has announced terms of the sale yesterday of this state-owned tobacco monopoly by private placement and

has informed potential bidders that an 'intellectual capital account' is likely to be published shortly. Marzio Basile's intentions for the commissioned intellectual capital accounts are to secure and hold the estimated sale price if volatility of the capital markets continues downwards and possibly to increase the sale price by demonstrating the significant transformations he has undertaken in the business over the past three years. The sale of this business is estimated to fetch between €1.5 billion and €2.0 billion despite the negative fallout from a chain of tobacco litigations and anti-smoking campaigns in the Italian media.

Ente Tabacchi Italiano (Eti) is one of the world's last state-owned tobacco groups in a country of heavy cigarette smokers. Italy is one of the largest markets for cigarettes in Europe, second only to Germany. The current state monopoly controls a major distribution network of 58,000 tobacconists (*sale e tabacchi*) around the country. These tobacconists are a familiar part of the Italian landscape and hold the same high regard as Vespa scooters and Fiat 500s in the Italian psyche. The tobacco group also owns an e-commerce venture firm that supplies this network of tobacconists, who are slowly transforming themselves into small retail outlets or betting shops. In addition, Eti manufactures on behalf of Philip Morris, a US multinational, 25 per cent of cigarettes sold in Italy by this group.

Mr Basile, a 53-year-old Neopolitan, was brought in by the government three years ago to transform and restructure the unwieldy and inefficient state monopoly into a leaner, more competitive group. He had had considerable experience of liquidating or privatising complex and troubled state-owned assets such as hospitals and steel plants. At the outset, he found Eti was an inefficient public sector entity that was responsible for tobacco as well as state salt mines. It had managed to give over a major share of the Italian cigarette market to Philip Morris in a misguided licensing agreement. Eti controlled more than 73 per cent share of the Italian tobacco market more than twenty years ago, with Philip Morris having less than a 20 per cent share. Now, Philip Morris commands 62 per cent of the market compared with 27 per cent for domestic brands.

Mr Basile based his transformation strategy on refocusing Eti on its core tobacco business and shedding non-tobacco assets such as its salt mines. He improved productivity of the tobacco operations and rejuvenated the cigarette and cigar brands through increased advertising as well as launching two new brands. Productivity was extremely low, with a rate of 11,000 kilos a year per employee compared with a European benchmark of 35,000 to 40,000 kilos a year per employee. Mr Basile closed seven of Eti's sixteen plants and reduced the staff from 7,000 to 3,500 employees. These reductions resulted in no strikes as they were managed through early retirements, redeployments and other incentives. The annual per capita productivity rate has risen as a result to around 30,000 kilos. Eti has also secured a union agreement to reduce staff by a further 1,300 people down to 2,200 employees by the end of next year. This is likely to increase productivity rates to 45,000 kilos per capita.

Mr Basile has also renegotiated two production and distribution agreements with Philip Morris. The first four-year production partnership allows Eti to manufacture 16 million kilograms of cigarettes for Philip Morris on a cost and fee basis. This deal accounts for 35 per cent of Eti's annual cigarette production. The second agreement involves a three-year distribution deal for Philip Morris brands in Italy. The tobacco group's distribution company has established an e-commerce joint venture with the Italian post office and the Italian Federation of Tobacconists to offer internet services to the national network of tobacconists. Sales for this financial year will total €650 million, with a gross operating profit expected at around €150 million.

The potential bidders include tobacco multinationals wishing to enter one of Europe's largest tobacco markets and provide a threat to the leading market share of Philip Morris. These multinational include British American Tobacco (one of the world's largest cigarette manufacturers, second only to Philip Morris), Altadis (a Franco-Spanish group with 1 per cent share of current market), JTI-Japan Tobacco (5–6 per cent of current market share) and Swedish Match (heavily focused on cigars). The main rivals to these multinationals are Italian investors wishing to invest in the distribution power of the tobacconists and to develop stylish cigarettes and cigars. The potential Italian candidates include Imprenditori Associati (a group of Italian entrepreneurs), Lottomatica (a group that has close ties with the network of tobacconists and operates the Lotto gambling game) and various Italian banks and venture capitalists.

Source: Adapted from article by Paul Betts, *Financial Times*, 31 July 2002

Questions

1 Discuss how you intend to produce an 'intellectual capital account' within the short time frame of three weeks, taking into account the nature of potential bidders.

2 How do you suggest that a valuation model can be developed to assess a fair value for intellectual capital given that Eti is currently a state-owned group? Is any estimated figure likely to be meaningful?

3 If you were to produce a narrative on intellectual capital, how would this differ from the marketing material already supplied by the Italian treasury to each potential bidder?

4 If you were to be retained by the successful bidder to produce its annual intellectual capital accounts, discuss how your approach may differ from the current assignment.

Summary

This chapter has elaborated five main themes:

1 An international consensus among firms, governments and regulatory bodies that intellectual capital is the critical factor in future growth and prosperity.

2 Traditional financial measures cannot capture the richness and diversity of intellectual capital within an organisation.

3 Intellectual capital frameworks used in practice tend to centre around the notions of human capital, organisational capital and customer capital.

4 Increased importance of firms to strategically manage their intellectual property.

5 The use of narratives for reporting intellectual capital accounts.

QUESTIONS FOR FURTHER THOUGHT

1 David Bowie has undergone several transformations from Ziggy Stardust to the Thin White Duke over three decades in the music industry. The capital markets have seen considerable value in his talents. He became the first person in the music industry to float a bond issue for a total cost of $50 million. The entire issue was sold within one hour. Can we consider David Bowie's talents as intellectual capital? How would you have reliably valued his talents earlier in his life when he was Ziggy Stardust?

2 How does one identify an emerging knowledge process and add a value to it when one may not know whether it will contribute to the future success of an organisation or not? Is developing scenarios enough?

3 What are the likely positive and negative consequences of 'method of doing business' patents? How would patent offices be able to distinguish between two MDB patents such as toasting a piece of bread?

4 How could you determine the shelf life of intellectual capital? For example, is any attempt to measure intellectual capital valid for only three months?

5 How can we reliably account for the depreciation in intellectual assets in a firm?

6 How can the manipulation of intangible assets be curtailed?

7 What are the dangers of high levels of social capital within an organisation?

8 Are intellectual capital accounts likely to increase spurious reporting and financial engineering of company accounts?

9 What are the advantages and disadvantages of an international agreement on intellectual capital accounts led by the WTO or OECD?

10 If an intellectual capital narrative is based on a company's culture and values, how can an analyst make meaningful comparisons between firms in the same industry or other industries?

Further reading

1 Stewart 1997 provides a well-researched and readable book on intellectual capital.

2 Edvinsson and Malone 1997 shows how intellectual capital was first used in Skandia's annual report and how the 'Skandia Navigator' was developed for managing a firm's intellectual capital.

References

Andriessen, D. (2002) 'Weightless wealth: four modifications to standard IC theory', *Journal of Intellectual Capital*, 2(3), 204–214.

Barnard, C. I. (1956) *The Functions of the Executive*, Harvard University Press, Cambridge, MA.

Becker, G. S. (1964) *Human Capital*, University of Chicago Press, Chicago.

Bertels, T. and Savage, C. M. (1998) 'Tough questions on knowledge measurement', *Knowing in Firms. Understanding, Managing and Measuring Knowledge*, G. von Krough, J. Roos and D. Kleine, eds, Sage, London.

Boland, R. J. and Schultze, U. (1996) 'Narrating accountability: cognition and the production of the accountable self', *Accountability. Power, Ethos and The Technologies of Managing*, R. Munro and J. Mouritsen, eds, Thomson Business Press, London.

Boudreau, J. W. and Ramstad, P. M. (1997) 'Measuring intellectual capital: learning from financial history', *Human Resource Management*, 36(3), 343–56.

Brooking, A. (1996) *Intellectual Capital*, Thomson Business Press, London.

Czarniawska, B. (1997) *Narrating the Organization: Dramas of Institutional Identity*, University of Chicago Press, Chicago.

Danish Confederation of Trade Unions (1999) 'Your knowledge – can you book it?', *International Symposium Measuring and Reporting Intellectual Capital: Experiences, Issues and Prospects*, Amsterdam.

Davenport, T. H. and Prusak, L. (1998) *Working Knowledge: How Organizations Manage What They Know*, Harvard Business School Press, Boston, MA.

Eccles, R. and Nohria, N. (1992) *Beyond the Hype: Rediscovering the Essence of Management*, Harvard Business School Press, Cambridge, MA.

Edvinsson, L. and Malone, M. S. (1997) *Intellectual Capital: Realizing Your Company's True Value by Finding Its Hidden Brainpower*, Judy Piatkus (Publishers) Ltd, London.

European Commission (2000) *Proposal for a Directive of the European Parliament and the Council amending Directives 78/660/EEC as regards the valuation rules forth e annual and consolidated accounts of certain types of companies*, 24 February.

FASB (1999) 'Preliminary views on major issues related to reporting financial instruments and certain related assets and liabilities at fair value', *Financial Accounting*, Series No. 204–B(December 14).

Hamel, G. and Prahalad, C. K. (1994) *Competing for the Future*, Harvard Business School Press, Boston, MA.

International Accounting Standards Committee (IASC) (1998) *IAS 38 Intangible Assets*, International Accounting Standards Committee, London.

International Federation of Accountants (IFAC) (1998) T*he Measurement and Management of Intellectual Capital: An Introduction*, International Federation of Accountants (IFAC), New York.

Kaplan, R. S. and Norton, D. P. (1992) 'The balanced scorecard as a strategic management system', *Harvard Business Review*, 70(1), 71–9.

Kogut, B. and Zander, U. (1996) 'What firms do? Coordination, identity and learning', *Organization Science*, 7, 502–518.

Kossovsky, N. (2002) 'Fair value of intellectual property', *Journal of Intellectual Capital*, 3(1), 62–70.

Lang, J. C. (2001) 'Managerial concerns in knowledge management', *Journal of Knowledge Management*, 5(1), 43–57.

Lowendahl, B. (1997) *Strategic Management of Professional Service Firms*, Handelshojskolens Forlag, Copenhagen.

Machlup, F. (1984) *Knowledge: Its Creation, Distribution, and Economic Significance: Vol. 3. The Economics of Information and Human Capital*, Princeton University Press, Princeton.

Maxwell, R. (2002) 'Smart patents: is your intellectual capital at risk?', *Harvard Business Review*, March/April, 18–19.

Morgan, J. (1992) 'Human resource information: a strategic tool', *Strategies for Human Resource Management*, M. Armstrong, ed., Kogan Page, London.

Mouritsen, J., Bukh, P. N., Larsen, H. T. and Johansen, M. R. (2002) 'Developing and managing knowledge through intellectual capital statements', *Journal of Intellectual Capital*, 3(1), 10–29.

Nahapiet, J. and Ghoshal, S. (1998) 'Social capital, intellectual capital, and the organizational advantage', *Academy of Management Review*, 23(2), 242–66.

OECD (1999) 'Guidelines and instructions for OECD symposium', *International Symposium Measuring and Reporting Intellectual Capital: Experiences, Issues and Prospects*, Amsterdam.

Petrash, G. (1996) 'Dow's journey to a knowledge value management culture', *European Management Journal*, 14(4), 365–73 reprinted with permission from Elsevier.

Reinhardt, R., Bournemann, M., Pawlowsky, P. and Schneider, U. (2001) 'Intellectual capital and knowledge management: perspectives on measuring knowledge', M. Dierkes, A. B. Antal, J. Child and I. Nanaka, eds, Oxford University Press, Oxford, 794–820.

Rivette, K. G. and Kline, D. (2000) 'Discovering new value in intellectual property', *Harvard Business Review*, 78(1), 54–66.

Roos, J., Roos, G., Edvinsson, L. and Dragonetti, N. C. (1997) *Intellectual Capital: Navigating in the New Business Landscape*, Macmillan Business, Houndsmils.

Schultz, T. W. (1961) 'Investment in human capital', *American Economic Review*, 51(1), 1–17.

Skyrme, D. J. and Amidon, D. M. (1997) *Creating the Knowledge-Based Business*, Business Intelligence, London.

Smith, T. (1992) *Accounting for Growth*, Century Business Books, London.

Stewart, T. A. (1997) *Intellectual Capital: The New Wealth of Organizations*, Doubleday/Currency, New York.

Sullivan, P. H. (1998) *Profiting from intellectual capital: extracting value from innovation*, Wiley, London.

Svieby, K. (1997) The *new organizational wealth: managing and measuring knowledge-based assets*, Berrett-Koehler, San Francisco.

Tobin, J. (1969) 'A general equilibrium approach to monetary theory', *Journal of Money, Credit and Banking*, 1, 15–29.

Tomer, J. F. (1987) *Organizational Capital: The Path to Higher Productivity and Wellbeing*, Praeger, New York.

Tomer, J. F. (1998) 'Organizational capital and joining-up: linking the individual to the organization and to society', *Human Relations*, 51, 825–46.

Truch, E. (2001) 'Knowledge management: auditing and reporting intellectual capital', *Journal of General Management*, 26(3), 26–40.

Knowledge management

**DISCOVERING
KNOWLEDGE**
Data, information & knowledge
History of managing knowledge
Philosophical perspectives on knowledge

**LEVERAGING
KNOWLEDGE**
Knowledge management
in the learning organisation
Intellectual capital

**KNOWLEDGE
MANAGEMENT
CYCLE**

**GENERATING
KNOWLEDGE**
Organisational learning
Knowledge management
Tools & technology

**SHARING
KNOWLEDGE**
Knowledge management
and culture
Change management

**EVALUATING
KNOWLEDGE**
Knowledge management systems
Strategic management perspectives:
knowledge management strategy

Epilogue

Introduction

The depth and breadth of material in this book has tried to demonstrate that knowledge management is more than a management fad or buzzword and has established itself as an important area of inquiry for practitioners, consultants, researchers and academics. The fact that this emerging discipline is highly fashionable need not detract from the fact that it aims to contribute to real-life problems and issues which organisations face today.

Knowledge is not new and has been part of human experience from the beginning of time. The current challenge is developing our theoretical and practical understanding of this concept. One approach is to engage practitioners, researchers and consultants with fellow philosophers on this journey to help move beyond our simplistic notions of this prized entity. In general, philosophy tends to be neglected in many business schools and for years the relevance of ontological and epistemological issues on academic curricula has been widely debated. This is not surprising as business studies as a major academic discipline has a pedigree from around the1960s. In its attempt to gain legitimacy as a serious discipline, it has adopted the rigours of the scientific approach in the main. However, there have been healthy signs questioning this orthodoxy and its shortcomings. The emergence of knowledge management may help shape those debates as it is critical that we understand the nature of knowledge beyond a scientific paradigm before we attempt to manage it.

The importance of knowledge management derives from an assumption that we are moving into a post-industrial society or a knowledge-based economy (Bell 1973). Former factors of production in the economy such as technical and craft skills of mass production are less important than the more intangible and intellectual skills concerning 'knowledge'. These intangible resources are considered valuable as they constitute the difference between an 'excellent' and a mediocre organisation. Such assumptions imply significant changes in our society, particularly as new classes emerge on the basis of their control over knowledge (Kalling and Styhre 2003).

Even though the notion of knowledge management may have a recent lineage, the idea of managing knowledge has existed among practitioners and scholars for much longer than is commonly assumed (Etzioni 1964). The literature concerning knowledge management derives from the more mature field of organisational learning and the more recent applications of information technology to capture, organise, evaluate, share and store knowledge in organisations. Without this technology, knowledge management would have laid dormant within the organisational learning and strategy literatures. Technology, and in particular web-based technologies, have provided major advances in this field but have been found wanting with their preoccupation with historic and explicit knowledge. The Holy Grail of knowledge management is the ability for organisations to capture and use their tacit knowledge in original and creative ways that differentiate them from their competitors. In the financial sector, the life of many newly developed financial instruments has been shown to be limited to a maximum of three months. Firms make their profits during this brief period before competitors copy the instruments and profit margins disappear. Such knowledge-intensive industries are indicative of competitive environments pervading more traditional industries such as construction where knowledge and creativity have become key drivers.

The rest of this chapter shall attempt to draw on key lessons learnt on our journey of knowledge management throughout this book and summarise the current status of this discipline, its shortcomings and potential ways forward.

Wrestling with knowledge: some reflections

How do we develop a consensus on the nature of knowledge in organisations when philosophers have been unable to derive a consensus on this valuable asset from their studies over 2,000 years? A useful starting point might be that an absolute consensus on the nature of knowledge may remain elusive indefinitely and that any conclusion about its nature can be only temporary as we wrestle with the shortcomings of our own arguments in relation to it. A Socratic approach to questioning is suggested as the optimal way forward.

From a scholarly perspective, another approach is the recognition that each scholar views knowledge from a particular ontological and epistemological perspective (Burrell and Morgan 1979), as shown in Figure 11.1 (p. 293). A useful analogy is to imagine practitioners, researchers and consultants wearing 'invisible coloured glasses'. Each of these glasses bears different assumptions written all over them whether the wearer is aware of them or not. In the final analysis, these 'coloured glasses' or our 'theory-laden' perceptions are 'value neutral', implying that no particular ontological or epistemological understanding of reality has a monopoly over truth. Each has its contribution to knowledge which adds to the richness and diversity of our understanding of organisations. Such a liberal or possibly a radical perspective to some will undoubtedly be challenged by the dominant orthodoxy in any discipline but it acts to question the established norms and values within a field. For example, the dominant positivist, functionalist paradigm pervasive in management research and literature can suffocate scholarship and threaten the development of new possibilities in this field. A frequent response to the failure of aspiring doctoral students to explore different paradigms or 'coloured glasses' found at the Academy of Management was (Morgan 1990):

'Those who do so will fail to "get published", and fail to "get tenure".'

Figure 11.1 Burrell and Morgan's four paradigms and different epistemologies (adapted from Burrell and Morgan 1979)

In a similar manner, the current dominant notions of knowledge are the distinctions between 'tacit' and 'explicit' knowledge (Polanyi 1967; Ryle 1949). This book has argued that many of the current typologies of knowledge are little more than abstractions to denote the continuum between 'know how' and 'know that'. However, there are green shoots developing in the literature that are providing a more sophisticated and critical postmodernist perspective (Hassard and Kelemen 2002; Kalling and Styhre 2003; Styhre 2003). This increasing diversity within the literature and continued questioning of the dominant tacit–explicit distinction is likely to lead to a deepening and greater maturity of our understanding of knowledge management.

At practitioner level, knowledge tends to be characterised in its relation to data and information. Simplistically, data is perceived as a signal acquired through our senses. It is important to recognise that our senses and our minds are not 'theory neutral', meaning that we project our stored mental images on to any data we may observe. We are not neutral observers and are informed by our experiences and cultural backgrounds. Information can be considered as organised data where we endow meaning, relevance and purpose to it (Meadows 2001). In this conception, many scholars consider knowledge as information that allows us to act in any given situation or context. Action becomes the distinguishing feature of knowledge. However, action may come at the price of reflection. In many organisations, there may be dangers of neglecting the 'reflection' phase of knowledge development, particularly if organisations are engaged in 'action-fixated' learning cycles. In pressurised business environments focused on results, it is not difficult to see the negative consequences of a lack of reflection or foresight on impending problems, particularly when there are continual competitive demands on people's time.

The practical implication of these debates is to ascertain the most effective way to conceptualise knowledge in organisations. Is it using the distinction between tacit and explicit knowledge? Or is it considering knowledge as 'actionable information'? The predominant difficulty arises in articulating the subtle differences in common language between notions such as tacit knowledge, knowing and intelligence in organisations.

Knowledge management – is there an optimal approach?

Numerous knowledge management models and frameworks have been forwarded in the literature. There is little consensus among practitioners or academics on the optimal approach but these are early days on a burgeoning literature. However, there are some strands and commonalities that link them together. Some models come from a human resource perspective, focusing more on learning processes, whereas others come from a technological perspective, focusing more on information systems to transform an organisation. The approach adopted in this book has been to integrate these two dominant dimensions of knowledge management under a coherent model, as shown in Figure 11.2.

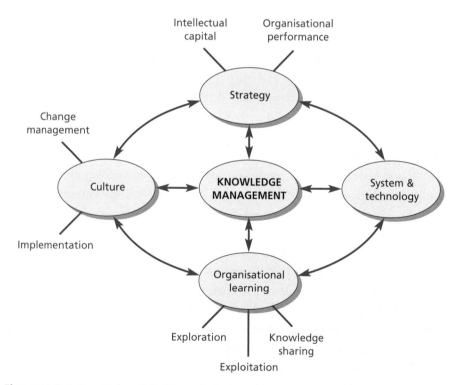

Figure 11.2 Integrated model of knowledge management

An alternative and popular framework in knowledge management literature is one that develops a hypothesis of the four modes of knowledge (tacit and explicit) conversion (Nonaka 1991; Nonaka 1994). Processes are forwarded such as 'externalisation' where an organisation may use metaphors and figurative language to help convert its tacit base to explicit knowledge. The conceptual gap in this framework is that it considers tacit and explicit knowledge as distinct entities rather than existing along a continuum as commonly understood (Polanyi 1967). The assumption is that organisational knowledge can somehow be 'ground, lost or reconstituted' (Tsoukas 1996). Tacit knowledge as an entity is much more sophisticated and may come in different forms. The fashionable knowledge conversion framework does not acknowledge that things may remain unspoken in a workplace (tacit knowledge) based on a wide variety of reasons such as (Boisot 1998):

- things that everyone understands and takes for granted;
- things that nobody understands;
- things that may have a personal cost to the individual if spoken.

Organisational gymnastics: balancing learning with routines and dynamic capabilities

Moderate levels of failure may be good for organisations, as shown in Figure 11.3. This is our conclusion from studying the organisational learning literature. Success can result in maintaining the status quo, complacency and risk aversion as managers follow tried and tested patterns of behaviour. This 'exploitation' of past behaviours may lead to greater efficiency in organisations but may not save them in dynamic environments where greater innovation rather than efficiency is required. In contrast, moderate levels

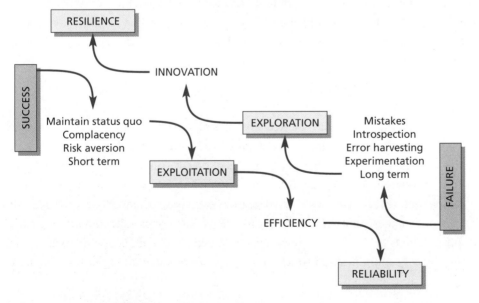

Figure 11.3 Success and failure in organisations

of failure and making mistakes can lead to 'exploration' behaviours where people are more inclined to reflect and experiment with new strategies, procedures and processes.

One of the enduring organisational learning frameworks that has attempted to integrate different dimensions of the literature comes from an information-processing perspective and focuses on four constructs (Huber 1991): knowledge acquisition, information distribution, information interpretation and organisational memory. A common criticism of this approach is that it tends to focus more on the outputs of learning rather than its processes. To overcome this criticism, one can explore the different facets of organisational learning in relation to processes characterised as single-loop and double-loop learning. Single-loop learning is considered as behavioural learning where organisations follow their traditional ways and patterns in response to a problem. In contrast, double-loop learning is considered as cognitive learning where organisations question their underlying assumptions and values and explore new ways of responding to a problem (Argyris and Schon 1978).

There are similarities between single and double-loop learning and the more recent notions of organisational routines and dynamic capabilities. Organisational routines are regular and predictable patterns of behaviour whereas dynamic routines are a firm's ability to integrate, build and reconfigure its competences to address dynamic environments. One could argue that the former concept appears to be a reworking of single-loop learning whereas the latter one is of double-loop learning. Is this an example of old wine in new bottles or are there real and major distinctions with earlier concepts?

Knowledge management technology and systems

A useful typology for grouping different knowledge technologies is one that acknowledges the knowledge development cycle, as shown in Figure 11.4 (p. 297). Even though many technologies tend to focus on explicit knowledge, tools for capturing the elusive tacit knowledge can be found in:

- tools for capturing knowledge, particularly using cognitive mapping and mind mapping tools;
- tools for sharing knowledge, particularly utilising the power of the internet, intranet, extranets and e-mail to share tacit knowledge over a firm's value chain. The technologies can be used to develop virtual communities of practice online to help share ideas and tacit knowledge. Another tool is 'expertise yellow pages' to assist in finding the right people with the relevant tacit knowledge to solve pressing organisational problems. This cannot be underestimated in large organisations. The use of videoconferencing allows organisations to share tacit knowledge over geographic boundaries and maintain the richness of communication which derives from a combination of our body language, spoken words and tone of voice.

More traditional tools for codifying, storing and evaluating explicit knowledge include:

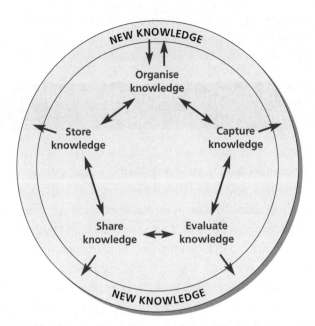

Figure 11.4 A typology of knowledge tools and component technologies

- Tools for organising knowledge, which include ontology and taxonomy generation tools. The challenge is maintaining taxonomies with high levels of flexibility so that they can respond dynamically to our changing perceptions of concepts and schemas over time;
- Tools for storing knowledge, which include sophisticated datawarehouses that have the ability to store and summarise internal and external data over different time horizons;
- Tools for evaluating knowledge, which include data mining, OLAP, case-based reasoning and machine-based learning tools. Interpretation of knowledge using these tools needs to be carefully handled as patterns and relationships may be suggested that are misleading to the untrained eye. Most tools tend to adopt statistical and probabilistic analyses rather than more qualitative insights into a particular problem.

The types of KM systems employed in many organisations include:

- document management systems – involve getting the right information or knowledge to the right person at the right time;
- decision support systems – entail creating and evaluating knowledge through data analysis or using sophisticated models to support decision making;
- group support systems – designed to enhance communication, knowledge sharing, cooperation, coordination and social encounters within groups;
- executive information systems – provide high-quality information and knowledge to executives to aid strategic planning and control processes;
- workflow management systems – integrate knowledge associated with workflows and alignment of 'cases' with resources such as employees;

- customer relationship management systems – develop knowledge about customers' individual preferences and needs using knowledge repositories and knowledge-discovery techniques.

Institutionalist perspective and the knowledge-based view of the firm

Much strategic management theory and practice today is based on assumptions of the industrial organisation tradition (Ansoff 1965; Chandler 1962; Porter 1980). Here the relationship between the firm and the market structures of any given industry is deemed critical. Rational microeconomic theory is the mode of analysis concerned more with the price elasticity or inelasticity of demand. Firms can reduce competition by collusion, creating higher barriers to entry, differentiating their products and services or lowering their costs. This industrial organisation tradition has influenced the dominant planning approaches to strategy prevalent on MBA programmes across the world. The assumption is that executives can use their prized strategy tools to plan ahead effectively each year. The fact that these strategic plans have often been found wanting on implementation strategies is often telling. It is not surprising that only a small proportion of formulated strategies ever gets implemented in organisations (Mintzberg *et al.* 1998).

An alternative approach that has been argued in this book is the institutionalist perspective (Barney 2001; Penrose 1959; Selznick 1957). Institutional theory tries to explore the homogeneity between organisations in an industry and places greater emphasis on the individual in an organisation and their day-to-day learning. Strategy is considered synonymous with strategic change and is informed by a manager's learning and understanding of a situation over time. From this perspective, competition and strategic change are intimately linked. Core competences of a firm (Prahalad and Hamel 1990) become much more important in defining superior performance as the collective learning of a firm depends on these capabilities.

Such core competences or firm's resources that lead to competitive advantage are premised on the 'resource-based theory' of the firm (Barney 2001). This assumes that it is the firm's internal resources, tangible and intangible, that lead to competitive advantage. These internal resources are seen as rare, valuable and not easily replicated or transferable. One subset of the resource-based view of the firm has been the emergence of a knowledge-based view (Grant 1996; Spender 1996). Here the most important internal resource of an organisation is argued to be its tacit and explicit knowledge. Knowledge sharing and knowledge integration become key factors in achieving competitive advantage from this perspective.

From a knowledge-based view of the firm, the most common form of knowledge management strategies found among US management consultancy firms were 'codification' and 'personalisation' strategies (Hansen *et al.* 1999). A dialectic of knowledge management strategies that develops these findings is shown in Figure 11.5 (p. 299).

Codification strategies are heavily based on technology and use large databases to codify and store explicit knowledge. In contrast, personalisation strategies are less about

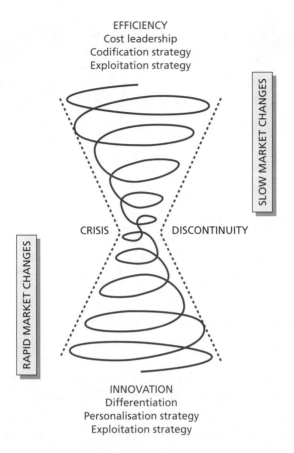

EFFICIENCY
Cost leadership
Codification strategy
Exploitation strategy

SLOW MARKET CHANGES

RAPID MARKET CHANGES

CRISIS   DISCONTINUITY

INNOVATION
Differentiation
Personalisation strategy
Exploitation strategy

Figure 11.5 The dialectic of knowledge management strategies

technology and more about getting people together to share their tacit knowledge over any given problem. As suggested in Figure 11.5, codification strategies are likely to be more prevalent in organisations where competitive forces based on efficiency are dominant. Similarly, personalisation strategies are likely to be found in firms where creative insight and innovation are prevailing forces. Knowledge management strategies have been conceptualised as a dialectic as firms exist in dynamic market environments where the strength of external competitive forces may vary considerably over time.

Communities of practice

One of the key channels for enhancing tacit knowledge sharing in organisations is the promotion of 'communities of practice'. The World Bank sees communities of practice as the main component of its knowledge management strategy to fulfil its aims of becoming a 'knowledge bank'. Communities of practice are informal, self-selecting groups that are open ended without any deadlines or deliverables (Wenger *et al.* 2002). They can be informal groups that meet regularly around physical environments such as

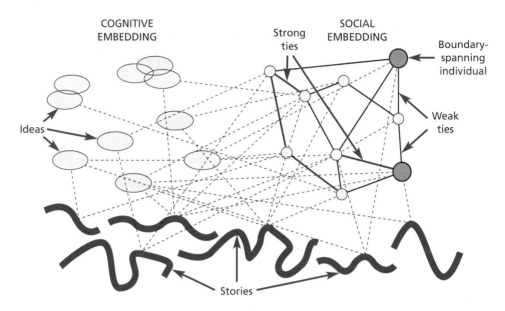

Figure 11.6 The ontology of storytelling

water coolers or canteens or they may be virtual communities that meet in discussion forums over the internet. They are not formalised work groups or project teams but are like-minded individuals who share similar problems and outlooks.

The informal interactions found in communities of practice tend to encourage reflection of practice rather than simply reworking everyday processes. Storytelling and narratives play an important role in embedding tacit knowledge socially and making it 'sticky', namely, making it difficult for competitors to replicate such socially embedded knowledge. One of the potential dangers of communities of practice is that they may become self-reinforcing and self-deluding, turning core competencies of an organisation into core rigidities. An ontology of storytelling showing how stories embed tacit knowledge cognitively in the form of ideas or socially in the relationships between community members is shown in Figure 11.6.

Personal knowledge management

If knowledge is likely to be the core commodity of future 'knowledge' markets, there is relatively little literature on its implications for the individual. Each individual's worth on the market could be described as their personal capital. Like other forms of capital on the stock market, personal capital has a value dependent on the demand for certain capabilities and a cost related to acquiring certain levels of knowledge and skills. In a knowledge era, it is argued that each of us needs to take our personal capital seriously and take ownership for the development and maintenance of our knowledge. Like many commodities, it may soon become outdated and valueless.

One model forwarded for exploring ways we acquire and distribute our personal capital is the 'K-profile' (Cope 2000), as shown in Figure 11.7. This model is based on different facets of an individual knowledge cycle from discovering new knowledge to delivering it to market. The model makes a distinction between our tacit and explicit knowledge base (termed 'knowledge stock') and our knowledge currency. The knowledge currency is the different ways we use to acquire new knowledge and exchange it with the world. It is suggested that this knowledge currency has three principal components:

- head – representing our thinking and cognitive abilities;
- hand – representing how we act or behave in a situation;
- heart – representing our emotions and ways we manage our relationships with ourselves and others.

The three components of knowledge currency are easily identified in relation to explicit knowledge. However, these distinctions can break down in relation to tacit knowledge. Do intuitive insights or knowledge arise as a consequence of a person's cognitive or emotional abilities or both? Also, the model does not acknowledge that tacit and explicit knowledge may exist along a continuum rather than behave as distinct entities. However, the strength of the model is its ability to allow individuals the ability to reflect on different dimensions of their personal capital along a knowledge cycle, from discovering new knowledge to delivering it to market. Like the use of psychometrics in the field of personality measurement, the K-profile allows individuals to assess their strengths and weaknesses in relation to their personal capital and take restorative measures as necessary.

Personal K-profile		Discover — New knowledge	Delay — Stored knowledge	Discard — Redundant knowledge	Diffuse — Shared knowledge	Deliver — Market knowledge
EXPLICIT	HEAD (our thoughts) HAND (our actions) HEART (our emotions)	Acquire new codified knowledge	Store codified knowledge for later retrieval	Discard codified knowledge	Share codified knowledge	Sell codified knowledge in the market
TACIT	HEAD (our thoughts) HAND (our actions) HEART (our emotions)	Acquire new intuitive knowledge	Store intuitive knowledge for later retrieval	Discard intuitive knowledge	Share intuitive knowledge	Sell intuitive knowledge in the market

Figure 11.7 **The personal knowledge map or K-profile (Cole, 2000)**

Knowledge management between nations

As with personal knowledge management, the current literature has paid scant attention to knowledge flows and exchanges between nations, assuming that we are moving towards a global knowledge-based economy. The unit of analysis in knowledge management has remained at the level of the organisation. Many bodies such as the World Bank and the United Nations have become increasingly concerned at the relative lack of knowledge transfer to local communities on major funded projects. There are difficulties in sustaining knowledge generated on these projects or embedding knowledge deeply in everyday roles and practices of local communities. Such development projects can provide an insight into knowledge management between nations, particularly when there is a diverse number of countries involved and collaborating over a common concern. Civil servants in each country act as guardians of governmental knowledge and can play an important role in promoting knowledge sharing or inhibiting its progress. Political sensitivities come to the fore as well as cultural and historic differences between countries. Tensions may also exist between different government ministries that may contribute towards a lack of cooperation and knowledge sharing resulting in suboptimal practices.

For example, a United Nations Development Programme project named 'PEMSEA' involving twelve nations in the Far East (Ganapin *et al.* 2003) showed that there were differences in organisational learning within local communities in each of these countries. One major distinction was between 'centralised learning' and 'decentralised learning', as shown in Figure 11.8 (p. 303). Project sites based in command economies such as China and Vietnam favoured centralised learning aimed more at mobilising committees rather than communities. Progress in these countries appeared much faster due to the strong committee decision-making structures in local government. In contrast, decentralised learning was much more evident at project sites such as Bali based more on community-oriented decision making. Progress appeared to be much slower as greater efforts were made to mobilise community leaders and local stakeholders.

Concluding remarks

Conclusions have no major status in Socratic dialogue. They are purely temporary and tell us which point we have reached in our understanding at any moment in time. They are dynamic and likely to change dependent on our continuous questioning of the status quo. The starting point behind the current knowledge management literature is that it is no longer resources such as land, technology or manual labour that are primary factors of production in society but rather intellectual resources such as knowledge that are the dominant concern. This assumption has led to the emergence of notions such as knowledge economies and knowledge societies.

In the knowledge management arena, there still exist two dominant camps, championed on one side by human resource professionals and on the other by technologically oriented information systems ones. Similar in fate to modern-day architects and engineers, the language and discourse of each side can be incomprehensible to the other. This book has been an attempt to break down these barriers and integrate these two perspectives by providing a language for mutual dialogue (Styhre 2003). Each has valuable lessons to challenge and enhance the other. One cannot remain blind to the incredible technological advances such as the internet that allows us to almost instantaneously share knowledge across the world. Nor can firms remain blind to the fact that their intellectual capital is primarily driven by people. Out of organisational necessity, firms need to foster and develop their human and social capital as a matter of competitive survival.

Beyond these two common approaches, the book has examined knowledge management strategy in organisations from an institutionalist perspective and has challenged the common orthodoxy of the industrial organisation tradition. The individual and the spoils of their learning are placed more centrally in an organisation as the source for competitive success. Such assumptions have led to the emerging knowledge-based view of the firm.

The most pressing challenge in knowledge management today is around fostering and cultivating knowledge sharing in organisations. Explicit knowledge is relatively easy to codify and transfer around an organisation using tools such as data warehouses. However, the ability to share tacit knowledge is much more elusive. Much of the knowledge-sharing literature is concerned with how the more intangible tacit knowledge can be transferred, diffused and disseminated in an organisation. This may occur through formal teams, formal and informal networks and across organisational boundaries (Kalling and Styhre 2003).

Figure 11.8 Organisational learning at national levels

One of the principal aspects of knowledge sharing appears to be the ability of organisations to create environments that foster dialogue between related groups. The importance of dialogue is that it allows us to tap into the rich tacit base in organisations and to play with ideas. It is unclear whether formal groupings can suffice in generating this tacit knowledge through tools such as brainstorming or whether there is a need for more informal groupings termed as 'communities of practice'.

Finally, as a caution, the reader needs to guard against the 'old wine in new bottles' syndrome that may exist in some writings in this field. Like Alice in Wonderland, different terms can become confused as they mean the same thing. Despite this shortcoming, this book has demonstrated the breadth and depth of the corpus of knowledge underlying a serious and emerging discipline. Knowledge management and its practices have significant contributions to make in the reality of a knowledge-based economy. Like the development of English as a discipline in the early twentieth century, the study of knowledge management is here to stay and likely to pervade every facet of organisational life.

Further reading

1 Newell *et al.* 2002 is a good all-round book on knowledge management predominantly from a human resource perspective and contains some good case study material. I have used it successfully with postgraduate students.

2 Davenport and Prusak 1998 helped popularise the field of knowledge management and comes from a consultancy and practitioner background.

3 Styhre 2003 is an excellent book providing a much-needed critique of our current understanding of knowledge management from a postmodern perspective.

4 Cope 2000 is the only book that explores the notion of personal knowledge management. This may be useful for readers wishing to reflect on their personal capital profiles and explore ways of overcoming blocks or shortcomings such as marketing their knowledge more appropriately.

References

Ansoff, H. I. (1965) *Corporate Strategy*, McGraw Hill, New York.

Argyris, C. and Schon, D. A. (1978) *Organizational Learning: A Theory of Action Perspective*, Addison-Wesley, Reading, MA.

Barney, J. B. (2001) 'Resource-based theories of competitive advantage: ten-year retrospective of the resource-based view', *Journal of Management*, 27, 643–650.

Bell, D. (1973) *The Coming Post-industrial Society*, Basic Books, New York.

Boisot, M. H. (1998) *Knowledge Assets: Securing Competitive Advantage in the Information Economy*, Oxford University Press, New York.

Burrell, G. and Morgan, M. (1979) *Sociological Paradigms and Organizational Analysis*, Heinemann, London.

Chandler, A. D. (1962) *Strategy and Structure. Chapters in the History of the Industrial Enterprise*, The MIT Press, Cambridge, MA.

Cope, M. (2000) *Know Your Value? Value What You Know*, Prentice Hall, Harlow, Essex.

Davenport, T. H. and Prusak, L. (1998) *Working Knowledge: How Organizations Manage What They Know*, Harvard Business School Press, Boston, MA.

Etzioni, A. (1964). *Modern Organizations*, Prentice-Hall, Englewood Cliffs, NJ.

Ganapin, D., Burbridge, P. and Jashapara, A. (2003) *Building Partnerships in Environmental Management for the Seas of East Asia (PEMSEA)*: Mid-Term Evaluation, United Nations, New York.

Grant, R. M. (1996) 'Toward a knowledge-based theory of the firm', *Strategic Management Journal*, 17, 109–22.

Hansen, M., Nohria, N. and Tierney, T. (1999). 'What's your strategy for managing knowledge?', *Harvard Business Review*, March–April, 106–16.

Hassard, J. and Kelemen, M. (2002) 'Production and consumption in organizational knowledge: the case of the "paradigms debate"', *Organization*, 9(2), 331–355.

Huber, G. P. (1991) 'Organizational learning: the contributing processes and the literatures', *Organization Science*, 2, 88–115.

Kalling, T. and Styhre, A. (2003) *Knowledge Sharing in Organizations*, Copenhagen Business School Press, Copenhagen.

Meadows, J. (2001) *Understanding Information*, K.G. Saur, München.

Mintzberg, H., Ahlstrand, B. and Lampel, J. (1998) *Strategy Safari*, Pearson Education Limited, Harlow, Essex.

Morgan, G. (1990) 'Paradigm diversity in organizational research', *The Theory and Philosophy of Organizations*, J. Hassard and D. Pym, eds, Routledge, London.

Newell, S., Robertson, M., Scarbrough, H. and Swan, J. (2002) *Managing Knowledge Work*, Palgrave, Basingstoke, Hampshire.

Nonaka, I. (1991) 'The knowledge-creating company', *Harvard Business Review*, 69(November–December), 96–104.

Nonaka, I. (1994) 'A dynamic theory of organizational knowledge creation', *Organization Science*, 5(1), 14–37.

Penrose, E. T. (1959) *The Theory of Growth of the Firm*, Blackwell, Oxford.

Polanyi, M. (1967) *The Tacit Dimension*, Doubleday, New York.

Porter, M. (1980) *Competitive Strategy*, Free Press, New York.

Prahalad, C. K. and Hamel, G. (1990) 'The core competence of the corporation', *Harvard Business Review*, 68(3), 79–91.

Ryle, G. (1949) *The Concept of Mind*, Hutcheson, London.

Selznick, P. (1957) *Leadership in Administration: A Sociological Interpretation*, Row, Peterson and Co., Evanston, IL.

Spender, J. C. (1996) 'Making knowledge the basis of a dynamic theory of the firm', *Strategic Management Journal*, 17, 45–62.

Styhre, A. (2003) *Understanding Knowledge Management – Critical and Postmodern Perspectives*, Copenhagen Business School Press, Copenhagen.

Tsoukas, H. (1996) 'The firm as a distributed knowledge system: a constructionist approach', *Strategic Management Journal*, 17, 11–25.

Wenger, E. C., McDermott, R. and Snyder, W. M. (2002). *Cultivating Communities of Practice: A Guide to Managing Knowledge*, Harvard Business School Press, Boston, MA.

Glossary

A posteriori presupposes our sensory experience and reasons information derived through our sense perceptions.

A priori is taken to be independent of sensory experience and reasons from abstract general premises.

Abductive inquiry presenting theories for consideration.

Adaptability the ability of an organisation to adapt to internal or external changes in its environment.

Agent technology computer systems that are capable of autonomous action in certain environments to fulfil their design objectives.

Artefacts can be material objects, physical layouts, technology, language and behavioural patterns.

Associative memories where pairs of associated data are memorised using a long-term memory network model.

Ba' physical, virtual or mental space for helping convert tacit into explicit knowledge and vice versa.

Balanced scorecard a balanced approach to organisational performance which takes into account the customer, innovation and learning and internal business processes as well as traditional financial measures.

Behaviourism body of psychological theory concerned with identifying conditions that stimulate patterns of human behaviour.

Boolean operators locate records containing matching terms (AND, NOT, OR) in specified fields.

Business process re-engineering (BPR) rethinking and radical redesign of business processes.

Case-based reasoning information retrieval systems that allow the storage of past problems, their solutions and their reasoning for future retrieval.

Cleavage paralysis arising from two or more forces confronting each other in an organisation.

Clustering techniques the grouping together of closely related data.

Coaching where instructor observes student completing tasks and provides helpful hints, suggestions and feedback as needed.

Codification strategy heavily based on technology and uses large databases to codify and store knowledge.

Cognitive mapping visual representation of a domain through concepts and their interrelationships.

Cognitive perspective the study of mental processes associated with perception, learning, reasoning and memory.

Communities of practice groups of people who share a common concern or passion and interact informally on an ongoing basis.

Configuration competitive state when one external force dominates.

Congenital learning learning influenced by the founding fathers of an organisation.

Contamination problem when the dominant external force undermines equally valid forces.

Conversion move from one competitive force and form in an organisation to another.

Core competence proposition that competition between firms is as much a race for competence mastery as it is for market position and power.

Crawlers software programs that send requests to remote web servers looking for new or updated pages.

Customer capital the value of organisational relationships with customers including their intangible loyalty.

Customer relationship management (CRM) systems systems that integrate technology and business processes to meet customer requirements at any given moment.

Data known facts or things used as a basis of inference or reckoning.

Data processing (DP) use of technology to automate tasks.

Data warehouses large physical databases that hold vast amounts of information.

Decision support systems (DSS) systems that combine data analysis and sophisticated models to support non-routine decision-making.

Decision tree a graphical representation of a decision process drawn as branches of a tree stemming from the initial decision point to the final outcomes.

Deductive inquiry preparing theories for test.

Dialectic fundamental process of development in thought and reality from thesis to antithesis to synthesis.

Dialogue involves active listening and the suspension of one's assumptions to explore complex issues and divergent thinking.

Discussion involves presentation and defence of different views to find the best view to support a decision or convergent thinking.

Document management systems the systematic management of documents in an organisation.

Double-loop learning doing things differently or doing different things.

Dynamic capabilities the learning abilities of organisations to adapt their daily routines to meet the challenges of volatile environments.

Economic rent profits to any asset whose sale exceeds its competitive price.

Effectiveness the ability to meet customer requirements on product or service features at a given cost.

Efficiency developing cost advantages of operations.

E-learning education delivered via the internet.

Empiricism reliance on experience as the source of ideas and knowledge.

Employee involvement engagement of employees in order to gain commitment.

Encryption security measure to prevent non-authorised party from reading or changing data.

Epistemology relates to our grounds of knowledge and what we can know.

Excellence and turnaround perspective centred around managerial remedies and recipes of successful companies.

Executive information systems (EIS) systems to enhance strategic planning and control by summarising large quantities of data and allowing the user to drill down to different levels of detail.

Existentialism emphasises the primacy of individual existence and its unqualified freedom.

Experiential learning learning acquired from direct experience.

Expert systems systems designed to mimic the reasoning skills of experts.

Expertise 'yellow pages' list of employees in an organisation with a summary of their knowledge, skills and expertise.

Explicit knowledge 'know that'.

Exploitation learning to perform the same processes better or faster.

Exploration experimenting with new strategies, procedures and processes to work differently.

Figurative language not literal form of speech.

Forcefield analysis examines the driving and restraining forces in any change process.

Fuzzy expressions use a thesaurus to expand a query into related terms.

Genetic algorithms involve complex data structures and are based on biological mechanisms.

Grafting employing new members with the knowledge or skills required rather than developing them in-house.

Group support systems systems to aid communication, knowledge sharing, cooperation and coordination in groups.

Groupware tools software that allows groups of people to collaborate on a project using the internet or intranet.

Human capital the value on the knowledge, skills and abilities that allow individuals to produce goods and services.

Human resource management a managerial perspective which argues for integrated personnel policies in alignment with organisational strategy.

I

Idealism belief that only mental entities are real, so that physical things exist only in the sense that they are perceived.

Inductive inquiry assessing results of test.

Industrial organisation tradition design and planning model of strategy where the relationships between the firm, industry and market structures are central to competitive advantage.

Information systematically organised data.

Information overload the saturation of information by an individual leading to impaired reasoning and judgement.

Information systems interrelated components working together to collect, process, store and disseminate information to aid organisational activities.

Information systems (IS) capability relates to an organisation's information system's capability as a source of competitive advantage.

Institutionalist perspective belief that experience and learning of individuals is central to competitive advantage.

Intellectual capital the economic value of two categories of intangible assets of a company: organisational capital and human capital.

Intellectual property the collective intellectual assets such as documents, drawings, software programs, data, inventions and processes.

Intelligence know how or tacit knowledge.

Internet an international collection of computer networks.

Intranet a collection of private computer networks within an organisation.

Inverted file a list of words in a set of documents and their occurrences in terms of their precise storage locations.

J

Just-in-time production (JIT) integration of automation with production information system to deliver any part in the necessary quantity at the right time.

K

Knowledge philosophically there is no consensus on term. Practically may be regarded as actionable information or tacit or explicit knowledge.

Knowledge economy an economy based fundamentally around knowledge rather than other factors of production such as labour or technology.

Knowledge management the effective learning processes associated with exploration, exploitation and sharing of human knowledge (tacit and explicit) that use appropriate technology and cultural environments to enhance an organisation's intellectual capital and performance.

Knowledge workers individuals who need to use a high level of knowledge in their everyday activities.

L

Leadership situational skills learning the appropriate use of 'telling', 'selling', 'participating' and 'delegating' interventions.

Lean production form of manufacturing that uses less human effort, manufacturing space, tools, hours and inventory compared with mass production.

Learning organisation organisation that sustains competitive advantage through learning faster than its competitors.

Lexical analysis identifies the words in the text and their interrelationships.

M

Machine-based learning the ability of a machine to improve its performance based on previous results.

Management information system (MIS) system to provide managers with information for monitoring and controlling their business processes.

Mentoring learning process where a mentor can serve as a role model, counsellor or teacher.

Metaphor imaginative use of a name or description for an object or action to which it is not literally applicable.

Method-of-doing business (MDB) patent patent to provide protection of a firm's business methods.

N

Networks of practice more formalised networks such as professional networks where power relations may become more prominent.

Neural networks tools to mimic the physical thought processes of the brain.

Norms expectations of appropriate or inappropriate behaviour.

Noun groups clustering nouns found near each other into a single indexing component.

Online analytical processing (OLAP) allows organisations to analyse large sets of data along more than three dimensions.

Ontology (philosophy) relates to our assumptions of reality such as whether it is external or a construct of our minds.

Ontology (systems) overall conceptualisation of a field of knowledge that may not be represented in a hierarchical manner.

Organisational alignment the ability of an organisation to align its processes with changes in the external environment.

Organisational capital the value of the knowledge assets remaining in the organisation when people have left their workplace.

Organisational climate an understanding of social environments where individuals are considered separate from their environments.

Organisational culture a study of social environments predominantly from an anthropological or sociological perspective.

Organisational learning the processes of improving organisational actions through better knowledge and understanding.

Organisational routines repeated patterns of behaviour and processes in organisations.

Personal knowledge management ways of developing and managing an individual's personal capital.

Personalisation strategy focused on gaining deeper insights into problems through people rather than technology.

Perspective making process by which a community of practice develops its knowledge domain.

Petri nets allow processes to be described graphically in terms of places and transitions.

Phenomenology the description of experience through careful analysis of intellectual processes.

Positivism belief that the natural sciences comprise the whole of human knowledge.

Postmodernism expresses grave doubts about universal truth, rejects artificially sharp dichotomies and delights in the ironies of language and life.

Pragmatism explains meaning and truth in terms of the application of ideas or beliefs to observable actions.

Probabilistic expressions assign probabilities to documents that the query assumes users will find relevant.

Rationalism reliance on reason as the only reliable source of human knowledge.

RDF Resource Description Framework is a metadata standard.

Realism belief that universals exist independently of the particulars that instantiate them.

Resource-based view belief in the firm's resources as the principal determinant of (RBV) competitive advantage.

Rule induction statistical techniques to discover rules related to frequency of correlation and accuracy of predictions.

Semantic web an extension of the current web in which information is given well-defined meaning, better enabling computers and people to work in cooperation.

Signature files index structures that divide text into blocks for analysis, primarily to aid retrieval.

Single-loop learning doings things better.

Slogan a short catchy phrase.

Smart patents a method of extending the life of a patent through using continuation patents.

Social capital the value on the strength of linkages, connections, interactions and shared understandings among social networks in organisations.

Stemming removal of affixes of a word to improve retrieval.

Stopwords words that occur too frequently in the text that do not provide good discriminators for the purposes of retrieval.

Strategic information systems (SIS) systems that integrate customers more fully in business process, develop new products based on information and provide support for strategy development and implementation.

Strategic intent a firm's obsession with winning in the short or long term.

Strategic management includes an understanding of a firm's strategic position, its strategic choices and ways of turning its strategy into action.

Strategic positioning is concerned with impact of strategy on the external environment, a firm's internal resources and expectations of its stakeholders.

Strategy plan of actions to achieve one's goals.

Suffix file forms a tree data structure of words in the text.

Symbols can occur as words, statements, actions or a material phenomenon.

Systems thinking focuses on the way that a system's constituent parts interrelate and how systems work over time and within the context of larger systems.

Tacit knowledge 'know how' or intelligence.

Taxonomy the hierarchical structuring of knowledge in subcategories related to its essential qualities.

Team learning ability to balance dialogue and discussion in groups as necessary.

Text-based conferencing internet-based discussion forums or chat groups.

Tobin's q ratio compares the market value of an asset with its replacement cost (book value).

Total quality management (TQM) structured system of integrating the business environment and continuous improvement with development, improvement and cultural change.

Unlearning process by which individuals discard obsolete or misleading information.

Vector expressions assign weights to index terms linked to their frequency in a document.

Vicarious learning imitating strategies, practices or technologies of competitors.

Videoconferencing conferencing with people through the use of video and computer technology.

Visualisation technology that allows users to understand complex information through use of rich computer graphics.

Wisdom ability to act critically or practically in a given situation.

Workflow management systems effectively model organisational processes into workflows and allow the efficient processing of large numbers of cases through predefined cases.

XML eXtensible Markup Language. A subset of SGML constituting a particular text markup language for interchange of structured data

Index